Bravo! Fantastic!
I love the tone, content and spirit of t
Tim Mayotte, former World top 10 and Wimbledon semifinalist!

Manuel's Book "What Tennis Pros Don't Teach", shows Manuel's conscientious attitude, professional manner and expertise in all aspects of the game, and makes him an easy recommendation for an "up and comer" junior or adult, Tennis Coach, or Professional player aspiring to enhance their Tennis skills and knowledge in a short time span. I am a huge advocate for Manuel's work as Tennis Professional, as a writer, and his program in NW Arkansas...
Peter Doohan, former NCAA Champ, Davis Cup Rep (Australia), and World Top 50 Singles and Top 10 Doubles!

THIS GEM HAS SOMETHING FOR EVERY TENNIS JUNKIE. WRITTEN BY A PRO WITH PASSION, KNOWLEDGE, AND LOVE; READ IT SLOWLY, THERE IS A LOT TO ABSORB AND TO LEARN!
Best regards. Cliff
Cliff Drysdale is a well known and respected Tennis TV analyst and commentator. He beat Rod Laver in the US Open singles in 1968 and was doubles champion in 1972. He became President of the Association of Tennis Professionals (ATP) in 1972. Drysdale was ranked World No. 4 in 1965

This tennis book is unlike any other, period. Part instructional, part philosophy, part memoir, it touches on more subjects tennis related than anything written before. Everyone will find something of interest in this truly remarkable book. Congratulations to my friend Manuel who with his passion and dedication to the sport has given us all a wonderful gift to savor.
Ross Walker: Italia Cup USA Team 1988 Runner Up to West Germany, USTA National 35s Indoor Champion 1987, USTA National 35s Clay Courts Runner Up 1987, 3 time All American University of Houston 1972-1974, National Amateur Clay Court Champion 1972, National Junior College Champion 1972.

What Tennis Pros Don't Teach is an exceptionally good book written in plain English. I have read a lot of books on tennis, and I can confidently say that WTPDT is a super book that pulls no punches. Within its pages, there is great common sense, advice, and instruction based on real life examples. WTPDT does a good job of explaining coaching principles; it is valuable to parents who want to help their children become as good as they want to be by finding the right coach. Cervantes focuses on a bevy of topics: The passion for the game, developing a strong body in order to have a strong mind, solid technical and training practices, the role of the tennis professional, and he even tackles a few controversial issues. Both coaches and parents should read this book.

JP Weber played tennis as a junior, collegiate and senior player. Over 30 plus years he has coached and developed all levels of tennis players. JP is the Host of the **We Coach Tennis** Radio Program in Blog Radio. **Director of Tennis** *for the Laurel Park Tennis Center in Marietta, GA. and owner of Tennis Dynamics, LLC.*

Cervantes' book should be kept beside the Bible as the next go-to book for dealing with all the sins in life and the problems of the World. Instead of reading the New York Times, read WTPDT, and you'll learn as much about the World as you want or should know. Steve Ersinghaus

Steve Ersinghaus is an English Professor at Tunxis Community College and a freelance writer and poet. He also does editing work for his friends. Attended University of Texas at El Paso, lives in Simsbury, CT, Steve has been a Tennis player since he was child.

WHAT TENNIS PROS DON'T TEACH
(WTPDT)

Wisdom Tennis 101

Manuel S. Cervantes

Master Tennis Professional

Copyright © 2015 by Manuel S. Cervantes.

Library of Congress Control Number:		2015917942
ISBN:	Hardcover	978-1-5144-2092-8
	Softcover	978-1-5144-2093-5
	eBook	978-1-5144-2091-1

All rights reserved. No part of this book may be reproduced or transmitted in any form or by any means, electronic or mechanical, including photocopying, recording, or by any information storage and retrieval system, without permission in writing from the copyright owner.

Any people depicted in stock imagery provided by Thinkstock are models, and such images are being used for illustrative purposes only.
Certain stock imagery © Thinkstock.

Print information available on the last page.

Rev. date: 11/05/2015

To order additional copies of this book, contact:
Xlibris
1-888-795-4274
www.Xlibris.com
Orders@Xlibris.com
542091
manuelscervantes@gmail.com

CONTENTS

DEDICATIONS xiii
FOREWORD xv
ACKNOWLEDGEMENTS xvii
INTRODUCTION xix

SECTION I
FOUNDATIONS, SETTING THE STAGE

LOVE OF THE GAME 3
HEALTH BENEFITS OF PLAYING TENNIS 5
SPORTSMANSHIP, ETHICS, VALUES 6
NOBODY KNOWS IT ALL 8
WHAT IS TENNIS-PRO OR COACH CERTIFICATION? 13
FINDING THE RIGHT TENNIS-PRO/COACH AND
    PROGRAM/ACADEMY 15
WHAT WE NEED TO LEARN FROM A TENNIS PRO/COACH? 22
ASSISTANT TENNIS PROFESSIONALS 24
WHAT IS THE RIGHT ATMOSPHERE FOR ME AS A TENNIS
    PLAYER? 26
WHO SHOULD GO FOR TENNIS? IS TENNIS FOR MY KIDS? 29
ORGANIZED TENNIS, TENNIS ASSOCIATIONS, AND
    FEDERATIONS 31
DEVELOPING THE ATHLETE FIRST AND THEN THE TENNIS
    PLAYER 33
WHAT'S A GOOD AGE TO START IN JUNIOR TENNIS? 34
HOW MUCH SHOULD PARENTS GET INVOLVED? 35
A LETTER TO ALL TENNIS DADS AND MOMS 37
TRAVELING WITH JUNIORS 39
COACHING IN TENNIS 43
CREATING A VISION... LIVING THE DREAM! 47

SECTION II
SOME TECHNICAL STUFF

- DIFFERENT TYPES OF TENNIS LESSONS 55
  - HITTING LESSONS 55
  - POINT-PLAY LESSONS 56
  - THE 30-MINUTE LESSON 56
  - SEMI-PRIVATE 56
  - GROUP LESSONS OR DRILLS 57
  - VIDEO ANALYSIS LESSONS 57
  - ACCELERATED LEARNING LESSONS 58
  - MENTAL TOUGHNESS AND EMOTIONAL CONTROL LESSONS 58
  - HAND-FED DRILLS 59
  - BALL FEEDING 59
  - SERVING PRACTICE AND LESSONS 59
  - BALL MACHINE LESSONS 60
- BALL MACHINE DRILLS 62
  - 1) AEROBIC CARDIO WORKOUT: 62
    - CARDIO WORKOUT TIPS: 63
  - 2) APPROACH SHOT TECHNICAL WORKOUT: 64
    - APPROACH SHOTS TECHNICAL TIPS: 65
  - 3) BACKHAND TECHNICAL WORKOUT: 66
    - BACKHAND TECHNICAL TIPS: 67
  - 4) FOREHAND TECHNICAL WORKOUT: 68
    - FOREHAND TECHNICAL TIPS: 69
  - 5) HALF-VOLLEY TECHNICAL WORKOUT: 70
    - HALF VOLLEY TECHNICAL TIPS: 71
  - 6) LOB TECHNICAL WORKOUT: 72
    - LOB TECHNICAL TIPS: 73
  - 7) OVERHEAD TECHNICAL WORKOUT: 73
    - OVERHEAD TECHNICAL TIPS: 74
  - 8) QUICK REACTION VOLLEYS: 75
    - QUICK REACTION VOLLEYS TIPS: 76
  - 9) RETURN OF SERVE: 77
    - RETURN OF SERVE TIPS: 78
  - 10) VOLLEY TECHNICAL WORKOUT: 79
    - VOLLEY TECHNICAL TIPS: 80

11) PASSING SHOTS:	81
PASSING SHOT TIPS:	82
12) SWINGING VOLLEYS TECHNICAL WORKOUT:	83
SWINGING VOLLEYS TECHNICAL TIPS:	84
13) BM DRILL FOR 2 OR MORE PLAYERS:	85
BM DRILLS FOR 2 OR MORE PLAYERS TECHNICAL TIPS:	87
BALL MACHINES OPERATION INSTRUCTIONS	88
QUICKSTART TENNIS! HOW GOOD IS IT? DO WE NEED TRANSITION BALLS?	89
HOW MUCH TENNIS SHOULD WE PLAY?	94
THE 6 HOUR A DAY JUNIOR TENNIS CAMP	96
HOW LONG DOES IT TAKE TO LEARN A STROKE?	97
TALENT VERSUS MOTIVATION	99
SETTING GOALS	101
DOING IT ON OUR OWN	105
HOW TO GET BETTER NO MATTER WHAT	108
HITTING ON THE WALL	110
TENNIS CARDIO WORKOUTS	112
WHAT SHOULD A PLAYER'S STROKES LOOK LIKE?	113
IS MY TECHNIQUE SOUND?	115
GRIPS ADVANTAGES AND DISADVANTAGES	118
THE IMPORTANCE OF THE NON-DOMINANT ARM	123
FOOTWORK IN TENNIS	125
THE SPLIT STEP	125
ADJUSTING STEPS	126
THE DROP-STEP	127
THE CARIOCA STEP	127
SHUFFLING STEPS	128
THE KILL SHOT SKIP	129
THE SCISSOR KICK	129
SERVING SPLIT RECOVERY STEP	130
LOADING	130
CLOSED STANCE VERSUS OPEN STANCE	130
SLIDING ON CLAY	132
ANTICIPATION	134

PLAYING STYLES, STRENGTHS, AND WEAKNESSES 136
      THE AGGRESSIVE BASELINER 136
      THE COUNTER PUNCHER 138
      SERVE AND VOLLEY/NET RUSHING PLAYERS 139
      ALL COURT PLAYERS 140
ONE HANDED VS TWO HANDED BACKHANDS 142
WEAPON DEVELOPMENT 145
PRACTICE SPECIFICITY; PRACTICE AS WE WOULD PLAY 147
THE GAMES APPROACH TO LEARNING TENNIS 149
GAMES APPROACH DRILL MENU 150
SERVING 157
RETURN OF SERVE 161
GROUNDSTROKES AND BASELINE PLAY 164
HITTING ON THE RISE 167
BREATHING AND GRUNTING IN TENNIS 169
TIMING 171
VOLLEYS AND NET PLAY 173
PASSING SHOTS 178
DROP SHOTS AND DROP VOLLEYS 180
EXTREME SHOTS! WHY WE NEED TO LEARN THEM? 182
THE UTMOST STAGE 187
SPINS 190
THE SECRET OF THE HEAVY BALL 193
REDIRECTION, HITTING THE BALL
    BACK BY DEFLECTION 194
POWER VS FINESSE 196
COMPETITION AND MATCHPLAY 198
POST MATCH PRACTICE, THE MINI LESSON 200
THE ART OF SEEING/WATCHING THE BALL 201

SECTION III
MIND OVER MATTER

STRATEGY 207
MOON BALLS AND DROP SHOTS 211
PLAYING THE ELEMENTS 212
DEALING WITH ALTITUDE 215
TURNING DEFENSE INTO OFFENSE 218

HIGH PERCENTAGE TENNIS.. 220
THE 4X4 RULE 223
STATISTICS, WHAT DO THEY MEAN TO US? 224
TEMPO ON COURT, ESTABLISHING RHYTHM AND PACE...... 229
CLOSING MATCHES AND MOMENTUM................................ 231
COMING FROM BEHIND AND SHIFTING THE MOMENTUM
    OF A MATCH... 235
DEALING WITH DEFEAT 238
SCOUTING.. 241
GETTING READY FOR MATCHES 245
TRANSITIONING 248
    TRANSITIONING FROM 10s TO 12s.......................... 250
    TRANSITIONING FROM 12s TO 14s.......................... 250
    TRANSITIONING FROM 14s TO 16s.......................... 251
    TRANSITIONING FROM THE 16s INTO THE 18s 252
    FROM JUNIOR TENNIS TO COLLEGE TENNIS................ 253
    THE ULTIMATE CHALLENGE, GOING FOR THE PROS... 254
CONFIDENCE... WHERE DO WE GET IT? WHAT IS IT?........... 259
MATCHPLAY AND PERFORMING UNDER PRESSURE 262
HOW MUCH IS TOO MUCH?.. 266
DOUBLES! WHAT COULD BE MORE FUN IN TENNIS? 268
WHY NOT DOUBLES INSTEAD OF SINGLES? ARE WE
    MISSING THE BOAT? 275
PRESSURE AND BURNOUT IN JUNIOR TENNIS 279
WHAT IS MENTAL TOUGHNESS? 283
DIG, DIG, DIG!.. 295
PLAYING A CHEATER AND HIS/HER PARENTS..................... 297
VISUALIZATION AND IMAGERY 299
DO RULES MATTER? HOW WELL SHOULD I KNOW
    THE RULEBOOK?... 301

SECTION IV
MATTER OVER MIND

FITNESS AND CONDITIONING... 305
TENNIS TRAINING TESTING.. 307
WTPDT FITNESS TRAINING PROTOCOL 311
SPORTS SCIENCE, WHAT IS IT? HOW DO WE APPLY IT? 313

PERIODIZATION	314
WEIGHT TRAINING	321
STRETCHING FOR TENNIS	324
INJURIES	326
CRAMPS	330
NUTRITION, HYDRATION, AND SLEEP	332
PROPER EATING	332
HYDRATION, DRINKING, AND ELECTROLYTES	333
SLEEP	334
A WORD ON COFFEE	335

SECTION V
GEAR AND EQUIPMENT

RACQUETS FOR CHILDREN	339
RACQUETS… THE TRUTH!	340
TENNIS BALLS	342
CLOTHING FOR TENNIS	344
TENNIS SHOES	346
SOCKS FOR TENNIS	349
STRINGS, STRINGING MACHINES AND RACQUET STRINGING	351
BREAKING STRINGS	356
STRINGING MACHINES	358
SURFACES FOR TENNIS	365

SECTION VI
CONTROVERSIAL STUFF

DAVIS CUP, FEDERATION CUP, OLYMPICS, GRAND SLAM AND JUNIOR TENNIS	375
THE CODE (CHANGING THE CULTURE OF OUR TEAM)	378
DEVELOPING OUR PHILOSOPHY	382
SPORTS THAT ROBBED FROM TENNIS AND COMPETE WITH TENNIS	385
POLITICS AND DRAMA, THE DARK SIDE OF TENNIS	387

SECTION VII
WHO WE ARE

TENNIS PRO'S IMAGE: WHO ARE WE? WHAT DO TENNIS
  PROS DO? 395
WHY I STARTED PLAYING TENNIS AND HOW? 398
HANGING WITH THE RIGHT CROWD 402
REMEMBRANCES IN TENNIS AND STORIES FROM
  THE PROS 404

SECTION VIII
WISDOM TENNIS 101

101 TENNIS TIPS WITHOUT DIAGRAMS... MY WISDOM
  TENNIS CONNECTION 419
101 SPORTS SCIENCE AND SPORTS MEDICINE BASED
  PRACTICAL TIPS 436
101 RULES THAT MATTER... SPECIAL CASES 453
101 QUOTES PLUS MORE FROM THE PROFESSIONALS 467
101 THINGS WE MAY NEED TO CARRY IN OUR
  TENNIS BAG 478
101 EXCUSES FOR LOSING IN TENNIS 485
101 REASONS WHY WE PLAY TENNIS 491
101 QUESTIONS... WHAT TENNIS PROS DON'T TEACH
  QUIZ 503
QUIZ KEY 534
EPILOGUE 539
WHAT TENNIS PROS DON'T TEACH VIDEO SERIES LINKS 541

DEDICATIONS

This book is dedicated to Tennis players around the World trying to improve and seek a deeper understanding and appreciation of the game. To the all-time greats of Tennis, who have provided inspiration for me to persist in the sport for nearly fifty years. Some of my all time favorites are Pancho Gonzalez, Margaret Court, Roy Emerson, Rod Laver, Manuel Santana, Stan Smith, Arthur Ashe, John Newcombe, Tony Roche, Manuel Orantes, Guillermo Vilas, Vitas Gerulaitis, John McEnroe, Stefan Edberg, Steffi Graf, Pete Sampras, Patrick Rafter, Roger Federer, Maria Sharapova, Serena Williams, Ana Ivanovic and our own, nearly forgotten Rafael Osuna, who led Mexico to its only Davis Cup final versus Australia in the 1960s.

To my dear family, Carmen, and Anasazi, this book is also dedicated in a very special way. "Thanks for putting up with me for so long, and for supporting all my crazy ideas all these years. I know that you surely have suffered, for I have devoted pretty serious time and effort to the completion of this project". "Remember that any achievements I might have are also your achievements and were only possible thanks to your everyday support".

FOREWORD

by Jorge Lozano

This book, "What Tennis Pros Don't Teach" tells the story like it is! Many junior players and their parents, as well as Tennis players of all levels, enter the World of Tennis not knowing the different aspects of the game. This book will give a pretty good idea of what knowledge is needed coming into this World. Manuel Cervantes is a great friend of mine who has devoted most of his life to Tennis. He was a very dedicated Tennis player, and now is more dedicated to learning everything there is to know about this discipline. In this book, he tells the truth about coaches, what should be expected in a lesson, and what values a Tennis coach must have. Also, he gives great advice to parents, and what they must do in order to have a happy child learning the sport. He covers all the angles Tennis players should master, and most importantly what their goals should be. The section on "Tips" is an excellent piece that every Tennis player should benefit from reading. I fully recommend this book not only for the knowledge that was put into writing it, but also for the values it covers, like sportsmanship and honesty that we rarely see these days on a Tennis court.

Jorge Lozano, a three-time All-American at the University of Southern California, '82-'86, was ranked 51 in the World in the ATP rankings in singles and fourth in doubles in 1988. Jorge represented Mexico in Davis Cup competition for 15 years, 1981-1995. He was the Mexican Davis Cup Captain from 2008 to 2014. Now, he is the Athletic Director for the University Tec de Monterrey, Campus Guadalajara. Lozano is better known as "El Pantera" among his friends, because of his speed on the court, and his characteristic gait similar to the "Pink Panther" in the famous cartoons!

ACKNOWLEDGEMENTS

It is important to include in this thankful paragraph my uncle Manuel Guerra, who placed that old wooden Wilson Jack Kramer racquet in my hand when I was 9 years old, and walked me to the practice wall in The Club Guadalajara in Mexico. To my Mom, who was always so encouraging to me. Also, thanks go to my Dad, who never really accepted Tennis as a way of life, but he understood very well he needed to let me forge my destiny. One day, my Dad took me to the ticket counter of the airline AeroMexico, pulled his credit card out, and purchased a one-way ticket to Dallas, Texas, when I received a scholarship to play collegiate Tennis in the United States. He always provided for me and for our huge family unconditionally, and for that I want to thank him deeply. Finally, I want to acknowledge my brother Luis the studious. When we were kids, he would get Tennis books from libraries to study them, and later he would explain them to me. I remember him handing me money from his own savings to buy Tennis balls or to string racquets. He also gave me some good advice on how to make time to write more, and also helped with a detailed revision of this work. "You have been a great big brother and role model to me, thank you, Luis!"

Thanks also to other coaches, friends, mentors and players of yesteryear and today who influenced me in many different ways. They were a positive force in my life as a Tennis player and the man I have become. Some of them have passed away already, and I think of them often for inspiration. In silence, I ask them questions on and off the court. Questions regarding Tennis and life, they are, Victor Hernández Sr., Rubén Nápoles, Pancho Esparza, Ezequiel Mercado, Ross Walker, and José Quirarte.

A note of appreciation is also in place to some of my friends and other family members who helped polish this work. They are: Sisters Alma and Laura; my lifetime friend, Jorge Lozano "Thank you, amigo."

To my friend Ross Walker "Thank you for your valuable insight and support on reviewing this manuscript. You always found a way to raise the bar a little higher for me, and in regards to this book it was no different. Thanks for the advice and support. You know I think the World of you."

Also big thanks and appreciation goes to Tim Mayotte, Cliff Drysdale, Peter Doohan and son John, thank you for your ideas, enthusiasm, and support."

To JP Weber, "thank you JP for your insights and support. You were always a dreamer, a radical and a visionary, keep dreaming; it's free and its fun".

Jess Donham, thanks for the help reviewing my manuscript, you are without a doubt the most voracious and amazing reader I have known; what in the World were you doing working at a Tennis shop?

Thanks also go to all Tennis players of yesterday, today, and tomorrow around the World for making this game what it is today, and especially all dedicated junior players! "All of you have been a source of inspiration and commitment my entire career!"

Last but by no means least I am forever indebted and thankful to my great friend and editor Steve Ersinghaus, the English Master, Poet, and Philosopher. "Thanks Steve for your guidance, inspiration, motivation and daily hard work." Steve and I go back a long time. We worked at El Paso Tennis Club in El Paso, Texas back in the 1980s. We became friends through Tennis and many other mutual interests such as chess and camping. Back in those years, Steve traveled with me deep into Mexico as part of my support team pursuing Professional Tournaments. Although Steve was not pursuing professional Tennis, he was a good Tennis player and a great sparring partner for me! We had some good times and some rough times! But he was always adventurous and positive! "Gracias Amigo".

INTRODUCTION

What Tennis Pros Don't Teach was written with the every-day Tennis player in mind. *What Tennis Pros Don't Teach* was also written with the everyday Tennis pro in mind, and *What Tennis Pros Don't Teach* was written with the everyday junior Tennis player and his or her family in mind. This book is not your typical Tennis book with lots of pictures and complicated technical stuff nobody can understand. This book is an effort to compile in a practical and useful way knowledge accumulated in my years devoted to Tennis as a junior, college, and professional player. Also, as a coach, and finally, as the dad of a junior Tennis player.

This book is an effort to break away from the stereotyped Tennis Professionals we have all around the World. This book is a work of love of the game and an attempt to help the Tennis hungry player. Hungry to be better, hungry to know more about the game, hungry to learn and understand Tennis, or hungry to be the very best he or she can be! Yes, it's all about hunger!

It is not the intention of this author to pitch himself as a *know-it-all* but to offer a guide and a hand to those in search of answers in the complex World of Tennis. Neither is it the intention of this author to dip into political issues or be critical of others but to provide a different perspective.

The writing of *What Tennis Pros Don't Teach* has been an unfulfilled responsibility in the back of my mind for many years now. The idea of the title came to mind several years ago. And I had started writing at least an equal number of times and an equal number of times I had lacked the discipline, inspiration, and sheer drive to take it to completion. As the book materialized little by little, it became more of an urge, and, like the snowball effect; the more I wrote, the more the urge grew stronger to continue.

The title *What Tennis Pros Don't Teach,* also refers to the fact that a student can go a lifetime taking Tennis lessons from numerous coaches and still come away from such instruction with significant gaps. This book is also an attempt to plug some of these holes.

This book is an effort to compile a knowledge base for anyone wanting to read and learn. A lot of people have paid pretty huge sums of money for some of the information contained in these pages. And then again, all the money they have paid did not get them even close to having all the information presented here. Although, no player in the World needs to know all there is to Tennis, every player in the World would benefit in several ways from at least some of the concepts, ideas, and information on *What Tennis Pros Don't Teach*.

The word *Wisdom* is used in this book as part of the subtitle. Webster's definition of wisdom is *accumulated philosophic or scientific learning, knowledge, insight, good sense, judgment, a wise attitude or course of action.* There are several books that include this word in their titles. How about the *Bible's Book of Wisdom*! All the information in these pages involves the above definition in practical and applicable solutions to problems that present themselves on and off the Tennis court.

Several of the principles presented here, such as those in *Section III, Subtitle: Transitioning,* apply more directly to junior Tennis and junior development. However, we can find information applicable to any Tennis player at any stage or level of development, regardless of age or gender.

Dive in with an open mind, this is not a novel to be read from page one to the end of the book. But go ahead and read the whole thing; then come back and underline what seems relevant, and then come back and read what was underlined yet again. Make notes on sticky pieces of paper and place them on the underlined sections where the notes came from. Once having done this, use this book as a reference; throw it in the Tennis bag and take it to the court everywhere to play Tennis. It will be like having a Tennis coach at hand all the time. The idea of carrying a book in the bag; is not a new one. I have seen some really good players do this in the past. It is also very common to see a player sitting on a changeover reading notes on his or her lap. These notes are probably coming from books or their coaches.

I am confident every Tennis player in the World could benefit one way or another from reading this book.

SECTION I

FOUNDATIONS, SETTING THE STAGE

LOVE OF THE GAME

For this book to make sense to the aspiring junior or anyone trying to develop their game, there needs to be a secret ingredient. Although, this ingredient is not a secret at all, it's called *love of the game*. However, it seems to be a secret; since there are so many coaches, children, dads and moms try to get their kids into Tennis without realizing this in the first place. Without love of the game, this book makes little sense and will be pointless. As Coaches and Tennis Pros, we need to have a deep love of the game in order to be able to instill that attitude in all our students and players. If we don't sincerely love Tennis, how can we teach it to anyone? Or how can we be role models for our kids and students so that they learn to love it as well? And how can we expect our children to invest the huge effort and lots of time needed for Tennis if we don't show them how to love every minute of it?

In order to help develop a full understanding of the value of Tennis, as Coaches, we have to be models for our students, and as parents we have to be models for our children. Players have to learn to enjoy every step of the way, good or bad. Tennis is an incredibly tough challenge, but it is one worth undertaking because it helps people forge their lives in so many ways. Consider these quotes "Love what you do, and do what you love" or "Fight for what you love." How will anyone fight and sacrifice for something they don't love?

The word sacrifice should not be taken lightly. This word needs to be explained to junior players very carefully. Sacrifice encompasses a lot of things, here is a short list: Going to practice instead of to a friend's party. Choosing to play in a tournament over going on a vacation. Or going to sleep early in order to be 100% the next morning, instead of staying up late watching a movie or show on TV. Also, going the extra mile on the Tennis court, by spending additional time practicing after junior drills or lessons to polish technique. Eating more nutritiously instead of all the sweets, desserts, and greasy foods that probably taste better, but are not good for our body. For a teenager, these challenges are incredibly difficult since they have to spend a lot less time socializing and being kids and a lot more time on the Tennis court. Kids who sacrifice for Tennis have to give up a lot because they don't have time for what other kids do. Said another way, kids who love the game of Tennis and sacrifice for it are a little different because they understand that they are pursuing a significantly higher goal. We have to help them understand these contrasts better so they persist regardless of how insurmountable the challenges may seem. In Tennis, as in anything in life, the only way to reach and exceed dreams is to be passionate about them! How can anyone be passionate about anything they don't love? How about this quote? "Without love, I am nothing." Does it sound familiar? (Corinthians, 7.25.14)

My daughter drew a pink heart on a sticky piece of paper with the well-known phrase: I (love) Tennis; she is only ten years old! I dated it and placed it inside the front cover of one of our favorite classic collection books, and maybe, she will stumble upon it one day when I am gone... and remember!

HEALTH BENEFITS OF PLAYING TENNIS

As mentioned elsewhere in this book, it has been scientifically proven that Tennis will prevent death for all reasons combined as much as 50%. This statistic is true if we play Tennis two or more times per week for periods of 45 minutes or more.

What else do we want?

Tennis increases strength, stamina, reflexes, flexibility, coordination, as well as mental toughness. In other words, Tennis teaches how to deal with pressure and problem-solving when under the gun. All of these things ought to make everyone think they need to be playing Tennis at least a couple of times per week. In addition, how can anyone afford not to play Tennis? This study was published in the *New England Journal of Medicine* back in the early 90s by Dr. Ralph Paffenbarger. He conducted a study with over 10,000 individuals over a 20 year period.

On top of all the above reasons for playing our awesome sport, Tennis is great fun! Take a look at the 101 reasons for playing Tennis in the 101 Section of this book.

SPORTSMANSHIP, ETHICS, VALUES

The single most important aspect of a Tennis Professional's job is to teach a player sportsmanship. Tennis coaches need to reinforce what I am sure parents want for their kid out of Tennis: to play by the rules in a level field and to understand that winning is worthless without sportsmanship and ethics. Respect must be shown to all opponents, officials and anyone involved in the Tennis milieu. Players must make the right calls to the best of their ability and conduct themselves properly on and off the court in tournaments and Tennis facilities.

Sportsmanship should be one of the greatest priorities in Tennis. Show manners and respect, address officials and tournament personnel with the utmost politeness on and off the court, and keep strong talk and negative conduct out of the equation no matter what.

The philosophy of winning at all costs and the "Whatever It Takes (WIT)" philosophy is fundamentally wrong. I have seen these initials on some college campuses and wonder who sanctions this; a college campus... really? Who in their right mind would allow WIT or promote this kind of mentality? We are a decaying society in some ways!

Winning in Tennis (and so it should be in all other sports as in life itself) is only valid and worthy if promoted ethically. Players, coaches and parents who think otherwise have their values messed up.

Unfortunately, I have seen this WIT mentality exercised by parents and even some coaches many times. Parents who are okay with their kids making bad calls in order to win a match are not all that uncommon. It is not uncommon to encounter coaches who say nothing to their players after a close match, where the player made a bad call at just the right moment at a crucial point. How distasteful is it to hear players bragging about bad calls to other players and how they got away with it?

Something hard to understand is when players sign up for a tournament in a lower division than their ability level calls for, so they can win more easily. Is there merit to this? Is there glory? I wonder what it feels like to just beat up on players who are inferior in caliber. Can it possibly feel good?

It's a tough call; that's all. When our opponent makes a great shot on the line at a crucial moment in the match; ethical play indicates that the right thing to do is to make the correct call. The player who lost the point needs to be thinking something like this: "If he or she can raise his or her game to that level now, so can I. Here we go." If the match is lost, so be it, shake the opponent's hand, congratulate him or her, smile, learn from the loss and move on. I will personally give athletes a pat on the back and take my hat off to them for being ethical and true sportsmen. In my mind, the loser is the true winner here, and I can see a bright future.

If a player is truly trying to make it all the way by cheating, bending the rules and maneuvering others, eventually he or she is going to hit a brick wall. Because the higher the level of competition players engage in, the more refereeing these dishonest players will encounter. Umpires and officials will eventually stop them down the road. In other words, unethical play and cheating will lead to nothing. It's a dead end.

The only real way to win is through ethical play! Anything outside of this simple definition is probably not winning but losing; losing the opportunity to do the right thing, and feeling good about it regardless of the result. A player cannot possibly feel good about "winning a match" if he or she resorted to gamesmanship and cheating.

NOBODY KNOWS IT ALL

Nobody knows everything there is to know about Tennis. Nobody can write everything there is to be written about Tennis in a single volume such as this one. I consider myself knowledgeable about Tennis because I have played for 45 years and have taught for over 30 years. I have been through all stages of the game as a player and as a coach; from tiny tot to junior Tennis, then college Tennis and ultimately through Professional Tennis. Even though, I have all this experience; I still get surprised all the time by outcomes or predictions that were flat out wrong! I have to say then... Nobody knows *nothing about nothing* when it comes to Tennis!

In order to agree fully with someone, we have to hear what they have to say about whatever subject, be it Tennis or anything else. Opinions in Tennis are as varied as there are stars in the sky. What may be the worst thing ever for one person, may actually work just fine for someone else. This theory will hold true even when talking about high caliber Tennis. The moment someone says something is impossible or wrong, the next thing we know, here is an awesome player proving everyone ignorant or presumptuous. A simple illustration of this would be the great Monica Seles with her two-handed forehand and backhand. Not an acceptable technique and many thought she had very few chances of making it to the top. A few years later, she was No. 1 in the World.

Here is an interesting story: In Washington, D.C. I believe the year was in 2001, I attended the USTA High-Performance Training Program School. That same week the US Open Series tournament The Legg Mason Tennis Classic Championships was being played. So several of us attending the training thought it was a good idea to swing by and catch some top notch professional Tennis first hand. I spent all my afternoons there watching players from all over the World training and playing matches. The Bryan brothers were barely starting their professional career. On the last day of the conference, I had a conversation with the USTA program director. I was telling him how impressed I was with the Bryan brothers with their big serving and lightening speed, creativity and shot making. At which he said to me that they had no chance of making it in professional Tennis, and they were on their way out. He also said something about their father being their coach getting in the way of their development or something like that. So here we are in 2014, thirteen years later, and the Bryan Brothers are still going strong and are considered to be the best doubles team in the history of Tennis. They have to their credit a record number of Grand Slam Titles, Olympic Gold Medals, and Davis Cup Titles. How is that for going for predictions and being an expert in Tennis?

Another mishap of this nature coming from an "expert" occurred at Roland Garros in 2014: Sharapova is playing versus Muguruza in the quarterfinals. Muguruza is playing great and takes the first set handily 6/1; in the second set Sharapova starts lightening up as her game and great mental toughness start surfacing. They play really close all the way to 5 all. At that point, Sharapova is serving as Muguruza gets up 15/30 in the score during that game. By now I am getting a little irritated because our expert TV commentator keeps making remark after remark about how good Muguruza is and how she looks like she is going to win this match. But we all know what Maria is made out of. We have seen her come back once and again from pretty intricate situations. However, our TV commentator mentions how Muguruza is *only 6 points* away from winning the match; which meant that in order for her to win she needed to break Sharapova and hold serve. Now, we know that in Tennis, things don't work out that way, especially when we are dealing with awesome competitors like Maria Sharapova. Our "Expert", was also referring to the 6 points needed to be won; to be pretty much done in a row, or almost in a row, because we know that in Tennis, we can go to deuce back and forth many times in a game. When was the last time we saw a player win 6 points in a row if playing against a good opponent? It does sometimes happen when someone is totally dominating someone else, but in close matches it is very uncommon. Winning 6 points is no easy task, and it may be easier to climb Mount Everest! Of course, Maria ended up winning that 2nd set 7/5 and the 3rd 6/1. How is that for misleading the audience? Right about the time the erroneous and out of place comment was made Maria was grasping the momentum of the match. When she did, she never let go and ended up winning the 3rd set pretty easily! Situations and comments like this happen all the time on TV and around Tennis courts and facilities. Don't believe everything that's coming from the so called gurus, experts or professionals. Be skeptical and quizzical, investigate and find the truth!

At the 2015 Wimbledon, Sam Groth faced Fed in the third round. The big Australian was trying his heart out to serve smart to be able to hold in order to maybe force a tiebreaker to give himself a better chance. That much he did achieve in the 3rd set winning it 7/6. From the beginning of the match, two famous commentators were talking about how small Groth's chances were since Fed had been playing really well throughout the tournament to that point. Since Groth possesses one of the hardest serves in the World, our two commentators kept talking about how all he should be focusing on is breaking the record for the fastest serve in Wimbledon's history of 148 mph set by Taylor Dent in 2010. I find that ludicrous to say the least. As a player, Sam was obviously trying to figure out ways to win and was very nervous throughout the majority of the match versus the legendary Roger Federer. I think that going for the record of the fastest serve ever at Wimbledon was low on his bucket list for that match, and our commentators obviously misled the audience. Professional Tennis players want to win matches to move up in the rankings and make money. Sooner or later somebody would come and break the fastest serve ever recorded at Wimbledon anyway. That's what always happens to speed records, so who cares? It is impressive to see someone serve that hard, I agree, but I will take winning and serving effectiveness anytime over speed records of any type any day!

The previous stories remind me of the old quote from Le Petit Prince: "Here is my secret. It is very simple: One sees well only with the heart. The essential is invisible to the eyes."

When my wife Carmen and I got married, we had the print shop put this quote from *The Little Prince* in the back of the invitation cards.

In the heat of battle, we can see the struggle, the fight, the punches coming and going. But we cannot see the feelings, the fire, the emotions, the determination and the drive. Such things make the heart of a champion, thus only with the heart can one perceive them!

Another good example of Tennis experts making wrong assumptions and comments happens when players switch grips the wrong way. Some of these players (no need to mention names) are or have been ranked top 100 in the World. These players switch grips in a reverse way. The normal way to switch grips is as follows: Observing the player from behind, he or she will switch the grip by rotating the racquet clockwise to obtain the backhand grip and counterclockwise for the forehand grip. Some "experts" say that doing it any other way is a flaw and not acceptable. But how do we argue with success?

WHAT TENNIS PROS DON'T TEACH (WTPDT)

At the USPTA Winter Southern Conference in Memphis in 2012, one of the speakers presenting a seminar on Junior Development, mentioned that one of the pro players participating in the US National Indoor Tennis Championships, played at the Racquet Club of Memphis, taking place simultaneously with the conference, had this problem, and therefore he would not make it. At the beginning of the seminar, he was quizzing the audience to see if anyone had caught the switching grips technicality during a match most of us had attended the night before. Towards the end of 2014, this player was already ranked in the 42nd spot in the ATP World Rankings. Is that not successful? I guess we would have to define success to begin with. By the way, at the time of this writing this player is only 22 years old and on his way up.

Anyway, the question remains: is the way these professionals actually switch grips, clockwise or counterclockwise, correct or incorrect? Here is how these pros do it: "incorrect or correct?" The racquet only turns in one direction, to either go to a backhand grip or to get back to the forehand grip; only clockwise for a right handed player and only counterclockwise for a lefty. In other words, from his/her regular forehand grip, he/she spins the racquet from left to right or clockwise, to switch to his/her two-handed backhand grip, and from the two-handed backhand grip, he/she goes back to the forehand grip by spinning the racquet in the same direction (clockwise as well), instead of going in the opposite direction or counter-clockwise! Going from the backhand to the forehand, these players actually use the standard or normal method of grip switching! But when switching from forehand to the backhand for top-spin shots, they end up hitting the ball with the same side of the racquet face, and this is perceived by some coaches as incorrect technique! This situation is only sort of common with players who utilize a western or a semi-western grip.

It is often difficult to determine what is right or wrong on a Tennis court. What works for some might not work for others. We do have certain boundaries and standard approaches for the development of solid technique. These should not be set aside, like generating racquet head speed through the proper utilization of our whole body and not just our arm or hand. As a coach, always apply the principle that: *if it ain't broke, don't fix it*. Any stroke in Tennis, be it a serve, a groundstroke or any other technique, which gets the job done, should not be messed with. Unless we, as coaches, are 100% sure that it will far surpass the way it performs now!

As Tennis pros, we shouldn't get all fluffed up about ourselves. We need to recognize our limitations. We may not be able to coach every player on this planet. We need to recognize when a player outgrows us. We need even to help him or her move on to the next level by finding the right coach or Tennis professional or program. It would be wise if Professional Tennis Associations developed a more standardized way to qualify their professionals. We need specialists for kids 7 years of age and under, specialists for 8 to 10 and 11 to 13, and finally 14 to 18 year-olds. Specialists for College-player-level training would be a significant change and even specialists for professionals. We even need specialists for adults and seniors. It would be great if we could get to the point where there is a specialist for the beginner, intermediate and advanced player in all the stages of Tennis. Specialization should be the job of the Tennis professional himself and not the Tennis organizations across the planet. In a way, Tennis coaches and professionals have their niche of comfort. For the most part, we already have several of these specialists. However, in failing to recognize our own niche, we will encounter the problem everywhere. If too broad a spectrum of players was taken up or was put into our hands and we end up doing a mediocre job of it all.

One of our main deficiencies as Tennis Professionals is that we try to cover too much ground. Instead of doing an excellent job in one area and expand within this area, a lot of times we end up doing a poor job in all areas. On top of all Tennis know-how, Tennis Pros are also demanded to be administrators of Tennis programs, Tennis facilities, and budgets.

Nobody knows everything about Tennis and nobody can solve every problem in the game. Eventually, Tennis Pros will need to move into a more specific way of doing things.

There should be no Tennis Directors as we know them today. Being a Tennis Director is a full-time job in the sense that at most Tennis facilities, the administrative part of the job is already full time. On top of the amount of administrative work, Tennis Directors are also expected to teach a pretty full schedule of lessons, and their teaching must encompass all levels. That is absolutely crazy and virtually impossible to do successfully unless this Tennis Pro is Superhuman! Instead, let's put in place a Tennis administrator or manager, who is trained to do what they do best: run the business. At some facilities, Tennis pros are even required to do maintenance work... That needs to change!

WHAT IS TENNIS-PRO OR COACH CERTIFICATION?

Tennis associations and federations like USPTA, USPTR, USTA, ITF and others provide some low-level coaching certifications, that, in theory, qualify someone to teach Tennis. These so-called certifications, to me, are at best, equivalent to a high school diploma in the majority of cases. It should by no means, in my mind, allow someone to teach Tennis, at least to junior players; until they have done their homework in the form of a dissertation or thesis. Especially problematic are the so-called coaches who teach but who have had very little to no experience as players. They learn how to play Tennis to a level of 3.5 or 4.0 (A or B level in most other countries in the World), and then they are let loose to teach juniors at some country club or Tennis club. Many of these so-called Tennis teachers work at public courts. It must be said that an aspiring Tennis teacher should have at least competitive junior and college Tennis experience.

A much more rigorous certification process needs to be instilled into the system. This way when players seek out a certified Tennis professional, they can trust that they have found someone knowledgeable in the sport, someone who has truly earned the title through experience, study, and training! This level of certification is more common in Europe, and that is part of the reason they are producing so many more players than we are here in America.

A promising 6 or 7-year-old with the right athletic and mental ability will be lost if he or she spends any amount of time in the hands of the wrong "Tennis Pro". Moreover, a child's successful development with the right physiological makeup, commitment and support system will be 100% the result of the quality of the coaching provided!

Having a license to teach or exert influence in many other professions is regulated, in some instances, by state or federal laws. Why then are we not placing the same emphasis on Tennis, when we know how character-building, or how life-defining Tennis can be in a child's development?

There are, of course, some anecdotal stories "So and so are really good coaches, but they never were strong players" in their defense. Let me answer that, as in everything else, the exception confirms the rule! I too have seen some good coaches who have had very little experience as players!

FINDING THE RIGHT TENNIS-PRO/ COACH AND PROGRAM/ACADEMY

Not all good coaches can work with all students. Through experimentation and study, it has been found that Tennis coaches need to adopt a persuasive style of teaching. Even players that are not self-motivated or have lost interest in Tennis for one reason or another can be persuaded to work hard or get back at it by a good coach. Neither authoritative nor submissive approaches will work. The thing here is that in order to persuade players, coaches need to set the tone for how things are done. How can coaches convince players to work hard, eat healthily, and play for all the right reasons if coaches don't act as role models, mentors, and friends?

Unfortunately, players will not have that many exceptional coaches to choose from. Ideally, a coach who has a similar playing style as the player in question will probably make a better coach, but by no means is this a rule. A coach ought to be able to coach all different styles successfully. Players and parents should have a close look at a Tennis Pro's current or previous students. If possible, they should get an opinion from those students before signing up to work with the coach. A coach does not have to be active in tournaments, but it helps if the coach is active in Tennis recreationally and/or for fitness, as well as developmentally. We want a coach who can play points and hit lots of balls for long periods of time. If he or she is too old, maybe he/she can hit half court, while the student has to cover the whole playing area. After all, it is the student who will be the one playing in the tournaments and winning or losing matches, not the coach.

Personality plays a big role in finding the right coach. Relaxed personalities may not feel comfortable with someone who is aggressive in his or her approach. Or if a player likes to take their time getting ready, make sure the coach is fine with this tempo. A player doesn't need someone next to him who is going to bring anxiety before big matches. The bottom line is that what is important to players, what they enjoy doing on a Tennis court, or on tournament trips, and what makes a difference to them, should matter equally to the coach, or at least be fully understood by him or her. This way a coach will be able to deliver what is needed to make his or her player more effective, confident and comfortable.

Questions to ask when taking a Tennis lesson or signing up to do some work with a Tennis Pro or coach:

1- What are we working on today?
2- What are our goals?
3- Can we summarize what we did in our last lesson?
4- Are we hitting, drilling, talking or playing points?
5- Can we spend some time doing such and such? (Things the student wants to work on)
6- What would be our next most immediate goal as a team and for me as a player?
7- How about this new technique or shot I have been trying?
8- Any suggestions or new ideas for stuff or a more detailed routine I need to do to stay calm before big points?
9- Etc...

Mutual understanding and trust between coaches, players, as well as their parents in the case of juniors, is paramount. Here is an anonymous quote: "Earn a coach's trust, and he or she will go any distance for his/her students." Once a coach trusts the player, parent, or just a fervent supporter, unseen benefits, and attention will result because now the initial relationship of student-coach has been surpassed. The player has an ally and a friend.

Good Tennis coaches are few and far in between. It could be that in a whole region of several communities, there isn't even one who players should consider for lessons, advice or instruction. The fact that someone is a respectable player does not and should not automatically qualify him/her to be a Tennis Pro or coach. Worse yet, there are plenty of mediocre players who will claim to be the next greatest thing since Nick Bollettieri or the Great Harry Hopman. A mediocre player can potentially become a good Tennis coach, but it will be a lot more difficult having to supplement playing ability and tournament and competitive experience with only knowledge and understanding of the sport. A coach who was a good player will find it a lot easier to work with advanced players. He/she can more easily coach at a high level given he or she has taken the time to learn what it takes to be a true teacher. It is a sad but kind of a common situation to see a player totally intimidate a coach in the juniors; because the junior player is way better than the coach. Of course, a hard-working junior player will eventually far surpass his or her coach, but by the time that happens, a solid working relationship has already proved to have been in place for a while.

Finally, just because someone is USPTA, USPTR or ITF certified, does not guarantee success. Unfortunately I have met plenty of terrible Tennis pros who were certified, and could not even teach the basic technique of the different strokes. Let me say that there are plenty of people out there who have taken lessons for years and do not know what a Continental grip or a split step is. And the Tennis Pro or coach they took lessons from was certified and had been teaching for many years.

It is very simple; why would a Tennis coach not teach the right technique or footwork on all the strokes? Why would a coach not take the time to go into detail with a student about mental toughness and how to develop it? Why is it so difficult to work on strategy and tactics? The answer to these questions is unfortunately not what players would like to hear. Because excellent coaching is a detailed, painstaking process, that takes lots of time and effort.

A great Tennis teacher is an avid observer of Tennis players on and off the court. He/she has played or still plays a lot of Tennis, and it may be that he/she is still spending endless hours working on his/her own game! One very sad thing is that many Tennis Pros, nowadays, don't even follow pro Tennis on TV or the Internet. A lot of them don't even know the names of a few of the players in the top 20 in the men's and women's sides.

I used to get carried away. I would spend way too many hours in front of a TV. As a kid, I was obsessed with following Tennis tournaments on TV. Nowadays with the TV coverage we have, it can be dangerous. My wife and my daughter get on my case about it all the time. So much so, that I decided to cut off all Tennis Programming from our TV satellite signal. Now, I only pay attention to Davis Cup and Grand Slam Tennis. What I am getting to, is that one can learn so much from paying attention to the really good players, the professionals. Let me add that a lot of what I know and teach today came from watching Pro Tennis on TV. There is so much to learn from just watching, observing good Tennis players. And I can assure anyone that all good players, all times included, learned this way! They were influenced by competent coaches and friends as well as relentless effort.

Finally getting back to the above question regarding how to finding a good Tennis coach/pro. Part of the trick is in understanding the fact that no good players were developed under a bad coach. They either did it on their own or were lucky to fall into the hands of someone capable of getting them to where they are. Before jumping on board with these coaches, listen to him/her teaching or coaching and then ask many questions, such as how long has he or she been teaching? How did he or she get into Tennis? What is his/her teaching philosophy on junior Tennis or adults? What experience does he/she have as a player? Who is the best player he or she has ever coached? And for how long did he/she work with this player?

For a Tennis Pro or coach to really go the extra mile, there needs to be more incentive than just a paycheck. Ethically it is true that any professional in any field will get the job done, or will he or she? In reality, students want an all out effort and full commitment mentally, emotionally and physically from their coach. Coaches need to pay attention to all details: Tournament schedule, training routine, practice matches, nutrition, and more. As coaches, we like to have pride in the players we work with; this means that lessons will be more focused, more intense. Moreover, players will always come back for as much as they can.

This environment will more likely produce the results everyone is looking for.

More often than not some of these so called Tennis Pros work only for the money. In other words, true vocation, devotion and passion for the game are not necessarily a part of their motivation. As coaches, we need to be passionate about our players, their results, and goals! Let me give some examples of sure giveaway signs of bad or mediocre Tennis coaches:

1. The Tennis Pro who is out of shape. Either overweight or cannot hit for more than 15 minutes at a time without running out of breath (the exception here is a Tennis coach who is overweight or out of shape because of health issues). Tennis Pros don't have to be in perfect shape, but they do need to be able to take some heat from students and show strong physical presence on and off the court.
2. The one who never hits Tennis balls or play Tennis just for fun.
3. Amigos who have competed very little or not at all.
4. The so-called Tennis Pros who don't continue to practice and try to keep their games at a respectable level. We, as Tennis teachers, owe it to our clients and ourselves to keep as high a level of play as age allows.

WHAT TENNIS PROS DON'T TEACH (WTPDT)

5. Tennis Pros who smoke or chew tobacco in the presence of students or clientele.
6. Tennis Pros who drink in excess, especially in front of their students and clientele.
7. Tennis Pros who swear in front of students and peers.
8. Tennis Pros who don't listen to students and pretend to know everything.
9. Tennis Pros who never mention the importance of the non-dominant arm and how to utilize it.
10. Tennis pros going on court to work with just one racquet in their hand. Tennis pros should walk on the court with a bag full of equipment. A Tennis bag is a true Tennis Pro's office on and off the court.
11. Tennis Pros who don't take notes during lessons or tournaments.
12. Tennis pros who don't feed enough balls to their students. A true high-performance coach will feed 10,000+ balls per week!
13. Tennis coaches or pros who talk and text on their cell phones in excess.
14. Tennis coaches who always sit down while his or her students pick up balls to replenish the teaching cart.
15. Coaches who ignore incorrect technique. Letting the students continue to practice the wrong moves.
16. Tennis pros that are not in love with the game and are not absolutely passionate about Tennis! It is not difficult to figure out if a Tennis pro or coach loves the game and how passionate they are about Tennis. A 5-minute conversation about his or her game, best students, or big projects will provide enough information.
17. Pros or Coaches who don't help their students pick up balls when the basket depletes.
18. Pros who don't clean up on a regular basis by trying to look decent for their clientele.
19. Coaches and Pros who let students socialize and talk in excess while everyone is hitting serves.
20. Coaches or pros who hardly ever attend tournaments to watch their students compete or play matches.
21. Coaches who let students make bad calls during matches or practices and say nothing about it to the student or parents.

22. Pros or coaches who are consistently late for lessons and not ever make up the time.
23. Pros or coaches who play loud music during drills or lessons. This practice is intolerable since, for full concentration and an efficient practice session, we need as few distractions as possible. Also, if music enhanced the quality of Tennis, we would hear it during professional tournaments.
24. Pros that have not been able to hold a job for at least three years in a row at a time.
25. Coaches who claim to be the best or greatest, bragging about having the best and most equipment, and latest teaching gadgetry on the market.
26. Tennis pros or coaches who peg or hit their students with the ball when playing in with them.
27. Pros or coaches who ridicule or make fun of their students.
28. Coaches who don't listen or show a legitimate concern for students when they are down or having some sort of problem.
29. Coaches who wrestle or horse around with students at the same time overpowering them.
30. Coaches or Tennis pros who get visibly/audible upset and emotionally out of control when playing/losing against their own students.

And the list goes on...

If a Tennis Pro takes notes or has a notebook all the time; that is a sign of a good Tennis Pro or coach. Taking notes is easy, and it adds a great deal to the image of the coach. Taking notes is part of carrying the office to the court. Taking notes is a valuable skill. I cannot remember how many times I came up with some awesome idea, only to get lost in my deficient memory banks. The problem ended a long time ago. When I decided to carry a small journal in my bag at all times (I call this little journal my "Genius Ideas Journal"). The idea and the title of this book came about this way!

As Coaches, we need to be mentors, leaders, and role models for all involved. My students call me *the life coach* because my speeches to them involve a lot more content than just Tennis related material. To me, it is an honor to be called *Manuel, the life coach,* by my students.

As far as finding the right Tennis program, let us just say that finding the right coach far outweighs finding the right program. The right coach will figure out ways to get players moving forward with their game and will come up with all necessary and appropriate training. The coach will provide a roadmap to follow to the desired destination. Players need to trust their coaches, be open about problems they may be having, and resolve any that may be arising. The solution to each issue will reinforce the relationship of the coach-player-parent team.

Another thing to remember is that a coach will expect loyalty from players. It is not a great idea to take lessons with one coach and do drills and clinics under another coach. However, sometimes this is necessary due to the limitations of courts or assistant coaches as well as other factors at some Tennis facilities, programs or academies.

Tennis is fundamentally an individual sport, and the right coach/player relationship will be a big determining factor in whether a player is successful or not. Tennis players need other good players to practice with, but let the coach determine how to come up with the right balance. Sometimes, the solution to this problem may take a little time, but he/she will figure it out. At the same time, coaches need feedback from players in order to be able to satisfy the student or persuade him or her they are doing the right thing! Always remember that it is not what a player can get out of a program or academy, but what he/she can bring to it that will matter. It is fine for developing players to hit with lesser players a couple of times a week, as long as this player works hard and challenges himself. Just imagine if the only way to get better was to hit with better players, then what would happen with top professionals? They very rarely get to hit with players better than themselves! A lot of times, they just hire a local teaching pro, former college player or assistant pro, get them on the court and beat up on them! One thing is for sure, I guarantee these professionals are working at 120% intensity, even though; their practice opponent is not a top 100 in the World Tennis professional.

Let me just add that as coaches, we do serve as hitting and sparring partners. However, the one thing that never fails to irritate me more than anything else is when I feel that I am working harder than my students. A coach is unlikely to want to work with students who don't go all out at least 90% of the time. Good coaches are always booked and most probably have a waiting list of players and students trying to get a spot in their schedule.

WHAT WE NEED TO LEARN FROM A TENNIS PRO/COACH?

Does everyone know what they need or want to learn from a Tennis Pro? True fundamentals and sound principles are simple in Tennis. It is easy to figure out what they are. Observe the good players and touring professionals. Don't follow the ball or pay any attention to power. Study the player, the movements of their body. Notice the balance, the eye and hand coordination. Students, as well as coaches, should build a mental profile for what a solid forehand or serve needs to look like. Modeling a game after someone else's is a good idea; modeling strokes to look like different players is encouraged, such as Federer's forehand, Sampras's serve, and McEnroe's volleys.

A good Tennis Pro needs to have a clear, preconceived idea of what solid strokes need to contain and how to teach them. Personally, I tweak the player's movements until they look sound to me. If a stroke is not solid, I am going to stay on it until it is, no matter how long it takes.

A Tennis Pro or coach should be able to demonstrate and present accurately the information regarding all the different strokes to a child or adult. This way he or she will able to understand what to do or how to move the racquet/body combination. As we explain something, and if the player is not able of doing it or reproducing it, then we need to come up with a different way of explaining things. The process goes on until the student fully understands and is at least able to perform the movements or technique to an effective or acceptable degree.

One thing is to be able to hit a Tennis ball with the right technique, and a complete other is to have the right shot selection and on court positioning under all kinds of different circumstances. Experienced former players have a huge advantage in understanding strategy and tactics and explaining these to students. Something as simple as a drill where a student hits a couple groundstrokes, followed by an approach, volleys, and overheads. Will immediately give away a player lacking experience because of improper shot selection, positioning, footwork and simple tactics. For instance, when a deep, wide fed ball is aimed to the player's backhand. He or she may go for a down the line shot low over the net, which would be wrong shot selection under most matchplay circumstances. Instead, this student needed to go for an arching trajectory shot 5 to 10 feet over the net, preferably with topspin in a crosscourt or down the middle direction. A low short fed ball, bouncing about one foot off the ground, three feet inside the serviceline, may be handled wrong by the student trying to rip a hard flat shot into the net or long. Instead of a heavy slice or topspin approach shot down the line followed by some smooth volleys. Examples such as this abound at the developmental stage. Tennis coaches and Tennis pros need to deliver solid advice and positive critique of any such happenings. Each and every ball and shot can be hit in a variety of ways and options are numerous for direction, speed, spin, trajectory, depth, etc… Developmental players have the opportunity to learn something and improve a little infinitesimal bit each and every shot hit. But a wide-open mind needs to be in place. A critical eye to see what really is going on and what can be done to make it better.

As Tennis coaches, we need to be able to deliver comprehensive understanding of the game in all the different stages. We have to be able to help others reinforce or assimilate all they need to know in order to improve their games.

ASSISTANT TENNIS PROFESSIONALS

Assistant Tennis Professionals or assistant coaches are at every Tennis facility or every Tennis program or academy. We will usually have a Director of Tennis, a Head Tennis Pro, sometimes a High-Performance Coach or Director of Junior Tennis, and two or more assistant Tennis professionals. These coaches can be good or bad. Parents and players need to identify what they are dealing with when it comes to working with them. It is often the case that a Director of Tennis or Head Pro will pass some lessons of his down to the assistants. Lack of time is usually the reason to take care of them themselves, or just to give added opportunity to the up and comer junior to practice and hone his or her skills.

Most assistant Pros come from the different college Tennis ranks. Most of them are getting into teaching Tennis because they need some cash to go on with schooling, or maybe they just want a job for the summer to get cash for gas and partying. Very few of them are working Tennis related jobs out of a sense of vocation, meaning they love Tennis and want to make a career out of teaching Tennis. Look for someone who is a good player and has had some pretty serious experience playing college Tennis or some entry level pro tournaments. Former college or professional players present us with a good opportunity to get in some pretty serious hitting at sometimes bargain lesson or hitting fees.

An assistant pro's hitting session will usually be 30% to 40% less expensive than the Head Pro or Director of Tennis. If a really good player is available to hit with some juniors for a lower fee, the opportunity exists to capitalize on some high caliber practice sessions. These guys may not be great at teaching the intricacies and detail needed for great shot production, but they can definitely transmit some serious confidence, momentum, and rhythm to an enthusiastic junior.

Be cautious here. It is not uncommon to see players or parents get too excited about a new pro or coach. A lot of times, they will jump ship from their regular coach when they find a situation like this within their reach.

Chances are these younger pros will not cut it as full-time coaches just because they came from a Division I university program where they played varsity Tennis or simply because they are fantastic players. These assistants can indeed provide some solid hitting, and point play session opportunities. They can do a great job when it comes to shot selection, strategy, and tactics. Another area, where these assistant coaches or pros fit in well, is by getting some good input regarding fitness and conditioning for Tennis.

Another word of caution is needed here regarding technique instruction. These new, young coaches or pros may have some suggestions or input regarding hitting technique. But this information should only be transmitted via the actual player's coach; confusion and loss of confidence in strokes are pretty common as a result of conflicting information regarding technique. So anything technical, and I would suggest even tactical, requires collaboration with the existing player's coach to avoid problems and setbacks in a player's development.

College players and assistant coaches present a good and refreshing opportunity for developing players. But it is better to watch them give lessons to others and ask other parents or players already hitting with them about their experiences. At first go for a couple of hitting sessions with them, and based on solid feedback, maybe sign up for a permanent lesson or weekly hitting session.

WHAT IS THE RIGHT ATMOSPHERE FOR ME AS A TENNIS PLAYER?

Some Tennis Programs are user-friendly and just about anyone seems to fit just fine. But at the same time, these may be programs where students attend for years and years and don't really ever break beyond a certain level or limit.

Other academies or junior development programs offer stiffer work regimens. These academies include fitness training, a lot of times off site at a gym, school or track somewhere, as well as mental toughness specialists and a full array of all kinds of Tennis Coaches. This kind of program may be the one that fits serious students of the game. For access to this kind of program, the player may have to leave home at an early age, sacrificing family, social development and life, and lots of money. The bottom line, this is not always a sure shot solution to developing a player's potential. Remember: personality must match the program.

I don't believe there is a program or academy anywhere that is a good fit for everyone looking to reach their potential as a player. Often, players require a more personalized approach. Plenty of fantastic players have come from a personalized program. As an example, let's say a player does private lessons twice a week with their main coach. He/she drills at a separate facility under the vigilance of other coaches and some additional training and match-play on his or her own. On top of that, the player may have a fitness training schedule tailored to his/her specific needs.

Fun, challenge, thirst for learning and hard work are the ingredients needed to fall in love and stay with Tennis for years and years.

An atmosphere, where there are lots of pretty good players of all different ages, is also a very important ticket here; this shows continuity in a program.

It is not uncommon to find a coach with four or five players all in the same division or developmental stage playing pretty good Tennis. This situation, to me, shows a lack of continuity. This coach probably got lucky and was able to recruit these players to train together. Often, the coach running such a program is not the true developer of the players, and chances are these players may have been poached or stolen from other academies and programs in the area. If such a situation is suspected, the parents of the players as well as the players themselves should be consulted. Find out a little about their background and figure out where they really came from. Healthy programs often develop players over their lifetime or demonstrate a range of veterans and newcomers.

I call coaches who poach from other junior programs, Pirates. For the most part, this kind of program tends to vanish and disappear. Unfortunately, in the meantime, some players will suffer, and a lot of times see the end of their junior career under such pirates. Some of these pirate programs and coaches will go as far as to invite some good players in an area or city to train under them for free! Offering scholarships and discounts can be destructive and is an outrageous situation that in the end will hurt the player. Parents may fall for such a scam. In reality, the pirate coach is utilizing this player's level, and reputation to recruit other players for his or her benefit or to help grow a program or academy. Parents should be wary of this situation. In the majority of cases, this is a destructive atmosphere that will ultimately end up hurting the family of the player(s) involved.

When I worked in Ciudad Juarez, Mexico, I had these two pairs of really good sisters fully developed in my Tennis school, winning tournaments at the sectional level on both sides of the Rio Grande. They ranged from 8-14 years of age. They were entirely a result of my program. There was some serious talent and drive from all of them. A new little Tennis academy sprouted nearby and a few months later, all four of them started acting a little strange. Skipping some drills or practices and traveling to some unscheduled tournaments. Before long they dropped out of my program on the basis of some silly excuses. They would say something like "The caliber of training is not there, and the assistant coaches are not doing their job" and so on. I was perplexed but suspicious. In Tennis circles, all is known sooner or later. Later on, I found out that all four of them were training for free in this new academy. Sadly but surely, a couple years later all except one of them had quit Tennis!

Technically, players in this situation are being used as moving billboards. Promising, disciplined, hard working players will hardly ever benefit under these circumstances. When this happens, the "hired junior player", will probably end up being the best or one of the best players in the program. Unfortunately, most of the hitting and training he/she will be doing, will most probably be against lesser skilled juniors.

Let me add that there may be some well-established academies or programs out there that do offer legitimate scholarships for some players in financial need. Parents should do their research, making sure they are not falling for one of these self-serving pirates.

WHO SHOULD GO FOR TENNIS? IS TENNIS FOR MY KIDS?

It could be said that Tennis is for everyone, but let me start by reminding everyone that Tennis is, for the most part, an individual sport, with the exception of Team Tennis and doubles. About 80% of all Tennis played will be individual. Parents should ask the following questions: Is my child independent? Can he/she be on his own and figure out solutions to problems independently? Is he self-motivated? Is he enthusiastic and out-going? Is he physically active? If the answer to any of the above interrogatives is yes, then parents should encourage their children to give Tennis a try! Tennis will help children forge life skills like few other sports.

Which Dad or Mom, in their right mind, would not want their children to have the above qualities? Tennis is indeed for all and parents want their child to develop that freedom... right? Then get them into Tennis. Under the right tutelage, they will flourish.

On the subject of serious junior and professional Tennis, it could be said that Tennis is not for everyone. Tennis is for those who like to be out there pushing themselves, proving they can do it. Tennis is for those willing to discipline and work extra hard every step of the way. Tennis is also for those that love every second of the process. Real Tennis players will take the good and the bad equally, the wins or losses, the good tournaments and the tough ones where things did not go as expected or anticipated, the great and poor performances. There will be plenty of all of these. Tennis is for those who are willing to get back up, over and over, after having fallen for the nth time. Tennis is for those who love a fight on a one on one basis. Tennis is for those who are independent thinkers, self-reliant and determined.

What is the risk? As the old adage goes *the greatest risk is to not take one*. What parent in his or her right mind would not want his child to become independent? Who in their right mind would not want to teach their child problem-solving and self-reliance? Tennis may not be the only way to learn these things, but it sure is a great way to do it.

Let me also add, that if a child thrives in team sports and loves the groups, the teammates, and the camaraderie that goes with it. If he or she loves the social side of the team thing and is always talking about his or her friends and spending time with them. I'll have to say that Tennis may be a hard sale and may not work out for this kid. In this situation is where Team Tennis and doubles can come into play and maybe this way we can keep some of these troopers in the sport long enough for them to start going for it on their own. Unfortunately, as mentioned elsewhere in this book, doubles has lost so much ground in Tennis that it may be too late to rescue it from how much it has been minimized by some of our Tennis organizations.

ORGANIZED TENNIS, TENNIS ASSOCIATIONS, AND FEDERATIONS

All around the World we have thousands of different kinds of Tennis organizations. These organizations are responsible for delivering an escalated leveled field of competition in all stages of the game. Organized Tennis, without a doubt, is something we need. Therefore, it should be supported. These organizations need support from players, coaches, parents, and all different kinds of sponsors.

There comes a point in the developmental process when a child or player has to be signed up for official tournaments. Matches are essential to player development regardless of age and gender. In early stages of development, official and formal matches are not necessary. A player just needs some matches for fun and recreation. As long as the player has competitive matches, he or she does not have to play in official or sanctioned events or tournaments just yet. Once higher level of competition is required by an up and coming junior player. It may be that a state or sectional ranking is needed in order to be able to enter even bigger events. At this point, it is time to join in the Tennis association and maybe start traveling a little to some out of town tournaments. At first, about $1/3^{rd}$ of the time on court needs to be devoted to pointplay and matchplay. This percentage will increase as the player continues to learn and develop more skills. A coach should be able to come up with the right amounts of matchplay versus lessons or just recreational hitting. If time allows, the player with the right motivation should be exposed to as much matchplay and fun situational point play as possible. As long as this is done in a fun environment where the right amount of pressure is present, we can be sure our player is continuing to develop. One has to be careful, not to lose sight of technical development, as well as potential burnout in this context.

It really does not matter how old the player is. He or she has to aspire to competitive matches whether it is in a tournament setting or just a friendly encounter at a public facility. When possible try to have children, play friendly matches from start to finish though. When possible, reproduce the scenario of a real tournament match in order to gain the full experience of the opportunity.

Another good reason for joining a Tennis association is to support the sport. Tennis associations and federations around the World subsist thanks to member fees, sponsors, and all kinds of contributors. All lovers of Tennis should support their local, sectional and national associations.

For the most part, organized Tennis is run by volunteers or retirees; they don't always have effective leadership or knowledge needed for the job. It is what it is and either get involved or stay out of it. If someone feels he or she is knowledgeable and would like to make things better, he or she should try to join a board or committee serving the local Tennis association. We cannot be too critical of something we are not contributing to in any way ourselves as parents, players or coaches.

It must be said that without the aid, enthusiasm for the sport and leadership of all these individuals, Tennis would not be the great sport that it is all around the World. The ITF, ATP, WTA, FMT, USTA, USPTA, etc… all add up to making Tennis an incredibly internationalized sport that is nothing but awesome, in how it works out. Also, consider that historically, organized Tennis has impacted so many peoples' lives in a positive way.

DEVELOPING THE ATHLETE FIRST AND THEN THE TENNIS PLAYER

Many Tennis academies and Tennis programs have hand-eye coordination or motor skills clinics. Here the idea is to teach kids how to run... how to move... how to jump . . . how to throw.... Training and teaching children like this is all a big mess because kids shouldn't be subjected to this sort of boring torture.

Children should get involved in different sports and disciplines at an early age: soccer, basketball, baseball, ballet, karate or gymnastics. Kids need to get involved in at least two or three of these beneficial activities by age 4 or 5 until they are at least 10-years-old, so they develop all the skills necessary to play Tennis effectively. In other words, they should develop into athletes first then start or continue their careers in Tennis. By the time they are 12 to 14 years old, they will make up their minds as to what they want to do. By then they will be fully developed as athletes and prepared to become good Tennis players if this is their inclination. Of course, all this development needs to include Tennis as part of the equation from day one. For instance, if a seven-year-old loves Tennis, he/she needs to be hitting a lot of Tennis balls on a weekly basis. However, this child should also be included in other sports on his or her schedule.

By doing this, we are also allowing kids to experience the differences in the atmosphere of the individual versus the team sports, which helps them develop socially.

Having said that, instead of sending kids to speed school at some gym, sign them up for soccer or track. Instead of sending them to some trainer to learn motor skills, sign them up for baseball or basketball camp, and so on and so forth... How about that? More fun and better results!

WHAT'S A GOOD AGE TO START IN JUNIOR TENNIS?

A child can be exposed to some of the fundamentals of Tennis the day he or she is born. Competition can start as early as 5 or 6 years old, something very simple, like a little fun match against another kid the same age and ability level. Also, little games with Tennis balls during a group clinic or semi-private lesson.

Formal competition is probably better introduced later at about age 7 or 8 years old. If the kid has already acquired enough proficiency and skill to sign up for a tournament and participate successfully. By saying "successfully," I don't necessarily mean winning; I mean the kid likes to play and has a positive experience. Parents should be aware that it is okay for a child to lose, especially at the beginning of formal competition. Parents and coaches should be supportive and show excitement. This kind of early competition should all be about learning and having fun, and learning how to compete and understanding that it is okay to lose as long effort is made to win. Pressure should be minimized. Several of my students throughout my career as a coach have entered competition before they were ten years of age. Some of them propelled the rest of their Tennis career from those fun little in-house pseudo-tournaments or childrens' matches. A few of them got burned out because it was more the parents than the kids, themselves, who wanted it. Something as simple as a couple of sets against any of the other kids that are going for Tennis is fine. It does not matter that they make lots of errors and scoring mistakes, all that matters at this stage is that they have fun and learn from the experience.

HOW MUCH SHOULD PARENTS GET INVOLVED?

This is a tough question. Parents might think, "Well, as much as possible". But that is random and not necessarily correct. Parents need to get involved a lot and work as part of a three-way team with the coach and the player(s). Parents have to be supportive, caring (but not babysitters and or slaves for their children). Winning-at-all-cost parents... Always pushing to win no matter what and trying to have their children on the court drilling and taking lessons for many hours, and playing 30 tournaments per year usually end up burning kids out of Tennis. There has got to be a balance. One of the primary reasons to have kids play competitive Tennis at an early age is to help them build character so they can perform well under real life situations in the future. If a professional player emerges, that is awesome, but the chances of this happening are one in thousands. Parents need to support their kids emotionally, on and off the court in a professional way. Parents need to help with what they can financially, such as paying for some lessons if possible and arranging for tournament travel, as well as obviously taking care of entry fees. Making hotel reservations, and planning trips to tournaments is a parent's job up to a point. At the same time, it could and should be said that a family should not be burdened or suffer because of the financial costs of lessons, drills, tournament fees, and travel. If this is the case, there is a real chance a child will feel the pressure and sooner or later will stop playing Tennis.

When watching a match, parents need to sit quietly on the side and be supportive and enthusiastic but not to the point where they annoy the opponent and distract their own kid. Great concentration is needed for Tennis, and if Mom or Dad is on the side screaming after every point, how can the player concentrate? Disapproving of bad conduct on court is a role that parents and coaches need to play. After the match is over, it has to be mentioned and greatly discouraged. Parents need to make their kids understand that making bad calls is wrong and worthless as a strategy for winning. Coaches should work with parents on correcting disruptive conduct.

A big problem with inexperienced parents also is for them to be visibly disturbed by mistakes and or bad play. When a player misses an easy shot on a big point, parents and coaches need to look unaffected by the incident and remain calm and quiet. With younger kids who still rely on their parents, there is a good chance they will be looking at their parents after every missed shot. Under tough circumstances, a sincere smile and firm sitting stance is probably good medicine to help with emotional control and to help them regroup.

Kids should be discouraged from looking at parents and coaches during play. A casual look here and there is okay. There is nothing that can be done from the outside to help him or her win a match. As the old saying goes, "Tennis matches are won inside the court." Kids have to keep all their concentration, all their effort and focus inside the court. It is also wrong, for players to be looking at other courts and points on adjacent matches. Even if it is a team competition, and the player wants to root for his/her teammates playing on nearby courts. The best cheering and rooting he or she can do is to try to win his/her own match first, and then worry about other team members.

Parents along with players should take care of the sleeping, the nutrition and hydration of their kids, especially during tournament play. Coaches can and should advise in this regard. But ultimately, parents and players need to be aware that. Not paying full attention to nutrition, hydration, and sleep, will greatly reduce the chances of the player performing at the top of his/her ability level. (See chapter on nutrition, hydration, and sleep)

What follows is a letter I wrote to all parents from our program before a big tournament:

A LETTER TO ALL TENNIS DADS AND MOMS

Dear Moms and Dads, here are some thoughts to help in understanding and supporting better all children's efforts and results during drills, practices, lessons and tournament matches.

As dads and moms, if our kid makes a bad call in favor or against himself or herself. Or if he or she messes up the score. Or if he or she is distracted and does not call a ball out that was clearly out. Or if he or she hands a couple points or games to her opponent because she is not concentrating, maybe because he/she is nervous and does not know the score. Or if he or she is having too much fun by just hitting away mindlessly. Or if he/she does not look like he/she is trying hard enough to win every point; all of those things are okay, let him/her... he/she is okay! Don't try to disrupt a natural process. Learning is a natural thing for sure! Dads and Moms, I cannot over-emphasize enough how important it is to step aside and let the Professionals do their job. When it comes to coaching on and off the court, and when they are doing lessons, and they messed up or did not listen or pay attention to instruction, just let them be. In fact, if, as parents, we cannot do all of these things; it will better for the child, the coach and ourselves to just leave. As the old Led Zeppelin song goes, *Leave the kids alone!* They will learn and be okay, guaranteed 100%... It has been done so many times in the past with no consequence and amazing results. There is no reason our kid should not be able to do it on his or her own... *Leave the kids alone!* If we cannot sit still, quietly and smiling on the side of the court, no matter what is going on... we are better off not being there at all. It will be better for everyone involved, especially our own kids. Let us all do ourselves a favor and our child; either learn self-control and restraint or step aside. Also, parents that pick up balls during practices, drills and lessons are great as long as they don't interfere at all with the lessons or instructions the coaches are imparting. They can ask questions or make comments later and talk to their kids after practice has been done. Again, the consequences of not listening to this advice can be very adverse... resulting, at best, on children frustrated with Tennis wanting to quit the sport... A sport they once seemed to love and have so much fun with!

Maybe we should not watch his or her matches and practices. This may sound pretty radical, but think about it. If by us; Dads and Moms, not being there, the kid's performance is going to be enhanced, then just drop him off at the tournament site, stay home, go shopping, etc... let the kid set himself free. Remember it is not about us! It is about the child's life and development. We as parents know we don't want to impose pressure, well not so much pressure that we push them out of the sport..!

Note: The response to this letter from parents was pretty interesting; the letter originally went to about 30 parents. About 80% of them mentioned to me later that they felt I had written the letter specifically for them. Funny!

TRAVELING WITH JUNIORS

Let's talk about traveling with juniors to tournaments. Traveling to tournaments with other players is usually a good time and a team effort. Everyone cooperates. Players have a foundation to fall back on and a support system. Lots of players will travel to tournaments without parents for different reasons. These reasons could be financial, or they could be time restrictions or other family commitments. A lot of juniors prefer to travel without dad or mom because they feel more freedom and less pressure. This freedom and the fact that the player is feeling less pressure will oftentimes result in better performances. From the developmental standpoint, this situation should be encouraged since a player who is by himself will have to be accountable for his/her acts. Sure he/she will have his or her coach for direction and advice. However, as coaches we help players get ready for matches, but we are not babysitters. An example of that would be a couple juniors who are rooming together, and they did not go to sleep early for whatever reason. Behaving this way, is irresponsible on their part and will backfire on the court the next day. As coaches, we need to give precise instructions to juniors as to what to do all the time. But there is no way a coach can keep track of 15 - 20 juniors during a big event played in multiple facilities. Kids traveling with their folks will have a lot of the work done for them. A coach does not worry so much about these players outside the court.

Good communication with all players, parents and other coaches is paramount during traveling events. Besides the spoken and person to person communication, nowadays texting with cell phones is the most common and practical way to be in touch during the event. During the weeks leading up to the event, e-mail is an effective communication tool. As coaches, we need to talk to all the players before and after matches. We want our players to be warmed up, hydrated and in the right frame of mind before stepping on the court. Touching base with all players a few times per day during tournaments; becomes a necessity to keep players on track. Young junior players will want to spend their time running around and getting exhausted before and in between matches, and by the time they need to get on the court, they have no energy left. Players need to relax, hydrate, eat and rest before or in between matches. This is a perfect time to look for some scouting opportunities. A good team player may aid with the warm up of another player, or support a teammate from the sidelines by applauding and cheering while he or she waits. It is probably not a good idea for a junior who has one or two matches left to spend all his or her time doing this. Some rest and relaxation are important as part of being ready. Listening to music, reading a good book, a game of checkers or chess, watching TV or any other relaxing activity in the shade, or in a players lounge; is probably not a bad idea while waiting their turn to go on court for a match.

Here is a list of all the things a coach needs to do when traveling to tournaments with juniors:

a) Send at least two e-mail reminders to all juniors and parents about the deadline of a traveling tournament coming up; the first one a few weeks out and the second one two or three days before the deadline. In the second e-mail, ask about doubles partners to make sure everyone is playing doubles and has a partner. At most tournaments, the deadline for doubles is one or two days after the deadline for singles.

b) After the deadline, make e-mail and texting distribution lists of all players and parents traveling. Send an e-mail with a phone list of everyone's cell phone information on it for added team communication purposes.

c) Send e-mail information to all regarding the tournamen, check in procedures, special regulations for the event, traveling fees, coaching fees, hotel information, directions, addresses and phone numbers for Tennis facilities, the tournament director and the referees. For the most part, this information will be found on the tournament website, but this is a good way to make sure to emphasize the most important points in it.

d) Send information concerning age group warm up, practice times, and places. (Arrangements have to be made in advance to make sure sufficient courts and locations are available for this purpose) For first rounds, we usually have a team warm up 1 hour and 30 minutes before the start of the first match. Typically, these practices/warm-ups are one hour long. Practice/Warm-up serves several purposes:

to relax and loosen players, so they are ready for their matches, as well as talk about strategy and tactical stuff with some or all of the players. Practice/Warm-up is of particular importance if players have matches starting the same day they traveled.

e) Usually, a coach will travel in a team van or SUV. Via e-mail a coach needs to find out who will be traveling alone without parents. Time and place for departure need to be known at this time. We usually meet outside the Tennis Shop at our Tennis facility to load up luggage.

f) Traveling by plane requires arrangements to be made further in advance. Time to meet at airport, rental vehicle, hotel reservations, etc...

g) At the main tournament site, we usually have a team camp under a large tent or gazebo with coolers, water, ice, granola bars, sports drinks, folding chairs, a couple sets of chess or checkers and even mats or blankets so a player can lie down and stretch, or just relax while waiting in between matches. I like to carry a banner with our logo and slogan on it and will tie it to the top edge of the gazebo for identification and promotional purposes. Also, a ball hopper full of good Tennis balls is always handy in the camp, so any player wanting to do some extra fine tuning or serving on his/her own, before, or in between matches, can do so.

h) Another e-mail to the team asking players for performance and result goals is a good idea. Players need to share goals in writing with coaches before their first round of play.

i) Additional information regarding uniforms, playing conditions, scouting, coaching, hydration, rules regarding conduct around tournament site or hotel. Cheering should also be spoken of, encouraging team players to sit down and watch teammates competing even for a few points if possible.

j) Team Dinner. We always have a team dinner the second day of a tournament. It is not mandatory because it has to be scheduled at an early enough time so everyone goes to bed at a respectable hour and sometimes there may still be matches going on. Players, parents, and peers or friends love team dinners. I usually let the parents pick the restaurants, as long as it's a place with a healthy atmosphere and decent food choices. A team dinner is a great opportunity to visit with everyone and to share tournament tales. Team dinners also make a great recruiting tool, since oftentimes, a player or parent may ask a friend to join, and the next thing we know, is that another kid joins my program. Having dinner with teammates is not a formal event, and almost everyone will show up in Tennis clothes.

Once the tournament is finished, I like to write individual reports to all players and parents regarding observations, overall performance, and future goals. Writing reports from tournament observations is a great way to continue to build rapport with the team and momentum for the next event, be it traveling or local.

Throughout my career, I have spent thousands of hours watching player's matches. This is the single most satisfying part of my job and the one I absolutely love the most. When traveling to tournaments, a coach will have lots of things to worry about, but it will all be worth it the moment he/she sits down on the sidelines, and starts taking in the shot making, the tactical moves, and overall performances. It's time to harvest!

COACHING IN TENNIS

Historically, coaching has been allowed in Tennis when played as a Team Sport. This has been good and has added excitement and dimension to the game. In doubles, of course, coaching happens all the time. One player may be coaching the other player as when we see a seasoned veteran and a less experienced player competing together. It may be that both players are assisting each other. Coaching has been a tradition in High School Tennis, College Tennis, and at the Davis Cup and Federation Cup levels.

Coaching rules have changed recently allowing some degree of coaching in junior Tennis, and in some women's professional events. In my mind, this is not a good idea since we are stealing away juniors' opportunity to develop on their own and learn independently. Until when, will a player continue to have a coach to fall back on? Or until when, will he/she be independent enough and mature enough to get out there and figure it all out on his or her own? Independent learning encourages confidence, maturity, growth as well as self-correction. Are we babying our future champions-in-the-making too much? Are we inhibiting their development by not allowing them to fully be independent thinkers? Too much intervention could easily lead to players maturing later as opposed to earlier. This should be an issue of major concern for a lot of coaches, parents, and players. Reaching Tennis maturity simultaneously with physical prime is not always possible. Some players reach their potential technically and tactically when they are in their mid and late twenties. Optimally, however, players want to reach Tennis maturity in their early twenties.

It seems to me that coaching from the sideline at the junior level is counterproductive. Instead of accelerating development, it slows it down! Juniors need to learn hard lessons that are going to lead them to become better at everything and anything they end up doing in life. Kids need to make mistakes now while they are kids and not later when they are men and women entrenched in real life. Mistakes later in life tend to be a lot more costly!

In addition to developmental and maturity factors, there are other aspects that seem to point to excessive coaching as not being such a great idea. What I am referring to is the fact that not all juniors can afford a coach. As in so many things in life, "We get what we pay for." I cannot remember how many times, I have walked on court after two players split sets, and sat down with one of my juniors, and spoke to him/her openly about how to play a match tiebreak or a third set. At the same time, I felt bad for the other player who either did not have a coach or anyone else to talk to or at best his/her mom or friend. Let me say that I am not such great coach that my players always won under these circumstances. My players have lost at least 20% of those matches, which is humbling to me and at the same time, I have tipped my hat and congratulated the winners.

It is definitely not fair to allow some players the benefit of coaching while others get zip. On or off-court coaching should not be allowed in junior Tennis or in any other type of individual competition. It is fundamentally flawed, and it is a rule that needs to be revised quickly. Associations and Federations need to either rule out all coaching or provide a qualified coach for all those who don't have one in sanctioned tournaments!

As a player of many years, let me now say, that it would not feel good to me to win a match having had an unfair advantage over my opponent, such as a good coach, while he had none.

On the other hand, there are many reasons why coaching can be a good idea. It does provide an opportunity to make ourselves helpful to our players in many ways. It is not only about strategy and tactics, or making our player aware of his or her opponent's flaws and weaknesses, as well as strengths, but also giving advise regarding mental toughness and emotional control. Factors such as getting the player calmed down, hydrated, cooled down or refocused on effective play will come into the conversation. Another common coaching tip in these circumstances is to get the player accelerating or decelerating the pace of the match. Coaching allows for close and personal influence of a junior player's performance in the heat of battle. Coaching at this level is a sacred thing. Let me add that we should not be messing with it unless we are 100% and totally engaged in what we are doing!

Coaching matters to players, parents and tournament organizers, as well as associations and federations. It matters because it makes a difference, and a lot of people are willing and able to pay large sums of money to get the absolute best coaching they can. Unfortunately, not everyone has this chance; it is not a fair World. But Tennis is still a game, and we can help by leveling the field and having the right rules in place and enforcing them.

It is also worth mentioning that coaches and parents who insist on coaching players illicitly are doing them a tremendous disfavor. We send a strong message to junior players that it is okay to cheat and act unethically and dishonestly in order to obtain what we want. Rule-bending or outright rule-breaking should be punished with hard fines, violations, and hard suspensions for offending coaches and parents from tournament participation. Less attention and less severity should be given to the players themselves, whose fault may be difficult to determine.

At this point, I'd like to make mention of a few great coaches in the history of Tennis. Let's start of course by making mention of Harry Hopman, the great Australian coach who was all discipline and whose understanding of the game has not been matched to date. Also José Higueras, who has coached and influenced so many top juniors and professionals in recent history and has a staggering and profound record as a Tennis analytic. One of my favorites is also Brad Gilbert with his best seller "Winning Ugly" and his peculiar and practical way of coaching that led champions like Andre Agassi and Andy Roddick to great heights. Lennart Bergelin, who was Bjorn Borg's coach, with his secretive but effective coaching techniques. Tom Gorman stands in my mind as one of the greats since he had such an unbelievable record as a Davis Cup Captain and Coach for the USA squad. In Mexico, we had a great Davis Cup Captain and Coach who really knew how to get into the players' heads by the name of Ives Lemaitre. Another one is Pancho Contreras, who defeated the US and Australia in an epoch when that was a forbidden thing to do. Many other names deserve mention and an incomplete list is all I can jot down at this time, Dennis Van Der Meer, John Newcombe, Ivan Lendl, Paul Annacone, Tony Roche, Larry Stefanki, Darren Cahill, Jimmy Connors, Jim Courier, Chris Evert, and many more. This list does not account for many of the great coaches I have met throughout my life. High honors to them, too. The cases above are all former top players. I'll let the reader draw their own conclusions about that.

In professional Tennis, there is a mantra, "Don't hire a Coach, who has not been ranked in the top 100 in the World." Personally I could not make this cut. At the same time, players can't be blamed for this unwritten rule. Maybe the exemption confirms the rule.

To all great coaches of yesterday, today and tomorrow my hat is off for all the great contributions to the game and the forging of men, women and children all around the World. Coaches are teachers, and they will be received in the afterlife with high honors at the end of days… let us all be teachers of the truth and what is right!

CREATING A VISION... LIVING THE DREAM!

All high aspiring and up and coming Tennis players in the World should have a vision. A vision that will help them see where they will be 5 years out, and maybe as far as 10 years down the road. Creating a vision is not easy and is not for everyone. This applies more to Tennis players who have shown pretty serious commitment and have fallen in love with the game of Tennis. These players are ready to go to the next level in how they train and what they expect to do with their Tennis. It is difficult for children under the ages of 12 or 13 to have this clear vision. At this stage of development, they don't yet have the maturity and autonomy to determine with certainty how much they will be committing to Tennis or the consequences and sacrifices derived from this commitment. Serious players should have a clear idea of what kind of player they will become down the road. Several interrogatives come to mind. Here is a list of questions that demand some thought if a player is to go the distance necessary to achieve their goals and full potential:

1) What will his/her playing style be?

    a) All court?
    b) Counter Puncher?
    c) Aggressive Baseliner?
    d) Serve and volley or net rushing?

2) Will the player be well rounded physically, technically, emotionally and spiritually?
3) What will his or her strokes look like? Will he/she have smooth, efficient strokes? Or is his/her technique going to be forceful and unorthodox?
4) What about on-court personality? Will he/she be well behaved and under control? Or maybe his or her personality lends itself more to

the kind of player that is more challenging and emotionally involved with opponents and all else in and around Tennis courts.
5) How far and how much is he or she willing to commit to Tennis? Is he or she willing and able to sacrifice lots of things for Tennis knowing that the rewards will be tenfold?
6) What about fitness level? Will he or she be a fit player who does not ever get tired, moves super fast and is very flexible and agile on the court? Is this player going to be willing to spend the time adhering to a fitness routine that helps him or her get the job done? Given genetic makeup or tendency, it is possible to predict with some accuracy the answer to these and many other questions.
7) How much time and money will be needed for coaching, traveling, tournament entry fees, training, equipment? Where will this money and resources come from?

These seven questions cover the most critical areas of player development. They not only apply to juniors, but also, for anyone seriously interested in Tennis, and even players who have been at it for years.

A critical route needs to be traced or planned for the player(s) in question. This plan should resolve the seven questions. A detailed periodization schedule (as shown elsewhere in this manuscript) is an absolute must for the committed player; this should be a weekly routine for all activities pertaining to Tennis, on or off the court.

The purpose of this plan is to have a clear road map to the final and ultimate vision of the player he or she eventually wants to be. This plan, therefore, needs to be in writing. It is very important to take into account input from players, coaches, and parents. Of course, out of the whole team, it is easiest for a coach to see the potential in a player and he can start the conversation with parents and player. Parents have to be on board and understand their role in the process as well as the financial and time commitments their kid is undertaking. And if the money is a problem (as is the case a lot of times), suggestions for alternatives have to be considered by all parties involved. Commonly it would be the coach who leads this team effort, but parents could also. If the player is mature enough, he or she could be in charge of making sure the plan is accurate and executed correctly.

It is not a bad idea to take a player on the professional tour as a role model, especially when visualizing a game style. This player needs to be someone who the up and coming player admires; a good role model makes it is easier to come up with a well defined and accurate vision. For instance, if someone is developing as an all-court player, use as role model Roger Federer. A great model for a counter puncher could be David Ferrer. A solid model for an aggressive baseliner could be Maria Sharapova, and so on and so forth. It is important to consider all possible factors and variables. At least to a certain degree, the physical makeup and personality of the player being modeled needs to match the student's physical makeup and personality. These are important considerations so that the vision can actually be realized.

It is not recommended to spend too much time on a project like this before full commitment is observed from the player in question. Children who are too young will generally say "yes" to everything we ask of them. But in the majority of cases when they get to the teen years, they veer into other activities. So, in the case of juniors and as a coach or parent, we have to wait until the player reaches 13 or 14 years of age and has shown a full intention to go the distance.

As mentioned above, characteristics such as temperament and genetic make-up must be seriously taken into account. Will the player be tall and slender? Bulky and muscle bound? Or will he or she be hot tempered and explosive or more quiet and controlled? Will this player be fast on the court or not so much? What about agility and natural athletic ability? How does all this fit into the whole equation? The genes or genetic make-up should help determine the vision!

Here is an example of a vision for a 13-year-old girl who has been playing committed Tennis with respectable results for over 5 years. She wants to play Division 1 Tennis at some top notch university and maybe professional Tennis after that.

Her dad is fit at 180 lbs and a very athletic 5' 11" in height. He is a former Tennis professional who adopted the all-court style.

Her mom is 5' 7" and also of slender build, athletic with great hand-eye coordination for just about anything she does.

This girl is already 5' 5" and still growing. An anticipated growth curve indicates she will be 5' 9" or taller. This girl's temper is kind of explosive, but she knows how to keep it under control. Physically she is very strong but flexible, with respectable mobility. She is working hard to improve this area of her game. She can hit the ball with great power already for someone her age and loves to go for it when in halfway good position. We will call this girl Cassandra for practical purposes.

Based on the knowledge presented, here is a proposed vision for Cassandra, given she does not deviate from her current path:

Cassandra is an aggressive baseliner with a well-rounded game. She has solid and efficient strokes. She has two main weapons: her serve and forehand with which she can win points consistently. Cassandra can also hit her two-handed backhand with solid control and power. She knows how to slice the ball well off both wings having a one handed backhand slice. She can finesse some really good drop shots when good opportunities present themselves, especially off the backhand since she disguises it perfectly.

Cassandra's inside-out forehand, right along with her serve, are her best shots. Her first and second serves are delivered with an effective variety of spins (flat, slice, topspin, and kick). But she can also hit the serve hard and flat (sometimes 110 MPH) with good consistency. Cassandra's slice, topspin, and flat backhands are used a lot more to set up the forehand and as a means to move the opponent around and construct the point. Cassandra's net game and volleys are solid, and she is not afraid to press forward to close out a point or as a tactical move to pressure an opponent who is a counter puncher. Cassandra also has variety from the baseline; she can employ topspin, slice, and flat shots tactically or defensively as needed.

Cassandra is competitive on the Tennis court and will keep on fighting hard regardless of the score, playing conditions or opponent. She is in pretty awesome shape and can handle back to back matches. Fatigue is a non-issue, she always seems to have plenty of energy and motivation for the next match. Cassandra has a strong temperament on the court, but she controls her emotions well. This mental control provides mental toughness, and so she is capable of dealing with controversy during matches as well as the capacity of coming back when behind in the score. She is always very thoughtful of her strategy against the different opponents she faces and understands game plans, tactical Tennis and the momentum swings of a Tennis match. She identifies these situations and knows how to keep the momentum of a match flowing in her favor.

Another characteristic worth noting about Cassandra's game is that while she moves fairly well, her mobility isn't excellent, but she is improving in this area. She is very good at anticipating and knowing where to position herself on the court. Sometimes her shot selection looks a little reckless because she hits so hard, but her targets generally fall into big areas of the court, allowing herself a better chance to stay in the points longer as needed.

WHAT TENNIS PROS DON'T TEACH (WTPDT)

Cassandra's Dad has set up a budget to manage the resources and a fund from which to draw money to support her development. She also gets help from a couple of private supporters and financial aid from Tennis organizations. She does not take this for granted, and she is well aware of all that is being done to help her be successful in her endeavors. She knows that what others require of her is maximum effort, concentrating on the performance more than the outcome. She understands that without the right frame of mind, the desired outcomes will not be there!

SECTION II
SOME TECHNICAL STUFF

DIFFERENT TYPES OF TENNIS LESSONS

There are many kinds of Tennis lessons. Often a combination of two and even three or four types of lessons may occur during a single session. Time has to be utilized wisely in order to maximize a developmental player's growth. A player, doing the same thing for the entire lesson, like hitting topspin groundstrokes for a period of 60 minutes straight is probably not the best way to spend a lesson with a Tennis pro.

Hitting lessons: Nothing beats a hard hitting session with emphasis on different aspects of someone's game that needs work. Things such as consistency, accuracy, technique, even strategy and mental toughness can be addressed; this is why it is very important for a Tennis Pro to be able to hit and play at as high a level as possible. Generally, if a coach misses more shots than the student, the coach needs to get on the court and practice and or get fit. If the coach is older, a good hitter may be needed and have the coach teaching from the side of the court. This is a best case scenario since a good coach on the side observing will probably do a better job of detecting problems and give better advice.

Backboard or wall lessons: An overlooked way to take lessons is through the use of a backboard or hitting wall. A coach can stand next to a student and address details as they do all the hitting and moving. Nowadays, Tennis players practice very little on walls. By doing lessons this way; students are assured that the coach is going to pick up on everything that needs to be addressed.

Ball feeding or drilling (dead ball drills): This kind of lesson can be very valuable for highly technical instruction. This type of lesson can also be used to work on mental toughness, or a player's personal image control and management. This type of training is done between rounds, as the player is recovering for the next series of shots or balls fed by the coach. These lessons emphasize repetition until the student gets a feel for the technique, and he or she will know what to do when practicing on his/her own.

Point-play lessons: This is a very good idea especially when the student is preparing for tournament competition. About two weeks out, 90% of the time spent in lessons should be point play related. The coach should focus on strategy and shot selection through point play situations that expose a player's weaknesses and, therefore, can be improved. Short games to seven or eleven points should be played; sometimes little games with the regular Tennis scoring system can be used, such as 15-love, 30-love, and 30-15. Instead of regular serves, the player and coach can just drop feed a ball in order to focus on the task at hand (the tactical objective). Getting to play a lot more points this way; this is also a good time to throw in some seven or ten-point tiebreakers. Full matches are too time-consuming, and it is not recommended that they are played against a coach or Tennis pro all that much. Matches should be scheduled by the player on his/her own. If help is needed to come up with the right balance, a coach can provide some names, phone numbers, and e-mails. Also, during a group drill, matches can be set up to be played under the supervision of one or two coaches. Sometimes it is a good idea to play a few games or half sets during junior drills for the sake of saving time and variety. At the same time, it is important that some full matches are played as prep work leading up to a tournament.

The 30-minute lesson: In my own personal experience this is probably the best deal in town. Short and concise, 30-minute lessons are a lot cheaper. They put the coach in a situation where he really has to think about how he will spend this precious time with players. In some instances, the one-hour private lesson is too long. The player should do all the actual hours of grinding and practicing on his own or in a group drill setting. Let me go as far as to say that a disciplined hard working player can achieve full potential doing one 30-minute lesson once a week and practicing on his/her own the rest of the time.

Semi-private: This is also a great way to take a Tennis lesson. Players should take this kind of lesson with someone of similar level. Both players will benefit from hitting with one another; the coach, moreover, can take the time to talk and work with each player. There will be several instances where information coming from the coach applies to both students. The cost for the lesson is divided up between the two. Semi-private lessons lend themselves to good observations coming from the coach on a consistent basis for both players involved. The semi-private lesson is ideal to address pointplay situations, strategy, shot selection, mental toughness or on court tempo.

Group lessons or drills: This can be a meaningful way to spend time on the court for a lot of players. Drills can be anywhere from 1 hour to 3 hours or in some cases longer. All exercises should be set-up so that generalities of the game are addressed. Everyone should do some warm-up and stretching, and everyone should do some basic practice with all the strokes. All should do some point play situations or full sets or even matches. However, each player should have their individual goals for every different drill. Neglecting a specific goal for every ball hit on the practice court is wasted time; random practices and hitting will lead to random results.

Drilling is convenient in that it should deliver observations and guidelines from coaches. The different formats, such as everybody hitting one-on-one volleys will be set up by the coach as needed. Here is where the *games approach* (Look for subtitle *The Games Approach*) is one of the best ways to organize practice. Kids love it. This approach makes them work hard, and it produces results.

Let me add that the hard earned dollar is stretched doing group drills. But the supervision is obviously not 100% since it has to be divided amongst all players involved. It is definitely worth mentioning that if a family's budget is tight, this kind of training is not necessary, as long as players, children, or their parents are able and willing to set up practice sessions with other players on their own. Do not interpret this as saying let Dad or Mom be the coach or run the drill. Get some players of similar caliber on the court and let them lose to hit on their own. The only thing I would probably de-emphasize is to allow for too much social interaction, not serious hitting, or playing of points or matches carelessly or recklessly.

Drilling in a group should always have a format for players to follow. Unfortunately, the drills and the formats used may not always be fitting to players with varied needs. That is why I really believe a player who wants to go the distance is almost always better off on his/her own, setting up drills and practices with a like minded player of similar level. Players may need some guidance from a coach to do this, but it certainly can be done.

Video Analysis Lessons: Very few Tennis pros do video analysis. Video is one of the greatest tools Tennis pros have to analyze a player's strokes, strategy, and on-court personality. The main drawback is that it can be time-consuming and technically challenging. However, slowing video down from normal speed can improve observations. A player ought to see himself hitting the ball and walking the court; the players and the coach can really pick up clues on shot selection criteria as well as strategy and technique.

Here is the catch; huge amounts of money aren't required. Players can have a friend film them with a cell phone during matches or practice and study it later in slow motion on a computer or TV. A player can share video with a coach and have him go through it in the office as part of a lesson. The computer programs specialized in video analysis are expensive, and the user's manuals are the size of the Bible. I have done a lot of on-court video analysis with my students' own cell phones, no additional fees or time consumed getting in the office on a computer. There are free apps for smartphones out there. One of them is the "Swing Reader." Although it was designed for golf, it really works for Tennis, too. It slows the player to a frame by frame speed. It is incredible. Another good application is "Slow Pro." This one may be even better since pictures of amazing resolution can be subtracted for comparison purposes.

Accelerated Learning Lessons: On a few occasions I have had Moms or Dads show up to their kid's lessons and film almost the entire lesson. They may use a video camera, an iPad or even their cell phones. I don't mind because I know they are just trying to make the best of their money and time on the court with me. Having the student review the video a few times, is an awesome way to capitalize 100% on the material covered in the lesson. The student gets to hear the corrections verbally from the coach, see himself/herself executing the technique as well as see the coach demonstrate. It's an all in one kind of deal. I had this one mom (Koven White) that even asked permission to stand behind me and film all the demonstrations and catch the audio up close. Her son improved incredibly fast and caught up to other kids that had been playing Tennis for a lot longer than him in a relatively short period of time.

Mental Toughness and emotional control Lessons: Very few Tennis pros teach these kinds of lessons or integrate them as a daily routine. Mental toughness lessons have to be done on-court intermixed with other hitting drills. The mental toughness exercises should be addressed in between feedings, rallies or points. The student needs to have very specific routines to follow in between mental toughness exercises. Everyone needs mental toughness training. What we do, how we do it, what we think in between points, or on changeovers directly impacts our performance and emotional control. These things are what mainly differentiates good, consistent, and stable players from the ones who struggle.

Mental toughness exercises can be as simple as practicing certain rituals between rallies and points. When the ball is not in the air, thoughts, feelings, emotions, and appearance will directly impact whether a point or match is lost or won (See section on mental toughness training)

Players should ask that coaches or Tennis pros to include this kind of training into lessons. This is the one way, to take full advantage of every minute spent on the court with the coach, even when not hitting balls. In fact, mental toughness training should always be part of the equation when on a Tennis court, whether the player is practicing or playing matches.

Hand-fed drills: Lessons where the coach or Tennis Pro hand feeds balls are effective. However, they should not be used exclusively in a lesson. Having the coach nearby telling students how to hit, how to walk or move their feet, how to look, and how to breathe. Informing them of what they did correctly or incorrectly for fifteen or twenty minutes is valuable. These should never take precedence over all court hitting.

Warning: The proximity of the coach tossing balls with his/her hand makes for very easy conversation. Players and coaches shouldn't fall into this trap (the chat trap) and forget their reason for being there.

Ball feeding: When a coach feeds all the balls from the service line or closer to the net, this is not what we call Tennis-specific feeding. Balls need to be fed from all different positions of the court: the sides, the baseline, and no-man's land. The feeding should be varied depending on the task at hand. For instance, if I want my student to work on ground stroke exchanges, such as hitting baseline to baseline, then my feeds need to come from around the baseline. If I want him or her to work on re-direction, then, I need to have the balls fed from one side of the court, near the baseline, or from no-mans land, towards one of the singles lines and have the student hit the balls back to the opposite side of the court. Again, please remember that in higher developmental levels, ball feeding drills are good for ten to twenty minutes tops.

Serving practice and lessons: Highly underrated, a serving lesson can be very valuable. The serve is and will always be the single most important shot in the game of Tennis. Players should spend up to one-third or more of all their practice time working on and improving their serve. The serve is the only shot players can practice on their own. Players have whatever time they need to serve each ball. It really does not take that much time to get in a good service practice session. Sometimes 15 minutes is all that is needed. 80-100 serves can be hit in this amount of time. A coach should find ways for the player to serve more efficiently, consistently, and effectively. Also placement, consistency, variety, and power or spins are all important considerations when practicing service. Once the basic service motion has been learned, tossing technique, and tossing consistency are probably the most important technical aspects of serving. Try to be specific when working on the serve; meaning, try to practice one thing at the time.

A Tennis mom once said to me "Manuel, can we start a daily 30 minute serving lesson for my kids?" Because she was so frustrated with the double faulting and ineffectiveness of her children's serving in tournaments. So, I went "That is the most intelligent lesson request I have ever had"

Serve two to four balls in each service box, alternating for 15 to 20 minutes. Mix in different spins and placements. A good server should be able to hit the ball with every variety of serve: flat, slice, topspin, and American Twist or Kick and all variations of them. Also wide, down the T or the curving can-openers into the body. Also, practice serving all along the baseline from both, the add side, as well as the deuce side.

A coach should demonstrate any of these varieties, understand and be able to teach all the intricacies of different serving techniques, such as the different grips, toss placement, racket path, racket acceleration and angle, as well as differing points of impact.

There is so much to serving effectiveness that is not covered anywhere in the literature. It seems as if a lot of this information is simply passed along from great coaches to players, generation after generation without it ever finding its rightful place in the written word.

Ball Machine Lessons: Lessons on a ball machine can be effective in many ways. The coach watches the student up close and personal. He does not have to shout across the net or observe the player hit at the same time he himself is concentrating on a return shot; this is also an easy way to score on some video analysis with cell phone or tablet device. One of the drawbacks is that, even though, most ball machines are computerized nowadays, they cannot reproduce even remotely what a good Tennis-pro can do when feeding the ball by himself/herself. A very simple drill, one of my favorites, is what I call the six ball drill. It goes like this: One forehand, one backhand, an approach, a forehand volley, a backhand volley and, finally, an overhead. Most ball machines are too dumb for this kind of simple pattern. Even though, I have not seen them myself, there are ball machines capable of a lot more sophisticated patterns, but I am sure they would be terribly expensive.

Ball machines cannot yet mix spin, depth, and speed. However, for serious random side to side practice with a definite amount of spin repetition, speed, and depth, the ball machine is a good tool. Players have to vary the position of the ball machine on the court to make practices more realistic. Also, it is highly recommended to use one of those ball mowers to aid with ball pickup. It is also a good idea to have parents on the court to help pickup while the junior does all the hitting. Ball pickup can get pretty cardio, and it is a good compromise for all parties involved. Finally, practice on a ball machine is great with two like players or friends practicing simultaneously. They can take turns hitting or picking up balls, or they can hit at the same time and then pickup together. This makes for a much more enjoyable practice session, and ball pickup is faster and more efficient.

What follows is a series of drills designed for practicing with ball machines:

BALL MACHINE DRILLS

1) Aerobic Cardio Workout:

- Set Ball Machine (BM) on or near court's Center Mark.
- Adjust feed to shoot balls to places where player has to move at least 5 feet for every shot; he/she should be able to get to the impact point and stop before swinging.
- Feed rate should be set to anywhere between 2 to 4 seconds for each shot depending on aerobic capacity and speed of ball.
- Make sure to load BM to its full capacity in order to go non-stop for a while. Players want the BM to operate for at least 15 to 20 minutes non-stop if possible; that's why it may be better to go with the ball feed every 4 seconds.

WHAT TENNIS PROS DON'T TEACH (WTPDT)

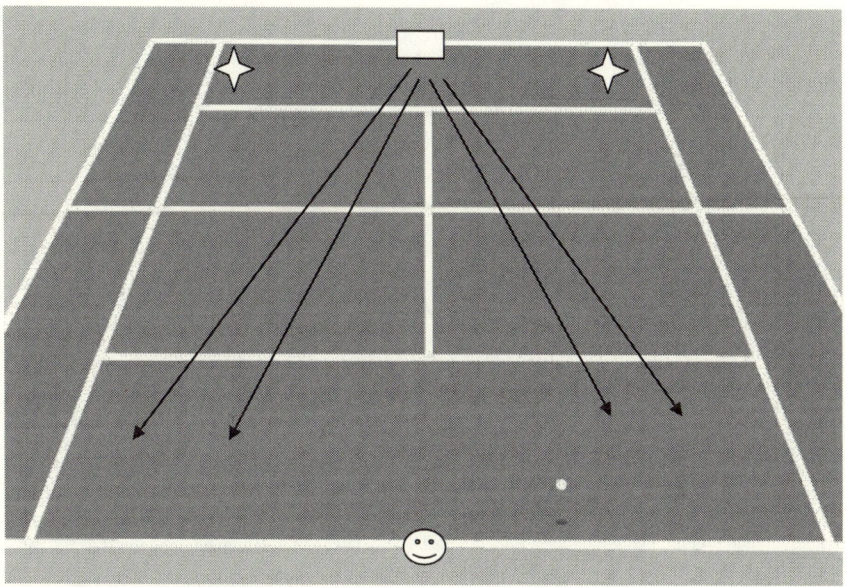

Fig. 1)Aerobic Cardio Workout
☐ -Ball Machine (BM)   ☺ -Player,   ✧ -Targets

Cardio Workout Tips:

- Player should position about one or two steps behind baseline.
- Players can also do this drill with volleys or overheads as long as they keep moving for at least 15 to 20 minutes non-stop.
- In between feeds, players have to keep bouncing around on their toes in order to keep the heart pumping at a regular (aerobic) rate.
- Be careful not to set BM at a rate so tough that the player cannot keep up with it.
- If set up at a ball feed rate, where the player runs out of balls before 15 to 20 minutes at least (or whatever the target time was), in order to complete the workout make sure to pick balls up at a trot. Do not use a ball hopper to get them up. Try panning them up on the racquet face and run from ball to ball to keep the heart rate up (when racquet face is full of balls run back to BM and dump balls in), if done before the target time. Crank the BM again for another round.

➤ It is also a good idea to work on developing a breathing technique. Inhale while back-swinging, exhale with contact. A little "grunt" can be added for better timing and a more relaxed action.

Note: See video of Ball Machine cardio workout at https://youtu.be/x3zxmfoL6Xk

2) Approach Shot Technical Workout:

- Set Ball Machine (BM) as indicated on the diagram
- Set BM on random direction to work on both wings; or to the deuce or ad court if work only on either forehand or backhand approach is needed. Go for approach shots shoulder, waist and knee height. BM feed to points A and B on diagram.
- For 3.5 (B level in other parts of the World) and above levels, set BM for top spin and under spin as well as flat shots.
- Interval or feed rate should be set for one ball every 4 to 6 seconds (should be able to go back and forth to the center mark or near the baseline after every shot)
- Speed of ball should be similar to players' level of play. A student wants to be able to hit solid, by getting to the ball on time for good contact.
- The approach needs to be executed coming in or running in (come in from or near the center mark after every shot) towards the net at different bouncing heights and speeds. Go for some down the line (most important for singles play) and cross court shots (better practice for doubles)
- Set targets on court as indicated and vary according to ability level

WHAT TENNIS PROS DON'T TEACH (WTPDT)

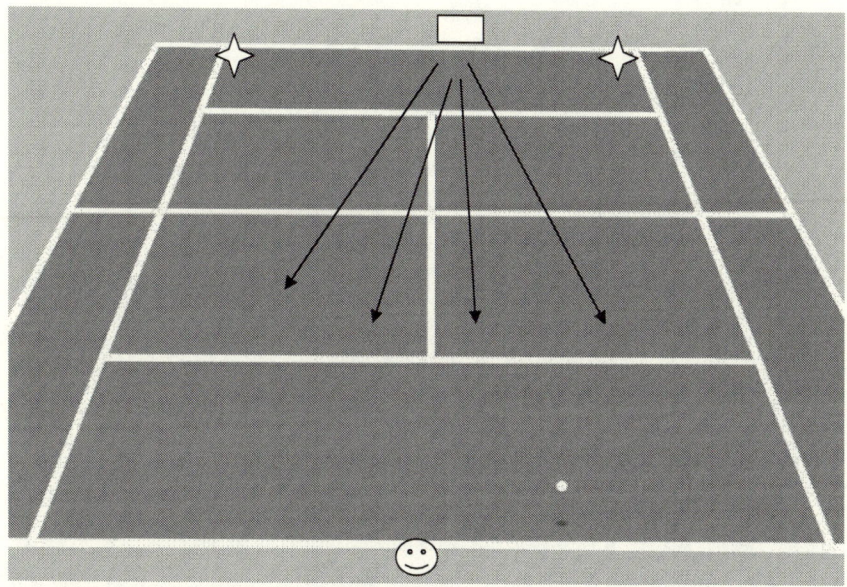

Fig. 2) Approach Shot Technical Workout
☐ -Ball Machine (BM),   ☺ -Player,   ✧ -Targets

Approach Shots Technical Tips:

> - The player has to shuffle back to the center mark or near the baseline after every shot in order to be able to hit running forward.
> - Try the double step (shuffle) on either forehand or two-handed backhand approach for closed stance technique.
> - If one-handed backhand go for the carioca step on slice approach to allow the body to remain sideways throughout the shot (Look for the unit on footwork in Tennis for an explanation of the carioca step)
> - On below net level approach, slice is a good idea, and if the ball is above waist level try some topspin or even flat (slice still probably a better option especially if the ball is moving pretty fast, like on the return of serve chip and charge technique)
> - Look for depth and placement rather than power.
> - When approaching a player is trying to set up for a volley, not trying to hit an outright winner.
> - After hitting the approach, the player wants to go forward two or three steps like he/she is pursuing a volley before he/she gets shuffling back to the baseline's center mark.

- ➤ -Players should pick their targets as they get back to the baseline and get going again for another approach.
- ➤ -Unless going for a very aggressive approach, the players need only about a ¾ backswing to hit an effective controlled approach.
- ➤ -Need to aim at the different targets. A lot of baseliners like a deep approach, and hate to have to go forward to deal with a low short approach to execute their passing shot.
- ➤ -Keeping the ball low to the ground makes for a much more challenging passing shot to go for.

3) Backhand Technical Workout:

- Set Ball Machine (BM) at a location appropriate for the kind of backhand shot to work on. (e. g. Crosscourt or down the line backhands) Set BM up on opposite corner near baseline. The More advanced levels should go for the ball coming in down the line and then change direction of ball by going cross court (and vice-versa)
- Have BM feed (ball feed set to shoot every 3 to 4 seconds) using settings 4, 6, 4, 6, on some panels to locations A and B (see court diagram) and shuffle back and forth to hit only backhands.
- Speed of ball coming out of BM set such that a player is able to get to hitting position with plenty of time.
- Set targets (plastic cones) at specific locations as shown in court diagram

WHAT TENNIS PROS DON'T TEACH (WTPDT)

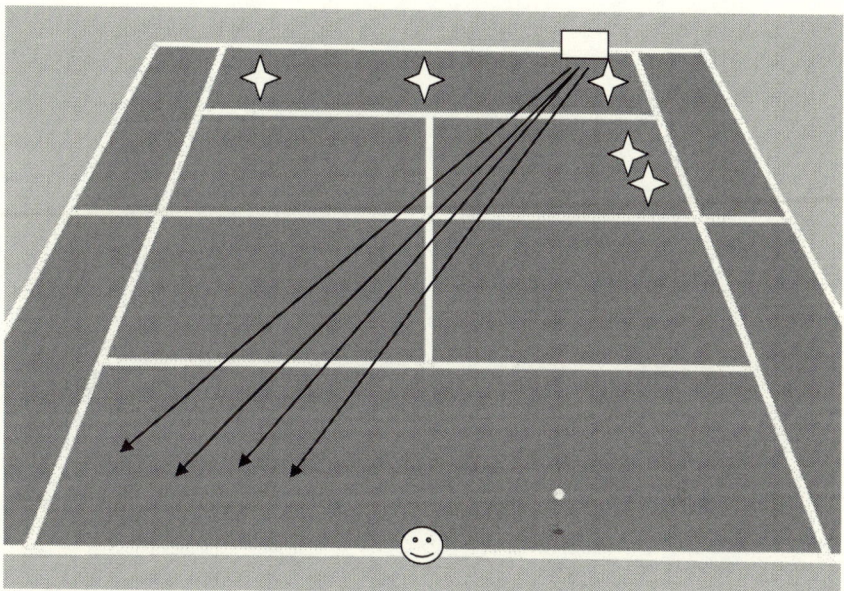

Fig. 3) Backhand Technical Workout
▢ -Ball Machine (BM)   ☺ -Player,   ✧ -Targets

Backhand Technical Tips:

> - Position player near center mark.
> - Make sure to split step synchronized to sound of ball as it is fed by the BM.
> - Whatever a player is working on, be sure he/she know what he/she is doing. The student could be reinforcing an already bad habit. Ask one of the coaches from Tennis Pro Staff if in doubt.
> - The player needs to be on his/her toes at all times (except for when hitting the ball) and be certain he/she is moving to the ball and stopping and setting up with stutter steps (small adjusting steps) before each shot.
> - One of the most common problems on ground strokes is hitting out of balance. Keep an eye for that. Vary the targets for more challenge. But do not worry too much if not hitting them.
> - Also vary the player's position to develop the ability to hit solid backhands from anywhere on the court.
> - Remember that when working technically, making the shots is not as important as working on technical corrections every single shot.

➢ European Tennis academies go for 150 good repetitions for each correction per day. American Tennis philosophy is about 50 good ones per session. I think 100 of each correction needing work on to be about right.

4) Forehand Technical Workout:

- Set the Ball Machine (BM) at a location appropriate for the kind of forehand shot needing to work on. (For example: For crosscourt forehands set it on the opposite corner near the baseline)
- Have BM feed (ball feed set to shoot every 3 to 4 seconds) to locations marked with targets (see court diagram) and shuffle back and forth to hit only forehands.
- Speed of ball set such that players are able to get to hitting position in time for solid balanced hits.
- Set targets (plastic cones) at specific locations as shown in court diagram
- The More advanced levels should go for the ball coming in down the line and then change direction of ball by going cross court (and vic-versa)

WHAT TENNIS PROS DON'T TEACH (WTPDT)

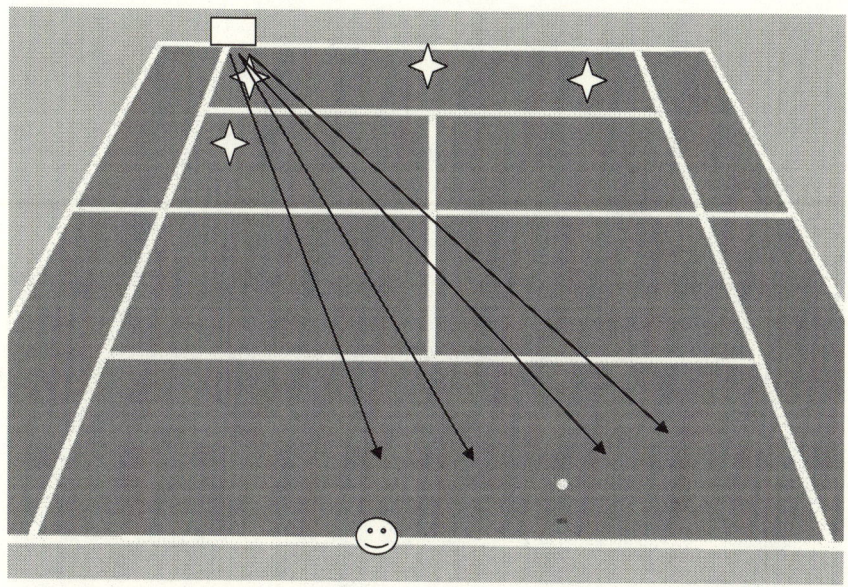

Fig. 4) Forehand Technical Workout
☐ -Ball Machine (BM) ☺ -Player, ✧ -Targets

Forehand Technical Tips:

➢ Position player near center mark.
➢ Make sure to split step synchronized to sound of the ball as it is fed by BM.
➢ Whatever the player is working on, make sure he/she knows what he/she is doing. Bad habits could be could be getting reinforced. Ask the Tennis Pro Staff if in doubt.
➢ Students need to be on their toes at all times and be certain to be moving to the ball and stopping before each shot.
➢ One of the most common problems on ground strokes is hitting out of balance. Keep an eye for that.
➢ Vary the location of the targets for more challenge. It is not that important if targets cannot be hit.
➢ Also vary the player's position on the court to develop ability to hit solid forehands from anywhere on court.
➢ Remember that when students are working technically, making the shots is not as important as working on the technical correction in every ball hit.

> European Tennis academies go for 150 good repetitions for each correction per day. American Tennis philosophy is about 50 good ones per session. I think 100 repetitions of each correction for what is needed to work on to be about right.

5) Half-Volley Technical Workout:

- Set Ball Machine (BM) as indicated on Diagram.
- Feed direction set on random
- Balls should land as indicated on diagram locations where arrows depict ball direction from BM.
- Feed rate should be set for one ball every 2 to 3 seconds.
- Ball speed should be similar to level of play.
- Players can work on both forehand and backhand or just one of the two. Either way, the players want to make sure they have to move a little to get to the ball for every shot.
- Work on half-volley from just inside service line, and from just inside baseline.
- Stand about a foot inside service line for short half-volleys and one foot inside baseline for deep half-volleys.

WHAT TENNIS PROS DON'T TEACH (WTPDT)

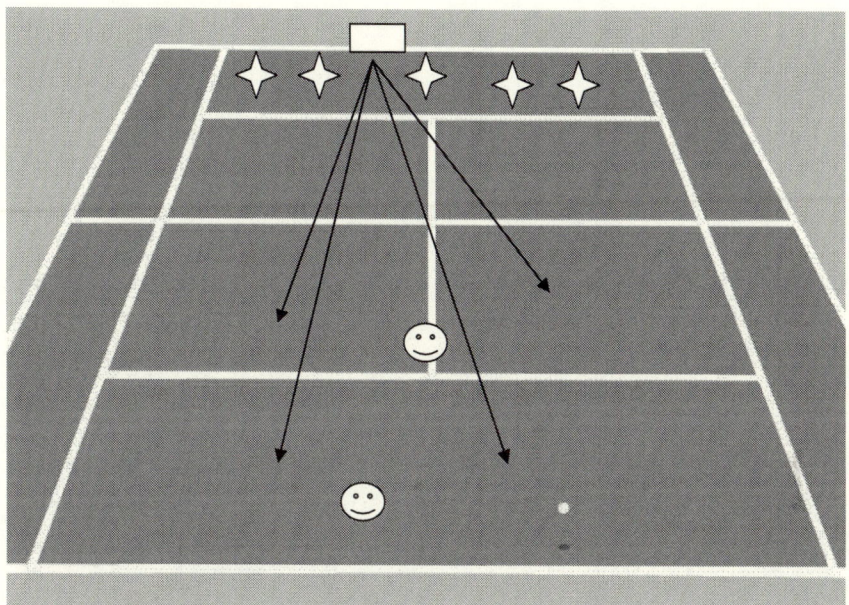

Fig. 5) Half Volley Technical Workout
☐ -Ball Machine (BM)   ☺ -Players,   ✧ -Targets

Half Volley Technical Tips:

➤ Use of underspin and topspin are appropriate for 3.5 and up levels.
➤ For effective half-volleys players really have to get their center of gravity low close to the ground by bending the knees.
➤ A very short backswing (or no backswing at all and even a negative or reverse backswing) is needed for a lot of the half-volleys near the service line. For half-volleys by baseline, a lot of times a player has to get some sort of backswing to be able to get ball back deep to opponents baseline. Emphasis on timing and control should be practiced, not power.
➤ Some topspin or underspin is in order for advanced levels, for 3.0 and below stay with simple blocking of ball flat or some naturally occurring underspin.
➤ Should try to hit back deep near the opponent's baseline if possible. Some players are very good at hitting unbelievable drop shots off half volleys by the net.

> When playing singles, a half volley is better directed towards the center of the court deep when going in.

6) Lob Technical Workout:

- Set the Ball Machine (BM) as indicated on the diagram. Set the BM on random feeding.
- Interval or feed rate should be set for one ball every 4 or 5 seconds for defensive lobs and every 2 to 3 seconds for offensive lob practice.
- For offensive lob practice have speed set low enough so as to be able to comfortably hit either forehands and/or backhands.
- Feed speed should be a lot faster if the player is working on defensive lobs. Players will get to the ball out of balance a lot of times, which is the way it is supposed to be in a specific real Tennis situation.

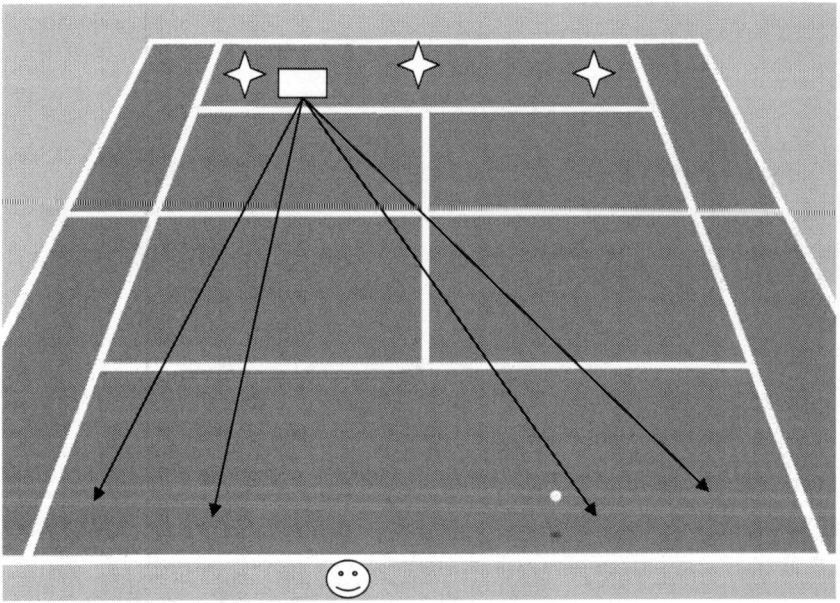

Fig. 6) Lob Technical Workout
☐ -Ball Machine (BM) ☺ -Players, ✧ -Targets

Lob Technical Tips:

- Stand 2 feet inside baseline to 3 feet behind baseline for offensive lob practice. 3 to 10 feet behind baseline for defensive lob practice. (Setup BM accordingly)
- For Offensive lob practice aim shots either down the line or crosscourt. In other words, try to place shots (shoot for the cones as shown on diagram; (T=cone targets) Try to aim about 20 feet over the net (usually light pole height). Offensive lobs are usually hit flat or with a little topspin.
- For Defensive lob practice, aim all lobs down the middle and a little higher. Go for about 30 feet over the net (10 feet over light pole height). Defensive lobs are usually hit with some underspin or flat.
- It is a good idea to work on disguising the offensive lobs. In other words, make the backswing look as if going to hit a regular ground stroke, and then hit the lob instead.
- A lot of defensive lobs have to be hit on the run and out of balance. Hit hard and try to get some height and depth near the center mark of opponent's court. Go for some half volleys as well as on the run lobs for more realistic practice!

7) Overhead Technical Workout:

- Set Ball Machine (BM) at location as indicated on diagram.
- Adjust elevation control to feed balls landing between service line and baseline. The height of ball should be about 10 to 30 feet above level of light posts (the higher, the more difficult)
- Set feed direction to random (fixed direction down the middle for 2.0-3.0 players or beginners)
- Interval or feed rate should be set to one ball every 3 to 4 seconds.
- Set targets on court as shown on diagram
- Player could practice either bouncing or out of the air overheads. (Bouncing overheads should also be practiced and usually require different footwork skills and also forces players to anticipate and track down the arching of the ball as it bounces off the surface)

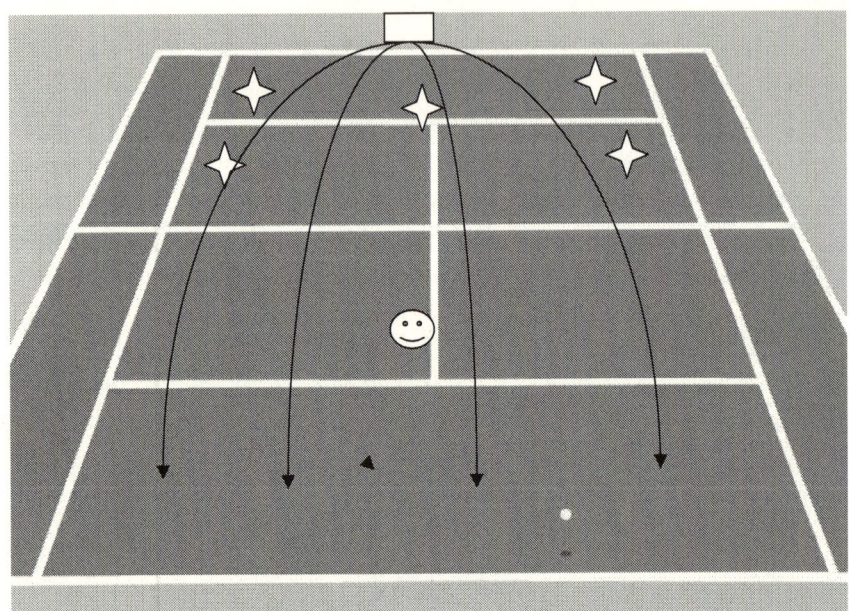

Fig. 7) Overhead Technical Workout
▢ -Ball Machine (BM)   ☺ -Players,   ✧ -Targets

Overhead Technical Tips:

- Position the player near or at the intersection of the service line and the center service line, (better known as the T) for out of the air overheads, and midway between service line and baseline for bouncing overheads.
- Make sure to split step synchronized to the sound of the ball as it is fed by BM
- Whatever the player is working on, make sure to know what proper technique. A bad habit could be getting reinforced. Ask someone from the Tennis Pro Staff if in doubt.
- Players need to be on their toes at all times and be certain to be moving to the ball before each shot. Players do not have to set perfect for either bouncing or out of the air overheads. Look for dynamic balance especially on difficult deep ones (not recommended for beginners or 2.0-3.0 players D or C level at most other places)

- One of the most common problems on overheads is a late wind up of the racquet. Make sure the racquet is ready (ready overhead position) by the time the ball reaches the summit or peak of the lob)
- Another common problem is to go for a circular wind up (like in the service motion) instead of the straight up racquet wind up. Ask a Tennis Pro Staff member if in doubt.
- Vary (pick targets in advance always) targets to make it more challenging.
- Also vary the players position on the court to develop ability to hit solid overheads from anywhere on it.
- Remember that when working technically, making the shots is not as important as working on technical correction every single shot.
- European Tennis academies go for 150 good repetitions for each correction per day. American Tennis philosophy is about 50 good ones per session. I think 100 of each correction to work on to be about right.

8) Quick reaction volleys:

- Set the Ball Machine (BM) in the middle of the court, between the service line and the baseline 5 to 8 feet off the center of the court.
- Adjust to random or unpredictable varied feeding.
- Feed rate should be one ball every 2 to 4 seconds (depending on ability level and the speed of the ball)
- Speed should be adjusted so that the player is able to get to 90% of balls (some shots should go past the player at net)
- If 3.5 or higher level use different spins (under and top spin)
- Take a break about every five minutes (no point depleting balls if not going all out 100%. When doing this drill, it really helps to have a remote control for the BM so a player can stop anytime he or she needs a breather)

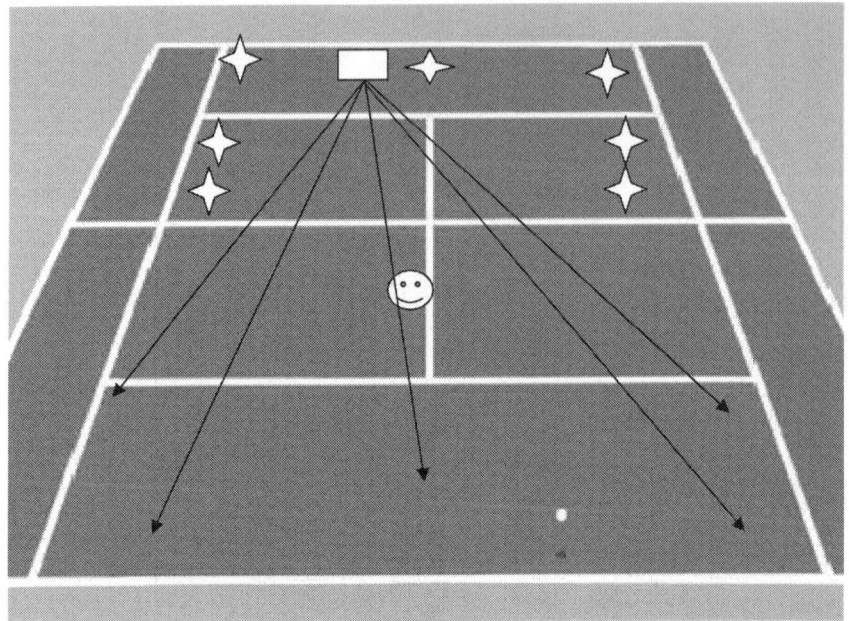

Fig. 8) Quick reaction volleys
☐ -Ball Machine (BM)   ☺ -Players,   ✧ -Targets

Quick Reaction Volleys Tips:

- Position anywhere between one step behind the service line and 5 feet from the net. Vary position according to the type of volley needed to work on and ability level. The higher level players should work from further away from the net at much higher speeds, spins, and feed rates.
- If a student does not use a continental grip, this is a great opportunity to start working on it. He/she should not switch grips when at net. Hitting forehand and backhand volleys with the same grip is extremely effective.
- Pick out a target (visualize) for each and every ball hit.
- Split step for every volley.
- Go for short, compact swings or stabbings with the racquet; the player should emphasize the use of body and shoulders and not the arm
- If a student figured out the BM feeding pattern, go ahead and change it to something more unpredictable so that he/she have to react accordingly.

- ➤ Work on deep first volleys, angles, and drop volleys, high and low over the net (where BM feeds high or low) volleys too.
- ➤ It is important to to go back to ready position after every volley.

9) Return of serve:

- Set the Ball Machine (BM) on baseline 3 ft (singles) or 10 ft (doubles) from the center mark.
- BM has to be set to random or unpredictable feeding.
- Ball has to land inside or near proper service box.
- Feeding rate has to be one ball every 5 seconds.
- Do 100 returns on each side, the deuce and the add (forehand and backhand sides of the court)
- Speed of the ball has to be equivalent or similar to playing ability.
- Besides the regular flat serve, mix in some top or under spin if you are a 3.5+ player. Use all flat feeding or flat for lower levels.
- For advanced return of serve practice, set BM to hit as hard as it can with as much topspin as possible. The ball machine should be positioned in such way as to have the ball land as close to the service box as possible. It may be that the BM may have to be set up all the way to the back fence. Make the BM shoot pretty high as the ball goes over the baseline on the same side; ball should clear the ground over the same baseline by about 9 – 10 feet. The topspin will make the ball land in the service box or close to it. This is great practice for the return of serve against kick servers and topspin servers. Players should work on moving their feet and trying to take the ball early before it kicks above shoulder level. Also, moving back and letting the ball come down to a height at which it can be handled with more ease.

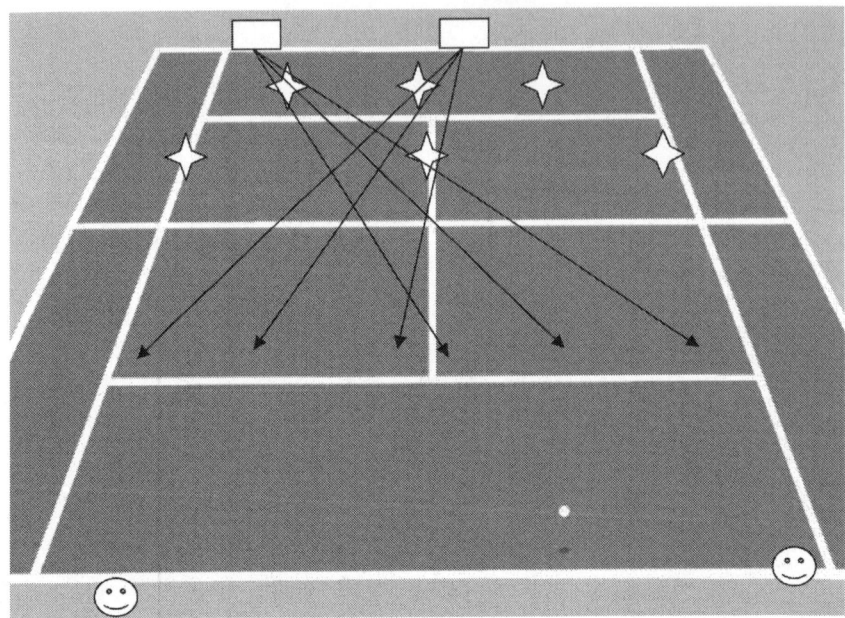

Fig. 9) Return of serve
☐ -Ball Machine (BM)   ☺ -Player   ✧ -Targets

Return of Serve Tips:

- Be on the ready position
- Make sure to always do a split step when the ball is feed.
- Commit to either forehand or backhand grip beforehand and switch accordingly.
- Look to hit the return at the peak of the bounce if possible.
- Make sure to pick a target (visualize return) every single time.
- Do not go for the same spot all the time. Use imagination and stay within ability level (Examples of shots to go for: angles, lobs, drop shots, slice, topspin, chip and charge (approach), as well as the regular down the line and cross court returns.
- If the player is not missing at least one in every four returns, increase the skill level. By Increasing the speed and/or spin of the BM; a player can also go for more difficult returns (going for more pace, or angle).
- Remember that for the return of serve, the backswing has to be shorter, for the most part. Anywhere from 20 to 80% shorter,

depending whether it is a first or second serve we are returning and obviously the speed of the ball coming towards us.
- ➤ Another important consideration is footwork. When it comes to return of serve, players better be on their toes moving with good intensity and focused concentration.
- ➤ Remember that this is the one area of the game where the most unforced errors are committed at all levels.

10) Volley Technical Workout:

- Set Ball Machine (BM) as indicated on the diagram.
- Set BM on random direction. Go for volleys about waist and knee height.
- For 3.5 and above levels, set BM for topspin and underspin.
- Interval or feed rate should be set for one ball every 2 to 3 seconds.
- Speed of the ball should be similar to student's level of play. A player wants to be able to hit solid, by getting to the ball on time for good contact.
- Practice volleys from one step behind the service line, (first volleys) and two steps inside service line. If a player develops solid volleys from this far from the net, up close to the net volleys are a lot easier to handle.
- Set targets on the court as indicated and vary accordingly. Try different patterns, for example, down the line followed by wide angle volleys.

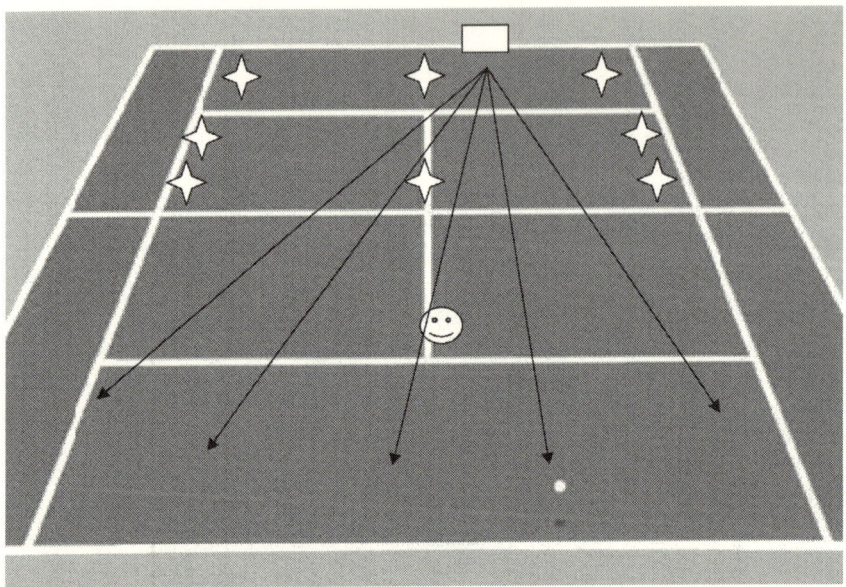

Fig. 10) Volley Technical Workout
☐ -Ball Machine (BM)   ☺ -Players,   ✧ -Targets

Volley Technical Tips:

- -This is a great opportunity to develop confidence on that continental grip for volleys (no grip changing)
- -Keep the racket head above wrist level at all times. This means that on low volleys students need to really bend their knees.
- -Some slice is in order on a lot of low volleys; on higher volleys a player may want to go for flat volleys. -For reaching out at very wide volleys, a little topspin may be in order (very advanced technique)
- -Avoid using the arm in excess or over-swinging. Try to develop racquet speed by moving forward, plus some shoulder and hip rotation. On top of that players can also work on some wrist acceleration.
- -Work on different types of volleys, deep, angle and drop shot volleys are all important. The first volley should be hit deep, as a player approaches the net, is the most fundamentally important of all, and where players want to spend most of their time.

> -Remember to turn a little sideways. A player does not have to turn all the way on most volleys, but for forehand volleys maybe about a one-third turn is about right.

Note: See video of volley techniques at https://youtu.be/YzbuiwuJUmg

11) Passing Shots:

- -Set BM at about the service line, plus or minus 5 feet inside or outside of the service box. Also, a good idea is to set BM near the singles lines and service line as well to make practice more realistic,
- -For the most part, a player needs moderate slice or topspin on the feeds from the BM. Adjust knobs accordingly. Many players approach or attack nowadays with topspin.
- -Balls coming from the BM should be landing about midway between the serviceline and the baseline, but vary the depth of the ball either shorter or deeper as needed.
- -The bounce of the ball should be pretty low, but this is also something students need to vary since conditions will change with different opponents' styles of play.
- -The frequency should be set, in such way, that the player is rushed a little to get in position in order to make practice more realistic. We cannot always set nicely to go for our passing shots. Vary the intensity of the drill to the individual needs.
- -Players need to set up some targets in specific areas of court as shown in diagram.

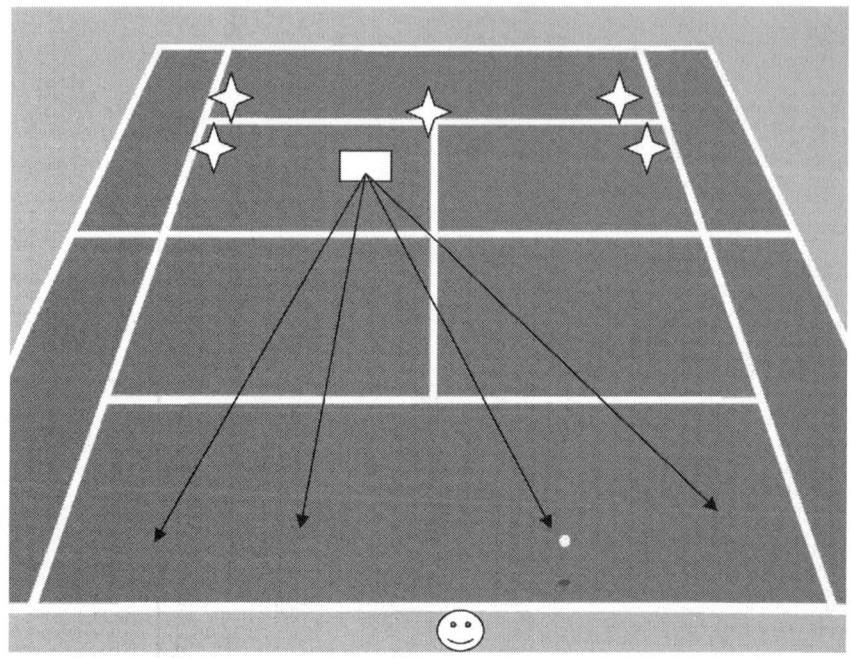

Fig. 11)Passing shots
☐ -Ball Machine (BM)   ☺ -Players,   ✧ -Targets

Passing Shot Tips:

> -Practice down the line, cross-court and angle passing shots.
> -Pay no attention to depth but be a lot more concerned with the height of the ball over the net. Passing shots generally need to be low over the net.
> -Students want to hit the ball at a nice intermediate to hard speed focusing a lot more on directional control than power.
> -The player should go low and hard down the middle, followed by either a cross-court or down the line passing shot, or even an offensive lob (The two shot passing shot look for subtitle on passing shots.)
> -Most passing shots should be hit with moderate to heavy topspin. Here and there players need to hit passes flat as well. If a player is really good with slice shots, he/she may want to spend some time practicing some slice passing shots, too!

WHAT TENNIS PROS DON'T TEACH (WTPDT)

> -Practice passing shots taking the ball early and on the rise. This is the way we deal with net rushing players most of the time. It is also a good idea to hit the ball after the peak of the bounce. We don't always have time to take the ball on the rise. Stay away from hitting on the rise if going for slice passing shots.

12) Swinging Volleys Technical Workout:

- -Set BM as indicated on diagram.
- -Set feed rate for one shot every 2-4 seconds on the random setting, or set direction depending on skill level. For lower skill levels, it is probably better to set BM to feed in a constant direction. Either way the player needs to try to keep his/her feet moving and then set up for the shot as he or she starts the aggressive forward swing.
- -If 3.5 or above set BM to shoot with topspin and underspin.
- -The ball should clear net by 10-15 Feet and be aimed to land a few feet inside the baseline.
- -Work on swinging volleys from 4 feet behind the serviceline to 4 feet inside it.

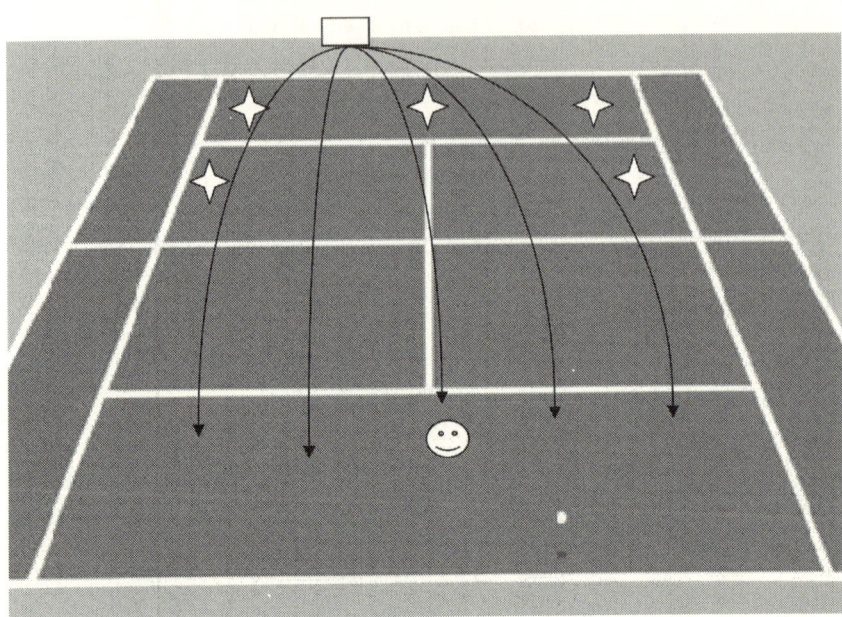

Fig. 12) Swinging Volleys Technical Workout
☐ -Ball Machine (BM)   ☺ -Players,   ✧ -Targets

Swinging volleys technical tips:

- -Use heavy to moderate top-spin on either side.
  -Make every attempt to hit the swinging volleys between waist and shoulder level by adjusting the position to the arching ball coming over the net.
- -Aim at fairly large areas of the court (use the 4x4 rule, look for subtitle "The 4x4 rule." See note below) set targets to go for as shown in the diagram.
- -Remember the swinging volley is a pretty hard shot that wins by speed more than accurate placement

Note: The 4x4 rule refers t aiming shots 4 feet from the baseline and 4 feet inside the singles lines.

WHAT TENNIS PROS DON'T TEACH (WTPDT)

13) BM Drill for 2 or more players:

Ball Machine Drills for 2-4 players at the same time:

- Setup BM in area as indicated in the diagram,
- The computerized panel needs to be set up to feed balls as indicated by arrows in diagram in an alternating fashion,
- If working with 2 players, feed rate needs to be pretty fast but alternating to the two ends of the court. Balls coming out of the BM every 1-2 seconds approximately,
- The direction settings can be fixed to hit to the same two spots or can be adjusted to hit about 10 feet from the previous shot to make the player move around more,
- For 3 players, we need one shot down one alley, the next down the middle and the third one down the other alley alternating in this same order every second approximately. The players have to move back and forth to hit forehands and backhands, or they can hit only forehands or only backhands if that is what they want to do,
- When 4 players are working simultaneously, one picks up balls while the other 3 hit balls. Once he or she has picked up a basket full, they rotate, and someone else picks up balls now. This way, they can keep practice going without pause,
- At the start of the drill fill the container in BM to the very top in order to keep the workout going longer since the BM will be shooting balls at an extremely fast rate.

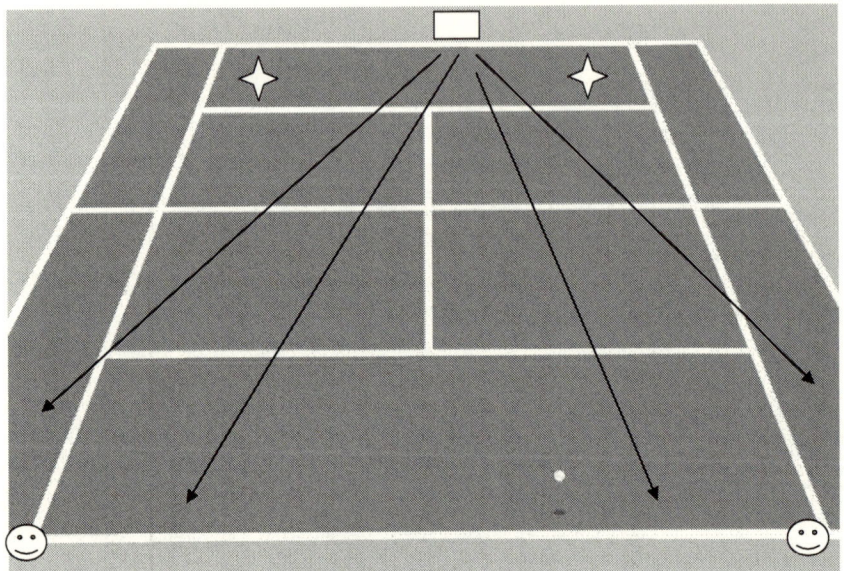

Fig. 13)Ball Machine drill for two players at the same time.
☐-Ball Machine (BM), ☺-Players, ✧-Targets

Fourth player picking up balls.

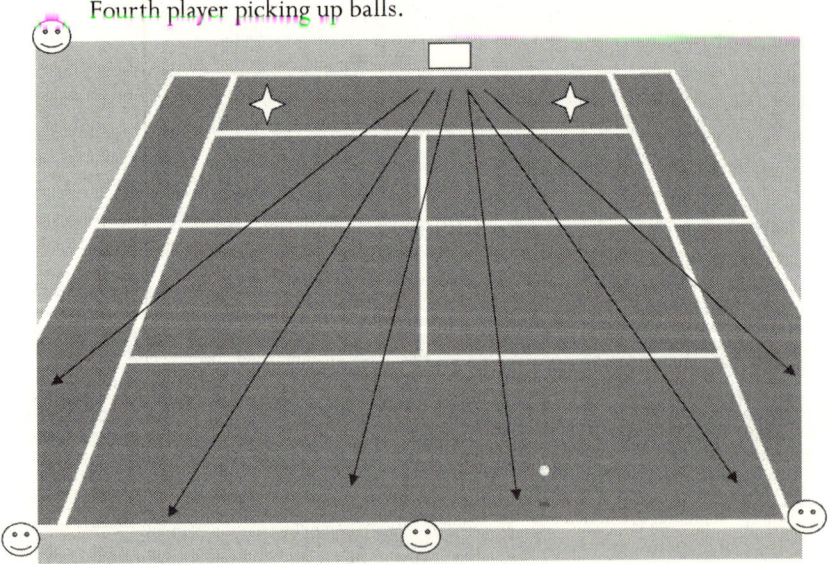

Fig. 14)Ball Machine drill for three or more players at the same time.
☐-Ball Machine (BM), ☺-Players, ✧-Targets

WHAT TENNIS PROS DON'T TEACH (WTPDT)

BM Drills for 2 or more players technical tips:

- ➤ Get balls from some of the pros teaching carts in order to have a full BM before the start of the drill
- ➤ Figure out what players will be working on beforehand, groundstrokes, volleys, or even overheads as desired
- ➤ Focus on the hitting and don't let the other players doing the drill be a distraction from our work
- ➤ Be ready to rotate to the next station when the player picking up balls is ready to enter the drill sequence. We do not want to turn off the BM when rotating. This way we can keep the drill going nonstop for everyone
- ➤ If alternating strokes, repeat the error. This means: keep hitting the same shot until hit right and with full satisfaction and then rotate

BALL MACHINES OPERATION INSTRUCTIONS

The operation of ball machines is kind of like the operations of vehicles. If a person can drive one vehicle, he or she can drive practically everyone out there. So here are some generalized operation instructions:

- Place Ball Machine (BM) at location needed for proper ball feed.
- Make sure cable is plugged into the electrical outlet on the side of the court unless BM is battery operated. If one's own, it is probably a smart idea to have a pretty long extension cord along with the BM.
- Set approximate ball speed, feed rate, spin and elevation knobs.
- In computerized machines, ball direction controls are set by adjusting the number dials to the indicated directions on the panel diagram.
- If on random feed, the BM will feed randomly on pre-program setting.
- If we want the BM to feed straight set all number dials to same number or block out all number dials except for the one intended for unidirectional use.
- If we have a remote control, set remote switch to remote position. If no remote, then set remote switch to manual position.
- When on remote, turn on BM and then go to the hitting position and press remote button to start ball feed.

Note: Always pick up all balls (inside and outside court) when done.
If help is needed setting BM up for drills, ask the Tennis Staff or Tennis Professionals for help when available.

QUICKSTART TENNIS! HOW GOOD IS IT? DO WE NEED TRANSITION BALLS?

QuickStart is a relatively new USTA mandate program whose results are still inconclusive. At the time of this writing, not all that much can be said. It could be said its Tennis made easier, for the twelve and under crowd: softer, lighter and slower balls, smaller courts and racquets and shorter format. I say its mandate because sanctioned events in the 8, 10 and even 12 and under divisions are being played with this transitional equipment as per the new rules here in the USA. Other countries are following this model but adjusting it in any way they see fit to do so.

The bottom line is that I am not 100% sure it will be better. A lot has been said by other experts in the field. Here is my two cents worth:

Pluses:

  a) Easier to control ball
  b) Easier to cover court
  c) Less time-consuming
  d) Less physical demands
  e) Kids can play like the pros at an early age. Perhaps!

Minuses:

  a) Tough transition to the regular ball and court
  b) Less discipline required from students
  c) Less physical demands can be viewed as a minus
  d) All made easier overall not necessarily a good thing
  e) Shorter format translates into fewer mental demands

f) As coaches, we need more gear, more balls, and we spend more money on equipment to implement QuickStart methods
g) Dads and Moms need to know the different rules for both regular and QuickStart format

Rules so far have been pretty inconsistent from State to State, Section to Section, country to country and even tournament to tournament; this is not good.

I cannot really say it is more fun than regular Tennis either. As a Coach, I can say that children had just as much fun with regular balls and courts. Let me also add that for what it's worth, it is extremely easy to convince dads and moms and their children to go for the real thing. They what the challenge, they want the real deal they want progress and solid learning!

My own daughter started with regular balls at a very early age and then went with squeegee balls for a few months. When she turned 8 we went back to regular balls again, and she seems to be doing just fine. She is pretty competitive in the 12s. We no longer hit with transition balls. I felt we were wasting time; my philosophy was "let's get going with the real thing." From previous experiences with other 9 year olds. When they practice with the regular balls and go back to the pressureless orange ball and the 60 foot courts, they tend to do a lot better and show easier transitioning down the road. I had a student who started practicing with the regular ball at 9 years old. Six months later he went to play in a Qualifier tournament and won in 10 and under with only one week of practice with the orange ball. Furthermore, he went on to take 5th place in the Southern tournament a few weeks later! How is that for an example? Final conclusions will be drawn 7-10 years from now (approximately in 2020), when players who started with this format reach developmental maturity!

Is making something easier to do, whatever it is, a good thing? I think not necessarily!

Following, we are going to take a look at some of Dr. Ray Brown's findings and conclusions thus far regarding (ROG) transition balls and other material regarding quick start Tennis. Ray Brown is a World recognized authority on the subject of player development. (The material presented here has been transcribed with Dr. Ray Brown's permission)

WHAT TENNIS PROS DON'T TEACH (WTPDT)

ROG AND TECHNIQUE

If ROG (Red, Orange, Green) transition balls promote the development of good technique one could use that technique to hit a yellow ball. But this is not what we see.

> So we ask, at what point in the ROG sequence does good technique develop and why? Is it between R and O or O and G? If so, exactly why does good technique appear at that point in the sequence and not before? What was not going right before the point was reached where good technique appeared? Was it neuromuscular development that was not in place? If so why?

If neuromuscular development was not in place, why would changing from R to O cause the development to appear? What is it about the human motor system that would cause neuromuscular development to appear just because one changed the color and compression of the ball?

It is a fact that a decompressed ball is easier to direct than a standard ball fresh out of the can. Hence, a student with poor technique can control a decompressed ball quite quickly but still cannot control a standard ball.

Part of the answer may lie in the fact that a decompressed ball will remain on the strings much longer than a standard ball (Standard balls remain in contact with strings from 0.005 to 0.007 seconds on the average). It is common to see two advanced students accidentally pick up a dead ball and begin to rally longer than they did with a new ball. Of course the sound of the ball at contact is a dead giveaway that the ball is dead, no pun intended.

Another part of the answer may lie in the fact that the decompressed ball deforms sufficiently on the strings to compensate for errors in racquet face orientation. If so, the ROG balls will not necessarily produce good technique and could even lead to developing bad habits.

It is easy to raise questions about ROG's efficiency as a technique development protocol, so easy that mandating ROG seems to not have been well thought out.

Where ROG shines is that it is far easier to control a decompressed ball without good technique than it is to control a standard ball without good technique. With a standard ball, errors of technique are immediate and provide good feedback that a technique problem exists that must be addressed. This feedback "test" is less likely to be available for decompressed balls. As an aside, the controllability of the ROG ball is a great equalizer in that a student without good technique can appear to be as good as a student with good technique.

The only thing that is clear is that a MANDATE for all to use ROG balls in sanctioned tournaments is unreasonable and penalizes capable students severely.

PERSONALITY SUGGESTS THE MOST INTRIGUING ROG QUESTION

Is the student that is attracted to ROG less aggressive, less mentally tough, less self-confident and less a self-advocate than the student who steps up to the challenge of standard tennis?

> *The inefficiency or efficiency of ROG may not be proven empirically for some years because the kids that are attracted to the greater challenge of standard tennis may beat the ROG kids simply because they are a tougher breed of kid*

Challenge is at the heart of growth and discovery. Removing challenge and choice is, therefore, a terrible disservice to our youth and our nation.

As noted, the ROG mandate has no scientific standing; it cuts our youth off at the legs. Our youth deserves better. They deserve respect and opportunity and the freedom of choice to go out and meet the challenges of today. Telling them that they are inadequate to do what previous generations were able to do will deaden their spirit and self-confidence. It promotes self-doubt. It institutionalizes mental weakness rather than building mental toughness.

We do not make a stronger generation by removing challenge. We make a weaker generation; and, by removing challenge we institutionalize a culture of weakness. We do not grow tennis by transmitting the message that it is a sport of weaklings. No one wants to be told that they are weak. Children want inspiration and strong leadership, not suppression.

As we can see, Dr. Ray Brown's theories are solid and make a lot of sense. Here are some more thoughts from this author on the ROGY experiment:

If the USTA or any other Tennis organization in the World wants to do experimental work to find out if the ROG system works, they should be utilizing mice or monkeys like real scientists do. Experimenting with children is not acceptable and will not be tolerated by this writer.

At the time of this writing, some experimental work was being done regarding the effect in the brain from hitting heavier regular yellow balls. Apparently some sort of chemical is released in the brain of the player that is addicting... the lighter the ball hit, the less of this chemical will be released and the less of the addicting effect the player will experience. Anyone that has played Tennis for any length of time can attest to the great feeling of hitting the snot out of the ball into the opponent's court for an outright winner; and what are feelings? Nothing but chemical substances in our brain, and in our body!

Brown's theories lead us to the conclusion that the ROG system is probably not as conducive to creating love of the game as the use of regular Tennis balls for developmental purposes. Therefore less desirable since love of the game is an essential ingredient in developing real Tennis players!

HOW MUCH TENNIS SHOULD WE PLAY?

At the young ages of 4 to 6 years of age, a couple of 30-minute sessions a week should be enough. Not so if the child wants to do more. Parents should provide as much opportunity as the child wishes but should not push them to do more than they really want to do.

Ages 7 to 9 will need two or three sessions of 45 min-1.5 hr. each. Again if the motivation is there for more, then by all means parents should go for it.

Depending on a player's developmental stage, more or less time on court hitting balls and playing matches is necessary. The amount of time devoted to Tennis will also depend on how much the child has learned to love Tennis and how passionate he or she has become. Take into account mental development and maturity. Some kids can handle a lot more than others; fathers and mothers know their children better than anyone. We want to put some pressure, but not too much... Be careful!

Ages 10 to 11 should go for three to five sessions of 1-1.5 hours.

It seems to me from experience, that once a child is 12 or 13-years of age, depending on physical and emotional development, as well as the level of maturity, they should be hitting a lot more. A 13-year old boy or girl has tons of energy. With the right motivation, this kid could be hitting in the neighborhood of 15 – 25 hours per week! Yes, it sounds crazy, but it is true. Motivated juniors don't mind half killing themselves on a Tennis court for hours on end, day in and day out, year in and year out until they get what they want. In the summertime vacation period, they may even hit more than that.

Once a junior player has developed the physical maturity to withstand the hard hours of work, there really is no limit to how much they should be hitting balls. It is more about motivation and determining the right goals.

However, do remember that quality over quantity will do the trick every time. Tons of random hours on court will most likely waste tons of time. The right balance of match play, stroke production, skill or weapon development, tournament play, and a well thought out supervised fitness regimen is what is needed here. Solid foundations and technique have to be in place for the player to actually have a chance to make it to the top of his or her potential, whatever that may be.

As a junior, I remember hearing people talk about Vilas and Navratilova, and later Lendl putting in 8 hours of training daily. That sounded like a lot to me. But I used to think, "Well, it is a full-time job; that ought to be the way to do it." But man… Was I wrong! I am pretty sure I put in the time, but I did not have the right coaching if any at all, and that is my excuse for not having made it to the top. Lots of Tennis freaks said to me as a junior that I had what was needed to make it… but something went missing along the way because I had a hell of a time trying to make it in the Pros. I never really got to the level I desired! The point here is that lots of hour on the court is not the solution. For the most part, a junior player needs guidance and supervision unless he is super smart and super mature.

At the end of the road, a developing junior player will need about 10,000 hours on court to fully develop their game. Doing the math, that is a massive amount of day to day work. At this point, it is valid to say that each player is different, and, of course, not everyone is willing to make this kind of sacrifice. Few people will make the kind of effort on court to make it to the top of their ability. A lot of players reach the 10,000 hour mark later in life, way after their physical prime. And that is the problem for most of us. In an ideal World, the 10,000 hour mark should be reached by age 21-26 for the player to actually be able to play to his potential. Only the absolutely most committed players ever make it!

THE 6 HOUR A DAY JUNIOR TENNIS CAMP

Some Tennis programs have 6-hour clinics or Tennis camps. Unless a child is at least 10-12 years old and already heavily involved in Tennis and loving it, I would highly discourage this sort of camp. They are just money making deals for the organizers, and it is a sure way to teach a 6, 7 or 8-year-old to learn to hate Tennis. Children in this age group are not ready for such rigorous training, and it is conducive to burnout. Instead, kids should be exposed to varied activities in different disciplines with lots of built-in breaks, including but not limited to recreational games that promote skill development to keep them motivated and energized.

Tennis camps for under 10-year-olds should be no more than 1.5 hours of continuous training. If the right motivation is present, another 1.5 hours session is possible later in the day. There should be at least a one-hour break in between. And in reality, this should be enough for one day. I have said this before, and I will say it again. Tennis is not a race to find out who can get there first, but an endurance test to find out who actually makes it to the end line! Staying in it for the long haul far outweighs trying to beat everyone at the beginning or the middle of the developmental process. The goal is not to get there first, but simply to make it!

When a 12-year-old child loses a match against a kid who is one or even two years younger--Hey, that's fine, just keep on working hard and time will tell. Let's see where we are at four years from now, or even 7 years from now... Then, we shall speak!

Take Tennis in a little at a time. A developing player needs to take it in little by little and build something very big after a long time. It is like a giant staircase to the Moon! Each ball well hit; each minute well-taken advantage of will get the player one step upwards towards the final goal. Imagine there are thousands and thousands of steps in this staircase... The player just has to keep climbing and climbing... it will take years to get there, no need to rush to the finish. Players that do, usually get tired and quit or burn out!

HOW LONG DOES IT TAKE TO LEARN A STROKE?

From 3 months to several years. That is the straight answer. However, it is not that simple. Even if a player gets help from a good Tennis professional, the actual mastering of a stroke takes a long time. Look at Gaby Sabatini's serve. She struggled with her serve during her entire career, never really developing a serve that measured up to the rest of her game and athletic ability. In fact, had she had a better serve, there is a good chance she might have won a lot more and sustained a higher ranking for longer periods of time throughout her career. Another example is Patrick Rafter's ball toss. He had a good serve, but oftentimes; he would toss the ball up to three times, at which point, he would simply hit the ball, whether it was a good toss or not. Going back in time, we can mention Yannick Noah's forehand. It was not the prettiest stroke, and he really never developed a good one. Other examples exist. These players learned to be successful with their deficiencies. They won a lot of matches, but I can guarantee that each and every one of them would have loved to have better technique on some of their strokes.

Within technical boundaries, there are ranges; this is why a great forehand from a player looks distinctly different from another great forehand from another player. However, players have to meet certain criteria. Some basic rules cannot be breached, or students will have technical difficulties, that in turn will become weaknesses, if, not resolved and addressed professionally.

There is no such thing as the perfect player. Some players enjoy what seems to be a perfect forehand or serve; however, his or her volleys or backhand may not be so perfect. Even Roger Federer, Andre Agassi, Martina Navratilova or Rod Laver as well as other great players could have improved their game in certain areas.

Going back to the question of how long it takes to learn a stroke; this has been mentioned elsewhere in this book. From my observations and other's it can be said that a player will need about 10,000 hours of training to fully develop. It will then take up that much time to fully develop any given stroke if the right commitment is shown all throughout this process. An effective stroke, be it a volley or a groundstroke, will take at least three months for the player to feel comfortable and somewhat confident with it. A technical adjustment to a stroke will take at least those three months, but a lot longer in most instances to fully master it. Mastery of a technique may never happen, and unfortunately it does not with the great majority of players.

At this point, we might say the question in this subtitle is too broad. And I agree because we need to define what we mean by "learn a stroke" or make a technical adjustment to a faulty technique. Talented and driven by motivation, players with great concentration and work ethic will conform to the "three month" rule. For most others, more time may be needed, and sometimes years will be required, and yes, lots of them will never learn proper form or technique. The great players of today and yesterday comprise less than 0.1% of all serious Tennis players. Those are the chosen few who learn in three months. All others mortals will suffer a lot more through this process. That is a tough but true statement to have to make. Some players are unteachable or incapable of learning!

One last encouraging comment here in regard to the 10,000 hour is that these 10,000 hours for someone who loves the game will be a road filled with fun, satisfaction, and great experiences. It will be a road of making memories that will stay with players forever. And these 10,000 hours encompass not only the technical, but also the tactical, emotional and even some spiritual stuff in the developmental field. It is, in fact, an awesome road to go through if Tennis is played for all the right reasons; this is a promise, and I say this from the bottom of my heart!

TALENT VERSUS MOTIVATION

Talented athletes are pretty common in Tennis. These are the players who make Tennis look easy to play. However, and, for the most part, these are not the players making it to the top, whatever the top is for our standards. Physically gifted athletes are usually filled with compliments from adults. It is not a good thing because these kids usually start developing a false sense of greatness and with this comes a lack of work ethic which in turn ends up hurting the athlete. These players have the tendency to lose perspective. They get lazy and casual about their training and effort in matches. Maybe they think that since they are so talented they should win by default, but they will get beat a lot and in the majority of cases ending up as just okay junior or college players at best.

It is indeed an unfortunate situation since there have been so many physically gifted players that let all the praise get to their heads preventing them from discovering on their own how good they can really become.

Dads or Moms of these super athletes should not offer them so much praise that they end up encouraging laziness. Children need to understand that greatness can only be achieved, through hard work. Parents need to talk to their kids about the value of ethical, hard work and day to day commitment and long range goals. The true potential of an individual should be based on their all out effort physically, mentally, and spiritually every minute of the road.

True talent should be measured in how much the athlete is willing to put in the time and effort into mastering a given discipline. Talent needs to be measured in units of hunger and determination he or she has to have success. If an athlete has this kind of desire and drive to go all the way. If he/she does not let all the praise get to his or her head, then this is the kind of athlete who is likely to escalate to the top of his or her potential.

If as a coach, one gets lucky and ends up instructing a very gifted athlete as our student. We want to make sure he or she understands that all the physical talent without discipline, drive, self-motivation, and determination is worthless! As a competitor at anything, results will be measured in relation to the effort put into achieving them. Anything that is given to us without effort on our part has less value. Whatever we are and whatever we want in this life needs to be earned in order for us to truly be able to say we have achieved anything!

SETTING GOALS

It is common for a coach to have no clue what students or parents want. Parents and players don't know what they want either a lot of times. Junior players need to have good communication with their coach. Coaches also need to have good communication with their juniors. All different types of communication are necessary here. Obviously, verbal communication is one of them, in the form of conversation. But also consider e-mail, texting or hand-written materials; such as notes on sticky pads as well as any of the social media means of communication. Even hand signals or facial expressions are good sometimes. Of course, we are not talking about hand signals during matches or communication during matches since this is against the rules of Tennis.

Coaches who communicate with students and parents of junior players on a daily basis are the best coaches. Players and parents need to know with clarity what is expected of them, and the coach needs to be aware of what players and parents want from him as a coach. The more communication we have, the better the results will be.

For good communication to happen there has to be chemistry among players, coaches and parents. If this chemistry is not present, it is better to find another coach until the right communication channels are found and open on a consistent basis.

Setting goals in Tennis is no different than setting goals in other areas of life. Players should have concise, short, mid, and long term goals. They should have performance and result oriented goals.

Performance goals are all those things that are 100% achievable and directly under the player's control. Good examples of these goals are, sleeping properly, eating a balanced diet, training the right number of hours per week, playing the right number of tournaments per season, keeping a good attitude at all times when on court, and working very hard at 100% intensity all the time during practice and matches.

Result oriented goals are those that may or may not happen, but students still have to have them, such as winning a predetermined number of matches in a tournament, playing well against all opponents, winning certain tournaments, or beating certain players. A result-oriented goal can also be to play college Tennis at an NCAA Division I school or to play professionally at a certain age.

Goals need to be often revised, at least three times per year if a player/coach/parent team is serious about this business and is intent on reaching the player's potential. These goals must be in writing and need to be shared and agreed on by all members of the team. Goals that are well thought out and realistic are great motivators for the day-to-day player. This is the kind of stimulus that makes a player go to the gym, hit Tennis balls for hours on end, go to bed early, and eat right.

Here is a list of goals to choose from for junior players. They can put check marks by the ones they intend to pursue. It is a good idea to do this at the beginning of the year, print the form, throw it in the Tennis bag, and look at it every week, to make sure to stay focused on our new year Tennis resolutions.

Goals Menu
Performance Oriented Goals

- ❖ Sleep at least 8 hour a day, preferably during my usual sleeping times
- ❖ Devote 10, 12, 15, 18, 20, 24+ hours a week to my Tennis (circle No. of hours)
- ❖ Hit 100, 200, 300, 400, 500, 600, 700, etc… No. of balls on the wall or the ball machine 2, 3, 4, 5, 6 days per week (circle appropriately)
- ❖ Play in 5, 10, 15, 20+ tournaments this year (circle No. of tournaments)
- ❖ Eat right and at the prescribed times to allow my body and mind to be at 100% for all my matches and practices
- ❖ Work at 100% mentally, physically and spiritually during practices and matches
- ❖ Abide by my fitness regimen on a weekly basis
- ❖ Follow instructions from coaches and parents week to week and in tournaments

WHAT TENNIS PROS DON'T TEACH (WTPDT)

- Work on my serve at least 4 times per week by hitting at least 50 serves
- Work on groundstrokes at least 4 times per week devoting a minimum of 1 hour of groundstroke practice every time
- Work on volleys at least 4 times per week devoting a minimum of 30 minutes each time
- Work on slice shots 3 times per week
- Work on topspin shots 3 times per week
- Work footwork 3 times per week
- Work on mental toughness every day by having a well-defined routine in between hitting balls for practices and matches
- Avoid time killers such as electronics, shopping (going to the mall) and/or TV in order to be able to achieve all my other goals
- Watch professional Tennis on TV 1, 2, 3 hrs per week (circle appropriately)
- Read inspirational material on the Internet or books to expand my Tennis knowledge and understanding
- During team travel to tournaments, make every single team practice in the mornings
- Be a team member to all practice partners and the rest of the team, as well as coaches and parents every day
- Hit every ball as if it was the last Tennis ball I will ever hit
- Don't be distracting to others or myself during group servicing or during any other type of drill or practice
- Drink lots of water every day, especially during tournaments
- Others (write them down)
- Don't miss drills or lessons over parties or social activities, sacrificing is part of my discipline and commitment to Tennis
- Play at least one practice match per week during the Spring, Summer, Fall and if possible even during the Winter
- Make sure my equipment and gear is complete and in proper working order before matches and practices or drills, strings fresh, overgrips clean, towels, caps, visors, Kleenex, etc...
- Other goals (write them down)

Result Oriented Goals

- ❖ Win at least 1, 2, 3 match(es) at every tournament I play in (circle appropriately)
- ❖ Win two, three, four, five, six tournaments this year (circle appropriately)
- ❖ Break into the top 3, 10, 15, 20, 50, 100 in the state, section, nationally this year (circle appropriately)
- ❖ Beat such and such players (write names of players)
- ❖ Control my emotions during important points
- ❖ Play smart tactically when it matters the most
- ❖ Play well against players that I am supposed to beat
- ❖ Play well all the time during practice, matches and tournaments
- ❖ Other goals (write them down)

DOING IT ON OUR OWN

I am going out on a limb on this one since I am a Tennis Pro myself and have made my living for 30 years teaching juniors how to play Tennis. However, it must be said, not everyone needs a Tennis coach to become a good Tennis player. All that is needed is true desire and some basic guidelines. I learned how to play by myself. As a junior I may have taken a total of 20 lessons over a period of 10 years. Most of them were just hitting sessions with the club's Tennis professional, Ruben Nápoles, who was indeed a very good player.

What I did do, though, is watch a lot of Tennis. I would sit down by any court where there were any decent players hitting balls. It was not difficult to determine who I needed to watch since good players are easy to identify even for a kid. Also back in the late 60s and 70s when I was learning, there would be a chance now and then to watch Davis Cup Tennis on TV. The occasions were extremely rare, but they would happen. And when they did, I was not going to miss anything. I remember watching entire Davis Cup matches between Mexico VS the USA, Spain or Canada. If it was on TV, I was there. It is funny, now that I remember; I seemed to always be by myself in the TV room. None of my brothers or sisters ever joined me, and guess who became, by far, the best and most committed player in the family? Of course... it was me.

Nowadays, I don't see too many people really sitting down to watch TV Tennis, especially junior players with any regularity. They really don't care about following Pro Tennis on TV. It does not make a difference at all, because trying to make them understand that they need to watch Tennis on TV one hour a week as part of their training, is like trying to make them understand Russian! Very rarely will they do it. The bottom line is that we learn by watching better than any other method. It is as simple as paying close attention to footwork, grips, swing paths, positioning, postures, shot selection, and strategy.

The only other thing needed to do is read some Tennis textbooks and Tennis magazines to support some of the technical applications. My oldest brother Luis and I used to check out books from our school library on Tennis strategy and technique. It was fascinating to study Tennis. To this day, I have no knowledge of how many books I have read, some really good, and some not so great or downright bad or boring, but I read them, looking for knowledge. I played college Tennis on an athletic scholarship in the US and played professionally in Mexico for 6 years with my fair share of success and failures along with it. I achieved a top 12 ranking in the nation professionally. Not bad for a self-taught junior with no resources or a coach!

Professionally as a Tennis Coach, my commitment has been to junior Tennis. Even after 40 plus years of experience, my main source of information on technique and strategy remains TV Professional Tennis, especially Davis Cup and Grand Slams. 80% of my coaching is based on information I pick up from Tennis on TV. Yes, I still read a whole bunch and attend conferences and seminars. However, it seems to me that observing players on Television is an excellent method of studying Tennis. The reason I don't follow lesser events is No. 1 because it takes too much of my time, but also because some of the top players don't always put in their best effort. In Davis Cup, the coaching involved in matches makes it that much more interesting. It is very helpful to follow a coach's strategy and efforts to outfox the other coaches and players in trying to get his or her team to beat tough opponents when faced with insurmountable odds.

Another fundamental key for players making it on their own is lots of match play. Sign up for all possible tournaments and play in as many events as the tournament director will allow. Even though, I love singles, doubles offers more lessons to be learned. Playing doubles accelerates understanding of the game. Tennis enthusiasts and aspiring students of the game should play as many doubles matches as possible. It is not a bad idea at all, for children in the 8-14 age range, to sign up for two doubles events in a tournament, instead of one singles and one doubles, especially with kids that are having a hard time with the pressure issue.

Players who want to teach themselves should hit tons of balls on walls, against ball machines and self hand-feed drills. Also, hit lots of baskets of serves. Players also of course need to have a list of friends to play with. As a junior developing in Guadalajara, Mexico, I played on just about every public and private Tennis court in the city in the 70s. I had everyone's phone number, and I would make day-to-day arrangements on my own to hit or play with someone at some obscure or remote court. Some of these courts were pavement or concrete or just plain dirt... but I was there hitting Tennis balls. During the weekends and holidays, my brother Luis and I used to keep a record of how many sets we could play in a single day. Beginning with a singles match at 7 am (or as soon as there was daylight at dawn), and finishing with some doubles in the evening at dusk… I guess we could play up to 12 sets or more in a single day all during daylight because back in those days lit courts were extremely rare. Out on the Tennis courts we were, playing Tennis with whoever was available; it was a lot of fun. Man… Those days are gone! I don't ever see any juniors putting in this kind of work. It makes me very sad!

Guadalajara in the 70s was already over 2 million in population, so the distances were pretty far. I took advantage of the urban transportation system, but most of the time I would ride my bicycle with my racquets strapped to my back everywhere no matter how far I had to travel! It was a great way to get fit. Of course, things have changed a lot, and it's difficult these days for a 12 to 15-year-old to ride around on his or her bicycle in a city of this magnitude in a country like Mexico. It is dangerous now, and kids will need help from parents and older siblings to get around.

HOW TO GET BETTER NO MATTER WHAT

Aspiring and developing players need to continue to work on their game's weaknesses. As Tennis players, it is very easy to get on the court and want to work only on things we are good at. We usually are less willing to put in the time to work on our weaknesses. I understand that if a player is about to participate in a tournament, the need to sharpen his/her strengths is paramount. But when in the low season; developing students need to address weak or underdeveloped areas of their game; this will continually force them to improve their technique and understanding of the game. Don't become one of those players whose game stagnates. In Tennis, there is always room for improvement. Tennis players should not settle for less than their best and absolute total potential, and since this absolute value, in reality, is not ever fully reached, players can always continue to improve their game no matter what. I know what everyone's argument and thinking will be here... Age! Right? I understand, but I know that athletes in Tennis, and many other disciplines of all ages in this World understand as well: Tennis can be our number one ally against old age, and I can prove it!

However, as the saying goes: "A Tennis player is only as good as the best competition he or she can find." Players will improve by exposing themselves to tougher and tougher opponents. By this, I don't mean to sign up for the toughest division players are eligible for, but they need to find competition in an ever escalating way. Play in tournaments where there is a challenge. Tournaments, where a player knows that he/she is going to win, should be avoided, for the most part. I like it better if it is a tournament where a player knows he or she might or should be able to win! Does that make sense? And, of course, the better the practice partners, the faster a player will improve, not to say that if someone practices hard with lesser practice partners they will not improve. Students will improve no matter what as long as they work hard and address their weaknesses. However, aspiring players should always look for the best partners possible for practice and competition.

WHAT TENNIS PROS DON'T TEACH (WTPDT)

As mentioned above, by just watching professional Tennis on TV in an objective way, players will improve their game; this is probably the cheapest lesson and one of the easiest ways to improve in Tennis. However, very few understand this and take advantage of this idea. Sit close by and watch a decent player taking a lesson from a good coach or Tennis Pro. Listen, pay close attention to what is being said and what is being done... Voila! A free Tennis lesson!

HITTING ON THE WALL

Hitting against a wall is probably the least appreciated form of practice, the least expensive, and very probably, even at the highest levels, one of the most effective ways to sharpen a player's game, polish their strokes, and learn new ones.

Hitting on a wall is relaxing, great cardio, and provides the needed repetition to instill solid strokes. Every stroke in Tennis can be practiced against a wall. A player only needs one or two balls to do it effectively (5 to 10 balls recommended for lower level players). It is fun, easily accessible, very efficient, and most of the time free.

We can find good concrete or wood walls at most public facilities, Tennis clubs, and country clubs around the World. I can say that I built my game hitting thousands upon thousands of balls off a wall. When I see one, I am attracted to it like a magnet. When I travel to tournaments with juniors, I always hit on the wall at whatever little chance I get. My students are usually very interested and inspired to see me do this since I am "so old" they cannot believe it. They probably wonder if I am still trying to improve. Well, the answer to that is "of course, yes". But more so, I am trying to keep my sanity. Working with a wall is such an escape from everything, even if just done for as little as 20 minutes. A wall can work miracles for anyone going for it. And yes… The cardio… Very few cardio workouts can pass by faster than a good solid hit on a wall where a Tennis player nearly smashes the wall to the ground with 700 plus strokes hit at full concentration and intensity. Passersby will take notice, because man… is it loud? Especially if it's a wooden wall; and if the player hitting on it, is pretty good, a crowd of spectators might start bunching up… *"pang-pang, pang-pang, pang-pang…"* 60 or more hits in a row without missing! It's awesome!

Players can come up with their own routines. I like to hit 600-900 strokes all depending on the available time; this usually takes me from 25 and up to 45 minutes to achieve depending on what I am working on. Of course, groundstrokes take longer than volleys. I count my hits and go for about 150 forehands, 150 backhands, 150 combined forehands and backhands, 100 slice forehands and backhands, 100 volleys, 50 overheads and 50 serves. That's right 750 hits! And I feel awesome when done. Also, if I was to get on a court later, the same or the next day, I will be hitting the covers off the balls with absolute control, because my timing and rhythm is so good from all that wall hitting! It's like magic. About half of the groundstrokes, I hit on a wall, will be double bounce. This way I can hit the ball harder at a further distance from the wall, which resembles the distance of a Tennis court from the baseline to the net. For all other groundstrokes, I work on turning my shoulders, moving my feet and back swinging early, hitting at or near full speed. This, makes a great practice for taking the ball on the rise and return of serve.

For volleys, I move to within five to seven feet of the wall and do different patterns, concentrating on form and timing as well as watching the ball. Volleys on a wall really strengthen your forearm. For overheads, I do a serve like hit to the ground 10 to 15 feet in front of me, and as the ball rebounds upwards I repeat the motion. This allows me to work on footwork, technique and keeping my eyes on the ball while hitting the overheads. It takes practice to get good at it but it is fun and challenging. Lobs off the wall will come off with a little underspin which resemble a defensive lob in actual play. For serving, I pace the distance from the wall to where the baseline would be and crank 50 plus serves, focusing on rhythm, technique, and spin. As the ball bounces back towards me, I just grab it and serve again! Fun and effective… Done!

Note: See video of how to practice on the wall at https://youtu.be/r9If8bdmEKU

TENNIS CARDIO WORKOUTS

There is a whole array of ways to do cardio training in combination with Tennis training. When doing this, time passes by fast and in a fun and productive way. Players are working on their game as much as they are working on their fitness all at the same time. A player can do these by signing up for some Cardio-Tennis drills at the local Tennis club, or country club, where a Pro feeds lots of balls and keeps the players involved running non-stop for 45 minutes to an hour hitting the different strokes or even playing points. Tennis is normally an anaerobic sport but can be practiced aerobically off a wall, ball machine, self-feeding or by serving in an aerobic non-stopping way.

Check out www.youtube.com for "What Tennis Pros Don't Teach" Cardio Ball Machine at https://youtu.be/x3zxmfoL6Xk, cardio serving at https://youtu.be/4TlxkXsC1Ss, cardio self-feed at https://youtu.be/bmFB6sqJeCU. View all strokes from Master Pro Manuel S. Cervantes

WHAT SHOULD A PLAYER'S STROKES LOOK LIKE?

It is not difficult to figure out whether a player hits the ball properly or not. By simply watching excellent players at a club or Tennis facility or the pros on TV, it is easy to tell whether or not strokes look good. If these kids don't look at least a little like these solid players, then chances are, they have deficient strokes. Solid strokes should be smooth, efficient, and powerful.

Watch a lot of good Tennis, create a mental file of what solid strokes should look like, and then emulate those strokes. Half the time this is probably a better way to learn the game than actually taking lessons from a Pro and spending a small fortune only to find out later that a player's strokes are faulty. Worse yet, now this player is going to have to undo what he or she is doing wrong and learn a whole new way of doing things more technically. I don't know how many times I have come across players, especially juniors, who were taught the wrong technique, who had to break down the old bad habits, in order to learn new ones. This is a very frustrating process, especially for the student. There it is; double the time and double the money!

Another example of poor coaching is when a Tennis Pro automatically teaches the two-handed backhand without regard to the potentiality of the player. The two-handed is a lot easier than the one-handed to teach, and that is why most pros automatically go there. The question that must be asked is this: Would Sampras, Federer, McEnroe, Navratilova, Henin, Sabatini, Graf and so many former professionals have been better or worse off? Had they employed a two-handed backhand? I say probably not! It is a known fact that Pete Sampras switched from a two handed to a one handed when he was 13 or 14 years old. Let me also ask, would have Roddick or Isner been better had they had a one-handed backhand? And so on… Again, probably so! Look at their playing styles and their physiques; amazing athletes, great work ethic, and a good support system. There is no excuse for the player not reaching his or her potential.

Another clear example of poor or lazy teaching is the lack of a continental grip or something close to it for serving and volleys. Just about any kid can learn this grip if taught right from the beginning. My own daughter Anasazi started serving successfully with a Continental grip when she was seven years old! I don't know how many times I have given lessons to students, juniors and adults alike who had these two problems. Many of them had been playing Tennis for a long time and had taken many lessons with so-called Tennis-pros.

Again, look at Federer's or Clijster's forehand and compare it to someone's technique on the same stroke. Are there resemblances? If not, I suggest this someone figures out a way to imitate what he/she is seeing on TV!

IS MY TECHNIQUE SOUND?

The first thing that will probably come to mind is to visit your Tennis Doctor, the local Tennis Pro for a stroke diagnosis. A good Tennis teacher can immediately tell if a technique is sound or not, but this would be the expensive way to do it. Spending money is not always the only or the best way to solve problems and is not always absolutely necessary. As mentioned in previous pages, studying video to compare technical moves to the Tennis Professionals is a good start. If there is not at least a little resemblance, then there probably is a situation of faulty technique. Another easy way to figure out whether someone's strokes are technically sound is to get in front of a practice wall and hit some shots… if this player cannot keep the ball going for at least ten shots consistently, then there is faulty technique. Some of the problems could stem from faulty footwork, but most likely it could be a technical flaw in the stroke itself. A simple example of that is a player trying to hit 10 shots in a row against the wall where all he or she hits are forehands. If this player is running all over and bending over backwards to make it happen, and he or she fails after two or three attempts, that is a sure indicator of bad technique.

One of the most common technical flaws is a late turn of the body or unit-turn in preparation and winding the body, arms, and racket or loading before the forward swing. Our body should be at least 70% turned sideways with the racquet back more or less 80% by the time the ball is bouncing on our side of the court. Wow! That's it, I said it… as simple as that… But it is a lot harder to actually accomplish! (Look at the WTPDT www.youtube.com video https://youtu.be/CRGMa0WhRcE on the right timing and form of the unit turn or proper body winding for groundstrokes)

Having awareness of what goes on the Tennis court is also important. Notice which shots we tend to miss the most; then figure out why. Again the problem could be footwork or timing, having nothing to do with the actual swinging technique.

Tennis players in the making need to do all they can on their own to develop sound technique. Another good way to have a player visualize himself or herself swinging is before a mirror or glass door. A cast shadow also works but, it gives a weird perspective. If a student can have his/her shadow cast on a vertical surface like a wall or door, the perspective is much better. Take some swings in front of this wall or mirror, see the shadow or image, and visualize the point of impact and how the body turns. Notice the swing path the racquet head follows and see if it resembles the Pros.

Developing sound technique is incredibly important in Tennis. With it we can go places, without it, we are not going anywhere, guaranteed! Obviously, taking lessons helps, but that can be expensive, and if a player falls into the wrong hands, then he or she will have spent a lot of money potentially developing bad habits. This poor individual may have to work double or triple the time undoing the wrong habits and learning the right ones.

I would suggest anyone looking to learn Tennis, first to learn to watch Tennis. Become a Tennis freak or aficionado by watching for fun, just like we would football, baseball or the Olympics; do it for fun and pay attention and learn what Tennis looks like. Get the children involved and get excited. Once they have developed a taste, and once they understand and have a vivid image of strokes and other elements, let them try it on their own. Grab a basket of 50 balls and head for the Tennis courts. A dad or mom with his or her children on a Tennis court, a couple of rackets, and some sort of an idea of what Tennis needs to look like from watching Tennis on TV, is all that is needed for now. The whole family will have a great time doing this.

One of the things that drew me to Tennis was its beauty, its artfulness. Artistic strokes are what we want to strive for. Tennis should look pretty, smooth, efficient, even poetic; Tennis should, to a certain extent, look effortless! There have always been a few players out there getting results with ugly technique or ugly strokes; personally I don't care too much for Tennis like this, but there are always exceptions to rules. More and more, I see players with what looks like ugly strokes and technique winning some big tournaments. Obviously, we need to show respect for these individuals because I can only imagine what they had to go through to achieve such level of play with such ugly technique. To me, a couple of the players who are winning nowadays are a total disgrace to Tennis and an insult to professional Tennis (no need to mention names… let the audience forge their own opinion. However, the ball does not care how one holds the racquet or what certain strokes look like, all it cares for, is to be hit right… and if that is being achieved, so the ball does what the player wants it to do! For the most part, I suggest that all aspiring players try to learn to hit the ball not only in a beautiful way, but in an efficient and effective way... it is a lot easier, more satisfactory and effective!

Unfortunately, a very small percentage of these unorthodox looking players are not only winning some tournaments but seem to be pretty seriously out of shape... I mean 15 or more pounds overweight! This is possible if a player goes for it all the time (in other words these players just go for winners off most shots). By playing like this, fitness level and mobility are not really challenged against a great majority of opponents. A player that just hits the ball as hard as he or she can will not have to move so much or work the point as much thus getting away with being out of shape! These players should not be winning, but they are... if only a little better strategy from more deserving players was utilized... mmh! Makes me wonder who is behind all this! Could it be poor coaching at the highest levels?

To me, unorthodox and out of shape players fit *"the exception confirms the rule"* principle and should not be used as models by anyone teaching or trying to learn how to play this game!

GRIPS ADVANTAGES AND DISADVANTAGES

There are different ways to hold a Tennis racquet: Eastern, Semi-western, Western, and Continental. Within this four major grip styles, I like also to discern what I would call radical and conservative extremes. Meaning a radical Eastern, will be at the edge of what is still considered an Eastern grip, but right before it could be called a Semi-Western. A conservative Eastern will be right where the grip is on the edge of going from Eastern to Continental. This particular grip used to be recognized as an Australian grip. And so it is with all four major gripping styles, we have radical and conservative conservatives. This is important because we all are a little different. If a player can hit a great forehand with a radical Semi-Western (which is almost a Western), he/she may not be so effective or feel as comfortable with a conservative Semi-Western, which is pretty close to a radical Eastern. Players should find out what feels better or produces the better results. The circumference around the racquet handle could be divided into 360 degrees, and each degree could be called something different. Of course, that would not be practical, and for simplification purposes these four techniques are what Tennis textbooks and observations have yielded over the years! The idea of radical and conservative grips is mine. I am sure that other Tennis professionals utilize similar teaching terminology and techniques.

For the Eastern forehand grip, the advantages are clear. Being the more traditional technique, it lends itself to flat, moderate and with the right swing path or technique even pretty heavy topspin facilitating knee to chest level strike zones. It is very simple and very flexible in that it can be adapted to all playing styles. Good examples of this grip are Pete Sampras, Roger Federer, Yevgeni Kafelnikov, Steffi Graf, Serena Williams, and many more. Lots of power can be generated with the Eastern forehand grip. This grip is also natural for underspin. Another clear advantage is how easy it is to handle low bouncing balls with fully controlled power as well as disguising drop shots because a player can learn to hit them without changing grips.

Another characteristic is the fact that it seems that the groundstrokes hit with an Eastern Forehand grip are more linear and less rotational. This is why players that use this technique are more classical looking, smooth and less prone to injuries. The point of impact does not have to be so far out in front of the body, and this makes for easier timing.

Some argue that the Eastern forehand grip is antiquated and obsolete, but I strongly disagree. Many extremely good players utilize this technique. The Eastern backhand is very similar in characteristics to the Eastern forehand, except that on the forehand side, for slice shots, sometimes players do have to switch their grip to a Continental. It is not as easy to disguise drop shots with it because the grip switch gives us away. Some players can hit good slice shots with their forehands with an Eastern forehand grip. Unless a player naturally utilizes a lot of slice in groundstroking from the baseline, and the opponent does not know whether another regular slice or a drop-shot is being hit.

Some disadvantages of the Eastern grip are that it is hard to handle higher bouncing balls. Some players find it hard to hit heavy topspin. Typically a player with these grips will not hit as may open and semi-open stance forehands and backhands, and this makes them a little less adaptable and flexible under some extreme situations.

The Semi-Western grip is maybe more conducive to top-spin and better for handling higher bouncing balls. It could probably be said, for now, that this is the most common technique in professional and high caliber Tennis in both the men and the women for hitting forehands. The Semi-western grip is very effective at generating great racquet head acceleration with huge rotation and lots of open and semi-open stance action from both sides. Players with solid technique will usually be the aggressive baseliners of this World; they will have tons of power and spin combinations. Players with great semi-western forehands are very common, such as Fernando Verdasco, David Ferrer, Sabine Lisicki, Justin Henin, and many more.

One of the drawbacks of the Semi-western grip, is the inadequacy in handling very low bouncing balls, and the tendency of a player to abuse the topspin, creating a weaker, less aggressive ball due to the excessive spin.

The Western grip is considered by many as too unorthodox for successful Tennis; however, it has been and continues to be used effectively. Typically the ball is hit way out in front of the player. The amount of rotational racquet speed is impressive on some of the better players. The Western grip is more conducive to handling high bouncing balls. It is very easy to come from under the ball and generate tremendous amounts of topspin. Hitting the ball with an open or semi-open stance is very typical.

Disadvantages are numerous: The grip switch path is the longest as compared to the other gripping techniques. In other words, the grip has to be rotated in the hand longer to reach any of the other grips for hitting backhands. That is why some top players switch grips in a reverse manner by rotating the racquet all in one direction instead of back and forth. It is not easy to hit low bouncing balls. The awkward swing path and enormous amounts of rotation are more prone to creating injuries in the lower back as well as in the arm and hip joints. Hitting slice shots with a Western grip is difficult, forcing the player to switch the grip thus he or she is unable to disguise the maneuver; because the racket has to be rotated in the hand quite a bit. This action can easily be detected by the opponent, and he or she will be able to anticipate what's coming. Most players hitting a Western forehand are somewhat unorthodox looking from the technical standpoint. And in my mind, anything that does not look technical and natural is probably not the best or greatest way to go! Some players have gone to what is called the super-Western grip, which is even past the radical edge for what could be recognized as a Western. Very extreme Western forehand grips lead to injury and sore arms, should be strongly discouraged, since it will be next to impossible to hit solid or with good consistency with this grip!

A word of caution is in place here. Junior players in early developmental stages need to be monitored very carefully as far as gripping techniques. A junior who starts with an Eastern forehand technique will end up with a western after a couple of years. In order to handle high bouncing balls, some of these juniors do this subconsciously, but it is self-destructive since, for the most part, the more natural or effective techniques, for hitting groundstrokes, are the Eastern and the Semi-western. No disrespect to all awesome Westerners out there. I had my fair number of losses to some of these guys. If a player with an awesome Western forehand comes my way, he pretty much is going to have to prove to me that he is indeed awesome with it. If the stroke is not performing well under pressure, there is a very good chance I might try to make the player switch to a Semi-Western.

As far as the Continental grip is concerned, it could be said, that for groundstroke purposes, this grip is obsolete except for slice shots. Especially with the one-handed backhand and some defensive and tactical slice forehands. This grip was widely used back in the old days. Players used only one grip to hit all the shots. And that was with the Continental grip. I guess that is where the name came from; continental, meaning, everything embraced within a single technique.

Still, nowadays, we will see a few players hitting balls with continental grips. For groundstrokes, players will be hitting very flat shots. Continental is excellent for slice and handling low bouncing balls. For the most part, the Continental grip is extremely important in that this is the right grip for volleys, overheads, and serves. In some cases, it is also used as a commanding grip for the two-handed backhand; this is good because players can disguise the slice backhand drop shot, without switching grips.

All of the explanations given above and the technical stuff talked about in this section refer to the grips in both the radical and the conservative extremes. A player who uses a Continental grip for his/her two-handed backhand may be radical or conservative, and both techniques would be acceptable. Same goes for any of the other gripping techniques. Many times, a Coach or Tennis Pro will make mistakes regarding technical changes such as the way a player holds the racket or other stuff of the sort. Sending the player into a spin where he or she may lose complete confidence on a stroke or strokes, this will affect not only the results but also the enjoyment of the game. Parents and players have to be aware of this situation!

One of the very first things a Tennis pro or coach will want to do for a new student is changing their technique, especially the grips. If the stroke in question is not causing any trouble, there should be no point in doing this. Let me finish by saying that, when changing a grip or a technique, the Coach needs to be 100% sure that the new technique will improve someone's game; and that this student is capable of learning these changes fairly fast (no longer than 6 months). If these criteria cannot be met with good confidence, then it is better to let things be as they are until a viable solution is found. Also, it is important that a player, who is already in an advanced developmental stage, be okay and fully on board with the changes being proposed.

As far as getting the right grip size for a player's hand, he/she needs to make sure there is a gap of about one-quarter of an inch to one-half inch between the base of the thumb and the tips of the middle and ring fingers. Different players like different feels. It is acceptable to be at either extreme of this range. Too small a grip, will not provide the right amount of traction on the hand/grip interface for hits outside the sweet spot of the racket strings. A small grip makes controlling the shot very difficult because of torque applied to the racquet head from heavy spins and hard hits. Too big a grip will not allow a player to apply enough pressure on the grip, especially when serving and ground-stroking, sometimes making the player lose the racquet in the air as he/she is making contact to the ball or swinging. The pressure we apply on the grip depends on what kind of shots we are going for. We want as lose a grip as possible without losing control of the racquet head as we strike the ball. On the ready and serving positions, we want a very relaxed grip as we get in position to start the point.

Avoid holding the racquet with a death or hammer grip. This is the kind of grip that looks just like the fist is closed with an object in the middle, and the fingers are all parallel to one another. We want the hand shaking grip or pistol grip where our hand and index finger shoots out diagonally upward towards the V of the racquet.

There is plenty of literature on gripping techniques; do some research if further understanding is needed; this is just a general overview of the different grips that should at least lead apprentices in the right direction.

For a short video of the different grips and right grip size in Tennis go to www.youtube.com What Tennis Pros Don't Teach Grips for Tennis https://youtu.be/SCmQduNiV1c

THE IMPORTANCE OF THE NON-DOMINANT ARM

The non-dominant arm plays a huge technical role in Tennis. It serves several purposes:

a) Balance on the run and when executing shots; this is obvious, as we see players reaching with their non-dominant arms out for balls on the run or at the net.
b) Cantilever on forehands and serves, aiding with the rotation of the shoulders; this may very well be one of the most overlooked but most important aspects of the left or non-dominant arm. It is simply difficult to hit the ball hard and rotate our body aggressively without the rotational swinging of the left arm. It is part of the kinetic chain process.
c) Depth perception on overheads, serves, forehand groundstrokes, and volleys. The left arm will be closest to the incoming ball and helps us determine when to start the forward acceleration of the racquet. In other words, the left arm helps tracking down the ball and measure the right distance to it as it approaches.
d) Cradle the racquet on the ready position and initial serving position.
e) If a two-handed backhand then the left arm is part of the technique all along the motion.
f) Helps get the racquet back into position for all shots; forehands, backhands, for groundstrokes, and volleys as well as overheads. The non-dominant arm and hand help in the maneuvering of the racquet into the right pre-acceleration position as we execute all shots.
g) The non-dominant hand really gets involved in the grip switching; it helps switch grips more efficiently and quickly.
h) Obviously for tossing the ball as part of the serve.

As can be seen, to disregard the non-dominant arm as a fundamental part of Tennis technique is a huge mistake. It is one of the most disregarded aspects of Tennis technique. If a coach has never addressed it, I would recommend players go elsewhere for help with their Tennis.

We don't naturally understand the biomechanics of what has been mentioned above, and we don't always naturally do what we are supposed to be doing with our left/non-dominant arm and hand. Unless a player is a pretty gifted athlete, he/she needs to pay attention to this analysis. I recommend anyone interested in learning how to use the non-dominant arm to turn on the TV again, and watch the touring professionals. Pay close attention to how much they use their non-dominant arm all the time. See video on www.youtube.com What Tennis Pros Don't Teach, The Use of the Non-Dominant Arm at https://youtu.be/8GHJh2CluoI

FOOTWORK IN TENNIS

Footwork is essential to good Tennis. There are plenty of players out there who polish and hone their strokes day in and day out, but devote very little time to mobility and footwork.

There is a best way to handle a shot for each and every shot a player hits. The position of his/her feet and body in relation to the ball cannot be exactly the same for hitting different types of shots. A down-the-line shot requires a different position of the feet and the body than would a crosscourt shot. Or a forehand volley angle off a low ball will demand a very different position of the body from a straight up drop-shot volley.

A simple explanation of the different footwork techniques is presented next. These are the most fundamental techniques, but by no means, am I saying these are the only techniques to move on a Tennis court. For the most part, all footwork techniques are based and will utilize part or all of the basic footwork patterns presented below.

THE SPLIT STEP

It seems we hear the word split step a lot. The split step is nothing more than a reaction step. In reality, the split step is a fight or flight reaction skip or step.

We have a Great Pyrenees dog at home that is extremely playful. As my daughter Anasazi and I start playing with her, she gets in what would be the equivalent to ready position for a dog, and as we make a move, she split steps and reacts at unbelievable speeds to whatever it is we are doing. She keeps doing the same thing over and over as needed depending on what game we are playing. This would be a great example of split or reaction stepping for kids.

Right as the opponent makes contact with the ball, a player should already be split stepping. By the time he/she comes out of this reaction step, the ball is on its way towards his/her side of the court, and he/she should be on his/her way already, moving to it, whether it is a volley, a groundstroke or a return of serve. Technically players should always split step in order to react quickly and efficiently to the approaching ball.

The reaction step should be fully automatic, but coaches may have to train some players to do it effectively. A good way to practice is on a ball machine or practice wall or board, where the player concentrates on this aspect of the footwork only. As the ball comes out of the ball machine or the wall, the player split-steps, moves to the ball and hits it over and over. Until he or she starts getting the feel for the correct timing, and it becomes second nature.

ADJUSTING STEPS

Another important aspect of footwork technique is what we call stutter steps, tiny steps, or what some pros call baby steps. These steps are nothing more than adjustment steps. As the ball is coming, a Tennis player may not always have sufficient time to do these tiny steps. Sometimes players are barely trying to get their racquet on the ball with little time to adjust distance, at such times obviously playing defense. But at any time it is possible, a player should try to take several extra little steps to fine tune his/her position to the ball. It is obvious when the player has lots of time and he or she can really fine tune the position for a very aggressive shot. Usually, 3 to 7 little steps are sufficient depending on different situations. Tennis players should take as many tiny adjusting steps as time allows for each and every ball hit. He or she has to continue to move his/her feet until the racquet starts the forward acceleration towards the ball.

Avoiding these extra steps when is a technical flaw. These little steps allow the player to hit with better overall technique just about any shot in the game, other than the serve; which requires no displacement of the body prior to the start of the motion. How we are positioned, or how our body is lined up as we approach the incoming ball, has everything to do with whether we hit the ball well or not.

Another important skill in Tennis is shuffling sideways, forward or backwards. When moving forward, it is a good idea to shuffle (galloping kind of footwork) leading with the opposite foot to the stroke we are about to hit, for at least the last two or three steps; meaning, that if I am going to hit a forehand, I shuffle leading with my left foot and vice-versa.

Shuffling as a recovery step is another important application of the sideways or shuffling steps. As a player recovers and before his/her opponent makes contact with the next ball, usually, he/she should be shuffling back to a neutral position and preparing for the next move. It is also common to see a player cross step and carioca step to get in position; this would be a necessary variation of the shuffling we talked about above. The player uses these stepping techniques to get in position for the hit as he or she is moving towards the ball. This may not be necessary if a player has anticipated where his/her opponent is going to hit the next shot. Anticipation is important and pretty common, and a whole sub-section covers some detail regarding the intricacies of it. Once our opponent makes contact with the ball, a player should be split stepping and moving in the right direction.

THE DROP-STEP

To get out of the split step, we need to utilize what is known as the drop-step. This drop-step is almost a myth; a lot of players and coaches have never even heard of it. The drop-step is just as important as the split-step, and there is no real substitute for it. Opposed to the reaction or split step, the drop-step is the first step we take as we start moving towards the next shot. The drop-step creates space and is sometimes taken at the same time or in coordination with the split-step.

The drop-step, is usually a step that is taken in the opposite direction from where a player wants to move. Usually one foot moves behind the other foot, as we lean in the general direction that we want to go, and as we step with this foot, the other foot is then able to get off the ground moving to the ball in the desired direction. This drop step is usually pretty small, but it can be bigger as needed.

In other words, a player is trying to get his/her body falling or out of balance in the general direction of the next shot so he/she can go there faster.

This whole thing is probably pretty hard to understand out of a piece of paper and a bunch of words, so it is a lot easier to demonstrate it in a video. Look at the www.youtube.com WTPDT video on footwork.

THE CARIOCA STEP

The carioca technique comes in handy when recovering after hitting a wide ball or when approaching the net. It provides more efficient and faster lateral movement than a sideways shuffle or lateral kind of gallop. Carioca running or shuffling could be described as running sideways while crisscrossing the legs. On the recovery, carioca helps a player's move in the desired direction more effectively as he or she recovers back to the proper position on the court. For approaching techniques, carioca running comes in handy especially if a player has a one-handed backhand slice. As a player approaches the ball (being a right-handed player), he or she steps to the ball with his/her right foot as he/she starts the swing, he/she moves the left foot by swinging it through the back of his/her right foot as he or she makes contact with the ball. It is a thing of beauty and difficult to explain in words. It looks like Ballet dancing. The technique can also be applied for approaching with a forehand slice as well as for forehand or backhand volleys as the player is transitioning or moving forward towards the net hitting the ball. When utilizing this technique in approaching or volleying, players only have to do one carioca step as they swing the racquet, but in recovery carioca, they may need to do several in order to get themselves back to the needed position on court.

The carioca step has the advantage of allowing the player to remain sideways longer as he or she executes the shot, be it a volley or an approach shot. This in turn, is conducive to much better directional control of the shot in question.

SHUFFLING STEPS

Shuffling sideways, or galloping steps are needed to set up for most shots. As a player approaches the ball, he or she getting really close and ready to hit it, he or she may start shuffling towards it, leading with the foot that will be planted in front. If it's a closed stance forehand, it will be the left foot for a right-handed player. If it is an open stance forehand, it will be the right foot. For the most part, the player will do two and usually not any more than three shuffles as he or she sets up for the shot.

Also, when a player is recovering towards the center of the court, after hitting the ball, shuffling steps will be useful in doing so. In case the ball is hit behind the player by his or her opponent, then he or she can go back to the same area where he/she just hit the previous shot, and hit it again without too much trouble.

Remember that for setting up for most shots, a maximum of two or three galloping or shuffling steps are needed. For recovery shuffle, more may be needed depending on how long it takes the opponent to hit the next shot. Because as soon as the ball is hit on the other side of the court, the shuffling player stops shuffling and he/she simply starts moving or running pretty fast towards the next shot.

In Tennis, it is very important to be able to move sideways since all shots need to be addressed with a somewhat sideways position. Shuffling or galloping is the way to do this. Under some extreme situations, shuffling may not be possible due to the time constraints placed on the player when on the run or defending.

THE KILL SHOT SKIP

The kill shot skip is a technique for hitting a short ball that is bouncing 3 feet or higher early and going for a winner or a very aggressive approach. There are basically two footwork patterns, the closed and the open stance techniques. The closed stance serves better the situation when the ball is moving fairly directly to the player. So the player runs straight forward, and as he or she gets closer to the ball, he or she takes two or maybe three shuffling or galloping steps, leading with the left foot (for right-handed player), swinging with full speed, rotation, and skipping off the ground with the left foot meeting the ball in mid air and landing with the same foot immediately after the hit. The right foot, does sort of a natural mule kick backwards, as the racket is meeting the ball. The open stance kill shot, serves better the situation when the ball is more out to the side of the player. So, the player moves in the direction of the ball, as he or she gets closer, steps in with the right foot (right-handed player) and as he or she swings he/she skips off the ground, leading with the left foot, landing with it immediately after making contact with the ball. For the most part, the shot needs to be taken somewhere between waist and shoulder level. Lower bouncing balls, should be treated as normal approach shots. In both techniques, the skipping foot should move in the direction the player wants the ball to go.

THE SCISSOR KICK

Utilized for overheads the scissor kick is the right technique for the player to be able to create enough acceleration with the racquet as he or she gets in the air jumping backwards. As he or she swings at the ball, the right foot goes forward, and the left foot backwards (right-handed player), creating a scissor-like motion with the legs that allows the body to rotate, and the player to hit the ball with sufficient force for an aggressive overhead. The player may shuffle backwards or crisscross run backwards, looking to get underneath the ball as it arches over the player, and as he or she gets closer, he jumps with both feet and executes the overhead with great power and accuracy. It is of extreme importance for net players and a very common technique.

SERVING SPLIT RECOVERY STEP

As the player is serving, he/she will lift off onto the court. Normally the player will land down with his/her left foot while doing a sort of mule kick with the right foot (right handed player). He/She will have to do a split recovery step, when not serve and volleying to be able to get back in position on/or behind the baseline, so he/she can deal with a deep fast return of serve from the opponent.

LOADING

Loading is nothing other than the player doing a sort of final touch-down or landing down by flexing of the knees getting down, in order to be able to explode out as he/she accelerates the racket at the ball. Normally, the player will have a nice stable stance with good feet width separation; be it open or closed depending on the type of shot to be executed.

CLOSED STANCE VERSUS OPEN STANCE

Traditionally, textbooks on Tennis taught us the closed stance was all there was. Nowadays we see all kinds of stances for execution of all the different shots. Open and closed stances are used for groundstrokes, volleys, and overheads. The feet or legs of the player should simply adapt to all the different situations on the court. What is most important is that the player shows good balance, either dynamic or static as he or she swings at the ball. Generally, open stance is great for handling wide far out balls, and closed stance is probably better for shots that are closer to the player or directly forward of the player. In closed stance forehands, the left foot (for right-handed player) will be closer to the approaching ball, and the player seems to be squared to the net, as he or she gets the racquet back and swings.

WHAT TENNIS PROS DON'T TEACH (WTPDT)

In this technique, there seems to be less rotation and the entire motion seems to be a little more linear. In the open stance forehand, the right foot (right-handed player) steps forward to the approaching ball. The player seems to be facing the net, but he or she coils the entire upper body (hips and shoulders) as he/she takes the racquet back. Racquet head acceleration comes more from rotation with this technique. With both techniques, great power can be applied to the ball. And both techniques are valid for volleys or overheads as well as groundstrokes. In fact a player that is looking to develop his/her entire game needs to learn to hit all shots (except for the serve) with an open or closed stance with total proficiency. What we call the semi-open, or semi-closed stances are techniques similar to either or both of these techniques. Years ago I presented a seminar at a Tennis Conference in Scottsdale, Arizona titled *The Anyhow Stance*. The idea is that juniors or aspiring Tennis students need to learn to hit their shots with any stance they can get their feet on where they have solid balance and good linear/rotational acceleration of the racquet. It really does not matter whether we use closed or open stance as long as the player is able to generate enough but controlled power.

For a long time now, I no longer tell my students to set their feet in any specific way. I simply observe them let them learn the closed, open and anyhow stances on their own. I might suggest a footwork pattern to them when I see them struggle with specific situations. Before they know it, they are naturally using open or closed stances successfully as well as different combinations of the two, *The Anyhow Stance!*

Go to the What Tennis Pros Don't Teach video on Footwork Techniques for Tennis on www.youtube.com at https://youtu.be/9xaCNSopSXs. Also see StellaLuna's split step at https://youtu.be/oMNuCzW1cbk

SLIDING ON CLAY

Sliding on clay seems to be so natural and easy for some players. On red clay, we see professionals make slide marks up to 13 feet long and sometimes more. It looks a little like surfing on the ground or gliding. Players don't lift their feet off the ground too much as they move on the dirt. Sliding on clay courts, be it red clay or Har-Tru (green clay) courts, is of extreme importance to successful play on these surfaces. Every year during the red clay court professional Tennis season, we are able to appreciate the technique. During the French open, and the other clay court tournaments, it is pretty common to see the long slide marks out wide, and from about the service line to the net, as players struggle to get wide balls and short drop shots, which are very common on this surface. Some new faces that have not been exposed to clay that developed their games on hard surfaces are at a distinct disadvantage. In the 2014 French Open, one such player was the French-Canadian Eugenie Bouchard. Even though she, at age 20, did well reaching the semifinal; it was easy to see how her mobility on the sandy surface was uncomfortable. Being able to slide on clay adds dimension to a player's game. He or she will be able to reach more balls and have better balance and control.

Sliding on clay is not always necessary. Sometimes a player may just take a step or two to set up for a shot. On clay courts, this may look a lot like ice skating. The player may slide a little to one side or the other, easing into the shot. The real sliding happens when a player has to sprint to a far away ball, picking up some serious speed in the process. As the player gets a few feet away from the ball, he/she applies the brakes by leaning slightly back, thus distributing weight opposite the direction of travel, and onto the back foot; leaving the front foot free to slide toward the point of impact to the ball. In order to stop or slow down, the player transfers his-her weight to the front foot. As he or she is doing this, he/she is also winding the racquet and upper body reading for the shot. Sliding on clay is not a precise science because the surface may vary from one area to the next causing players to over or under slide.

Sometimes the player stops just as he/she meets the ball and a lot more times he/she hits it while still sliding. The dampness of the surface determines how much a player will be able to slide on clay. Clay is more slippery when dry, but may have damped spots, which make smooth sliding more challenging. A player may be sliding nicely to a ball, and suddenly he or she hits a damped spot, and "slam." He/she stops suddenly, sometimes falling over or losing complete balance and control. Most players will slide better one way than the other, and most players will slide much better with one leg or foot than the other. It is rare to find a player who can slide equally well with the right leg and the left leg. In the case of right-handed players, the vast majority of them will slide with the right leg leading the slide to the right, as well as to the left and vice-versa for lefties. This player will hit the great majority of wide forehands with an open or semi-open stance and a closed or semi-closed stance for backhands. At the highest levels, we will see a lot more players capable of sliding equally both ways. It is a beautiful thing to see when done well. Sliding and mobility on red clay Tennis courts is an art! Kind of like figure ice skating!

On other surfaces, we see some players sliding to a lesser extent. On grass, it is a lot more common. Some players even slide on hard courts! It takes really strong and healthy legs and joints to be able to do that, it is not recommended to try this unless heavily and specifically trained.

Players who grew up on clay courts or spent a good amount of time training on these surfaces, develop this skill naturally while others can be trained. There are some simple exercises that will help us get more familiar and confident with these techniques. If practiced with some regularity, sliding will become second nature.

For a short video on sliding techniques go to www.youtube.com and see the What Tennis Pros Don't Teach Sliding on the Clay video at https://youtu.be/hCyMUh4QFR8

ANTICIPATION

A Tennis court is pretty big if we consider the speed at which the ball is traveling. The average groundstroke speed is about 50 miles per hour in professional Tennis. Serves sometimes are hit at over 140 miles per hour! Some hard groundstrokes will get to our side of the court at 90 mph and faster. Considering that the dimensions of a Tennis court are 78x27 feet, for high caliber Tennis. Players must know in advance where the ball is going most of the time if they are to be able to get their racquet on the incoming ball; this in Tennis is called anticipation.

Anticipation is about covering the open court, reading our opponent's moves as he or she swings and from these signs to know in advance where he or she is going with his or her shots. We could call it guessing, but in reality it is more of an educated guess. Another aspect of anticipation is to learn an opponent's tendencies and favorite shots. A player may just have a phenomenal down the line backhand or an impressive crosscourt forehand. This player will favor these tendencies, even when the court is open on the other side. Let me give an example of this: Fernando Gonzalez has a huge inside out crosscourt forehand; he will go for this shot even if the down the line is wide open. Or when Roger Federer is on the run, his backhand passing shot will be a crosscourt angle most of the time because he is so confident with this shot. Another unequivocal example of these tendencies was John McEnroe's serve from the add side. One could bet one's house he was going for the wide screwdriver serve on big points. His opponents knew this, and he still went for it, because it was such a heavy serve for the day, and he was successful with it in the great majority of occasions he hit it.

Every developed player on the planet will have tendencies and favorite shots. So players need to be covering these tendencies in order to be able to deal with them. Not to do this, is to allow our opponents to get away with it, and they will love it, they will just take the point away at every chance they get by doing the same thing over and over. By anticipating these tendencies, we force the opponent to go for alternative and perhaps less effective shots.

For example, Fernando Gonzalez will not hit that forehand down the line from the add side as well as his crosscourt inside-out. Federer will not pass as well down the line as he would crosscourt off his on-the-run backhand, and so on and so forth. Remember. Play to the opponent's weaknesses! In the case of Gonzalez or Federer, even their weaknesses are not that weak. They are just not as awesome as their preferred tendencies. In other words, cover the opponent's inclinations or tendencies by anticipating. Once a player has done that, Gonzalez may be going for the down-the-line forehand from the add side of the court, or Federer might start going for the down-the-line backhand passing shot on the run, and guess what? They will not be as effective!

Anticipation on a Tennis court is about using common sense. Where is my opponent going to hit the next shot? The obvious answer is: into the open court, right? Well, most of the time. But that is where we need to get moving after hitting the ball when we are pulled wide near the singles lines, back towards the opposite side of the court. Unless, as mentioned above, the opponent has showed that he or she likes to hit behind a player, or he or she likes to go with some tendency that they prefer, over just going for the open court.

Without anticipation, Tennis players have no chance of covering the court well. Some players are said to be extremely fast, but in reality these players just have great anticipation. So it seems as if they effortlessly get to every single ball no matter how far or fast it's moving. Anticipation makes up for the lack of mobility for a lot of players. Lindsay Davenport didn't move all that well, but she always seemed to be in the right place because her ability to anticipate was outstanding. John McEnroe was great at anticipating passing shots. Somehow the guy was nearly impassable once he was at the net. He also was pretty fast and athletic, and that also helped, but it was more his knowledge and understanding of the opponent's tendencies, and situational logistics of the point, that made him so awesome at the net.

In other words, anticipation is covering the opening, be it doubles or singles wherever this opening may be!

PLAYING STYLES, STRENGTHS, AND WEAKNESSES

There are four basic playing styles in Tennis: the aggressive baseliner, the counter-puncher, the serve-and-volley or net-rusher, and the all-court player. Coaches need to advise and present a vision of the playing style a junior needs to pursue by age 10 or 11. Coaches need to be able to identify what weapons, strengths, and weaknesses will be present as the player develops. In high-performance player development, at least one weapon needs to be nurtured at an early age. Solid fundamentals all around need to be in place and weaknesses need to be addressed on a daily basis on court.

THE AGGRESSIVE BASELINER

Aggressive baseliners are the hard hitters of this World, players who will dictate from the baseline with their ground strokes. They usually have one weapon. Most likely it will be the forehand, but it is not uncommon to find some juniors with solid backhands as weapons as well. The forehand, which is more complex than the more natural motion of the backhand, can sometimes pass as a weapon. However, in reality, it could easily become a weakness if properly challenged. Just because someone makes a couple of winners early in a match off the forehand side, does not mean this player has a great forehand. If he hits five winners the first three or four games, the opponent of this player needs to start adjusting his/her strategy and tactics in order to come up with ways to neutralize it or minimize its effects. A thing to do is to try to figure out if this aggressive baseliner can continue to hit winners when on the run or from different angles and heights. As an example of this, consider a player hitting winner after winner from a shoulder level ball near the midcourt court area. What happens if suddenly, he is forced to hit lower bouncing balls below waist level, such as a slice or a flatter and deeper ball? Unless we are talking about a very good player, chances are, this player will no longer be able to come up with the consistent winners.

Sometimes a player's effectiveness will diminish if we can make him/ her hit on the run or force them to deal with deeper shots. Also, consider that Tennis players need to understand that in order to neutralize a weapon, first of all, we need to be aware that this weapon exists.

Even balls that come straight to a player's body, where the player has to move out of the way to create room to swing, can neutralize his/her baseline weapons if hit well; as far as speed, spin and depth are concerned. Aggressive baseliners will be characterized by playing most points closer to the baseline; however they will generally have weaker volleys as well as not necessarily a big serve. A potentially good strategy could be to force them forward to the net via drop-shots or short low balls, assuming the skills to execute these shots effectively are present. Keep in mind that short high balls are sure death against players with big groundstrokes. This player likes controlled aggression but will take some chances in a cautious way. Once an aggressive baseliner gets going, it is hard to stop them. It takes a good strategy, variation as well as figuring out how to counter the hard groundstrokes and power game.

If going for the aggressive baseliner style of play, junior players need to really spend a lot of time nurturing groundstrokes, mastering topspin, as well as developing either a forehand or a backhand weapon. An aggressive baseliner needs to add some variety to the mix by being able to throw in a drop shot and or a heavy top-spin lob. As coaches, we need to make sure the player going for this style will naturally have the necessary power in his or her groundstrokes to be effective. If developing the big forehand, get really good at hitting big inside out crosscourt forehands from the add side of the court (for right-handed players). Also, spend some serious time learning how to run around the backhand with the right footwork under the right tactical situations. It is also important to add a decent slice backhand (preferably one-handed) and acceptable volleys to the mix of groundstrokes. We don't want to be the kind of players who can hit groundstrokes and nothing else. There will always be harder hitters! Also for consideration, it is well known that a lot of players just love to play against other players who hit hard. Players who have no natural power will feed off the power from the hard hit ball. Another important characteristic we don't want to overlook for this playing style, is that the aggressive baseline player, will usually have a pretty aggressive return of serve; capable of hitting forcing returns, or even winners right off a short or weak serve.

THE COUNTER PUNCHER

Counter punching is the most common playing style. Even at the pro level, we see lots of players who are just very consistent and move fairly well. Let me add that this kind of player is the benchmark at all levels. Counter punchers are the hardest to beat and probably most successful of all playing styles. Some awesome players who have been in the number one position in the World have been counter punchers, such as Bjorn Borg, Arantxa Sanchez, Layton Hewitt and Rafael Nadal. Of course, there are different levels of counter punching. At the pro level counter punchers come with at least one big weapon. These players are characterized by not having great volleys, but it will be common to find them more capable of net play than aggressive baseliners. A good strategy against the counter puncher that moves extremely well is to just hit down the middle hard until they hit a weak ball, one that we can really hurt them with or approach the net with. Counter punchers encourage unforced errors in their opponents, so one has to be very smart to be able to take them out; with outfoxing strategies. The baseline is the counter puncher's comfort zone. Making them go forward from the baseline is an effective strategy. But getting to the net in order to finish the point, needs to be part of the game plan as well since this forces them to go for lower percentage shots. This player will be characterized by leveled temperament and emotional control. Counter punchers will usually be in pretty awesome shape. The longer the match and the points last, the more the counter puncher is likely to walk out victorious. They don't mind being out there battling forever; they like the long points and don't mind having to hit the ball 20 times in order to win each and every point. Their return of serve will usually not be aggressive, but it will be very steady forcing opponents to hit the ball one more time and putting pressure on the opponent to earn each and every point.

For the most part, nobody likes playing against counter punchers because they will not beat themselves. They are accused of being pushers, hackers, and moon ball experts. But personally I have the utmost respect for them because I lost some matches to these guys. Just because a player does not hit hard and does not have flashy strokes does not mean you should not be respectful of his abilities. Telling a junior player to go for the counter puncher style may be a hard sell; nobody likes being called a pusher. Coaches need to pay attention to this issue and help juniors find the right style of play, one that is fitting for their physical make-up, and personality of each individual.

Watch the Spaniard David Ferrer for some ultimate counter punching at the highest level there is! David is not flashy, but he will give his opponents nothing! He has a decent everything and sometimes he can hurt opponents with his forehand. He is super steady and mentally he is a giant. He will cling to the opponent like a bulldog and not let go until it's all over.

SERVE AND VOLLEY/NET RUSHING PLAYERS

Serve and volley and net rushing is a rare, but effective playing style. This player will do everything and anything to try to get to the net and finish the opponent or put pressure on him to come up with the big passing shots. They serve and volley all the time, sometimes even on second serves; they chip and charge off the return of the first and especially the second serves. They just go forward, and the opponent on the other side of the net, is faced with the ever present situation of this net crawling *Spiderman* type player. It is a beautiful thing to see someone execute this strategy effectively, but it is very rare since more and more players are developing effective groundstrokes and returns of serves, thus neutralizing them. Effective strategies against the serve and volley player are to return low and lob over their heads as well as going for passing shots. In order to keep them honest, one must lob some, or else *Spiderman* will just get closer and closer to the net and it will be next to impossible to hit any successful passing shots. Another effective tactic against a net rushing style player is to take the net away from them by going to the net first; even if this is not a player's favorite thing to do. By doing this, we neutralize them by stealing their strength. Serve and volley players will generally not have good groundstrokes. Therefore, their passing shots will be weaker.

Serve and volley players' temperament, is characterized by a bold personality, someone who takes risks and is not afraid to go forward into unknown territory. They will have good volleys and good finesse at the net. They will also be very agile and athletic at the net. Serve and volley players are also pretty good servers; they have to be. Serve and volley players must master a variety of spins and serve placements. They will kick serve wide, come in and volley into the open court. Or they might slice-serve heavily down the T and volley behind the returning player, as he or she is getting back towards the middle of the court. They may just angle a drop shot volley off a low passing shot attempt from the opponent. Another common tactic is to serve a jamming slice serve to the opponent followed by a deep down the middle volley near the baseline, daring the opponent to go for the passing shot. All other things being equal, net players have, of course, the best volleys in comparison to the other playing styles. They win a lot of points by just putting pressure on their opponents to go for low percentage passing-shots. Another virtue of a good serve and volley player is that they are great at anticipating lobs, and they usually have very good overheads that they will simply put away most of the time. Serve and volley style players need to develop groundstrokes and returns of serve that are at least good enough so they can get into the point and then figure a way to get to the net. Sometimes they have a hard time breaking serve because they don't typically have consistent returns. A serve and volley style player will base his/her success on their ability to just hold serve over and over. They take chances when returning and eventually they may break serve, at which point, the opponent will be in trouble since it is so hard to break back the serve of a good serve and volleyer.

ALL COURT PLAYERS

In a way, all Tennis players are all court players in the sense that ultimately, they will all have to play from different parts of the court whether they like it or not, but very few ever master the true all court playing style. This player has all the above abilities combined but usually will not be as good at a specific style as the above specialists. As an illustration of this, and under the *all other things being equal* principle. Let me say that an all-court-player, will be able to hold his own at the baseline to a certain extent, but would be at a disadvantage against a counter-puncher or aggressive baseliner, if playing from the baseline and staying back was the entire strategy of the all-court-player. For further clarification, let it be understood, that an all-court-player needs a variety of tactics to deal with the other playing styles in order to come out the victor. An all court player's strategy will be a lot more elaborate and difficult to discern than strategies for the other playing styles. An all-court player may do some serve and volley, counterpunch, and go for some aggressive shots from the baseline all combined as needed to come up with a winning strategy against tough opponents. Usually, these players will have all the shots in the book and are extremely creative. It is common for all court players to sport a one-handed backhand that they can roll with topspin, hit flat or slice for deep low, consistent rallies, drop-shot or hit low angles. All-court-players take quite a bit longer to fully develop and start having some awesome results. Through the different developmental stages, they really struggle with strategy and are very confused about all the different strokes and abilities they have at hand. Shot selection training becomes very important. Some good examples of this playing style are Sampras, Safin, Federer, and some others.

If going for this style of play, one needs to be a very hard worker. Understand that all-courter players will take longer to develop, their results getting better later in the developmental curve. Hours upon hours polishing all the shots are necessary. An all-court-player's personality and/or mentality needs to be just like his/her game, malleable and creative. These players are a lot of fun to watch, and often have the most potential, but rarely reach it since they have so much ground to cover in the developmental race.

ONE HANDED VS TWO HANDED BACKHANDS

Deciding whether to go for a one-handed or a two-handed backhand is difficult. Say a 6 to 12-year-old-child comes over for his or her Tennis lesson for the first time; what is the Tennis-Pro going to do about the backhand? Most of the time with new students, Tennis coaches will go for the two-handed backhand. Tennis coaches should take into consideration two basic factors, athletic ability and personality. Find out if the kid can naturally move in such way so that he or she can hit the one-handed or the two-handed. Physiologically we are all built a little different from one another, and while the one-handed backhand may come somewhat naturally to some, it may well be impossible to hit for others. Also, if the kid is of aggressive and inquisitive resolve, his fit may be the one-handed backhand, as long as he is athletic. Since those two ingredients are needed in order to make an all-court player or serve and volley player out of him. At the same time, if the kid is more deliberate in his behavior, and seems patient in his decision-making and thought process. We may definitely go for the two-handed since this type of personality will serve better the purpose of a baseline player, be it a counter-puncher or an aggressive baseliner. Having said that, in the first few lessons, the backhand should be introduced as a one-handed slice backhand affair. Based on that experience, the final decision can be made later on, in the development of the kid. As the Pro gets to know the student, better judgment and decisions can be made as to how his or her technique is going to end up. In the meantime, the child will be learning a one handed backhand slice that he or she will have to have anyway as part of his or her repertoire.

There are advantages to the two-handed backhand. This technique provides more stability on hard hit balls, especially on returns of serve and basic baseline rallies. Also, it can be developed into a weapon more readily. Some of the disadvantages are that it is more restrictive to deal with jammed situations, or when stretching out for a ball. The two-handed backhand is more predictable, lending itself less to variety and disguise. Of lesser importance is the advantage that the two-handed backhand is easier to teach than the one-handed backhand. It is a more straightforward technique, and there are not a whole lot of things that can go wrong with it.

The one-handed backhand has as advantages that it is more flexible and adaptable to different situations. It is easy to mix and vary as needed, and in instances of jamming and having to stretch out for balls. The one-handed backhand has obvious advantages because the player hitting with one extremity opposed to two, has more reach or flexibility to deal with all kinds of different situations. In other words, a player with a one-handed backhand will handle better balls that are jamming him/her and balls that are out wide or out front pretty far than the player with the two handed. It naturally fits the volley game or transitional game; shots like half volleys, approach shots and drop shots come more naturally to the one-handed backhand than the two handed. A lot of players can even hit the ball harder with a one-handed backhand than a two-handed backhand since it is a longer kinetic chain and the racquet head ultimately, will pick up more speed at impact. The disadvantages are that it is not as solid for baseline exchanges, and definitely not as strong and reliable when returning serve. That alone could be the reason to stay with the two-handed since the return of serve is so important in Tennis.

As mentioned earlier in this discussion, the one-handed backhand slice should be introduced to the player first thing since he or she will need this shot either way. Let me say that with a good slice backhand, a player may not be capable of hitting too many winners outright. But this very technique, is responsible for setting up many situations where the next immediate shot is a winner. These are a few of the things that are naturally done with a one-handed slice:

a) Baseline rally, where the player simply stays in the point, waiting for an opportunity to either roll a topspin backhand or run around the ball and blast a forehand. A good slice backhand helps set up a player's weapons,

b) Hit a drop shot in a naturally disguised manner. Since the one-handed slice wind up always looks the same, the opponent never knows if a player is going for a drop shot or just another normal slice crosscourt or down the line,

c) Block/return of serve against someone with either a big flat or spin serve. Players can just slice it back deep near the baseline down the middle to get in the point very effortlessly,
d) Hit a defensive ball back in a jammed or stretched out situation where the player is able to get back to a neutral position and may be able to turn the situation to an offensive one because of it,
e) Hit angled or down the line low balls against a net-rushing player forcing him or her to volley upwards from below net level, setting the situation up for attempting a passing shot,
f) Defensive and offensive lobs are easy and natural with a one-handed slice,
g) Hit low short balls to get a baseline player out of his or her comfort zone by making them move into the court where they are not as effective as from the baseline,

As we can see, that is a pretty extensive list, so now let's ask ourselves: Do we need more reasons than all of these to go for it and just learn it? There is no substitute for this awesome tool in a Tennis player's arsenal!

As a 13-year-old, I had the opportunity to watch Rod Laver close and personal when he came to Mexico for some exhibition. All I could see is that effortless and flawless slice backhand land on the very corners of the court every single time with incredible consistency. The ball traveled pretty fast across the length of the court. It seemed to float kind of like a Frisbee in the air, only to hit very close to the corners every time, bouncing a few inches off the ground. It truly was beautiful! I developed a heavy slice backhand from those observations. Players often ask me how I do it, and all I say is that I learned it from Rod Laver! He did not teach it to me, he just showed me how it's done!

WEAPON DEVELOPMENT

We are not talking about missiles, machine guns, or nuclear weapons here. But in the context of Tennis, a player with one or two weapons definitely has a decisive edge when playing matches. A player with a weapon can more easily come up with a strategy, and the game of Tennis becomes more black and white. All he or she has to do is figure out ways to use this weapon(s) and apply it to his/her opponent's weaknesses. A weapon is a luxury on a Tennis court. There are many different weapons in Tennis. The most obvious one is the serve, (Roddick, Sampras, Isner, Ivanisevic, Tanner, Dibbley, Smith, McEnroe, Frazer, Federer, and Pancho Gonzalez are just a few examples). The serve is the best weapon to have in one's arsenal since we are going to hit it no matter what. Our opponents are going to have to deal with it whether they want it or not, and unlike other weapons, they cannot prevent us from using it. We are going to win a lot of points with it, and that is a good thing for those players that took the time to develop an awesome serve.

The second most common weapon is obviously the forehand. Federer, Sampras, Fernando Gonzalez, Nadal, and many more professionals possess this weapon. Players with a big forehand are always trying to figure out ways to use their forehand to control and finish points. Strategy is all about utilizing our strengths upon an opponent's weaknesses.

Backhands, volleys, returns of serve, can also be cataloged as weapons. Drop-shots or finesse shots can be weapons and even lobs used correctly could be used as weapons. Basically, just about any stroke can be developed into a weapon.

On the other hand, we have strengths and weaknesses; anything that can potentially be a strength can also be a weakness. Disguised strengths are those that are less obvious. Among some of these, at the top of the list we have mental toughness, intelligence, creativity on the court to come up with the right strategies and shot selection. A lot of times, these strengths are more difficult to deal with than actual weapons or technical strengths since they are not clearly visible. A mentally tough player will almost always come out a winner in close matches. And a fit player has a definite tactical and mental edge in tough battles; fit players tend to be more confident and mentally tough under the fire of competition; a major plus on a Tennis court.

Tennis Coaches and players need to identify which weapon is appropriate to develop. It would not make sense to try to develop a player's serve into a weapon if this player is only 5 feet 6 inches tall. Even though it can be done, but it is more likely to be a successful project if the player was at least 5 feet 11 inches or taller.

The number one factor in weapon development work is technique or mechanics! Without technique, even the greatest athlete will fail at mastering any given weapon.

A player who has natural power and racket acceleration off the forehand can be trained to utilize this power to dictate and finish the point given the right circumstances.

Personality, natural aggressive demeanor, and mentality are other important factors to consider in weapon development.

A kid with a naturally aggressive personality can be trained to go for his shots. He or she can learn to set up points, as well as to finish them with a forcing shot or winner at the first opportunity presented. This kind of personality should be taken advantage of. For a kid who is very athletic, where mobility is developed into a strength, and in order to take advantage of his/her aggressive nature, to teach a serve and volley or the all-court-game style that can be devastating and very effective if done correctly.

By the same token, players who are naturally calm, patient, and emotionally poised, can easily be developed into counter punchers. Players like this are consistent and don't mind having to work harder to earn points. If these players have the physical attributes, a weapon or two can be added, and then we are talking about a fantastic player in the making given all the right conditions.

Weapon development is fun, and it adds motivation, inspiration and passion to the game. To know that we will be able to finish a point with the right shot selection and strategy is something to look forward to.

PRACTICE SPECIFICITY; PRACTICE AS WE WOULD PLAY

The specificity principle applies to Tennis as much as it applies to fitness training for Tennis. The word specificity refers to avoid practicing stuff that will not be used much on a Tennis court.

Periodization and specificity are very important in competitive Tennis. To misunderstand and misapply some of the principles here is conducive to failure because an athlete will not maximize his/her efforts, and this could result in frustration and burnout.

Especially in the developmental stages of junior Tennis, as coaches and players, we need to be dealing with technical stuff all the time. Players may be in the process of change, be it a swing, the gripping technique, the racquet, the strings, as well as other equipment. All these things need to be happening away from important competition. As we approach competition, we need to have practices resembling matchplay and fitness training routines that closely emulate what we do on the court when playing Tennis.

Practicing the way we are going to play is not always possible. When a player is developing or getting used to a new technique, non-specific training is necessary. He or she has to hit the shot or make that movement over and over, thousands of times until it becomes automatic, and this is not specific! Meaning we don't hit the ball 200 times the same way when we play a match. However, as important tournaments approach, we need to program training in such a way so that we are done with all these technicalities, and hopefully already be in place and working. At least two or three weeks out, the player should be able to concentrate only on point play, tactical, and mental matters. All technicalities should already be mastered.

Two to three weeks out from a tournament, players need to only hit and move the way they will be playing, with very little to no technical coaching until after competition is over.

As an example of what happens during those two to three weeks before the competition arrives, let's look at the following situation: a player may be hitting long a lot off the groundstrokes. No technical advice should be offered or attempted at this point. Instead, a good coach needs to be saying things like: "Aim higher or lower, add top-spin, or aim further inside the lines." This kind of advice or coaching is not technical but tactical and mental. This way, players should be able to fix the problem on their own. Players have to learn to deal with their problems by being their own coaches on court making corrections themselves.

A player needs to know how to make these adjustments independent of a coach. Players messing with technical stuff during tournament matches are a formula for disaster. Some call it paralysis by analysis. The body is no longer able to process automatically and, therefore, is incapable to perform operations at the speed needed to hit the ball with any authority. At best, the player in question will start losing emotional control and confidence, rarely being able to regroup for a comeback.

THE GAMES APPROACH TO LEARNING TENNIS

The Games Approach is an idea that developed more than 20 years ago, but it had not really caught up to its potential till recently. Learning to play Tennis can be done through simple games that are fun and dynamic. They can be singles, doubles mixed, two on one or other combinations. If a Coach is involved, the better, since he or she can provide feedback and make observations on shot selection, technique or strategy. However, not having a coach should not be an impediment for applying this principle to practice sessions and everyday training.

Simple games like baseline to 21 points by drop feeding, or playing half court crosscourt or down the line games to 11 points, as well as what we used to call the Australian drill. The Australian drill was a game where we played points one up one back, half court, where the net player had to always feed the first ball from 5-7 feet behind the service line, and come into volleying. This game and others have been around forever.

Here is a list of some of my favorite drills and games that are very helpful in developing some of the different skills needed for successful competitive Tennis:

Note: This list of games and drills was designed to work with groups of junior players, but adjustments to these games can be made to fit all different combinations or number of players.

GAMES APPROACH DRILL MENU

1- Rotating Killer Ball

All four players start at the service line. We are going for doubles points. Pro stands to the side of doubles line, about five feet from the baseline, outside the court. Players rotate or switch positions on their side every point clockwise, hit balls randomly down the line at the switching player. Up to 4 players per side, play games to 7 or 11, depending on the number of players involved. Pegs count double!

2- TTF (Touch The Fence)

Four players stand by the baseline, two on each side of the court, the rest of the players stand in a single line behind either net post. Up to 8 players per court is good, but more is possible. The Pro feeds 5 feet away from either net pole, feeds go to either player on the side where the point was won last. Don't keep track of score, players that have a winner hit on them (their side of the court), are out of the game and have to do some fitness, like 15 push ups, ladder, medicine ball, Indian run, jumping jacks or pick up balls, etc... When a player misses a shot, he/she just gets back in line by the net post. 1st player in line takes up that spot on the court. When down to four players or less, the players have to touch the fence (back fence or side fence) or the net when they miss a shot. Last player standing is the winner of the game. A nice variation when smaller numbers of players, is singles TTF. Here players hit full-court one-on-one, and we have two or maybe three players in line as alternates. TTF is awesome for developing alertness, concentration, intensity, as well as teamwork when doubles TTF is being played.

WHAT TENNIS PROS DON'T TEACH (WTPDT)

3- Challenge Court

Divide the court in half lengthwise, using street chalk for hard courts or on clay just make a line with the edge of the racquet or a line sweeper. Add extra court by drawing lines down along the net poles to the baseline for added playing space. Pro feeds balls from King Side, two players (kings) on this side, 3 or more (up to maybe 5 or 6 is good) on the challenging side. Play points half court using the drawn extra court when possible. Players can go down the line or crosscourt, challengers have to win three points in a row to take over one of the two King sides. Challengers cannot play back to back against the same king. If two courts are adjacent, a coach can feed balls into both courts from the middle of the two courts near the baselines and do this drill where points are now played on a full court. A good idea is to have the players do 5 pushups if they miss the fed ball. Some variations include:

a) Serving and returning
b) All baseline
c) Australian Challenge (One up one back)
d) Approach/Passing shot

4- Olympics (use unit points)

This game works for either singles or doubles. An even or odd number of players can participate in this drill. We need at least 5 for doubles or 3 for singles. To get to the King side play either 2 out of 3; or 3 out of 5 points, depending on number of students. Also, if a winner on either side of the court is hit, the player that the winner was hit upon is out and back in line. Feeds come from the King side, anything goes, players can go to the net or stay back. When the King(s) is out, the Pro feeds a high lob to the next challenger to give the new king or kings (if doubles) time to get over to the king side. Keep track of Unit Points (games won from the King side)

A coach can feed balls on two courts at the same time when courts are side by side if there is no fence or low fence, and have a top court and a bottom court. When a player from the bottom court gets 5 unit points, he moves up to the top court and the player with the lowest unit points on the top court drops down to the bottom court.

5- Net Rush

Great for doubles and net rushing (serve and volleying skills). For this drill, we need a minimum of 5 players for doubles (3 for singles). The Pro feeds the balls by the baseline on the net rushing side, off to the side of the doubles alley. The players start behind the baseline, rushing in as the ball is being fed, and play the point out. Once they win the first point, they get to play the next two points starting at the net, if they win three in a row they go to the King side. When dealing with an odd number of students, the rushing players rotate on the rushing side. The players receiving, have to switch sides every single point to keep them on the move all the time. There are variations where the receivers or rushers are one up one back. In this situation, the feeding should go to the player that is back by the baseline on the king side.

6- Down the net volleys (warm up drill)

Need at least four players and good for up to 8 is still okay. Two players set up by the net pole on opposite sides at 5 - 10 feet away from the net, the farther from the net, the higher the level of difficulty.
Players go in pairs, volleying back and forth, along the entire length of net. From one net pole to the other, when they reach the far side net pole, players jog back to the end of the line, to the first net pole, and go again as their turn comes. They keep doing this for about 5 minutes, and then switch sides, so all players get to move along the net in both directions.
This drill really promotes lateral movement, split-step, ball control on volleys, intensity, and concentration.
Players self-feed. The game can be competitive by keeping track of misses each time. Hard hitting is not allowed; it is more of a control, footwork, and finesse drill; this is a great drill for warm-up purposes.

7- Fast Feed

On this drill, four players set up at the service line on each side of the net. Good for up to 6 players, 8 possible. The Pro feeds the ball in all imaginable ways to either side of the net. Keep track of the score, play to 6 points or more depending on number of players. Winner(s) stays, losers do fitness on the side of the court. Feeds can be a lob, an overhead, a hand fed drop-shot, and an angle, hard or very soft, right at them, or to the middle of both.

Keeps players on their toes and really promotes reaction, communication, imagination, finesse shots and shot selection. It is lots of fun for all!

8-Approach/Passing shot drill

This is a good drill for 2 or up to 5 players if on one court only. The player(s) on the King side has to go for the passing shots. The players stand on opposite sides of net, a couple feet from the baseline. The Coach feeds balls from behind one of the players to the challenger side. Feeds should be low bouncing, to either the forehand or the backhand. The player getting the feed, has to hit an approach and go to the net down-the-line (cross-court approaching is also good, but direction of approach is predetermined in advance, so the defending player; at least has a chance to make a move in the right direction). The player on the same side as the Coach has to try to win the point by hitting passing shots, a lob or just keeping it low to the center and maybe passing off the second shot. Keep track of the score, and either rotate players or switch them any which way is more suitable. Games are usually played to seven or eleven points. Variations of this game are great for doubles also with one up one back on each side approaching either down the line or crosscourt.

9- Around the World groundstrokes and volleys (warm up drill)

Up to 12 players can do this drill on a single court. Six players stand in a single line near the doubles alley by the baseline, (these players should be standing on the same alley side as the coach feeding balls from the opposite side of the net). The other six, stand in a single line near the center mark, inside the baseline on the feeding side. The Coach feeds from near the doubles alley about 6 feet inwards from the baseline. Feeds are directed one towards the middle and the next one towards the alley from the opposite side. The player receiving the feed runs along the baseline to the middle and hit the ball back down the middle and the second ball down the alley. Players standing near the center mark, on the same side as feeds are coming from, have to run in towards the net as the coach feeds the first ball, split step and put the volley away coming from the player hitting the fed ball, and then poach over to the left (or right depending where the fed ball comes from, and whether we are practicing backhands or forehands from the baseline), and put away the second volley coming up the alley as it is hit by the running player on the other side of the net. Once the players have done that, the player that hit the two groundstrokes, runs around the net pole and gets in line behind the center mark, and the player hitting the volleys, runs around same net pole and gets in line near the baseline, on the opposite side. All players should run around the net pole on the opposite side from where the feeds are being hit. The Coach keeps feeding two balls per turn to the baseline players. If the baseline player misses both groundstrokes, he has to do 5 push-ups or jumping jacks or other fitness related exercises. Keep track of missed shots to make it more competitive. Make players scream out loud their number of errors each time they miss a shot. Everyone keeps track of everyone else's errors this way. A nice variation from the normal way of doing it, when hitting the first down the middle ball from the backhand side, instead of hitting another backhand off the second feed, the player has to run around it, and hit a down the line (up the alley) forehand. This forces players to run even farther and work on anticipation!

10-Up and Back

This drill is good for singles or doubles. Up to 8 players are okay, but more is possible. Play short games to 3 or up to 6 points. Scoring length has to depend on the number of players doing the drill. Waiting participants should not have to wait longer than maybe one or two minutes to go back on court. Have one team or player start at the net and the other by the baseline. Feed the ball from the net pole to the baseline team or player, only if the team or player wins the point when they started at net, then we can count that point. If a player or team won the previous point, then he or she or they get the net position at the start of the next point. If the baseline team or player wins the point, then he/she/they get to start the point at net now, but they don't get a point until they win the next point starting from the net position. There are all kinds of variations where the players have to start the point behind the service line or on top of the net. Our imagination is the limit!

11-Razor

Four players start from the service line as in a doubles point. Max number of players for this game to work well is about 6, but more is possible. Play short games first to 3 - 6 points (scoring length depends on number of players doing the drill). When a team loses the game, both players have to race to the net or any of the fences around the court (Hence the name Razor). First one to hit the net/fence with his/her racquet gets to keep on playing; the other one gets back in line. First player in line has to jump into the spot left empty where feeds come in. Everyone rotates as needed to cover spot left by the player that lost race to the net. Feeds come down the line from outside the court near the alley by a pro (players can also self-feed). There are all kinds of variations of this drill; players can go to the baseline or the net, or do doubles formations or two players at the net and two at the baseline, etc...

12-Whale (3 Point Conversion)

This game can be done for singles or doubles. The Coach feeds the balls from the King side behind the King(s) back in the court. Players on the King side start every point by the baseline. Challenging players get one short feed so that they can come into the net and play the point. If they win it, they then get a volley feed, and if they win it they get an overhead feed. Winning all 3 points gets them to the King side. If a player or doubles team loses the point, they simply go back to the end of the line. The players challenging need to alternate sides for each round. This game really promotes point play and strategy on all areas of the court.

13-Masters and Slaves

Masters get the whole singles court, and slaves only half the doubles court. The slaves have to be able to hit ten shots in a row without missing into the half doubles court, while masters are trying to keep slaves from doing that. If a slave makes it to ten, then he becomes the master and the master the slave. When the slave misses two shots in a row, he has to do five lunges and 5 pushups. When masters miss the shot, the slaves keep their count. A coach can feed the ball to the slaves every time, or the masters can feed themselves. A coach can feed into two courts at the same time if the fencing is not too tall. A variation on two courts with 5 to 7 players could be that if a slave misses, he goes to a fitness station until another slave is out.

14-Fifty Drill

This drill is usually done on half court and alleys are good. Both players are trying to get to a total of fifty good shots. The game can also be done on a full court though. Players feed the ball underhand alternating one each. Every time one player hits the ball in it adds. Both players are trying to get to a total of fifty good shots. If a player hits it out, but the other player gets it back in, it counts as good for the player that got it in. Clean winners count double. Players should count out loud in order for each other to know what the other's score is. This is great practice for consistency and shot selection; it can get super intense with very long rallies. The counting out loud should be done as the ball lands on the other side, and it really makes players concentrate.

Note: It is a great idea to utilize regular Tennis scoring during some of these games (such as 15-love, 30-love, 30-15, deuce, add in or add out, game, set, etc…). This way practice becomes a little more specific to Tennis and players get to understand better how to play the bigger points in a game in a smarter way!

SERVING

I cannot even start overemphasizing the importance of serving in trying to describe the huge significance of it to Tennis players all over the World. It does not matter how much the experts and Pros from all walks of life say it. Serving is to Tennis what the queen is to Chess, in other words, serving in Tennis can be life and death. Serving is by far the most important shot in Tennis!

For starters allow me again to say that if the right technique is not in place, serving potential will be greatly diminished.

Serving in Tennis is such a complex motion, but at the same time, it is such a natural motion that if done properly, it looks effortless and simple. Some experts compare it to the baseball throwing motion. It has some similarities, except that it is as if a player is actually trying to throw his/her racket as far as he/she can. Using his/her whole body, legs, hips, shoulders and ultimately the arms. If the serve motion was compared to throwing a rock or ball, it would have to be the motion that we would do, if we were throwing the ball or rock upwards at a 45 to 60 degree angle approximately.

There are all kinds of good examples of solid serving in the Internet, or just turn on the TV again and pay close attention to the best teachers, the professionals.

Fundamentally there are four types of serves: Flat, slice, topspin and kick. There are several variations of these four, in terms of the amount of spin, power level, and ball placements. Such as down the T, down the center of the serviced box, body jammers, or wide and angle serves. The number one factor to take into consideration in serving has to be 1st serve percentage. Also, always remember that a player needs to take some chances off the 2nd serve by going for it a little. A player who does not ever double fault is not necessarily a player with a great second serve. But most likely, a player who does not take any chances with that 2nd serve is just dropping the ball in the box without any real action on it.

The greatest servers in history, were not necessarily players with the biggest or fastest serves, but the servers who had the most accuracy, consistency and variation on the serve. A server who is unpredictable with a fairly fast ball. One that we cannot ever predict as to what kind of serve he or she is going to throw at us is probably the hardest to deal with. Some of these great servers were able to utilize their 2nd serves as first serves. They often aced and hit serve winners with the second delivery. Achieving this level of accuracy, effectiveness and confidence is rare but possible.

If we want to reach our potential as a server, we must try to learn all four types of serves and dedicate about 30% of our practices to mastering the stroke. But the thing of it is, the deltoid or rotator cuff in our shoulder can only take so much. It is probably not a good idea to practice serves all out every day. Hitting 100 to 150 serves every day easily leads to injury. If one must practice every day, I recommend the player to hit 40-60 serves, no more than that. Three times a week is solid for going for 80-100 serves. Let's say a player hits serves Tue, Thu, and Sat, this allows his/her arm to rest from serving Mon, Wed, Fri, and Sun. If this player is in tournament mode, he or she may have to play two or three matches in a day. That much serving, will put a toll on his/her arm. Especially if he/she is not used to serving a lot of balls and the shoulder cannot take the load.

From a technical standpoint, serving well is all about rhythm, timing, fluidity and relaxation. When practicing try to get into a groove, feel the flow of the motion and unleash. Be loose, hold the racquet lightly and keep the technique simple. Watch some video and compare to some of the best servers. I see some very complicated motions. One of the most common is to start with the wrong posture. A loose balanced posture with the ball softly cradled on the joints of the tossing hand near the forward joints of the fingers, making contact to the racquet near the throat, preferably not too far forward. The server's body needs to rock back and forth, or maybe he/she can develop the oversimplified technique of starting with a leaning backward posture. Rocking forward as he/she tosses the ball (See picture below of correct technique for holding and tossing the ball)

WHAT TENNIS PROS DON'T TEACH (WTPDT)

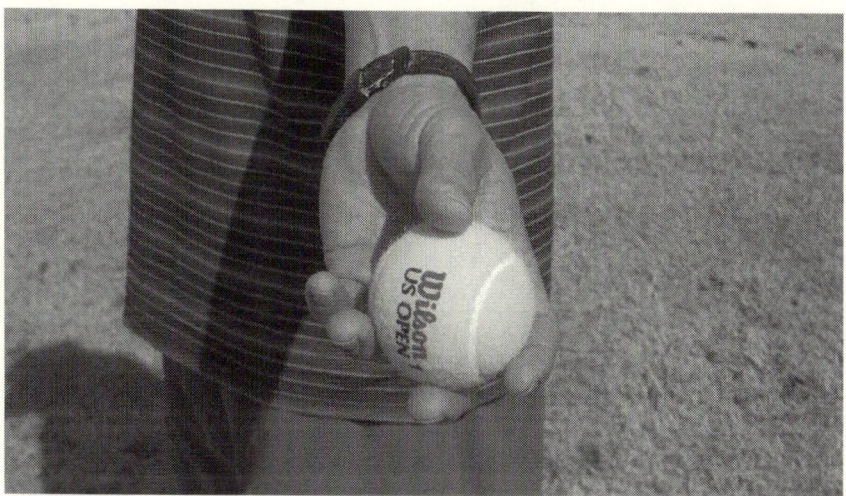

Fig 15)This is the right way to hold the ball for tossing when serving. Notice the ball is forward of the hand cradled in the joints of the forward part of the fingers and there is not tension at all.
The thumb is directly above middle finger on bottom for absolute releasing and tossing control.

See the What Tennis Pros Don't Teach video on www.youtube.com of the correct stance alternatives at https://youtu.be/N_FkQCV2wqc, Also the correct tossing technique at https://youtu.be/RFI4WnKDKtw

Federer and many other players place the ball in the throat of the racket on their initial serving posture. One cannot go wrong trying to imitate just about everything Federer does on the court. Both arms relaxed down at hip level or lower, and either leaning back or leaning forward to get into a natural rocking motion to start the serve. This natural rocking motion that we are talking about is very important. I see lots of people start the serve from a very static position. The body's center of gravity needs to lean forward then backwards and then forward again as a player tosses the ball. Another pretty common way to do it, is just to lean backwards, and as the player tosses the ball, he/she gets rocking or leaning forward starting the motion. Look out for some video and watch some good players' back and forth rocking rhythm at the onset of the serving motion.

Nobody is to blame for having a faulty serve but the player himself. There are many ways to practice it. And we can do it on our own. All we need is maybe ten balls, and that should be good enough to have a great serve practice session. The serve is the only shot where we can take our time and actually think through before we go for it. When serving, we can start with an offensive shot right off the bat... always! Yes, a player should be able to start every single point aggressively when serving, even if it is a 2nd serve! No excuses... Get out there and practice some more.

For some examples on serving and cardio serving go to https://youtu.be/4TlxkXsC1Ss

RETURN OF SERVE

Returning serve is one of the least practiced skills and one of the most valuable tools a Tennis player could ever have in his or her box of tricks. Failure to punish the server with a consistent and effective return is very frustrating. It leads to losing matches we could have won if we had been dealing with a weaker server or a serve that we could return with some consistency. To practice returns, it is required to have at least two players. But it can be done with three or more players on one court. This is a skill that like the serve should be practiced as often as possible. Unlike the serve, the return of serve can be practiced every day. Anytime someone is practicing serves; there should be someone else practicing the return of serve. What I mean by that is someone should be taking advantage of the opportunity to practice returns of serve while someone else practices his/her serve. Not to do this is wasting the unique opportunity to improve one's game.

Practice returns against all kinds of different types of serves: Flat hard and or soft serves, slice servers, top-spin serves and kick serves. But more than anything, we need to practice returns from left handed servers, especially left-handed spin serves. Without a doubt, the single toughest return of serve to handle is a heavy spin (topspin, kick or slice) serve out wide from a lefty. More so when we are failing to anticipate its variety. And yes, if a player is left-handed, he/she needs to really develop this serve. But at the same time, be prepared to deal with it as a returner, since we never know when we will have to play against one of these lefties ourselves.

Returning is all about reaction time, tracking down the ball, or seeing the ball carefully as it comes, and at the same time we are really moving into position to strike it back. The recommendation is to move forward and contact the ball with a short/compact swing. Attacking the ball with our body via intense footwork is very important especially dealing with heavy spin serves where the ball moves all over the place as it approaches the returner. On clay courts, it can get more challenging to take the ball early due to the uneven nature of the bounce. Tennis players may have to start further back so they can get a better look at the ball before they hit it.

Returning serve is where we see the most forced and unforced errors in Tennis. The tendency is to try to do too much with the return, resulting in mistakes and unforced errors. To go for an outright winner off the return of serve is generally the wrong thing to do; unless it is a very weak serve, we should generally put the ball into play. If dealing with a baseliner, be content to get the ball back down the middle with some depth off his or her first serve. Whether we block it by slicing it or hit it flat or with some topspin. We may be a little more aggressive off the return of the 2nd serve, but that will depend on its quality. There are plenty of players out there who have an awesome 2nd serve, and we need to treat these 2nd serves with equal respect as their 1st. If the 2nd serve is more manageable, it is a good idea to go for a little more by attacking the ball with an aggressive crosscourt return, where we get our opponent defending right off the bat. Down the line returning is the lowest percentage type of return and for the most part we need to stay away from it. Some net players like to chip and charge the second serve down the line. Be content to get some depth and pray for good timing, so the shot does not sit too long for the serving player to just rip a passing shot winner.

In order for us to be able to chip and charge in doubles or singles, the recommendation is to take the ball at the summit of the bounce or just as it breaks from the peak. A lot easier said than done since we don't know in advance how deep the serve is going to be. To be able to do this successfully requires good footwork, flawless timing and concentration from the returning player. McEnroe, Edberg, and Rafter were masters at this! And this strategy was more common a couple of generations ago, but not necessarily a bad one today given the right conditions! A player who charges the net behind the return puts tremendous pressure on the serving player. Pressure to get the first serve in, and also to go for bigger second serves which in turn encourages double faulting some of the time.

When dealing with net rushing and serve and volley players, the returner needs to focus on keeping the ball low as well as taking it early. Keeping the opponent from volleying from above net level, or getting too close to the net as they are hitting their first volley. The purpose is to make them hit the first volley from below net level as far away from the net as possible, providing opportunities for a lob or passing shot.

For the returning player, it is imperative to identify whether the serve and volley player is better off his forehand or backhand volley. Because although, he/she is not going for a winner off the return. He/She wants to make him hit the first volley off his or her weaker side by trying to place the return slightly to one side or the other.

In doubles, we want a low return crosscourt most of the time. If done right, doubles players should be serve and volleying every point. The return of serve in doubles should be cross court and more precise in order to keep the ball away from the threatening net player. However, some down the line will also be necessary to keep a poacher honest. Most poaching happens off the first serve, and very few players poach off the second serves. Finally, lobs off the return of serve over the net player add great variety to returning in doubles. If dealing with a big server, this is a fairly easy way to handle it, especially off the 2nd serve return since both players are anticipating a low or hard return. When we come up with a well timed lob over the net player successfully executed, this shot turns the returning team to offense right off the bat; it is awesome and smart.

One of the most challenging skills to develop as a Tennis player is the return off a heavy kick serve. Although we may not find too many players out there who can hit one consistently. The question is not whether we will have to deal with it or not but when we will, and when we do, we will have a nightmare of a time at it… Promised!

GROUNDSTROKES AND BASELINE PLAY

Big groundstrokes and baseline players are the vogue nowadays; it has been so for the last few years. Pete Sampras was the last very successful all court and serve and volley player. It seems that just about everyone is playing their matches from the baseline, and it is hard for those few guys who try to play the net rushing game to be successful. Passing shots and big returns of serve seem routine to a lot of these super solid baseliners.

As mentioned elsewhere in this book there are two basic styles to model for baseliners: the counter puncher and the aggressive baseliner. In today's World of Tennis, both styles of play require superior technique, smart shot selection, and good footwork.

One of the most fundamental factors influencing the success of a baseline player is variety. A baseliner needs to be able to hit topspin, slice and flat at will and as needed.

Tactically, if a player is dealing with someone stronger than himself. Given this opponent just loves to hit hard, the player in question needs to feed off the opponent's power not adding more to it by hitting hard himself. Good baseliners thrive on rhythm, as well as hard hitting, and a player needs to develop a taste for these two things if he/she is to become successful from the backcourt.

A lot of energy is needed to generate the huge racquet head acceleration off the ground. There is a large amount of rotation plus linear momentum applied to a hard hit ball. Fitness plays an important factor for a player to be able to repeat this over and over during a long match with sufficient power and control.

However, nothing beats solid technique. A player needs to use his or her kinetic link (legs, hips, shoulders, arms and wrist) efficiently to hit a solid ball. Through balance, anticipation, and good footwork. The player has to beat the ball to the point of impact and wait for it as he or she sets for the shot as the ball continues to approach him/her. It takes a lot longer to say this than it does to actually do it.

A player who is leaning backwards hitting off his back foot, or falling to the sides as he or she hits the ball is not under full control and will end up spraying or missing some shots. Remember though that not all is pink in this World, sometimes when defending, stretched out shots need to be hit with what appears to be an out of balance position or with the upper body leaning backwards.

Everyone should develop a slice backhand. Especially if a player has a one handed regular topspin or flat backhand, the one handed slice is a shot greatly needed. It adds variety and presents options when on the run defending or just as a change of pace during a hard baseline exchange.

Good baseline play goes hand in hand with good variety by adding drop shots and topspin lobs. Drop shots are a way to disrupt a complacent baseliner who sits comfortably in the backcourt all the time. Drop shots can also work as a weapon. When the player can potentially hit a kill shot from inside the baseline, but instead he or she chooses to go for a well-placed drop shot as the opponent is retrieving backwards towards the fence looking to defend. A player hitting topspin lobs breaks the rhythm of an opponent, forcing him/her backwards as he/she gains a positioning advantage.

All players need to get pretty good at hitting on the rise. Hitting on the rise takes time away from the opponent and adds juice to the groundstroke mix, at the same time giving a positioning advantage as the player takes the ball earlier. Hitting on the rise also helps to deal with players who just like to hit lots of high topspin balls, a tactic common with counter punchers.

One kind of groundstroke not mentioned in detail yet is the lob. Lobs play a very important part in ground stroking technique and baseline play. Players of all levels would benefit greatly from getting better at hitting lobs. Not only do lobs serve the purpose of getting the ball over our opponent's heads, but also work as good recovery shots when pulled wide, or even as a change of pace during baseline rallies.

Lobs add variety and creativity to a player's arsenal and should be practiced diligently just like any other shot. There are basically three kinds of lobs tactically speaking. One of them is the defensive lob. This is the ball we are just trying to get over the head of our opponent(s) when he or she is at the net, and we are just trying to stay in the point. This type of lob should be hit down the middle of the court, 30 feet high or a lot higher, and usually hit flat or with some underpin.

The second kind of lob is the offensive lob. When we hit this kind of lob, our purpose is to win the point outright. We need to hit this lob flat or with topspin, and it is better if placed either down the line or crosscourt. We are trying to get the ball to the area of the court where the ball, when bouncing, will be furthest from our opponent. The height of the offensive lob should be just barely over the opponent's racquet above his/her head maybe four or five feet.

The third kind of lob is the recovery lob. This lob is used more in singles. When the player is pulled wide, and he/she needs time to get back in position. It is a great idea to shoot the ball 10 to 20 feet over the net crosscourt or down the middle with some depth. Allowing time to get back into position. The recovery lob is usually hit with some underspin or topspin.

Groundstrokes are hit with an open, semi-open and closed stance. All of these techniques are valid and need to be learned by all players. Different on-court situations call for the different techniques to be applied as needed. (See the *Open Versus Closed Stance* subsection under the subtitle *Footwork in Tennis*)

HITTING ON THE RISE

Hitting on the rise is what we do when we catch the ball as it is still moving upwards after the bounce. Hitting the ball on the rise in Tennis can be considered a skill applied more in advanced levels. We see it to some extent at lower levels, but it is more deliberate and common with higher caliber players.

Hitting on the rise gives a player several advantages: A) To be able to maintain better positioning on the court. B) To take time away from an opponent to react to his/her shots. C) To take space away from the opponent to see the ball and react accordingly. D) To be able to hit the ball harder and more efficiently. Due to more stored kinetic energy in an upward moving ball.

If hitting on the rise presents all these advantages, then why doesn't everyone do it? Well, hitting on the rise has disadvantages. Since we are taking the ball so early, we have less time get in a good position for the solid execution of the shot. Moreover, we have less time to observe the ball's direction of rise. More of a problem on clay or grass courts, than on hard courts. Due to the uneven and less predictable nature of the surface. It's difficult to identify a heavy topspin ball's rise due to the steeper angle of incidence and racquet head also moving upwards as compared to a normal ball with little or no topspin. Hitting the ball with slice on the rise is not recommended. The upwards trajectory of the ball, right after the bounce, in contrast to the slightly open racquet face, going downwards as they meet, is not conducive to a solid shot, because it is extremely difficult to time the shot right. Not even the professionals go for the on-the-rise slice shots very often at all if ever!

Almost all aggressive baseliners will be more prone to hitting on the rise since they are more willing to take chances in order to finish the point. Counter punchers usually want to hit a very consistent ball that they can keep in play. All court players can do either or as needed.

Hitting on the rise should be done within the comfortable strike zone of the player. Somewhere between knee level and shoulder level is the norm for most players. On the rise hitting above shoulder, level, is not recommended since it is hard to create racquet head speed and truly control the shot from there. Good timing is a lot tougher to achieve the higher off the ground we hit the ball. When contact with the ball happens below knee level, on the rise hitting can be considered a half volley and it follows a whole different set of recommendations.

Hitting on the rise is offensive and deliberate; hitting half volleys is usually defensive and circumstantial. Hitting half volleys should be avoided when better options are available. Half volleys are more the result of a player getting caught helpless with the ball near his or her feet without too much time to do anything with it other than a simple half volley. There have been amazing players capable of incredible aggressive half volleys: McEnroe, Sampras, Agassi, and of course Federer and others, but these amigos are only a few out of thousands.

Hitting on the rise is something we want to do deliberately for offensive play. We can hit on the rise from just about anywhere on the court. It is most common from the baseline. A good example happens when the player moves in a little to handle a high bouncing ball. Allowing him/her to keep a good tactical position without having to back up all the way to the fence, which is probably what his/her opponent is trying to get the player to do.

We should be able to apply topspin to the ball as we hit it on the rise. This way we make this technique a little higher percentage and can use it with a lot more confidence and consistency. Because it is difficult to master, in early developmental players it is pretty common to see a lot of these shots hit flat. As mentioned above, slice on the rise should be avoided since it is next to impossible to hit with any degree of consistency.

When approaching the net, it is also recommended to take the ball on the rise any time it is possible. This allows the net-rushing player to get to the net a little earlier and takes time away from the opponent trying to get in position for the passing shot.

BREATHING AND GRUNTING IN TENNIS

Monica Seles, Jimmy Connors, Serena or Venus Williams, Rafa Nadal, Maria Sharapova and so many other awesome players, as well as thousands of martial arts enthusiasts and professionals could not possibly be wrong in their breathing/Screaming/Grunting techniques. As we wind up our body and racquet to make a hard hit, we inhale deeply, and as we make contact with the ball, we exhale hard, creating a sort of explosion. Grunting in Tennis helps time impact, as well as creates a cadence as we exchange groundstrokes. Letting out all air inside relaxes the body fully at contact, facilitating a cleaner and more explosive hit.

Grunting or yelling at impact happens naturally in Tennis, and it can be trained. In some cases, it can be very beneficial. Players who grunt will have great timing with most shots and will also have better cadence breathing during points. This helps them not as easily get winded. Grunting is a good thing as long as it is not overdone. Some players go overboard and get way too loud to the point of disrupting the opponent or other players on nearby courts with their exuberant decibels. I guess referees are not yet equipped with a decibel measuring device yet. Officials would be able to say "that grunt is too loud, and it needs to stop or lowered down since my decibel meter is telling me it is beyond the loudness permitted by the rules."

If we are getting winded as players, maybe we should consider adopting some sort of sound or grunt at impact for hard groundstrokes. I don't believe the grunt is as needed for serving, soft/finesse shots, most volleys or overheads, but only the player can decide what is right for him or her.

As a player, I get grunting some of the time. Other times I don't seem to need it. I am not sure when I got started doing it. All I know is that in my early 20s suddenly I was doing it. There are some players that don't seem to grunt at all. If you pay attention to Federer he seems to be hitting the ball quietly but he is not. As he hits, he is letting out this sort of moan. It is hardly audible but its there. There are players that get grunting louder as they get nervous or as the match gets tight. This seems to happen to most serious players out there.

There has been some talk amongst Tennis organizations in regards to the loudness of the grunt and how it disturbs other players that don't do it. But it has not gone anywhere. Grunting is not a bad thing; all we are doing is timing our breathing to our hitting; it works!

TIMING

Timing is everything on a Tennis court. Connecting with the ball at the right moment is of extreme importance to solid hitting, consistency, and technique; this can only be achieved through huge amounts of practice!

Timing goes hand in hand with hand-eye coordination obviously. Cross training in other sports helps players develop timing for Tennis.

So many things are happening simultaneously as we get ready to hit a Tennis ball, be it a serve, a volley or an on the run forehand. How and when we load our body for the shot and start the acceleration process; needs to be extremely accurate. Tennis players need to hit the ball in such a way that they are super efficient while applying the exact amount of force, be it a hard hit ball or a delicate drop shot or finesse angle winner.

On hard hits, always remember the hammer/nail relationship. If a man has a little nail and he has to hold it with his opposite hand as he winds up the big hammer; is he going to take a huge swing at it? No... He will probably hammer his hand... right? We need a short, accurate but fast swing, so we don't end up smashing our fingers, right? And once the nail is set in place, we can let it have it: "Pang."

This analogy applies to Tennis in that the length of the swing has to match the situation. When we have medium speed to fast moving balls we need pretty compact backswings, and on slower ones the swing starts getting a little bigger gradually. The bottom line is that we should hit the ball with the smallest swing possible that will achieve the purpose! Be it a groundstroke, a kill-shot put away ball moving forward on mid-court or a volley... I think this summarizes the idea pretty well. When backswinging, staying as compact as we can, is solid advice.

Also, in order to have good timing it is necessary to start early our unit turn. The racket wind up and unit turn should be completed before the ball bounces on our side of the court. Players with great groundstrokes are characterized by that early preparation; they seem to have so much time to hit the ball. Time the start of the wind up to the hit of the opponent, not the bounce of the ball on our side of the court.

As mentioned in the previous subsection, timing is oftentimes helped by grunting or deep exhaling as a player makes contact to the ball. Also, it is important to mention that great power is not possible without great timing!

Note: See video on timing and the unit turn at https://youtu.be/CRGMa0WhRcE

VOLLEYS AND NET PLAY

Net play is an endangered species; very few players at the professional level nowadays utilize this playing style. At the very top levels, we just don't see it that often anymore. Professionals set the tone for what everyone else is going to follow. And it seems that really good groundstrokes and baseline play are here to stay for a while. Although serve and volley will always be the style in doubles, and the most successful doubles teams in history have all been pretty serious serve and volley players, this is not the case in singles. However, as long as we are able to approach and hit a winner striking the ball out of the air, going to the net will continue have an advantage.

It is a lot easier to hit a winner or finish the point successfully as we get closer to the net. The court across from the net just keeps expanding. We have access to more angles, and at some point as we get closer and closer we can even hit down on the ball, an impossibility from the baseline.

There are different types of volleys, and a good net player will develop all of them. What is known as the first volley, is the volley we will hit, as we are either approaching the net; or serve and volleying. All other things being equal, and, for the most part, we will hit the majority of first volleys from around the service line as we transition forward towards the net. We need to have the ability to hit a sturdy volley deep into our opponent's court preferably down the line. It is also common to have to go crosscourt in order to pick on an opponent's weakness. In doubles, we almost always go crosscourt on this first volley; this sets up the situation for a putaway volley. This kill volley is usually an angled volley or just another volley into the open court. These examples can be considered textbook net play tactics for volleying in Tennis.

We all know things don't always go as planned, so we have to develop other kinds of volleys to make ourselves fully effective up at the net. Here is a list of all the types of volleys needed to master:

a) First Volleys: Deep volley as we approach or serve and volley. The goal is to make our opponent hit it on the run as the ball stays low. Normally a little underspin is good to better control pace and depth, but it can also be a flat ball. Practice this volley by hitting lots of balls moving forward starting about three to five feet behind the service line. We need to be proficient at it from different heights, all kinds of situations, and angles. In reality, our first volley is a transition volley that helps us get in further toward the net. This volley is by far the most important of all, and a player that develops a good one can usually master all others with a lot more ease.

b) Put away volley: This is the 2nd or sometimes it could be a 3rd volley as we get closer to the net and go for the kill volley. This volley is just stabbed into the open court usually for a winner. If the 1st volley was decent, that sets up the situation for an easy 2nd volley.

c) Drop volley: This is a good volley for situations when we were able to get our opponent pretty far back behind the baseline off the previous shot. We now are inside the service line getting ready for the kill. Requires great fines and lots of practice, it should be hit with underspin, and it can be either straightforward or at an angle placing the ball even further from the opponent. Some underspin is necessary to absorb the pace from the opponent's shot. It may also require a reverse or negative swing in order to be able to control pace and make the ball go softly over the net. It is better executed from waist level or lower balls. If above net height, it is probably better to go for a kill of regular put away type volley.

d) Angle volley: Very useful especially in doubles. This volley requires lots of practice, too, and requires the player to understand deflection of the ball from the racquet. It is more about redirecting the path of the ball. The player needs to think fast and be creative when going for it; it is a thing of beauty where the ball goes nowhere near where anybody can reach it in a path that no one anticipated. Also, hit with some underspin most of the time. Underspin helps absorb some of the pace of the incoming ball which in turn helps control direction and speed.

e) Defensive volley: this is what we have to do when the ball comes right at our body at high speed. Most of these situations should be handled with a backhand volley, given the greater range and flexibility of the elbow. There should not be such thing as running around the backhand when up at net. Most times we simply have to take a half sidestep diagonally forward with the right foot to hit a backhand volley or our left foot for a forehand volley. Other times we just put our racket in front of our body with a firm grip and block back with a backhand volley trying to keep it low. And yet other times, we need to get our arm/elbow behind our body in order to expose the racquet face to the incoming ball for a forehand volley, trying to keep it low as well. Sometimes we may be able to place these volleys, but it is more of a survival kind of volley. We should be happy to just get the ball back low allowing, ourselves a better opportunity for the next shot.

Fig. 16)Defensive backhand volley right at the body

Fig. 17)Defensive forehand volley with elbow tucked behind hip

f) Half volley: Another highly technical volley that is difficult to practice and master is the half volley. In reality, it is not a volley at all, and I am not sure why it is called a volley since the ball hits the ground before we hit it. Half volleys are those that bounce at the player's feet, therefore forcing them to hit the ball immediately after the bounce. There are different types of half volleys. When the player is near the net, all we need is to block the volley over hoping to get some depth on it keeping it low. After which the player tries to get in a better position for the next volley, often a putaway volley if the first half volley was executed properly. The half volley is an extremely tough shot to hit solidly with consistency. It is very difficult to even start practicing it, and, for the most part, it <u>is classified</u> as a defensive volley. Behind the service line and from the baseline, half volleys are hit more like regular ground strokes with shortened backswings and topspin or flat.

g) Swinging volley: When the approaching player is dealing with a ball that is floating over the net above waist level, and more commonly at about shoulder level. The volley can be hit like a regular flat or topspin groundstroke out of the air. Making it an effective way to hit a first volley very aggressively. We see the women in the pro tour do this more than the men. It is effective and easy to practice. It probably is a good idea to try to get good at timing the shot right. This shot is almost always better hit with some topspin and should be directed into the open court of our opponent. Not always a finishing shot but very effective at getting the player in position to finish it the next shot. A lot of times, it is just an aggressive first volley. Some coaches don't promote the use of this kind of volley in the argument that it is not technical, but when we see the pros use it all the time, we cannot argue.

h) Lob volley: This is the kind of volley we are going to go for when we got our opponent(s) at the net and closing. It is a great tool for getting them off their offensive mode and turning the situation for us from defensive to offensive. Lob volleys sometimes turn out to be outright winners because we get our opponent so off guard they don't expect this kind of reply. The timing of the lob volley needs to be precise. It has to be hit when our opponent is getting closer to the net and is already well inside the service line. If the timing to go for it is wrong, a player can end up having to deal with his/her opponents smashing overheads at him/her at close range! This volley should be hit with a little underspin to absorb the pace off the ball.

All this seems pretty complicated, and it probably is and we may need to practice all these types of volleys separately until we are pretty confident at each and every one of them. Go to www.youtube.com "What Tennis Pros Don't Teach" Volleys, Regular, Half Volleys, Survival Volleys, and Swinging Volleys at https://youtu.be/YzbuiwuJUmg

PASSING SHOTS

Passing shots are misunderstood in Tennis. Players from different levels neglect them by practicing standard groundstrokes rallying baseline to baseline. To begin with, this shot is better practiced with a player at the net and the other at the baseline, or by having one player approaching the net and volleying. With the ball machine, a student/player needs to set it up pretty close to the net, about midway between service line and the net, and have it shoot random balls flat or with moderate slice and pace. From practice to practice, players need to vary the position of the ball machine to either side, and up closer or farther from the net, to make practices more realistic, as well as, varying the pace and spin the machine is applying to the ball. Now and then we need to set up the ball machine for topspin remembering that not all approach shots and volleys are hit with underspin by the opponent.

Passing shots need to have different characteristics as compared to baseline groundstrokes. I would say the number one characteristic is that they need to be low. Because once a good net player meets a ball more than two feet above net level, the net player will simply put it away. Another characteristic would be ball direction. As a general rule of thumb, and under the *all other things being equal principle*, if the approaching player is still moving forward towards the net, a player should be hitting crosscourt passing shots most of the time, and if he or she is already pretty much established at the net, then our passes need to go down the line. These generalities apply under the premise of the all else being equal philosophy. Another thing to consider is the fact that placement is more important than pace; disguise, variety, and consistency will outweigh power as well.

Disguise and variety need to come in different forms. Sometimes we hit a low return of serve down the middle on a serve and volley player followed by a well placed passing shot. Another pattern or combination, would be to hit a low angle (it could even be a slice angle), followed by a down the line passing shot, as the net player is recovering towards the center. Assuming he/she volleyed deep down the line.

Most passing shots should be hit with either topspin or flat. If going for angle passing shots, heavy topspin may be necessary. Slice passing shots are rare; they belong to those who have developed this weapon. Slice passing shots, for the most part, come from players blessed with one-handed backhands, and like I said, they are very uncommon, but a beauty to watch. A well-hit heavy slice passing shot seems to set all in slow motion where the net player struggles to get to it, not quite being able ever to get his/her racquet on the ball.

Obviously net players inflict great pressure on their opponents. The number one factor here is to not over hit the ball when going for the passing. Secondly, to go for the wrong shot selection, meaning going down the line when we should be going crosscourt and vice versa. Other examples of incorrect shot selection are hitting a lob when we should be drilling the ball, or not drilling the ball or hitting it too gently when the player should be going all out for it. Also, keep in mind that if a player always goes for the same passing shot, a smart net player will anticipate these and simply volley all these ineffective attempts for winners. Therefore, as players going for passing shots, it is imperative that we mix directions. The passing player is pressured by time and the threatening position of the opposing player. To me, a solid passing shot hit from the baseline is one of the most beautiful and satisfying shots in Tennis.

Keep in mind the idea of the two-shot-passing-shot. Hit a forcing shot first, maybe low to the net rusher's ankles then the passing shot off the second shot either down the line or crosscourt or maybe even by hitting an offensive topspin lob winner!

DROP SHOTS AND DROP VOLLEYS

Drop shots are some of the best tools to have when it comes to variation and changes of pace. Drop shots can force an opponent out of his/her comfort zone, disrupt an opponent's baseline rhythm, and mess with someone's concentration. It is a good shot to go for when down in the score just looking for solutions or changes in strategy.

There are basically two types of drop-shots: Drop shots to finish the point and drop shots to gain a positioning advantage.

When going for the kill drop-shot we need to have the right shot selection. Any shot that presents an opportunity for a groundstroke kill, where our opponent might expect us to go for it, and he or she is moving backwards for defense, is also a good opportunity to pull the trigger on a drop shot. When going for this type of drop shot, we want to direct the ball over the section of the net that is closest to us, in order to have the ball in the air the least amount of time, and get it to quickly bounce twice.

Tactical drop-shots can be hit from further back near the baseline. The purpose here is not necessarily to finish the point but to get our opponent out of position and maybe set up a situation where we may be able to finish the point off at the next shot. When going for this type of drop shot we want to either place the ball down the line or cross-court near the singles lines depending on what we are trying to force our opponent to do. The idea is to make him or her cover some serious ground retrieving the ball, maneuvering them out of position. By hitting near the singles lines, we open up the court creating a situation where we may be able to go for a passing shot or topspin lob therefore winning the point off the next shot.

Drop volleys are drop shots hit out of the air. They require great finesse and racquet head control. Drop volleys are meant to be outright winners. Drop volleys can also be used to get the opponent out of position allowing a net player to put away the next volley. Drop volleys can be hit up the line or at an angle and should be hit with good slice or underspin.

All types of drop shots need to be practiced to develop confidence and proficiency with. The ball should technically bounce at least twice inside the service line, but it is a lot better if it bounces three or more times. When hitting a drop shot the ball should clear the net by about one to two feet. When higher, our opponent can get it easily since the ball will remain in the air longer after the bounce. Some really good players, know how to hit them with sidespin, in such way that, when the ball bounces, it not only stops moving forward, but it also bounces away from the running opponent, trying to get it back; this is a highly skilled shot that requires lots of spin control and practice. Drop shots are easy to practice with the ball machine or by hitting with a practice partner. We can also practice them on a wall by hitting hard followed by moving forward catching the ball at the summit of the bounce and slicing it softly over the white line on the practice board.

Drop shots add variety to one's game. Drop shots are a fun toy to have in the toolbox, and believe me; this shot can turn matches around and drive some players crazy!

EXTREME SHOTS! WHY WE NEED TO LEARN THEM?

There are a number of extreme shots that are not even mentioned in most Tennis books. These extreme shots will not be found in any of the regular literature. I call them extreme because they come in handy in extreme circumstances, and extreme technique and footwork is needed for proper execution. We are not going to cover all of them here, but we certainly are going to address the most important ones.

Here is a list of the most important extreme shots:

1) The tweener, or Yanick, since Yanick Noah was one of the first players to popularize this technique. The player simply runs down behind the lob, and as it goes down he/she hits it back between the legs while facing the back fence instead of the net. Normally, a player would be running to the side of the ball to return it with a normal forehand or backhand rescue or defensive shot. Instead, he/she gets close directly behind it, and as the ball bounces and starts coming down, the player gets on top of it with the ball right between both legs. Once the ball is about a foot from the ground, he/she hits it. A good player can hit the ball pretty hard, and place it down the line or crosscourt and even hit a lob off of it. It is a pretty impressive move.

    The tweener should not be a show off attempt, although it may appear so. This technique gives a player the only option to get the ball back in play and still have a chance to win the point. In the majority of cases, the opponent will rush into the net for the kill, and that is why a tweener lob is sometimes a good idea. The tweener is better hit with a continental grip or even past continental. It requires a lot of practice. Most players avoid the tweener, but once a feel for the shot's timing is acquired, it becomes second nature.

2) The reverse overhead: This is nothing other than a player hitting an overhead running down a bouncing lob in a reverse direction. The player runs down the lob, and as he/she gets closer, as the ball bounces fairly high, then the player can execute a reverse overhead. A reverse overhead is done in a reverse like manner, resembling the regular motion of a serve or overhead. A player needs a continental grip and he/she hits it over his/her left shoulder (right handed player). The player's wrist needs to be loose to allow the racket head to fully whip through the ball to create some racquet speed. When a player goes for this shot, he/she typically would have other options if he or she wanted since the ball bounced higher. However, the reverse overhead may well be the most aggressive or unexpected shot to play.

3) The low right hook: This is one of the most common rescue or defensive extreme shots for dealing with a lob from the opponent. It can be played offensively since quite a bit of power can be applied to the ball. The technique is very similar to the tweener's technique, but instead of having the player run directly behind the ball, he/she runs to the right of the ball (right handed player). As the ball descends, he/she strikes it with a continental grip, usually hit flat or with moderate slice/sidespin. It can also be a lob. This shot seems more normal to most players, and they will be willing to practice and learn it more so than the tweener.

4) The low left hook: Similar to the low right hook, this shot should be hit with a one-handed backhand and a continental grip. It is hit to the right of the player (right handed player) as he or she runs down a lob, and it usually can be hit with a little slice or pretty flat. A player will typically not be able to hit the ball with much power, so he or she needs to concentrate on keeping the ball low if the opponent is rushing the net. An easy alternative is simply to go for a lob.

5) The reverse low left hook: In my mind and from personal experience, this is the most difficult of all the extreme shots to master. A right handed player runs to the left of a lob. As the ball descends to about a foot from the court; the player hits with a continental or even an Eastern forehand grip. But instead of a backhand motion, he/she hits the ball with the face of the racket that would be used if a forehand was being hit. It is extremely hard to time the shot or to be able to see the ball because it's in a blind spot kind of like the blind spot

to the right of a vehicle while driving. More than power, a player requires placement. This shot can be hit with a little topspin as we let the wrist relax upwards through the ball. The great Ilie Nastase was a master at this trick or extreme shot. The opponent may even think that the point is over and suddenly, "bang," the ball is on its way back over the net. Wow! It's a pretty cool shot to witness and even cooler to be able to pull it off. Very few players ever learn how to hit this shot. I can see this shot may be very hard to visualize from just text, so a video of it and all other extreme shots was produced. The reverse left hook has the advantage over the regular low left hook in that it can be hit further behind the player giving us a little extra time to for the execution.

6) The underhand forehand slice serve: More than an extreme shot, this should be cataloged as a disrespectful trick serve during a serious Tennis match. But I would not avoid it altogether since, after all, we are trying to win the point and the match and not necessarily being disrespectful.

As a player gets ready to serve, standing in the serving position, and after his/her normal rituals of ball bouncing, etc… Instead of going for a regular toss, he/she just tosses the ball about a foot off the ground and slices the ball sideways with heavy spin into the service box. The ball should be very low over the net and have pretty heavy spin for it to be effective. A good underhand slice serve should be placed to either corner of the service box. For the right handed player, aiming about a foot to the right of the returning player, can severely jam the opponent if he/she did not anticipate the path and bounce of the ball. A continental or even extreme continental grip is used. The lower the ball is tossed, the better the chances are that the ball will bounce low. The opponent will have to deal with hitting a twisting ball that is curving from well below net level sometimes pretty close to the net.

The instance that stands out the most in the game's history is the time Michael Chang served an underhand sidespin ball to Ivan Lendl in the quarterfinals of the French Open. Winning the point and eventually the match, as well as the tournament back in the 80s. Michael Chang was suffering cramps and could not serve well, so he went for the underhanded serve. We don't know how much this got into Lendl's head. This sole move is given some credit for

Chang's win. A player should only go for this shot a couple of times in a match when he/she is in trouble, and it is only recommended if he/she is proficient with it.

A personal anecdote worth mentioning came to mind, when I was at a 16s clay court national tournament in Nashville, Tennessee with a junior player named Rafael Escobar. He was very talented and super competitive. Rafa had been having trouble with his rotator cuff in the weeks leading up to the national tournament, but he insisted on going nevertheless. He could only serve softly, and then used his awesome speed and skill to figure out ways to win points. During his matches, Rafael served a slice underhand better than 50% of the time and was able to win three matches this way. As he used it more and more, he improved the placement, speed, and spin, driving a couple of opponents half crazy.

7) The underhand backhand slice serve: This is also a trick serve and similar the forehand underhand slice serve, but sort of the reverse of it, executed from the initial serving position. The player tosses the ball to the left (right handed player) and forward about a foot, making contact with a slice one-handed backhand motion low near the ground with slice/sidespin to the service box. The ball will curve and bounce to the right of the opponent. If done correctly, the ball should stay low and severely kick to the side as it bounces. As we execute this shot, we need to keep our feet on the ground and twist from the waist and shoulders with a quick unexpected motion. It is pretty difficult and requires serious practice; I have only seen a couple of player with proficient technique over the years.

8) The backhand overhead: Although this shot may not be classed as an extreme shot since it looks like a high backhand volley, this shot can become an actual overhead weapon producing outright winners. In order to generate sufficient racket head speed to hit the ball with authority, the player needs to turn his/her body almost backwards to the net. As he/she jumps with the racquet head down over his left shoulder (right handed player) and snaps at the ball with full extension of the arm as he/she jumps out to it. A continental grip is needed, requiring good timing and repeated practice. The backhand overhead is one of the most athletic looking shots in Tennis, and it is beautiful.

As I talk about these uncommon shots, a lot of pros and coaches may say that all of this stuff is not necessary and is a waste of time. But I would strongly disagree since I believe learning all these shots is fun, promotes hand-eye coordination, develops racquet skills and adds dimension and unpredictability to a player's game. There are plenty of situations during point play, when one of these extreme shots will be the best option to go for, and in many occasions it may be the only one! Go to www.youtube.com for video on Extreme shots at https://youtu.be/kxDjHFucZpE

THE UTMOST STAGE

Doing extreme things successfully on court without thinking is not common. Players who are highly developed can do unimaginable stuff to most others in an instinctive, natural way. I call this the utmost stage. The utmost stage is reached when a player reaches a level of proficiency and familiarity with his/her racquet, the ball in flight, the court as well as technique. A level of confidence and control of the body/racquet/ball combination occurs that goes beyond previously conceived boundaries. When these players get in difficult situations during points, they might enter uncharted territory and come cook responses up we'd have a hard time finding anywhere in the literature. Players reaching this stage act out of pure instinct, athleticism, and dexterity. The task at hand is to get the ball back over the net in any number of meaningful ways. They just let their instincts take over to achieve their goal. Like when a player is able to hit a shot that seemed impossible to the spectator's awe!

For the purpose of illustration, I will cover only a few instances where an utmost stage player is able to pull one of his/her trickery to get the ball back in play. It may be of interest to know that half the time, the player himself may not even be aware he/she is capable of some of these stunts with the racquet and ball.

> ➢ A player approaches the net with a deep backhand slice crosscourt shot, the opponent comes up with a great angle low to the player's backhand. He/She reacts quickly but just a little late, getting there but is way out of position to do much other than maybe touch the ball with the racquet. Without thinking and in an unexpected move, he/she hits a low lunging backhand volley. In the process of doing it, perhaps assisted by the force of the incoming ball, he/she starts spinning counterclockwise. As soon as he/she is done hitting the ball, he/she is already turned over 180 degrees followed by completion of the 360-degree turn. By doing this, he/she was

able to recover for the next volley moving back towards the center of the court. By completing a full turn, this player does not waste any time in recovering and uses his/her rotational inertia to get back in position. Did he deliberately train this? Did some awesome coach teach him or her to do this? The answer to both questions is probably "no"; this player may not have even foreseen this ability or technique, thinking the point over. Completing the 360 degree turn is not always the most technical thing to do. A player doing this may have misjudged the direction of the opponent's passing shot and was unable to lunge forward to the ball. As a result his movement was more parallel to the net or even away from it. This gives him/her the inertia to spin around instead of simply shuffling back into position.

- Another scenario that occurs during net play or with less frequency at the baseline is a situation when the player cannot quite reach the ball with the center of the strings of his/her racket. Instinctively, this player will simply hold the racquet from further down the grip to add a couple extra inches of reach and hit the ball back in the court successfully. He/she may be holding the racquet by the very edge of the grip with the thumb, ring and middle fingers instead of the whole hand. Although not as firm a grip, this grip gives the player a little extra length that can be utilized to hit the ball in the center of the strings, and get it back, utilizing the power of the coming ball, controlling it back over the net. Instinct? Skill? Racquet head control? Utmost stage shot? "Yes, yes, yes and yes."

- A pretty uncommon and extreme scenario happens when the player needs to hit an angle volley, but he/she is already late to meet the ball and fully stretched out. The player will switch grips to what seems to be an Eastern or Semi-Western one-handed backhand grip and hit a sharp angle forehand volley successfully. Or an eastern or western forehand grip to do the same thing off the backhand. Often in these two situations, the player may also extend the racquet out a couple of inches. In order to get the extra length by holding the grip from the edge of the butt, with the thumb, index, and middle finger combination.

These and other extreme scenarios repeat themselves over and over during matchplay in top notch Tennis. Unfortunately, some of this stuff is so fast and subtle that we miss it. We may be able to catch some of it on slow motion replay; if a player returns a shot that seemed extraordinary, pay close of attention to the replay, if available.

These are only three examples of utmost development, but there are others. This stuff we don't practice; it just happens naturally during the heat of the battle. Players getting to this stage have hit thousands upon thousands of Tennis balls for thousands of hours!

SPINS

Topspin, slice, sidespin and other spins--what does this mean? Why must we know and understand all about spin in Tennis?

Starting with topspin, let's say that this spin is by far the single most important spin in Tennis. Topspin must be understood and learned at an early age; all good players use some topspin, some more than others depending on playing style and other factors such as power level and developmental stage of the players.

Without topspin, ball control would be impossible. Topspin keeps height, depth and speed under control. The ball, spinning forward on its way to the other side of the court, frictions with the air, making it drop sooner that if the ball was to fall or go down by just gravity forces. The combination of spin plus speed is what makes a ball feel heavy; it could be said that this is the secret of the so-called *heavy ball*.

Another attribute of topspin is the fact that it will not and cannot happen unless the ball is stroked with the proper technique. Meaning that if we are able to get a kid to hit consistent topspin, then this kid is most probably hitting the ball with sound and solid technique. So if we want to learn to hit the ball well; then try to learn topspin. One thing leads to the next, so we work on both simultaneously, always keeping in mind that topspin is essential to the full development of the player. Avoiding topspin instruction at an early age, really handicaps players in their development.

Nothing beats a hard, flat, well-placed ball. A very hard flat shot is one of the most effective ways to hit the ball in which we will potentially get a weak reply, or it will be an outright winner. Why? Because this type of shot is so fast and low bouncing. It is difficult to get set up on time for it and hit it back successfully, where we have at least a 50/50 chance of maybe winning the point. In other words, we will end up on the defensive more often than not when our opponent has hit a quality pretty fast flat ball.

Okay, I've said it. However, it is so difficult to hit hard and flat consistently. Even at the very highest levels, it is rare to see too many successful flat hitting players. And the guys/girls doing it are either up there on the unforced error charts or playing the match of their lives, which is probably a lot more unlikely to be the case.

Fortunately for all of us human beings, there is spin in Tennis. Topspin, underspin, sidespin, diagonal spin, and what we call the kick serve, is nothing other than diagonal top-spin. Diagonal spin is what makes the ball bounce to the side and up or down. It can either be diagonal topspin or diagonal underspin. Adding to all this confusion, all spins have variations in trajectory, RPM (revolutions per minute), speed and placement. All this stuff will drive anyone crazy.

Underspin or slice is easy to learn. Slice is obtained by chopping the ball with our racquet slightly open at an angle as it reaches the point of impact. For some good footage on solid slice techniques, watch Federer's backhand and defensive forehand slice on the run. Another very interesting player to watch is Feliciano Lopez from Spain. He has a variety of slice shots off the forehand and backhand similar to what Federer does; his defensive Tennis through the utilization of slice is pretty amazing. When approaching the net with a slice shot, the ball moves across the court slower than topspin. The gliding or soaring ball looks like a Frisbee in its trajectory. The slower travel speed allows the net-rushing player to get in good position for the next shot. However, if hit well, the heavy slice approach rarely allows the opponent to hit a clean pass right off the bat. Due to the fact that the ball bounces so low and the opponent has to really get the racquet under the ball to hit it, and the timing has to be just right. Correct timing is not easy since the ball skids across the surface, be it a hard, clay or grass court and just presents a very challenging shot to the opponent. When dealing with having to hit an effective passing shot off a very low, heavy slice ball, the thing to do is to try to keep the return low to the volleying player. Maybe get ourselves a chance to hit the pass on the second shot after the approach (the two shot passing shot).

Other examples of players with good slice backhands are Rafa Nadal and Ivo Karlovic and other classics before them, such as Laver, Roswell, Santana, Roche, and many others… Watching video is the best way to understand underspin. One thing to remember when practicing and learning to hit slice shots is the fact that a player should not try to hit it on the rise. Hitting slice shots on the rise is very difficult to do consistently due to the non-conducive angle of incidence between the rising ball and the open and downward moving racquet face.

Sidespin adds a degree of difficulty to spin shots. Sidespins will make the ball kick either towards or away from a player. Side-spins will drive some opponents crazy. Kicking topspin groundstrokes are so difficult to time and return successfully. A player really needs to practice against players that do this stuff so he/she can get used to it. Unfortunately, ball machines don't have a setting for side spins; only for topspin, underspin or no spin. Set up the ball machine to hit some serious topspin and slice and practice against this heavy ball anyway. But side spins are a totally different animal. I have been blamed for some pretty radical training methods in the past. One thing I have done is set up the ball machine at an angle. Tilt the ball machine a little with some boards or books on its legs on one side or the other; in order to have it sit sideways to get it to shoot side spins! Learn to anticipate the bounce of the different spins by reading our opponents swinging paths. Different degrees of side spins are very common in Tennis; the more the hitting is done against this type of balls, the more second nature and comfortable a player will be dealing with them.

Go online and see some video of Nadal's forehand kicking topspin. We virtually see the ball curving in the air, sometimes going around the net pole down the line only to end up bouncing one foot inside the singles line; it is amazing! Some obvious side slice shots can be seen on video when the player hits a down the line backhand drop shot with heavy sidespin. The ball bounces away from the singles line getting further away from the desperate player trying to get to it; it is a thing of beauty.

Developing and aspiring junior players need to learn all these skills in today's World of Tennis. It just adds to the toolbox and honestly if a player does not have at least some of them, he/she will be at a huge disadvantage.

THE SECRET OF THE HEAVY BALL

By the rules, all Tennis balls should weigh about two ounces. However, a Tennis ball in motion can feel like it is a lot heavier when the right characteristics of spin plus speed are added to it. We hear the experts say stuff like, "He hits such a heavy ball off his forehand" or "he is serving bricks" That's weird stuff!

Yes, all balls weight the same, but not when they are in motion. The secret to "weight" is spin plus velocity. A heavy ball can be a heavy slice or a heavy topspin ball or any heavy spin shot or serve. Heavy balls have more Kinetic or dynamic energy in them as they move; Kinetic Energy is energy in motion. Volleys seldom can be classified as heavy since we hardly ever need to hit them with a ton of spin and/or speed.

Roger Federer's forehand or Rafa Nadal's ground strokes, especially the forehand, are good examples of heavy ball hitters. Heavy servers include Andy Roddick, Pete Sampras, Milos Roanic, Goran Ivanisevic, and many more. A slice shot, especially off the backhand side can be hit pretty heavy if plenty of speed and spin are applied to the shot.

So, how much spin plus linear speed can a player apply to a Tennis ball? Hitting a heavy ball requires large amounts of racquet head acceleration. Be in serving or ground stroking, in order to develop this ability, a player has to hone his weapons for years; a lot of it is fitness related. Players need to be pretty strong in their core muscles, and more than anything, explosive on their rotation and swinging as they create the needed racquet head acceleration. A lot easier said than done!

On top of proper technique, players need explosive fitness training in order to create the power needed to hit heavy balls.

REDIRECTION, HITTING THE BALL BACK BY DEFLECTION

The easiest way to hit a ball back over the net and back into the court; is by hitting it in the same direction from which it came. Unfortunately, that usually means we are hitting back to our opponent's racket! We definitely want to master redirecting the ball and placing it. For that to happen, we have to be able to change the ball's path and in some instances this is very difficult. We need to position our body differently and meet the ball either further out front or further back. In reality, we meet the ball at the same point in relation to our body but relative to the court, we don't. Visualize a stray bullet bouncing off a hard stone wall. Where will this bullet go? That will depend on the angle of deflection the wall has in relation to the traveling bullet. Another good example is how light bounces off a mirror towards whatever angle we want it to. That is redirection in Tennis. We make the racquet meet the ball at an angle, so the ball bounces off the strings at a different direction from which it came from.

 Someone that spends lots of time rallying down the middle as part of their practice will struggle with point play once he/she start going full court. Hitting down the middle is not bad practice, but it is not specific to the varying needs of real play. Hitting down the middle is enjoyable because it requires so little mind and body adjustment.

 Dealing with a shot that is coming at a crosscourt angle from the opposite side of the court, and we have to move towards the corner to hit it back down the line. That is one tough thing to do consistently. We see even the pros make the most mistakes when doing this. Especially if they are going for it on the run and they are hitting from a position near or outside the singles lines. Worse yet when they have to do it from behind the baseline.

 When going down the line, as a player gets moving towards the center of the court, and farther away from the outside singles lines, the better his/her chances of making the shot. Also, if the ball is coming at the player from a down the line direction, it should be a higher percentage situation because we are not having to redirect as much. But if it is coming from the cross court direction, then we have to redirect it, and it becomes much lower percentage, especially if we are on the run.

Hitting the ball back cross court from an incoming down the line shot is a lot easier to make since we have so much more court to shoot into and the extra margin works in our favor.

Again, this skill needs to be repeatedly practiced until it is automatic. Redirecting the ball is crucial to tactical success in general on a Tennis court whether we are playing singles or doubles.

One very effective way to practice redirecting the ball; but it is also a very advanced way to do it, is to do the famous butterfly drill or exercise. In the butterfly drill, one player hits down the line, and the other one hits crosscourt. Requiring great skill and fitness as well as accurate footwork for proper shot execution. We used to do this drill "playing points." The players were required to make the shot to the designated half of the court or he/she lost the point. We did it drop serving and with normal serving. It is an extremely advanced drill! Give it a try and unless we are talking about Roger Federer or Rafa Nadal other players may get frustrated pretty fast!

Another way to tackle this skill is to use targets and get that ball machine out where it is moving the player all over the court, and he/she has to aim for specific targets. Set targets so the player has to redirect the ball every time. Practice redirection with all imaginable different scenarios. Mix in spins in the process. Practice the skill with volleys, return of serve, and groundstrokes at different speeds and angles. Have the ball machine set up near the singles or doubles lines for more realistic and specific training.

When hitting returns of serve, it is a lot lower percentage to try to redirect. Here is where we need to be content to hit the ball right back to our opponent if he or she has a good serve, especially off the first serve. (See section on return of serve)

POWER VS FINESSE

The word *power* sells more in Tennis than any other connotation. Adding the word power to racquet and string advertising, training routines, and training, aids as well as anything else that has anything to do with Tennis or sports performance. The simple use of the word "power" will make it sell quicker. Everyone wants more power on their groundstrokes and serves. Everyone wants to be able to rip the covers off the balls. Honestly, I cannot blame them for it because it feels great to be able to hit it super hard and see the ball go in. Watching the pros do it effortlessly is what fans pay big bucks for. Players that have this ability will have a decided edge if they know how to use it intelligently.

However, finesse can also be beautiful to see and execute and also effective if utilized correctly.

Not everyone has the luxury of power, but by the same token, not everyone has the luxury of finesse either. The pros usually have both. Both of them are excellent tools to have as part of our repertoire. We should really not talk about them as countering or opposing things; they are just different, and both serve the same purpose on a Tennis court of being able to finish the point outright!

Let me start by stating an anonymous quote: "There will always be someone that can hit the ball harder" Are we getting the idea? Power is not everything; we want it if we can win points consistently against an opponent. Keep in mind that a lot of players out there love to be fed power, and they play way better when we do just that! A combination of power, finesse, and other variations is much better and will yield better results. That is why a player that can combine his power serve and groundstrokes, plus a few drop shots or sharp low angles, is so much tougher to deal with. Than one that just pounds the ball from the baseline as hard as he or she can. A winner from the baseline or an ace serve is a thing of beauty, but a winning drop shot executed with great finesse is also a thing of even more beauty sometimes!

A lot of players are just gifted in that they have natural power built in their strokes. Most have to develop it through fitness training and improved technique. On the other hand, finesse is something that does not come naturally to all players either. Some players have great touch, but most others have to develop it. The point is that whether we have power and finesse or neither is not as important as the fact that if we don't have it we can develop both. If a player is serious about his/her Tennis, and means to reach his/her potential, power and finesse will be an absolute must.

Power and finesse go hand in hand with the subject of weapon development mentioned elsewhere in this book. Both of them can be means to the development of weapons. If we can consistently use one or the other or a combination of both to hit winners then these are weapons and we will be feared because of our skill. And if our opponent is fearful of us, we will have already won half the battle.

COMPETITION AND MATCHPLAY

How do we know a player is ready to compete? The answer is simple: If the player can hit serves and basic groundstrokes, he or she should be immediately subjected to matchplay. Matchplay teaches all kinds of good things that cannot be learned any other way. Tournaments provide matchplay that forces us to deal with losing. It also forces us to deal with pressure. Matchplay teaches us how to control our emotions. Even though winning is a wonderful thing. My late uncle Federico Cervantes, who played Davis Cup for Mexico, used to tell me that losing was not such a bad thing since when we lost we learned. And a lot of times, when we won, we didn't!

Matchplay gives us experience, and there is no substitute for this. Experience, what a precious thing; matchplay provides it, and there is no other way to get it. We have to get ourselves on the line, sign up for the tournaments and compete in order to develop as players. We can play friendly matches, hit tons of balls, and do a lot of lessons. But until we have to play tournament matches against tough players whom we are expected to beat, we will not have dealt yet with the whole experience. And we are missing out on an important element in the player's developmental process.

Here is a good rule of thumb for parents and coaches to figure out what division to sign up their kids for. If they can win two back to back tournaments then sign them up in the next upper division. And by the same token, if they lose two back to back first rounds, then they need to drop down a level in order to win at least some matches. Remember, the developmental player in question needs to be winning about 60% of the matches in which he or she is playing.

How much is too much? This is a difficult question to answer because every player is different. It is true that if we play a lot of tournaments, we get match-tough and perform better at them. At the same time, we need to be careful of burnout. Watch for signs of burn out all the time as explained elsewhere in this book. We need to be at or near the maximum matchplay allowed by a player without crossing this invisible barrier; we just have

WHAT TENNIS PROS DON'T TEACH (WTPDT)

to go with our gut instinct on where this barrier is. For a 12-year-old it may be about 10 evenly spaced tournaments in a year, some can handle a lot more. Maybe a 15-year-old can play in 17 tournaments in one year. More is definitely not necessarily better. We need to find the right balance for the player, and this is usually pretty obvious. If a player is not fully excited about a tournament or seems tired, we better watch it. Observe the player in practice; is he giving it 100% mentally, emotionally, physically and spiritually? Or is he/she coasting? As coaches and parents, it is very important to look for all these signs very closely. Refer to the chapter on Burnout.

There are different ways to get used to matchplay. We may get started on some casual point play with a kid; this helps them understand shot selection and strategy. Play lots of friendly 7-point and match-tiebreakers. Just play a bunch of points where one player or the coach serves a ball and play the point out. Don't keep track of the score, when keeping track of the score everything changes and some children cannot handle it. Let them serve the ball to us and play the point paying attention to shot selection and basic tactical stuff such as positioning and shot selection. Again, as soon as we start keeping track of the score, if they are not winning with some consistency, they start getting upset and lose motivation by getting all frustrated. Do lots of this non-scoring point play practice a lot until they get much better, and more mature. And then a little at the time, play some short games. Again, play lots of 7 and 10-point tie breakers rather than full sets and matches. As kids get ready and understand better how to play points, we can start signing them up for some lower level tournaments and start playing full sets and matches for practice in a gradual manner! Every kid is different, so the right balance for each and every player needs to be met by the coach or the player himself. For the most part, parents may need to talk to coaches, or coaches to parents in order to figure out whether a child is ready for tournament play or not.

POST MATCH PRACTICE, THE MINI LESSON

Something that I don't see often done at all is the post matchplay practice or the mini-lesson. Based on the match that was just played; especially if the player has more matches later in the tournament. It may be a good idea to hit some balls to clean up or make any corrections on strategy or technique. It is relaxing to the player and provides a great opportunity to really touch base in a very familiar setting with the coach. This may not always be possible or intelligent to do if the player had an exhausting match and must prepare for the next. But if there is time and an available court, by all means do it. Make sure this is done once the player has ingested sufficient water and had something to eat to start replenishing lost nutrients and energy. This practice does not have to be anything especial; 15 to 20 minutes of it is plenty. The player has already played, and we don't have to take too much time for an elaborate warm up. So as coaches, we don't take the time to warm up ourselves if we want to do this. A good coach is going to get warmed up on his/her own. Maybe on a wall or with another coach or student, and be ready for the mini lesson with his player when he or she is off the court. Better yet, if traveling with a group of players, we can get two players on the court at the same time. This way kill two birds with the same bullet by doing a mini-lesson with both.

Warm up for maybe 5 minutes, address the areas that need addressing for the rest of the time, stretch a little and talk a little, get off the court and let the players go rest!

THE ART OF SEEING/WATCHING THE BALL

Let's consider the following expressions that happen all the time during Tennis matches: "Watch the ball", "See the ball", "Keep your eye on the ball", "Track down the ball", "Look at the ball", "Focus on the ball" "Follow the ball", "Concentrate on the ball", and there may be others. Basically, all these phrases are saying the same thing. While playing Tennis nothing can be of more importance than knowing where the ball is, and where it is going, at what speed, what spin it has, etc... To a certain degree, all these terms are interchangeable depending on the different circumstances that happen on a Tennis court during play. Are we seeing as when we see something that gets in front of our eyes, and we cannot help to look at it? Or watching more like when we are paying attention to something and trying to concentrate on it by keeping our eye on it deliberately? I say a little of both are happening at all times. It is obvious we have to see the ball when we are playing Tennis; but how well are we seeing the ball? Or better yet, are we seeing the ball at all? There are different degrees of seeing/watching the Tennis ball; most of us don't really see it all that well. The majority of players will take their eyes off the ball when it's a few feet from the racket. Even at the professional level, we see pictures of players making contact or about to make contact to the ball looking straight forward and their eyes are nowhere near where the ball is at!

We've all seen pictures of Roger Federer looking straight at the ball as he is making contact. Experts say that he watches the ball 10% better than anybody else on tour. Is this true? I don't know the answer to that, but I can definitely see him looking down right at his racket head as he makes clean contact to the ball over and over. Another of yesteryear's players that was noted for doing that was Bjorn Borg, he seemed to always have a very still head as he was swinging, and his face was looking straight down to the strings-ball impacting one another. Do these awesome players see the ball better than the rest of us normal human beings? Yes, absolutely yes!

The good news is that we can get better at it. How? Practice watching the ball better. The same way we would practice our serve or volleys. Get out on the court, and hit some balls for 30 minutes every now and then, and the whole time, make it a point to see the ball impacting our rackets. All we will see is a yellow blur… but that's better than looking forward to where we are directing the next shot, which is typically what everyone does most of the time. One important technical aspect of being able to see the ball better is the fact that we need to have the ball in front of us, and our body is pretty much square towards it. If I have to turn my head to one side or the other to be able to see the ball at impact, chances are, I will not be as good at it as someone who is always turned or angled properly so that the ball is naturally in front of his/her eyes. Visualize someone hitting a forehand volley, if this player is a little sideways as he/she makes contact, he will naturally see the ball directly in front of his/her eyes. However, if the player did not turn his/her shoulders very much, he/she will have to turn his/her head to the right (right-handed player) in order to be able to see the ball better. Also, consider that when I want to pay close attention to something, I look at it straight on, not from the corner of my eye or with my peripheral vision. Straight on, that's the way we need to be looking at the ball all the time, where the ball is naturally in front of our eyes, and we don't have to turn our head or twist our neck to be able to see it. Another very important technical aspect for being able to watch the ball better is the fact that like Borg and Fed, we need to keep our head still as we swing. If we are out of balance or our head is moving or jerking as we are swinging, we can be assured of many solid frame shots… yes, shank, shank, shank…!

Scientific studies also show that when we are nervous we tend to blink our eyes more. The more nervous we are, the more we blink our eyes, and the less we see the ball. We hit the ball with the frame more and lose accuracy and confidence when we are nervous. If we could just remember to really watch the ball and let everything else unravel naturally, we can probably get over the nerves and start playing well.

Some techniques recommended for watching the ball better talk about watching the seams or the lettering on the Tennis balls in flight. Others recommend we watch the shadow on the bottom or the side of the ball as it approaches us, and we hit it. Yet others say we should really watch the ball as it bounces, and we should try to pin it down with our eyes as it comes off the surface toward our racket. I think all these ideas are great and can help someone train themselves to watch the ball better. The bottom line is that we need to get to the point where we are so used to seeing the ball through impact with our rackets, and that we do it naturally without additional or conscious effort.

Players that use a lot of topspin will be a lot more prone to framing the ball and have to be even better at watching the ball at impact. This happens because the angle of the racket frame and the ball at impact has to be very acute for the player to be able to apply the heavy topspin.

So there it is, yet another way to get better at Tennis, as simple as learning and training to watch the ball more closely as we hit it!

SECTION III
MIND OVER MATTER

STRATEGY

There's a lot of good literature on strategy in books, periodicals and on the Internet.

For practical purposes, we are not going to get deep into this subject since it is all out there already. Instead, we are going to come up with some practical and uncomplicated advice on what strategy is and the process of learning it.

Strategy is all about learning from matches played. Strategy can be summarized as knowing and understanding our shot selection and positioning options. In Tennis, we first learn how to hit the ball with the proper technique, but then we need to know where to hit it, how hard or high. Also, we now immediately have to know where to go after we have hit the ball.

Parents and players often ask my advice about strategy. They might say something like, "How is strategy learned in Tennis?" or "My son/daughter knows nothing about strategy, how can he/she learn this part of the game?" or "How do I need to play such and such player?" a student might say "Is there any time spent working on strategy and tactics during regular drills and lessons?"

Let's come up with a simple definition of strategy and tactics: Strategy is the overall game plan, and tactics refers more to the point to point shot selection and court positioning. These are oversimplifications but pretty much encompass what is most important.

A player will learn about tactics and strategy during point play practice and matchplay. Players need to play all scenarios in practice in order to see how successful they are in dealing with the different strategies and playing styles under different point play situations. Just talking about strategy to a player does not cut it and does very little for the player as far as really helping him, or her understand what it is all about.

One of the main sources of confusion comes when a player is told or coached to play outside of his/her boundaries. Meaning he or she is asked to do stuff he or she is not good at or does not even know how to do. Here is an example of a coach, sometimes parents or other players trying to give some advice or coaching on strategy and tactics to a player. "Tiffany is a really good baseliner, bring her to the net via short, low balls and drop-shots. As she approaches, try a low shot at her and follow with a passing shot or a lob as she closes the net." This tactical advice should sound simple enough to an advanced player. However, what if this player does not know how to hit low underspin or drop shots? Basically, in order to be able to hit low short balls, players need to have a pretty respectable slice off the forehand or the backhand or both. So here comes the player off the court very frustrated because he/she lost to Tiffany again, and her strategy did not work? Every time she hit short, the ball sat up in the air too long and Tiffany just came in and crushed it for winners over and over. There comes a point when a player should be able to modify this strategy if it is not working. Unfortunately, this player already was at a bigger than normal disadvantage since he/she walked on the court with the wrong strategy; one that made the match even easier for his/her opponent. This situation is pretty common in every tournament I go to with juniors and other players.

The first thing a player needs to do is recognize and define his/her boundaries. Know what he/she can or cannot do. Knowing ourselves as players will definitely help us understand strategy, game plans and shot selection that are effective for us. Knowing how to play this game involves a lot more than just knowing how to hit the ball well. Mobility, fitness, shot selection, strategy, tactics, mental toughness, determination to give it everything on every single point. All this factors and others have to be applied to win hard matches against tough opponents. Let's now consider a better example to deal with Tiffany: Anasazi is an aggressive baseliner, and she has to play Tiffany in the quarterfinals of the state qualifier tournament. Tiffany has always beat Anasazi, but they have had a couple close matches. Tiffany is just too consistent and has great anticipation and mental toughness. But Anasazi has a big game with hard groundstrokes, decent volleys and a pretty big 1st and 2nd serves. Anasazi's coach said to her that believing she could win was the main ingredient in her being able to come out the victor in this match. Her strategy is to mix around the first serve, aiming for a high percentage of 1st serves going in, to make a move early in the point, by either going for her groundstrokes, or coming in aggressively toward the net. When defending, she is to be patient and not go for too much by floating the ball back deep down the middle or crosscourt to be able to get back in position. Anytime Tiffany hits a medium to fairly easy shot; she is to take the initiative and start attacking. After a couple of nervous games from both sides, the match turns into a classic cat-mouse fight now. Anasazi lost the first set 6/4 but is leading in the second 5/2. Tiffany is serving; Anasazi gets her to 30/40 by playing fearlessly. Tiffany comes up with a couple really good shots and is able to get it back to deuce. Eventually, Tiffany holds, and the score is now 5/3. Anasazi can serve-out the set. She is visibly nervous; she is now aware this match is within her grasp, but she still has to win this game and the 3rd set. As she realizes this, she is getting herself too far ahead of herself. At moments such as this; players needs only to think of the next point. Anasazi gets broken at love; she lost her momentum, eventually losing the match in a tiebreaker; this is a pretty typical scenario. Tiffany came through because she is so mentally tough keeping herself under emotional control and within her tactical and technical boundaries. Anasazi's strategy paid off though, she at least did not lose because she got outplayed or because she had the wrong game plan beating herself. Her loss was more related to confidence, believing in herself and mental toughness. At some point at the end of that 2nd set Anasazi hesitated and missed a couple fairly easy shots; next thing we know, the match is over. At this point, Anasazi needs a good talk from her coach regarding these issues and how she has to learn to believe in herself, trusting her strategy and her game. Anasazi also needs to realize the importance of sustained momentum and keeping her mind on only the next point and the next point only.

How do players learn to win? The answer to that is simple: **By losing**; this is the cold truth and the way it is! Tennis players have to lose a lot in order to be able to win a lot. The more we lose, the more we will potentially be able to win. If players learn from their defeats, then this will result in better mental toughness and a better shot at success in the future. At the same time, players do have to try hard as hell to win! The mentality to go out there thinking we are just going to lose because eventually we will start winning is wrong too. We owe it to ourselves, our coaches, and everyone trying to help us become better at this crazy game to try our hearts out to win every single point we play. But we have to apply all the right forces to achieve it. Not bending over backwards and getting all frustrated and out of control about it. Losing will teach us how to win, given the right frame of mind is in its rightful place. There has to be a balance though; a developmental player needs to win some matches in order to stay motivated.

If he or she just loses over and over, eventually it will not be fun anymore, and he/she is likely to quit playing.

In reality, the only true way to benefit from Tennis is through the application of sportsmanship and ethics under competition and all throughout the developmental process. Ethics and values should always be of the highest priority for a player or a coach. Any strategy or tactical advice that deviates from this principle is basically flawed and worthless and should never be part of a game plan or strategy.

In summary, strategy is about knowing ourselves, and learning about our opponent's strengths and weaknesses over the length of a Tennis match. Players have to figure out a way to expose their strengths and apply them upon the opponent's weakness as best as they can. Also, players have to understand their boundaries; not playing within our boundaries will result in too many unforced errors and most likely more lost matches.

Two of the greatest attributes a player can have on a Tennis court are determination and patience. Another great attribute that develops and promotes the idea of mind over matter is clarity of thought and the capacity for intense relaxation and analysis of what is going on. In Tennis, we don't always have the time to come up with the right combination of variables applied to a match in order to win. Here is a good quote: "Half the time, we run out of time." when playing a match we might have won if we figured out what we needed to do earlier. I have witnessed way many matches where the player started a comeback too late; he or she was able to win two or three games and then it was over.

MOON BALLS AND DROP SHOTS

Right along strategy and tactics, I want to make special mention of these two huge game changers. Every player on the planet should know how to execute these two shots proficiently with the forehand and the backhand sides. Moon balls and drop shots are responsible for more momentum shifts and incredible comebacks than I care to tell about. These two techniques can save us when we run out of options. Against the counter punchers, bring them into the net out of their comfort zones with drop shots. Also, deal with their tremendous consistency by tossing some moon balls up in the air. If dealing with aggressive baseliners, break their rhythm with some moon balls or drop shots, and let them generate all the power and take all the risks. When dealing with players with weak volleys; bring them in with a nice drop shot, and once they are at the net, force them to volley. And don't forget the classical pattern of hitting a drop shot followed by a moon ball, if done right, this tactical move is guaranteed to drive anyone crazy pretty fast. By using moon balls and drop shots, we are taking advantage of the length of the court. Remember that a Tennis court is rectangular in shape, in other words, it is a lot longer than its width. The moon ball/drop shot pattern forces our opponents to move up and down the court much longer distances than if we were trying to move them from side to side.

In short, let me just say that the two shots in Tennis we all hate to deal with the most are the moon balls and the drop shots. It's not pretty Tennis, but it sure pays big dividends to know how to hit them, and they will add some dimension to our game. We want to spend some time learning how to hit them to perfection. Also, remember that the drop shot can even be considered a weapon if executed well.

PLAYING THE ELEMENTS

Playing conditions affect us all equally. How we deal with these challenges mentally and tactically have everything to do with how much we will enjoy the experience or whether we will be able to win not. The variables can be many, wind, sun, heat, humidity, cold, precipitation, dust, smoke, noise, smells, bugs, etc...

Players need to prepare mentally for Tennis in these conditions. Remember the conditions are always equal to all players on the court. A Tennis player needs to make sure to not use any of the playing conditions as an excuse and take whatever inconvenience as something that is going to keep him or her from going all out. As players, we cannot let the wind or the heat get into our head; this is the stuff where mentally tough players come out ahead of the game more often than not.

As players, we need to use every opportunity presented by playing conditions to our advantage. If the sun is bright on one side of the court, blind the opponent with some high lobs and also let him or her start serving from that side if possible. If the wind is really blowing towards us on our side of the court, we may want to hit a couple drop shots or really low short balls to drag our opponent forward even more than normal. Anticipation is key to dealing with the wind. Think of what the ball might do as we get ready to return serve or hit any other shot. If lobs are just soaring over our head, don't approach the net too deeply so that we can maybe hit overheads. If the wind is on our back, just aim a little lower, and maybe use a little extra topspin or slice to control the depth of our shots. When hitting into the wind, we need to hit harder and a little higher over the net depending on how strong the wind actually is. Also, when against the wind it is a good idea to play a foot or two further back than normal to be able to deal with the faster and deeper balls from our opponents. By the same token, play a foot or two closer to the baseline and the net when the wind is behind us. If crosswinds, we have to anticipate the curving path of the ball and do a good job of tracking down the ball the whole way to avoid being jammed or stretched out by it.

At the same time, we may want to use some heavy jamming or wide slice serves to disrupt the opponent's swings. A simple example of this would be a player serving to the deuce side with heavy slice to the T of the service box. If the right amount spin and crosswind combinations are happening, the ball is likely to jam the player returning; making it a lot harder for him or her to make a solid shot back over the net. One of the trickiest things to do on windy days is hit lobs and overheads. We need to develop an instinct for it. Players that are good dealing with the wind are always aware of what it is doing. If the wind is behind us, lobs should be softer and vice-versa. When windy, we really keep our eyes on the ball a little more and keep our feet moving as we set up for overheads. Anticipate a deeper soaring ball if the wind is in front of us and maybe a shorter one if behind us. In doubles, a player ought to adjust his/her initial position at the net a two or three feet further in or further back on windy days. If gusts of wind are happening, a smart player may wait a little for a wind gust to go by before attempting to serve. If our opponent decides to serve during a gust of wind, we should let him since there is a good chance his/her ball toss will be severely disrupted by the hard wind making him/her hit either a weak serve or a double fault. Another important consideration when dealing with cross winds is to avoid aiming to close to the side lines on the side where the cross wind may carry the ball out. Or if we do this, aim 3 or 4 feet further in than normal to compensate for the cross wind. If consistent play is needed, we need to concentrate on hitting to areas of the court where the wind will keep the ball inside the lines; preferably cross coourt. If the weather is hot and humid or both; the key to being able to put out 100% effort mentally and physically, is hydration. Drinking water and electrolytes more than we think we need will keep our body and mind operating just fine. Also, always have spare clothes at the ready just in case we get too wet; we can run to the bathroom and change. Another important consideration on humid days is maintaining a grip with sweaty hands. Carry towels, overgrips, sawdust or resin bag to keep our hand dried so that we are able to grip our racquet with authority. If cold then we need to wear three or up to five layers of thin, flexible clothing that is not too restricting and shed garments as needed.

An official will not call off a match or tournament because there are too many bugs on the court or exhaust fumes from a nearby roadway. We need to deal with these issues as best as we can. If a cloud of smoke from a big truck invaded the court, wait till it clears; if bug season then we need some bug spray in our bag, and so on and so forth… Be prepared and tackle each and every problem as it comes. Being prepared in advance is important and can easily be the difference between winning and losing. (See the subsection for the 101 things to carry in our racquet bag for a Tennis match in the 101 section of this book)

All in all the player that does not let conditions get into his or her head and the player that comes prepared will have the upper hand most of the time when dealing with tough on court variables. The players that use these conditions to their advantage every chance they get will have a definite edge.

DEALING WITH ALTITUDE

Tennis players need to understand altitude changes when traveling to tournaments in other regions. Altitude changes will affect a player's performance. He/she may not be able to execute his/her Tennis in a normal fashion and may end up playing poorly due to the lightness of the ball. The ball and the courts will feel different whether we go up or down in altitude. A player traveling to a different city needs to do some research. A period of adaptation will be needed. The greater the altitude change, the more time for adaptation is needed. Most professional tournaments nowadays are played at or near sea level. That is great for the pros, but what about juniors, college, or simply competitive players all over the World?

Traveling to a tournament to a city that is 1,500 feet above sea level or more will present pretty tough challenges. Suddenly the strings need to be tighter. Balls bounce faster and higher, and our shots just fly long or scatter left and right. On top of all that, we are running out of breath because there is less oxygen in the air at higher altitudes!

In a situation like this it would be ideal to arrive two or three days in advance. The problem is obvious; we may not be able to afford to do this. Getting there at least one full day in advance is necessary if we are not to get knocked out in the first round.

First of all, at higher altitudes we need to adjust the racquet string tension, something in the order of about 2-3 more pounds of tension for every 2,000 feet difference. So if I live at sea level, and I usually string my racquets at 57 pounds. When I play in a tournament at 2,000 feet above sea level, I need to go up in tension to about 59 pounds or maybe even a little higher. Also, all players should serve and play lots of points in order to get used to the thinner air, the faster points, and lighter balls. It is not that the balls are lighter, but they do feel lighter because the air is thinner, and gravity's pull is not as strong.

At 4,000 feet and above, pressureless or high altitude balls are required. These balls feel incredibly different on the racquet. Generally, they are a lot harder, making it more difficult to apply spin due to less deformation of the ball upon contact with the strings. Spin is important at high altitudes since it provides one solution to ball control. I have seen players from all over the World double fault 20-30 times per match because they could not control pressureless balls during Davis Cup competition in Mexico City where the altitude is near 8,000 feet above sea level. Typically these players arrived in Mexico City a full week in advance of the Davis Cup series to get adapted to the altitude and the lower oxygen levels in the thin air. At these altitudes, players need to get near the upper limit of string tension on their racquets in order to be able to control the ball.

Now, if we were traveling from Denver, Colorado, where the altitude is one mile at 5,280 feet above sea level, to Palm Desert, California for a tournament, which is only 224 feet above sea level, we will be dealing with a whole new and different set of challenges. Heavier conditions overall and much heavier balls on our strings. Our shots are likely to lack depth and power since we are so used to the higher altitude where we barely hit the ball, and the ball just keeps on going. We need to lower the tension on our racquets dramatically, hit the ball a lot harder, and with less spin. Maybe even add some weight in the form of lead tape to the frame of our racquet to increase mass and power. Going back to our example of string tension. If I typically string at 57 pounds, if going from Denver to Palm Desert, I would have to drop my tension by about 5 or 6 pounds to maybe 51 or 52 pounds.

Different playing styles are more or less likely to be successful at the different altitudes. Net rushers definitely have an edge at higher altitudes; baseliners have an edge as we get closer to sea level. The higher the altitude, the easier it is to hit winners since balls travel so much faster. As we get closer to sea level, points will be longer, and it will be harder to hit outright winners.

Going further into detail. Junior players developing at high altitudes are at a distinct and unique disadvantage if they are aspiring to play high caliber professional or college Tennis; because most big tournaments are played at or near sea level. So the junior developing at the high altitude situation will most likely lack a strong enough foundation for hard groundstrokes and power Tennis. He or she may develop great volleys and a pretty solid all court game, but will be at a disadvantage when facing juniors or players developed at sea level conditions when playing at or near sea level.

As mentioned above, most big tournaments and competition will happen at or near sea level. In countries like Mexico, where most junior development happens at pretty high altitudes, most players develop the all court or the serve and volley style, whether it fits them or not, because that is what works over there. As long as the tournaments are happening in cities like Mexico City, Guadalajara, Monterrey, Puebla, San Luis Potosi, Queretaro, etc… all big Tennis cities in Mexico and all high altitude cities! But as soon as they enter World competition, problems emerge. That is a big part of the reason Mexico is not a big producer of professional Tennis players. It sounds like an excuse, but it is a vexing issue.

TURNING DEFENSE INTO OFFENSE

We often hear commentators on TV and coaches talk about how he or she turned defense into offense. Basically, what they are saying is that a player who defends well eventually will have opportunities to be offensive. Nobody can hit all offensive back to back shots. So if a player defends and defends during a point, he or she will eventually be presented with a situation where he/she may or should be offensive. Playing Tennis expecting errors from our opponent is fundamentally incorrect. A player should be able to hit a winner now and then, and it does not have to be a hard hit ball, a winner can be anything. A drop shot, a topspin offensive lob, an angle, etc... but by doing this we are offensive. My advice to players is that they need to be hitting at least an average of one winner per game. And if they are not doing so, they need to step it up and start taking more chances by finding ways within their ability boundaries to hit them.

Turning defense into offense is nothing other than a player defending well and taking chances when he or she has them at hand. For instance, the aggressive baseliner will go for a down the center deep return off his/her opponent's big first serve. When the ball comes back, he or she may just rip a down the line winner off the second ball. An all-court player may hit a slice angled low ball as his or her opponent approaches the net, forcing him or her to volley upwards, and then, coming up with a clean passing shot down the line or offensive lob winner. A counter puncher will stay in the point for as long as he or she may need. Staying in the point until he or she gets such an easy shot, that he/she simply hits a winner into a wide-open court. Finally, a serve and volley player may come in behind his/her second spin serve, hit a deep half volley off a very aggressive return, closing the net in anticipation of the passing shot from the opponent, and then following up with a stab angle crosscourt volley winner. These are some simple examples of how all different playing styles ought to look for opportunities to turn defense into offense. More on clay than on other surfaces, we may see a player be able to run down balls corner to corner and just slice the ball back down the middle deep three or four times in a row. Or a player may anticipate well a couple put away overheads, getting them back deep into the opponent's court, after which he or she gets a chance to utilize his or her weapons, or at least be able to hit a neutral shot, and not just a defensive one, eventually turning the situation to his/her advantage. A typical situation occurs when we successfully hit a lob over the opponent's head, they run down the ball; then we filter into the net for a putaway overhead or volley against their desperate return. There we have it, defense into offense… At first we struggle to save our lives, next, we are the ones killing the opposition, it is awesome! Again, this can be said to be a quality belonging not only to the counter-puncher, but to all styles of play. Everyone should be able to apply this principle to different degrees. We need to be able to defend; in order to eventually, be able to attack!

HIGH PERCENTAGE TENNIS

We hear the terms high percentage or low percentage Tennis or low percentage shots all the time. What is high percentage Tennis? What is high percentage shot selection? These are important considerations in understanding Tennis. Just because we can hit the line some of the time does not mean we should be aiming at the lines all the time. Or just because we have hit some great down the line shots, does not mean we can get away with doing it repeatedly either.

Aiming too close to the lines and hitting down the line are potentially low percentage situations in Tennis. I suppose it is okay to aim for the line if we are going for our first serve, and the score is 40-0 or 40-15… But to go for the line with our the 2nd serve is very low percentage, meaning there is a very good chance a player will double-fault if he or she is feeling the pressure. Likewise, it would be low percentage to go for a 2nd serve by hitting it like a 1st serve. But this may be an acceptable risk if the player is feeling confident and the score is again 40-0 or 40-15, and even 40-30 or add in! When serving, it's reasonable that the player should pick a spot in the service box, and if it is a 2nd serve, visualize a spot a foot to two feet inside the service lines. Practice serves with targets, and develop confidence getting within a foot of these targets fairly consistently. Low percentage serving also refers to serving without enough spin to really harness the ball and force it into the service box. Spin serving will raise percentages. As stated in the Sub-section on serving, we need all kinds of spins to keep the ball under control.

When hitting groundstrokes, we would be smart to try to understand and study smart shot making and smart shot selection. Here is a short list of smart shot selection and high percentage

WHAT TENNIS PROS DON'T TEACH (WTPDT)

Tennis tips:

- If on the run go down the middle or crosscourt, especially if near the singles lines when making contact with the ball,
- When out of balance try to get the ball back in the court high down the middle and deep if possible, in order to stay in the point and make our opponent hit at least one more ball,
- For good consistency, aim four feet from the baseline and four feet from the singles line in singles. If doubles it will be four feet from the doubles lines (see subsection on *The 4x4 Rule*)
- The highest percentage groundstroke to go for in Tennis is midway between baseline and service line hit down the middle; against big servers we need to aim our returns in this area,
- If we hit a great shot and the ball comes back, for the most part, don't immediately try to hit another greater shot. Start the rally over and work on creating another opportunity to go for it again,
- Great shot making can only be said to be happening if shots are going in with regularity during a match. Hitting a couple of pretty good shots does not classify as great shot making, if the player missed another two after the first two. Great shot making should be consistent, and it is a very difficult thing to do,
- Just because the pros pull it off all the time does not mean we human beings can hit awesome shots down the line and angled winners. These displays of brilliance are derived from extreme confidence, great skill, and hundreds upon hundreds of hours practicing!
- A player needs to know his/her boundaries and stay within them! How hard can we hit the ball... consistently?
- Be aware of the different patterns of play: If missing long, apply more topspin or undersrpin or aim lower, and if missing in the net, aim higher! If missing wide, aim further inside the lines! If hitting too short, aim higher, hit harder or maybe take off topspin or underspin from some groundstrokes,
- For passing shot purposes, if our opponent hits a deep or very low approach, don't try to pass with the first shot. Maybe try to hit one low or hard right at him or her, and then maybe lob or pass with the second shot,

- During a baseline exchange, stay crosscourt for the most part and break away from it only if the opponent hits a short ball or one closer to the middle of the court,
- Aim for big areas of the court when under pressure. Meaning that instead of aiming four feet inside the baseline, aim 5 or 6 feet. If we want to make a second serve for sure, aim for the center of the center of the service box.

THE 4X4 RULE

The 4X4 rule does not refer to off road four wheeling. What it does refer to, is high percentage Tennis or smart Tennis and shot selection.

We want to aim for a spot four feet from the baseline and singles lines; this is a pretty high percentage target. I personally like to teach my students to go for midway between baseline and service line and four feet from the singles lines for purposes of baseline rallying. Depth control is harder to accomplish, and I feel this gives the student a better understanding of what a high percentage target is on a Tennis court. (See court diagram for high percentage and smart shot selection targets in Tennis Fig.18)

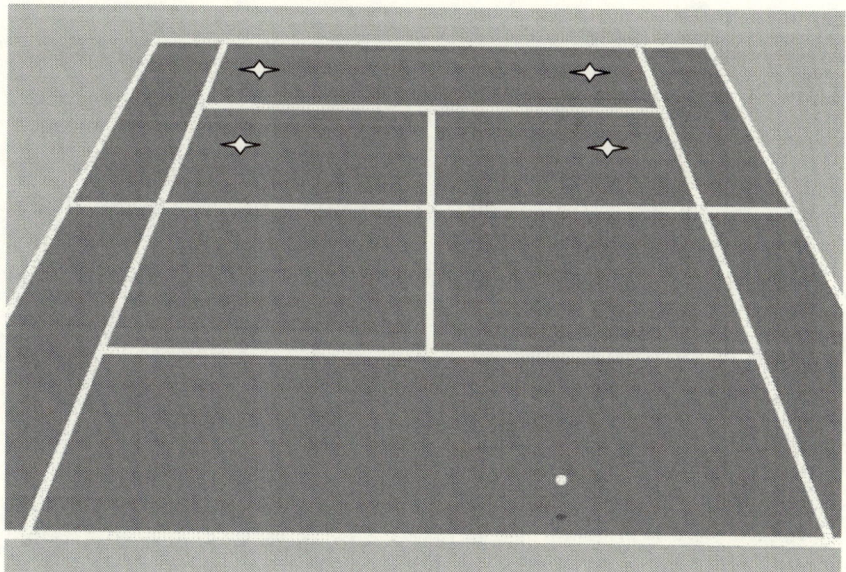

Fig.18) High percentage targets following the 4x4 rule of good shot selection for deep crosscourt and down the line shots as well as angled passing shots in Tennis.
✧ -Targets

STATISTICS, WHAT DO THEY MEAN TO US?

It is important to pay attention to match statistics. They mean a lot and they can help players predict the future, as well as aid in coming up with the right tactics or strategy under different circumstances.

There are only three ways we can win a point in Tennis: 1) by hitting a winner, 2) by forcing an error and 3) by getting an unforced error from our opponent. All points played in Tennis fall within one of these three categories.

In a fairly close match situation, a player playing near the top of his or her ability level will have pretty close to 33% of each of the three categories. Meaning that a player is controlling better than 60% of the points, therefore winning the majority of the points and games.

We need to be hitting some winners, forcing some errors, and want it or not, making some unforced errors as well.

How many winners? How many errors will we force? And how many errors will we coerce from our opponent? In a normal match of two developed individuals playing well, the answer to the above question is about 33% or one-third of each.

In order for us to apply this information to match play. Statistics of unforced errors, forced errors, and winners will lead us in the right direction. Granted the player in question is not hitting many winners at all, this player then needs to start taking some more chances with his/her shot selection and power. It may be that the player needs to advance to the net (since it is easier to hit winners at the net than from the baseline). Strategy or tactical changes are encouraged from the gathered information, and sometimes is extremely useful, especially if the player is losing. Plan B tactically, should not always be to play more conservative or consistent; sometimes we need to go for it more!

An important statistic in Tennis is obviously 1st and 2nd serve percentages. In singles, we want to hit in at least 60% of first serves, in doubles 70% or higher. Serving effectiveness is measured by what percentages of the points are won when the first serve or second serve is successful. Tactical adjustments will have to be made if we are not winning the point at least 60% of the time when hitting in our 1st serves or about 55% when going for 2nd serves. If a player is not holding serve at least 70% of the time, he or she will be in trouble and down in the score pretty soon and needs to make tactical or strategic adjustments. What adjustments though? Remember John McEnroe: "There is always a way to win".

One misunderstood statistic in Tennis goes like this: The more times player A loses to player B, the better the chances player A has of winning at their next meeting. Oftentimes, a player will go on court with a defeated attitude, because he or she is playing against someone that they have lost to a number of times. Not understanding very well that the pressure is totally on the other player, and they actually have a better chance this time around, than they did in all the previous matches they had played. In this situation, a player has to dig, dig, and dig! Remember Vitas Gerulaitis famous quote and story: Tennis player Vitas Gerulaitis lost 16 times in a row to Jimmy Connors. He then won a match versus Jimmy and said "and let that be a lesson to you all. Nobody beats Vitas Gerulaitis 17 times in a row".

Here follows a chart to keep statistics on a simple paper form on a clipboard. This chart has worked for me over the years. Providing an invaluable tool to help players figure out how aggressive or conservative they need to be playing, and how to manage their game better for more balanced and intelligent play.

Player's Name: Date: Event:

Player statistical evaluation form:
Players A_____ and B_____ // No of // Serves // Double // Score
Winners / Forced Errors / Unforced Errors / Hits / 1st/2nd // Faults // A / B
A / B // A / B // A / B // // / // // /

Nomenclature:

F = forehand
B = backhand
S1= first serve
S2= second serve
Vf= forehand volley
Vb= backhand volley
O = overhead
S = slice
ts= top spin
= = down the line
x = cross court
w = wide
a = angle
D = double fault
d = drop shot

Performance Chart: (grade 1-5, 5=excellent, 4=good, 3=okay, 2=poor and 1=weak
1st Set / 2nd set / 3rd set / 4th set / 5th set / Whole Match
Mental Toughness:
Strategy/Tactics:
Intensity:
Fitness:
Concentration:
Average from Above Scores:

Comments/Observations:_____
_____
_____

Coach's Name:_____

Fig 19)Blank supervision form. This template can be used to create or customize one's own format. It does take pretty serious concentration to keep this chart accurate. At least 4 games need to be charted to come up with any useful conclusions from observations. To make it a little simpler it is a good idea to use check marks at first and as we get better at it we may start using the nomenclature shown above to draw more information from our supervision and charting.

WHAT TENNIS PROS DON'T TEACH (WTPDT)

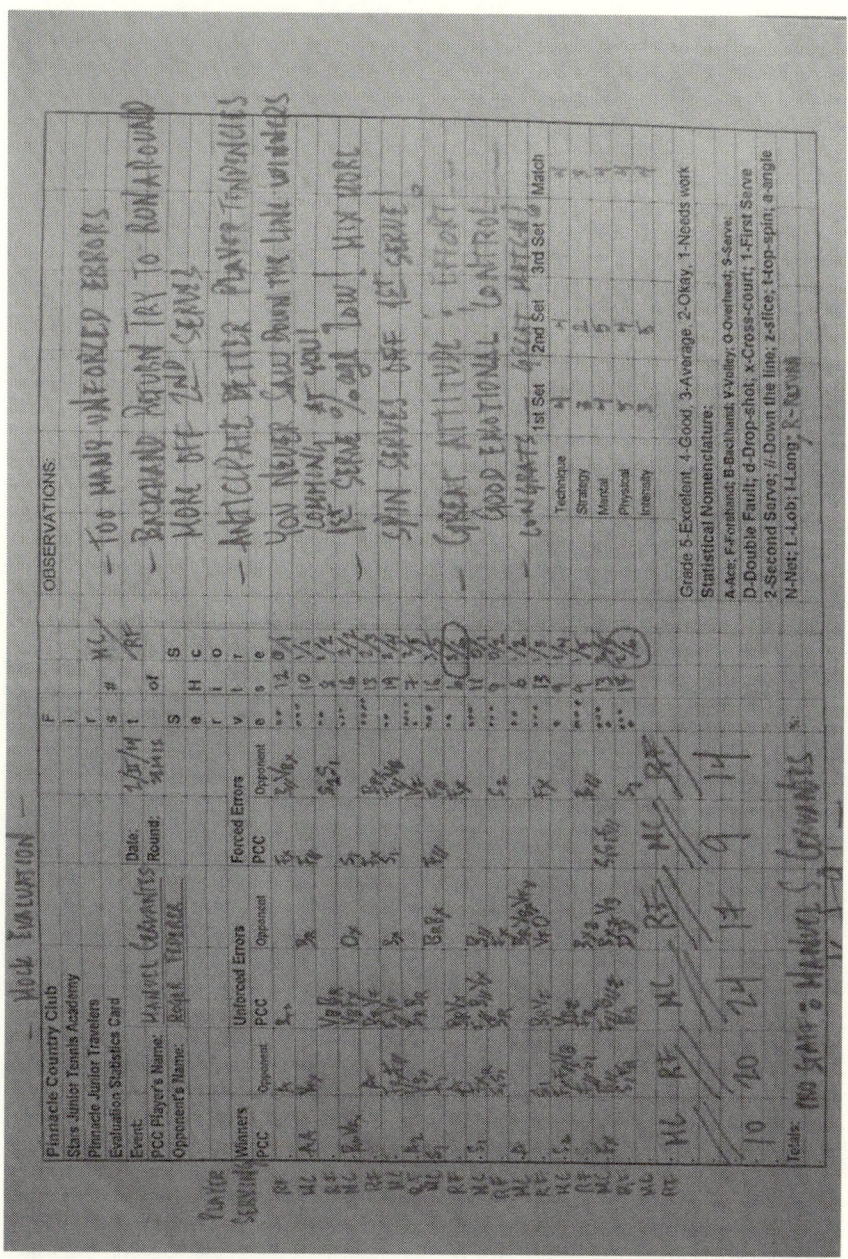

Fig 20) This is a picture of a mock Supervision Form filled-out of a match between Manuel Cervantes and Roger Federer. Notice Roger's 20 winners, 17 unforced errors and 14 forced errors VS Manuel's 10 winners, 24 unforced errors and 9 forced errors.

In the above statistical form, we can also see comments and the grades granted by the coach on the different Strategy, Mental, Physical and Intensity fields. With a little practice, different kinds of conclusion could be drawn from these statistics. For instance, we may find out that our opponent hit 10 winners off his/her forehand during a match we lost, but also made 12 unforced errors with it. Our player in question perceived his/her opponent's forehand as being something he/she needed to stay away from. But he/she never caught on to the fact that if he/she challenged this forehand more, he might end up winning more points and potentially the match. The above statistical form shows very balanced play from RF and not so balanced from MC since he committed too many unforced errors trying to play beyond his capability. We could conclude that in a match like this, the quality of play was pretty high given the number of winners and forced errors in contrast with the unforced errors. It is easy to conclude that RF outplayed MC. Note Roger's service percentage was near 70% and Manuel's only 42%... Serving a low percentage of 1st serves is a sure way to invite trouble!

Some coaches download an app for smart phones that does statistical analysis and e-mail the results to a computer or just draw conclusions on the phone. To me, as a Coach, it is difficult to manage apps when dealing with a variety of players. For me, keeping stats on paper is more manageable. Very rarely do I have the luxury of charting an entire match. It is a lot more common that I charted half a set or maybe a whole set, at least this gives me and the player, solid information as to how to proceed on future rounds and practices.

TEMPO ON COURT, ESTABLISHING RHYTHM AND PACE

Establishing tempo and pace in a match is a subject too few coaches teach their students. Establishing the tempo or pace that is appropriate for the player in question is of extreme importance. The tempo of a player should match his or her personality as well as his/her playing style and rhythm on court. There is fast, medium and slow tempo. We can see this executed by the different professionals. Some of them are very slow and deliberate, while others are extremely fast, wanting to move on with the match and trying to get the ball rolling as fast as possible after every point and changeover. The time taken between points and on changeovers varies from player to player. How a player handles himself/herself on the court varies from one individual to the next. Some walk very deliberately and slowly up to the baseline to serve or return: while others seem to be on turbo all the time. When playing against certain opponents a match seems just to flow while other times it is as if we are always waiting or being rushed.

We need to be able to establish our own rhythm when on a court, to not do that might mean losing and not being able to play our best Tennis. Players need to be aware of their own pace. As per the rules of Tennis, we are supposed to play at the server's tempo, but there are small ranges within this rule. Players that understand intervals and rhythm can definitely change the flow of matches in their favor.

So what is the right tempo for a player? Only the player can figure that out, maybe his/her coach can help. By all means stay within the allowed 25 seconds permitted between points and 90 seconds on changeovers. Practice this and get used to a rhythm that is comfortable.

A few examples of this are Andre Agassi or Andy Roddick as fast tempo individuals, and Ivan Lendl, Maria Sharapova, and Rafa Nadal as slow tempo players. Players with a tempo beyond the limits of what could be considered normal, either seem to move even faster or go even slower; the tougher the match gets or if they are playing badly and losing. Experienced players will do everything they can, to control the tempo of a match, especially if they are having a hard time.

Slow tempo players like to think things through as they recover from the previous point. They want to be very deliberate about everything they do before the next point starts. I was that kind of player. Some opponents/friends/official from the past used to give me a hard time about how slow I played… and yes, I did have a few time penalty warnings from officials.

As a final comment, it is important to understand that regardless of what our opponent's tempo or rhythm is, we have to do our best at staying within our range of comfortable tempo. Try to play at a quicker pace than what we are used to just for practice purposes. Identify the uncomfortable feelings associated with this. Make sure to not let the opponent dictate tempo during a match. As competitors, we need to figure out effective and legitimate ways to either speed up or slow down the match. Learning to have the right tempo for us may require practice; a simple wrist watch can help a player take note for how long he or she is taking between points or on changeovers. Time between points for different players ranges from about 7 seconds for fast paced to as much as over 20 seconds for slow tempo players.

As a general rule of thumb, increase tempo or play faster when winning and slow down tempo or play slower when losing!

Also, remember that one intelligent move when in trouble during a match is to do to our opponent what they are doing to us. Therefore, if someone's slow play or tempo is affecting my rhythm or quality of play. Then, I might attempt to play even slower than him or her to feel I am in command and then see what happens! Vice-versa in that if someone is playing fast and this is bothering my play, I may then start playing even faster than him or her!

CLOSING MATCHES AND MOMENTUM

Finishing a close match has to be one of the most difficult things to do in Tennis. We all know how hard it is to break serve and to finally win that coveted break point. But we also know how much more difficult it is getting to match point and winning that final point; this is obviously true only in cases when the match is close.

Closing a match requires fearlessness and clarity. A player needs to continue to go for his/her shots and play aggressive focusing on winning one point at the time. Once a player gets a lead, the goal is not to keep this lead but to try to increase it until the match expires. Tennis is not like many other sports where the length of the game is regulated by certain amount of time. In soccer, for instance, play is divided into 45-minute halves. The two teams fight one another for a total of 90 minutes, and regardless of what the score is, the game is over at the end of this predetermined amount of time. As in soccer and many other sports regulated by time, once a team gets a pretty good lead, they can play defense and wait out the clock. Tennis, however, is awesome because match point is a goal not governed by the clock. In Tennis, players have to keep beating the beast until it is very much dead. If the beast is still moving, it may come back and get us when we least expect it. Think about it, the rules say that we have not won a Tennis match until we have shaken hands with our opponent; this is part of the definition of winning in the rule book. Of course, in order to get there we should have won match point.

In Tennis the end of a match is dictated by the choices the players make; matches aren't over until they are over. And players have to take care of the business of finishing the match. And whatever got us to be in the lead, is in the majority of cases what we should continue to do in order to get us the win. As we step on a poisonous spider trying to kill it, she may still be moving a little. So back goes the sole of the shoe and twists on top of it to make sure she is not only dead, but very dead! Ugh!

No lead is large enough on a Tennis court! Players should never be content with a lead because it is very dangerous to do so. We need to keep doing what we are doing and as long as the lead continues to increase we will be fine. If the lead starts shrinking or staying the same, we may already be in trouble because momentum may be shifting against us, and we may not have noticed that yet. Being aware of these momentum shifts as soon as they begin happening is of extreme importance in Tennis. There have been so many big matches where a player comes back from being way down. No lead is enough on a Tennis court! Remember that line.

As a general rule of thumb, if we are winning, increasing pace or tempo a little is recommended, and whatever we are doing to win points start doing it more pointedly and aggressively. And if we are losing, then we need to slow down the tempo, be more deliberate, and try to counter whatever our opponent is doing to hurt us. At this point, some tactical changes need to come into play.

Tennis is a battle of the minds of two players as much as a battle of their strokes and physiques. Players who are capable of imposing their terms on other players, physically, mentally and spiritually, most likely will be the players who will win matches and tournaments.

Always remember the wounded bear principle: Once the hunter wounds a bear, the bear is 100 times more dangerous! To finish him will take bravery, intelligence, intensity, and concentration. Basically, this is what happens to a player when he or she is losing a match or has just lost the first set... Watch out! This player has now become the wounded bear!

Sure signs of momentum shifts to watch for are closely disputed games, streaks of three or more points in a row, and breaks of serve followed by holding serve. Games where the score keeps going back to deuce, are sure signs of the momentum trying to make a shift. A player has to win these games to maintain his or her momentum. Any time a player wins three or more points in a row is a sign of either him/her keeping the momentum and/or the momentum beginning to shift in the other player's favor. And holding serve immediately after a break is a sure sign that a player now has the momentum in his or her favor.

Grasping or keeping momentum at the beginning of the second set presents players with the opportunity to start a comeback. Players have to work hard at getting the first, second and even third games of this set. Those first few games of each new set can set the stage for what's to come for the rest of the set and even the match.

Another consideration in gaining momentum is to win the first point of each and every game. Giving us a chance to hopefully (especially if we are serving) close out the game without too much difficulty.

When receiving serve, with no add scoring, to be able to win the point at 15/30, presents a really good opportunity to grasp some serious momentum. Since the opponent now would have to win three points in a row, and each of these points is a breakpoint. The 15/30 is very big in regular scoring situations also. Players should always remember that the point previous to game point (whether serving or returning) is significant and carries more weight than other point situations.

A few more controllers that are key to grasping or keeping momentum are body language, on court tempo and recognition of the big points in each and every game. When a big point is played, smart players need to go for high percentage targets, at the same time staying aggressive while focusing on tactics and game plans.

For instance: Player A is controlling a match serving well and going for his/her shots from the baseline, player B has not yet found the right strategy to deal with A's shot-making. However, B is working hard and walking around the court with his head up in a strong posture. He/She is in the process of looking for solutions, he or she is taking his or her time between points, and he/she is fighting hard for every point. Suddenly, A misses a couple easy shots because he/she is feeling the pressure from B's strong on court image and slightly slower tempo. B wins the next point by bravely counterattacking from the baseline. As an experienced player, B is aware that he/she just won three points in a row, and A's confidence is trembling a little. B continues to counterattack the next few points and ends up winning the game. B now has found a better strategy and turned the momentum of this match in his favor.

Some statistical studies show that the player who wins the most points in a match will win the match; this makes sense and makes us wonder if every point should be played the same way tactically. However, in understanding momentum, remember that while all points count numerically equal, some carry a lot more weight than others. Other statistical studies show that winning the most bundles of three points in a row will win the match regardless of the score. (See Fig. 18 for a momentum chart that illustrates this point)

A competitive player needs to remember and be aware of these situations. For instance, when he or she has won or lost two points in a row; the next immediate point is more important and carries more weight regardless of the score. This point needs to be played with utmost concentration and in tow with solid tactics.

Other studies on momentum show that if a player is able to win the first three points of a tiebreaker, he or she has better than 60% chance of winning the set or match. This information is also something to be mindful of.

COMING FROM BEHIND AND SHIFTING THE MOMENTUM OF A MATCH

Remounting the score after being behind is always possible in Tennis. Remember that each game is a fresh start. If we are able to adjust our strategy and make the necessary changes, we can come back from being way down. In a close competitive game, a slight change in strategy may be enough, but if we are getting blown away, we need more radical changes in strategy. It is possible to shake the opponent and climb even the steepest of hills.

Uncomplicated strategy/tactical changes could be hitting harder, or it can be simply varying pace, or hitting more spin (topspin or slice) or hitting less spin. Also, hitting higher or lower, or placing the ball closer to the corners and lines. Maybe it can be just to hit more down the middle of the court and let our opponent take the chances and dictate by allowing him or her to get closer to the lines with his or her shots. A simple tempo/pace change can be all we need to do to start changing things on a Tennis court. Other things to try are switching to a racquet with looser strings, or maybe tighter strings, or it could be a lighter racquet or maybe a heavier racquet. Change something or do something different when in trouble on the Tennis court. Also consider hitting low short balls and dragging the opponent into the court or the net, and so on and so forth. The bottom line is we can come back, and we need to believe it is possible more in Tennis than in any other sport because of the unique characteristics of the scoring system.

We probably have seen comebacks in Tennis that were completely unlikely to happen but yet they did happen. A player who is losing a match needs always to remember that the final game or games of a match are the toughest to win. As long as he/she continues to fight, the opponent is likely to get a little nervous towards the end, presenting the opportunity to make a comeback.

Also, players coming back emerge out from the dig deep philosophy; a player, who is losing or just lost the first set, is very likely to bounce back strong in the second set. Remember "The Wounded Bear Syndrome" which means that a bear may be dangerous, but a wounded one is a lot more likely to hurt us. We see this repeat itself over and over every day, in every tournament. Even though, we know the wounded bear is there, a lot of times we fail to do anything about it and prevent the come back from happening; it is like a tremendous force. Momentum is so likely to shift sometimes, and once it gets going one way, it is very difficult to stop it or turn it! No one is immune to momentum shifts. These can and will happen to all Tennis players. At the same time, "Tennis players be cautious". If we've had momentum on our side for a while, chances of it shifting against us, in a fairly close match, are stronger and stronger as the match continues to evolve.

Never lose hope, never give up; always believe a comeback is possible. Again remember "There is always a way to win".

As overall general advise, I highly recommend that anytime practice matches are scheduled, to go ahead and play them with regular scoring, and not no-add scoring. Regular scoring promotes mental toughness development, and a better understanding of momentum or how it shifts. In regular scoring, the *luck* factor plays a much less important role in the outcome of matches. No add scoring, for the most part, is destructive to Tennis itself; and what makes Tennis so desirable a discipline at all levels.

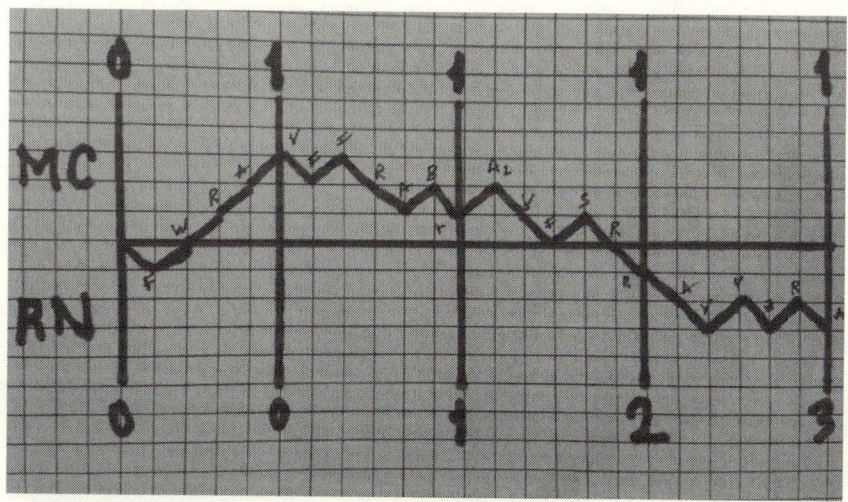

Fig 21)This chart shows the momentum flow or the first four games of the match between Manuel Cervantes (MC) and Rafa Nadal (RN). While MC grabbed some momentum in the first game, RF started controlling play and maintaining momentum the following 3 games. By graphing this way, it is an easy to follow momentum trends in a match. All you need is some graph paper and pay close attention to what goes on during matches. Each square is one point. You can come out with your own nomenclature, for instance, f=forehand, w=winner, A=ace, R=rally, v=volley, etc… and write down next to each diagonal line to make your chart more informational and conclusive.

DEALING WITH DEFEAT

Losing should be viewed as opportunity. We need to learn from losing. This is how we grow in Tennis, and in life we grow through learning from our mistakes. Children make mistakes all the time and the more mistakes they make, the wiser they become. The philosophy of "Learning the hard way" needs to be adopted by all Tennis players. Think about it: out of a tournament draw of 64 players, there will only be one player that will not have lost by the time the tournament is done!

Remember this quote: "Every defeat gets me that much closer to a victory." At first we see tears and great disappointment. It is very difficult for parents, coaches and friends to deal with crying children after they've lost. My Dad, who was not a huge advocate of Tennis, came to watch me during a match when I was like 11 years old. Being the first time he had ever come to see me play. Maybe I let the nerves get to me, and my opponent played great but I ended up losing in a close battle. As I got off the court, a couple tears rolled off my face as I approached Dad! He was quietly furious and whispered something like "Son, cut it out, if it's going to be like this, there is no need for me to see a Tennis court ever again". It happened a long time ago, and things have changed a lot now or have they? Are parents educated any better now to deal with their kids getting beaten?

Let me go out on a limb and say that at least 80% of all matches played, and tournaments entered in a player's early learning stages, will be developmental; which means the player will most likely get beat, and he/she knew that in advance of entering the tournament. Players, parents, and coaches should be prepared to deal and accept defeat when it comes, because come it will! In Tennis, there are not that many surprises at the developmental levels because as coaches we pretty much know who is going to win and who is going to lose before the start of the match. Parents, please be ready to deal with children's lost matches; also, coaches should help parents and players understand and anticipate defeat.

Players should know what their goals are when entering competition or playing matches. Winning, which is not wholly under our control, should not be a priority or the player's most important goal. Here are some of the reasons for entering competition and playing matches: a) development and learning, b) recreation and fun, c) learning what it takes to win.

While it is okay to lose, it is wrong to not try our absolute best to win. Tennis players and especially children need to understand this very well. They need to go on court and give it all, and if they lose, they need to learn to walk out of the court smiling and relaxed. Knowing that they achieved all their goals and that it is okay because they are that much better for having made the attempt. At the same time, players who stall or give up have to rethink their reasons or goals. Remember Tennis teaches us life lessons, and we cannot ever give up in the heat of battle. Sometimes juniors stop trying because they subconsciously are anticipating excuses for losing.

Now, it is important to say, that I have seen matches where someone is playing possum. A player may be acting as if he or she was not trying his or her hardest in order to get the other player to lose focus or momentum, and get overconfident. But then, they come back stronger than before to end up maybe winning the match. Not trying or pretending to not be trying, could be considered gamesmanship to a point, but it is real, and it is part of Tennis. It is not over until it is over... Always keep in mind that we cannot lose focus on a Tennis court!

The meaning of losing is an important part of development. We have to be prepared mentally, emotionally and spiritually to deal with it. Defeat is not a question of if but of when. We can see it coming, and we need to do all we can to receive it and take with us the good and leave the bad in the past. Here is what Michael Jordan, the famous professional basketball player, said about losing: *"I've missed more than 9000 shots in my career. I've lost almost 300 games. 26 times, I've been trusted to take the game-winning shot and missed. I've failed over and over and over again in my life. And that is why I succeed."*

Lost matches require evaluation by players, coaches, family, and friends. It is important for a parent, coach or friend to realize that the timing for talking to the player needs to be appropriate. Most of the time, it is difficult to approach the player right after the match is done, he or she may not be very receptive to our input and critique. As the player gets off the court a firm handshake, high five or a good pat on the back followed by something like "Tough match" is all that is needed. Most of the time, I might add "Hey Robert, come talk to me when ready." And then, when the player comes back, go into detail with the player in order for him or her to fully understand what happened and learn from the experiences. It is a good idea to let the player do all the talking first if he or she is in the mood for doing so.

Losing is an opportunity to learn and move forward; that's all we can do, and that's all defeat needs to be. Every loss is an opportunity to improve. Tennis matches give us crystal clear ideas to improve. Tennis coaches need to watch players during matches to capture methods or points for improvement. A simple example of this follows: during his lessons and junior drills, Mike is focused and executes beautifully, but in tournaments he seems lethargic and flat losing matches he should be winning. He seems to get a lead often at the beginning of sets, but gets tight towards the end of each set and struggles to close the deal. In the process, he loses confidence and momentum and sometimes ends up losing the match to the lesser opponent. To the observing coach, it is obvious Mike is getting ahead of himself by looking at the end of the match and not the next point. Mike obviously needs help mentally, so he develops the ability to focus as the match goes on, and he starts getting a good lead. Mike needs to be a better forerunner by continuing to go for his shots, staying with the strategy that got him the lead to begin with.

I have always tried to explain to parents when we go to tournaments that the single most valuable thing they can get from me at a tournament is some solid supervision of their children's during matches. Not the warm up or even the coaching. By supervising I can pinpoint with precision what we will need to work on for the next few weeks if not months with a player.

SCOUTING

Before getting into scouting, let's explain what it is. We are not talking about the boy scouts or anything like that. Scouting in competitive Tennis refers to studying the opposition for future matches. Taking opportunities that present themselves in every Tournament to watch a specific player either practice for 15 minutes or play a few games in a previous or earlier round pays big dividends.Taking notes about this player's game, strengths, and weaknesses, on court tempo, etc… Then when the time comes to play against this player, as coaches we may talk to our students and discuss the strategy and tactics to follow. By doing this pre-match scouting, my player does not have to start from scratch, and he or she will be better equipped mentally and tactically to deal with what is coming his or her way.

Scouting is an overlooked area in competitive Tennis, especially in junior Tennis. I don't mean scouting in the sense of recruiting, but as coaches and/or players we should be observing or studying potential opponents when they are playing or practicing. Scouting will be better done by taking notes (preferably real, written notes, not mental ones). Keep a notebook or players log with names, dates, and observations/comments of the players scouted. Keep this at hand as a coach or as a player at all times. Oftentimes scouting will be the difference between life and death. Another thing about the little notebook is that we actually can build on previous scouting observations by adding to the same player we had already scouted. Observe players change from season to season. Techniques or strategies a player was not able to do three months ago, he or she is now capable of doing; this is more so in juniors than in college or professional Tennis. It is pretty common that a player encounters the same player over and again. Each time he/she plays against this opponent, he/she adds to the scouting notebook.

For me, a hard cover 3 by 6 inches notebook is good. I can throw it in my pocket or racquet bag, and it is handy at all times. I wrap a couple of thick rubber bands around it to keep it closed with one or two pens or pencils inside it, there it is, all ready to be utilized. Some of the books I used in the past, I went ahead and numbered the pages. And on the back pages, I write sort of an Index with the names of the players indicating where there is information about them. It is funny, how a lot of people have commented on the little notebook over the years. "So, what all is this writing about?". Or "It is very impressive always see a coach taking notes". Also, "We want that level of coaching for us, we don't see anyone else taking notes", "I love notes, keep them coming". A well-known junior coach once said to me: "What is this note-taking all the time? Just remember and store everything in here?" as he pointed towards his own head! I replied: "Yes, but I trust the written notes a lot more," as one of my players was hammering down one of his!

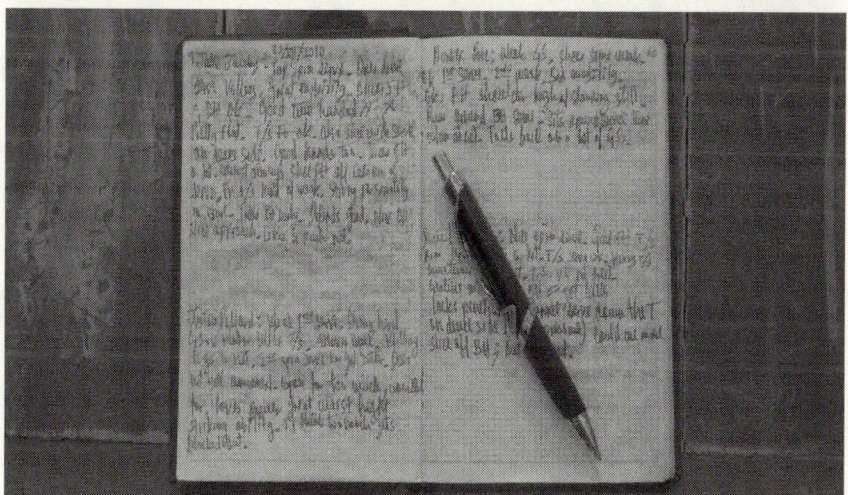

Fig 22)Two pictures of my Tennis journal. Top picture show journal with a couple rubber bands and a good pen, which are convenient to keep Journal shut and pen handy as needed. In bottom picture, you can see paragraphs with detail about four different players that were scouted on the date noted on top of left side page.

Going into detail even further, if we know in advance what a player is dealing with, we can write a pretty detailed description of the player on a small piece of paper; along with sound strategy and advice. My player can have it in his/her racquet bag or pocket and read it if needed while they are playing.

Improper scouting can result in ill advice to a player and result in unnecessary losses. Players and/or parents with some degree of knowledge can be sort of trusted, just be careful and pay attention as to where the scouting is coming from. A player, especially a junior, should learn and be encouraged to scout his or her opponents. Coaches should have their students sitting along the side of a court and make observations and notes on players. They need to see us do it, so we can teach them as their coach. They need to sense the importance of it; this is part of a coach's mentoring job.

GETTING READY FOR MATCHES

Last year I came up with what I thought was a great idea. To take notes on as many decent players as I could during tournament supervision. Transcribe and edit the notes onto a document, and keep them updated on my website on the Internet for all my junior players to use as reference. It has worked to a certain extent. Not all my juniors consult the document, and also it is an immense amount of work to keep updated. To this date, I have over 300 names with notes on detail about their games, strengths, and weaknesses. When looking at this information, players have to look at the date it was logged; because some of it could be outdated and useless.

The point to make here is that Tennis players don't go all the way to try to get ready for their matches. Some of the most important things competitive Tennis players should do are hydrate, eat right, sleep in sufficient amounts in a well-established routine, take time to warm-up well before matches. And, of course, get mentally ready for a match by coming up with a solid strategy before stepping out on court. One thing that I hardly ever see a student do is scout his or her opponent. A lot of my students ask me what they need to do against such and such players. If I know the player well, I tell them. But if I don't, I try to make the player understand that he or she needs to stay within their boundaries. And they have to come up with their own strategy, as well as apply what they are learning from each and every point played in a mindful manner. Simple things to remember; are to not go for silly shots that will most likely be errors, stick to our boundaries and playing style, go for it when clear opportunities present themselves, observe what our opponent does that hurts us, and what we do; hurts him or her. Counter his or her tendencies or favorite shots by anticipating, establish our own on-court tempo or rhythm, and so on and so forth.

Players should build a strategy by paying attention to an opponent's strengths, weaknesses, tendencies, as well as things they can do to win more points. How we counter these strengths and how we exploit a player's weaknesses and at the same time think of how we can apply our strengths and weapons more effectively.

A warm-up to get ready for matchplay should include all the following ingridients: A light three minute run, a few minutes of light stretching, a couple of minutes of soft hitting from the service line, up close to the net volleys for a good 5 minutes, baseline groundstrokes for at least 10 minutes; including crosscourt and down the line hitting, one up one back volleys/groundstrokes 5 minutes each player, 2 minutes for overheads and lobs, as well as up to 15 minutes for serves and returns with some point play combined. An all around warm-up routine, like the one described above, should be followed by a more in-depth 10-15 minute stretching routine.

A solid warm-up like the one described above should last from 30 minutes to an hour give and take a few minutes. It is sort of a luxury, but a player owes it to him/ herself to do it when possible or needed, so he or she has a better chance to perform at the top of his/her ability during the match. The presence of a coach in warm-up is good but not an absolute must. A player ought to be motivated enough to do all of these things on his/her own; a coach becomes a lot more important in earlier developmental stages. This routine should not result in a fatigued player. If the fitness factor is an issue for a player and playing conditions are tough, it is probably smart to keep the warm up short. A player should take a good 15 minutes after a nice warm up like this before getting on the court for the match. Make sure to drink plenty during and after warm up and replenish the carbohydrates spent by eating something within 30 minutes after getting off the court from warm up.

Getting ready for matches has to be taken seriously. Players that do everything under their control to be as ready as possible will win more matches, guaranteed! Change grips and check strings and all other equipment, caps, sunscreen, shoes, etc... Make sure to have all equipment handy in the racquet bag. Also, eat, drink, sleep, warm-up, stretch, write strategy, scout, etc... Our chances of being successful on court increase dramatically if we do all our prep work!

Tournament Match Checklist:

- ➢ -Sleeping
- ➢ -Hydration
- ➢ -Eating
- ➢ -Scout opponent

WHAT TENNIS PROS DON'T TEACH (WTPDT)

- ➤ -Game plans A and B
- ➤ -Speak to Coach
- ➤ -Visualization
- ➤ -Relaxation
- ➤ -Warm up
- ➤ -Stretching
- ➤ -Grips and equipment
- ➤ -Sunscreen
- ➤ -Cooler, water jug, ice
- -Etc…

Obviously a player may or may not be able to do all the stuff mentioned in this list, but needs to try to be as ready as possible before getting on the court.

TRANSITIONING

In Tennis, players have to think about transitioning from one level to the next, for example, from juniors to College Tennis play.

Transitioning is not well understood. It is not as simple as saying "Okay, this player is at the top of the World in Junior Tennis, therefore, he/she must be ready for the big leagues of professional Tennis." Or "He has won all the tournaments he or she has played in 10 and under, it is time for him or her to move up to 12s."

Parents and junior players are always looking for the next challenge but lose sight of many other factors before transitioning. We need to ask ourselves some questions: Is he or she physically and mentally ready? Will he or she be able to handle the beating that comes from pursuing tougher competition? Do we understand what we are trying to do? Who is pushing the transition? The Coach, the parents? Or is it the player? A lot of times, it is the player who wants to transition, because he or she is feeling the heat at the lower level. And by moving up, he or she is able to veer around this pressure, and play at a level where he or she is not expected to win many matches. Of course, ducking the proper competition level, would be the wrong reason for moving up. "Take the bull by the horns."

My personal formula goes something like this: If a player can win two back to back tournaments, then he or she is ready for the next level. And if he or she loses two first rounds, he or she should be dropping down a level. All others should remain where they are.

Now that we understand transitioning a little better let's talk about 10 and under and moving up to 12 and under.

Moving from 10s to 12s is a pretty big jump. Kids will be subjected not only to different and tougher competition, but to different rules, equipment, and playing conditions. As a junior player continues to improve, and right about the time they turn 9 and on their way to 10 they will be playing a lot better if they started at ages 6 or 7. These kids will already have some good experience in competition under their belts and, for the most part, will be getting ready for bigger and tougher opposition. This transition should be made as smooth as possible. At age 8 years old, juniors that started pretty early, need to start experimenting with the regular yellow balls in drills, lessons and games about 20-50% of the time. This way they start developing a taste and familiarity with the faster, heavier, bouncier ball, as well as the bigger dimensions of the court. By age 9, they pretty much should be doing most if not all of their hitting and playing with the regular balls. They have to start hitting with the 26 or 27 inch light racquet as early as 8.5 to 9.5 years old. By the time they enter the first few regular 12 and under events, they will be well on their way to adaptation to the bigger court, faster and heavier balls and bigger and heavier racquets. The key to it all is to start the change early to make the transition in a gradual and subtle way. Based on physical and technical development, different kids will be different in how early they transition. Some of them may start as early as 7-years-old. Not so much because they need to start playing in the 12s, as much as because they had been practicing with a group of kids who were one or two years older. And suddenly his or her whole group moves up to standard equipment, and balls and this 7-year-old might have been left behind. As coaches we cannot allow this to happen, at this point we need to be careful to not force the 7-year-old into the 12s. Commitment to the 10 and under tournaments and equipment should maybe be encouraged. This 7-year-old just had an early start on his/her transitioning.

Keep the child involved in cross training activities such as soccer, basketball, karate, etc... in order to continue to develop the athlete in him or her.

Transitions can be very complicated. Every individual case is a little different from the previous one. Coaches need to pay close attention to detail, and help parents understand what is going on in order to tailor the right balance. Tournament schedule, practice schedule, percentages of regular VS shorter court balls exposure for the player in question.

Transitioning in the 12s, 14s, 16s, and 18s as well as other transitions is not going to be as rough as the transition from 10s to 12s. However, coaches and parents need to be on board as to when to do it. Let me, at this point, go out on a limb and say that we do need to get started as early as possible on all transitions. By starting a player transitioning early, he or she will have more time and a better chance to be successful. Here are some examples of how to start a transition:

TRANSITIONING FROM 10s TO 12s

- Do at least 1 out of every 3 lessons with regular balls.
- Twice a month, do some ball machine or wall hitting with the regular balls.
- Make sure the player is not trying to get off the hook from playing 10 and under. When he or she is not ready for the 12s and is just trying to reduce the pressure, he or she may be feeling,
- Coaches need to be sure it is not the parents looking to make the change in an attempt to make the kid move faster through the ranks. Skipping divisions attempting to make a player develop quicker than his or her normal pace will have a reverse effect and make players move slower. We are not racing here, rather attempting to get to a final destination; a fully developed player.
- Get the 10 and under junior hitting some regular balls at least once per week with 12 and under players.
- Apply the formula: If a player wins two in a row back to back, then move up. If he/she loses two first rounds in a row, then move down. All others stay the same.
- Make sure the commitment from the player is in place for more time and effort put to Tennis; this applies only if the player is still going all out.
- Players need to be prepared and eager to increasing the number of hours devoted to Tennis. On and off the court, at this point, to about 10 to 20 per week. Depending where they are in the Tennis season, motivation level, and tournament schedule.
- When a player is pretty developed technically, he or she needs to make the move up to the regular ball and court permanently not looking back to the transition equipment anymore. Be extremely selective on tournaments at this point. This holds true even if the player in question is only 8 or 9 years of age! Keeping them training and playing with the transition equipment will severely slow down or hamper their chances development.

TRANSITIONING FROM 12s TO 14s

- Players are starting to play the game more the way they will be playing the rest of their Tennis careers.

- Playing style has been identified and is being pursued at this point.
- Further development of all strokes and techniques need to be clearly identified.
- Tactically and strategically, the player needs to know and understand game plans and playing styles in a much more comprehensive way as well as the mental implications and demands for successful Tennis.
- Players need to know how to use and expose strengths and work around weakness during matches.
- A more rigorous and detailed fitness regimen for Tennis needs to start at this point. Players entering early puberty will require that a pretty serious fitness training regimen be in place.
- Again, make sure the player is ready mentally, physically, and technically to make this transition; players and not parents, are the ones wanting to move forward to the next level.
- Number of hours devoted to Tennis on and off the court at this point should increase to 12 to 20 per week depending where the player is in the Tennis Season, level of motivation and tournament schedule.

TRANSITIONING FROM 14s TO 16s

- As juniors move up into the 16s, they will now be dealing with players that are a lot more developed as Tennis players as well as mentally. Especially girls since a lot of them have the tendency to mature and develop physically faster than boys.
- Make sure players transitioning at this point are ready physically through a well designed fitness program because at this level the physicality of the game increases dramatically. Now players will need more power, exert a lot more effort and energy to execute their game. The ball will be hit a lot harder, and points and matches will be longer.
- In the 16s, juniors and aspiring pros should be fully be enthralled and used to a personalized, well-defined fitness regimen.
- Every player should be in ownership of a weapon or two in their game or at least in the advanced stages of weapon development.
- At this point, the level of commitment should be clearly defined, time management needs to be really fine tuned, and the best of it should be made in practices and tournaments.

- A player may be looking into either college Tennis or if the resources and the right conditions are in place, may even consider taking a shot at professional Tennis. A word of caution is in place here. It is very important that the player and nobody else is wanting to go for either college Tennis or Professional Tennis at this point.
- Increase the number of hours devoted to Tennis on and off the court to an average of 15-25 depending on the time of the year and where players are in the Tennis season.
- Let me say again that it is possible professional help may be needed in time management for a player at this stage. He or she may be driving a car already, and they pretty much set their own schedule. As coaches and parents, we need to make sure he or she is making wise decisions about managing time.

Note: Keep in mind that regardless of what the player decides to do with his/her Tennis at this point, it is of foremost importance that he or she continues with his/her schooling and study responsibilities.

TRANSITIONING FROM THE 16s INTO THE 18s

- At this point it is not easy to keep the fire burning; full motivation needs to be in place more so than ever before. It is crunch time, and juniors at this point have been going for it for pretty long, some of them up to 10 or even 14 years!
- Tennis at this point is definitely a big part of a player's life. Some players might be betting everything on Tennis. Therefore, coaches, parents and all involved need to be fully supportive.
- Our formula still applies in that players have to win two back to back tourneys to move up or if they lose to back to back first rounds they move down.
- Players still are very much continuing to polish strokes and learning how to be more effective.
- The right match point/drilling/hitting/fitness/social/school/tournaments, etc… balance needs to be fully in place, at this point, time management needs to be carefully monitored. We need to make sure players are not wasting too much of their time socializing, be it on the phone or in person or maybe killing valuable time with electronics and other useless time absorbers. At this point, it is

extremely important that a player understands the sacrifice he/she is making socially; to have enough time to do everything else he/she needs to be doing in order to achieve the desired goals on the Tennis court.
- When making this transition, players are at a big crossroads. Junior Tennis is going to be over soon if not yet. And they have to commit fully to either going for college Tennis or maybe some of them may want to give professional Tennis a shot (give it a real shot though, not setting players for failure)
- Some players may have the vision of trying pro-Tennis after they are done with college Tennis, and this is very respectable and probably a good idea for a lot of juniors.

FROM JUNIOR TENNIS TO COLLEGE TENNIS

- This is a win-win situation. If going for college Tennis, there is a good chance a player can land some scholarship money. College Tennis is a good reward for the diligent and persistent junior.
- If a player is going for college Tennis, once he/she is committed to a school, he or she has to continue to work on his/her game. Oftentimes, players that landed a nice scholarship at some school get lazy and complacent. A college Tennis player owes it to his/her school to try to continue to excel at what is being done for him/her. Players have to keep working on their game and keep playing some tournaments, etc...
- School comes first and foremost for the college player, obviously. This does not mean a player can forget about training and continuing to polish his/her game,
- If in pursuit of a solid college coach, a player has to either look for a school that has the right coach. One that has a proven record of improving players in the four-year period. Or he/she has to go to a school that is in a town where some extra coaching can be contacted on the side. Unfortunately, a lot of college coaches place too much emphasis on winning and not enough on what's best for players. Of course, they want their players to make their grades because if they don't, that creates problems for all involved.
- If a player does decide to play college Tennis at the end of his/her senior year, he/she should be a much better player than he/she was

in his/her freshman year. Unfortunately, this is not always the case. I know of one too many cases where former players of mine went for college Tennis playing great and extremely motivated. At the end of four years, the players were no longer fit, the confidence and motivation were no longer there, and sometimes playing way worse than they did when they were 18 years old or so! It's sad, and this tells a story.

- If a player enters a college program with the proper guidance, they will graduate with a college degree, improved skills, and amazing stories to tell about their experience. An example of that, would be a player looking to continue to play Tennis, participate in tournaments, continue to practice, pass down his/her experiences about traveling with the college Tennis team, and some of the battles he/she endured during these years, as well as some friendships made that will last a lifetime.
- One of my own personal accomplishments in Tennis, and one that I don't brag too much about, once I was done with highs school, is that my family did not have to pay a dime for my education, my sustenance, or any of my Tennis expenses! This in itself is a very solid and achievable goal for a committed junior player, and a goal your whole family will fully respect and appreciate.

THE ULTIMATE CHALLENGE, GOING FOR THE PROS

Whether players are going for the pros right off the junior Tennis ranks or after they are done playing college Tennis, this is going to be the ultimate challenge for them as well as their families and coaches.

- Whether successful or unsuccessful in going for the pros, the benefits, in either case, can be astonishingly positive. The experiences on and off court, the traveling, and the huge commitment and discipline that come as a result of this endeavor are great.
- Players need to make sure they are ready mentally, physically, emotionally, financially and even spiritually to pursue professional Tennis. Obviously, taking this step, as in all other transitions, is the player's call, or so it should be anyway.

- In order to make sure players are ready for this, they, of course, want to get the opinion of their coach and for sure their family as well.
- If a player has had some solid results in juniors, this could be a pretty good indicator that he or she can probably go for it. But let's define in simple terms what we mean by solid results. A) He/She has ranked top 50 in the US, he/she has a ranking in the top 5 in his/her section or region, and/or he or she is or has been top 100 in the ITF (These results would have to be from either the 16s or most preferably the 18s. B) A player has beat or played fairly close against junior players ranked that high or higher. C) A player entered some open tournaments and he/she played against excellent college players or former professionals with good results. D) Someone with the right background or credentials, either a former professional or top player or a well known college or junior coach, mentioned or talked to a junior player or his/her family or coach about the possibility or feasibility of professional Tennis. E) If a player is getting scholarship offers and invitations from some of the top college Tennis programs in the US, that is also a good indicator that he/she may have the potential of turning professional as well.

If a player has had some of the above results or better, and a coach, former player, or anybody for that matter dares to tell him or her to forget it, and that he or she has no chance of making it, whoever these individuals are, they most probably don't know what they are talking about. Please don't listen to them! A 17 or 18-year-old kid is very susceptible to non-authorized voices. These weird voices are trying to kill some player's aspirations and rob them of their dreams. Don't allow it! I unfortunately was a subject of such bad influences. Back in the Guadalajara Club, some recreational Tennis players who were always there spoke as if they were knowledgeable, based on the fact that they had played Tennis for so long. But they were just avid okay Tennis players at best. Only because I was not winning professional tournaments at age 16, or was ranked No. 1 in the nation in the juniors, they would say stuff to me like, "Manuel, the train has already departed for you." Or "Manuel, look at such and such, they are going to make it, you're already too old and it's too late for you now." Or would go on with something like this "Manuel, just go to work and focus on your studies." As a self-taught junior without a coach, words like these resonated in my head from the time I was 16-years-old, all the way until after I was done with college Tennis. It is hard for me to explain why I listened, or why this happened to me. But it did impact me negatively in the worst possible way and made me lose motivation and drive. Now I know for sure that these voices or bad influences were completely wrong, that it is possible to make it if the right motivation, work ethic and the right set of circumstances are in place. If, for some reason, these circumstances are not there, then we have to think and come up with solutions or substitutions. Tennis is a very complicated puzzle, and a little at the time, a player can create the right set of circumstances and environments he/she needs to keep moving forward with his/her development.

In order to have a realistic chance to make it in the pros, there are four must ingredients. a) The passion, desire and drive from the player to go all the way, to continue to sacrifice more as well as apply unbending determination to his or her endeavor. The player needs to understand now that his/her approach to everything he/she does, has to be done in a professional and business-like manner. And that he or she will spend even more time, and sacrifice more things, to pursue this dream. b) The player's coach has to have the capacity and confidence to take him or her to that level, good indicators would be, 1) The coach has done this before with other players, 2) The coach wants to go for this, on the understanding that he or she is motivated and willing to travel to some far places, and is very enthusiastic about the idea, 3) The coach definitely has the knowledge and understanding to undertake this huge project, 4) The family is supportive and on board 100%, 5) Financial support must also be available if the family cannot afford this venture, a player must look for help. A player's coach, parents or family friends may be able to help. Sponsoring money is also possible to land. Some Tennis organizations have grant money for well presented and potentially feasible cases. Ask, look around, do some research. Everybody has to get involved in this process if need be. I might get chewed up for this one, but I would go as far as to say that a loan would not be a bad idea at this point. High school graduates get student loans to go to college, why not aspiring professional Tennis players? What the aspiring player will learn as well as the experiences in a three or four-year project will be at least as useful as a college degree anyway. A promising junior player without travel and coaching money is probably going to end up as another wasted talent due to lack of funding! At this point, I must add that the exception confirms the rule in all mentioned above. There have been professional players who did not follow the sequences mentioned above and developed under very different circumstances.

- Players in similar developmental circumstances can share costs. If two or even three or four players are ready to go for it, they can share the costs of coaching, hotels, car rentals, etc… Also this way, a player can set up his or her own practices and training sessions when on the road or at home, furthermore everyone helps everyone else scout as well as doing additional coaching. Players need to have some sort of code similar to the one presented elsewhere in this book.
- Be careful signing a contract with a coach, an academy, or a sponsor. Make sure to have this contract reviewed by a reputable lawyer. A contract is typically written in the best interest of the coach or academy. They are looking for financial security and want no competition in the matter. What happens if the coaching or academy is not working out for the player? A way out of this contract has to be part of one of the clauses if the results or goals are not being met. If starting with a new coach or Academy, a contract should not even be discussed the first 6 months of training. If the relationship between player and coach/academy is working out fine, then a contractual agreement is probably in order.
- Don't get discouraged. There is going to be a lot of losing for a while. A player has to learn to compete at this higher level, and it takes at least one full year, and as much as four years of some tough battles, psychologically the whole team needs to work together here.
- Put it all in writing. A written game plan with goals and much more information in the following areas is a good idea:

   a) Performance goals
   b) Result goals
   c) Budgeting, financial support via sponsors and/or family or other sources,
   d) Tournament and traveling schedule,

e) Training on and off the Tennis court regimen, short, medium, long-term,
f) Periodization applied to fitness training and on-court training as well as routines,
g) Vacation and cross training,
h) Create a vision and a mission that blends or is part of the whole developmental plan.

Writing it all is a good idea, so players know exactly where they are going, how they are going to do it, etc… This material will often be revised, at least every six months. But changes should be made in conjunction with the entire team.

Again, it's going to get rough and tough before it gets better. Be prepared mentally, physically, emotionally and spiritually.

Good luck and enjoy the ride!

CONFIDENCE... WHERE DO WE GET IT? WHAT IS IT?

Confidence is a non-tangible quality a player radiates on the Tennis court. It is the certainty players feel that they have what it takes to win matches and tournaments, and believing that positive results will come from their efforts.

There is no substitute for confidence. A confident player will win a lot more matches on average. Confidence comes from different sources: practice, winning, fitness, solid coaching, and mental toughness. Others making a difference for players in the confidence department are obviously family, friends and other players (Remember the anonymous quote: "If he/she did it, I can do it"). How much confidence is derived from this or that varies from player to player.

As coaches, we need to focus on the different sources of confidence. More emphasis may need to be placed on one specific way to build confidence depending on the different issues different players are having. A player that is not winning enough matches needs to boost his confidence by stepping down in competition level to where he or she can win about 60% of the time. If a player is losing because he or she is running out of steam, or out of lack of mobility and proper footwork, the moment that player gets fitter and quicker about the court, he or she will start winning more. Also, players who are super fit, project confidence and intimidate as soon as they step on the court. Fit players will give it 120% from start to finish, they are constantly sending a very strong message to their opponents; a message of confidence, energy, and power. These player are not going away; they will fight extremely hard from beginning to end!

Mental toughness training gives players faith and boosts belief in self; it impacts players' confidence in trained thought processes to follow certain rules or routines. Mental toughness training helps players harness emotions and thoughts which in turn help their confidence and keeps them focused. Finally, let me add that hitting thousands of balls every day, is eventually going to pay off in bigger wins and better results. Hitting a lot of balls will increase confidence greatly because of the immediate impact of improvement.

Another important concept in sports, is training or practicing to act as if we were confident; this is extremely effective in Tennis. Even if we don't feel confident, we need to act as if we were. If players act weak mentally and physically, their opponent and the rest of the World know it. Tennis players need to act as if they are under control. They need to make everyone out there believe they are good players, even if they don't truly believe it! A Tennis player needs to act as if he/she was No. 1 in the World. It is very easy to tell when a player is not confident. Unconfident players openly display anger. They relieve or release energy by smacking a ball towards the fence or violently smashing or tossing their racquets on the ground. They scream negatively out of control. They exhibit signs of lack of intensity and energy. They whine and complain about all kinds of things. Their body posture gives them away: how a player walks or his or her posture on court reflects what's happening in the head. Something is not right if a player is dragging his/her feet or persistently walks around the court with his/her head down looking at the ground in a negatively and defeated posture.

In many instances, losing is the consequence of not being able to get our mind to function in an efficient and effective way. Trying to instill these ideas into juniors will gather weird looks. Most junior players don't ever think about poise or demeanor. I might say something like: "As players, we have the option of listening or not; however, be forewarned, that the consequence of not listening is losing! Listening is up to the player… and then I may go on and add: "Does anyone like losing or wants to lose tough matches?"

Go out there looking like a million dollars. Players have to walk the court like they own it and pretend they are in full control at all times. There's a certain magic to acting as if we were winning, even if we are losing. Often confidence comes from the outside towards the inside. We act it, and then we magically start feeling it! It's magic!

It is also important to mention that a junior player needs to be smart about picking his or her friends and people with whom he or she is hanging out. These other kids will impact personality and confidence. As an up and coming junior player, it is probably better to have only one or two real friends. Real friends should be supportive and helpful all the time

WHAT TENNIS PROS DON'T TEACH (WTPDT)

unconditionally. Having a few well-selected friends is better than to be the most popular kid, but half of our so-called friends are either envious or will try to do something to hurt us or taunt us... This will undermine confidence and concentration. Friends should be picked with great care.

MATCHPLAY AND PERFORMING UNDER PRESSURE

Tennis players need to learn how to play under pressure. Why pressure? Because we place too much emphasis on what will happen if we win or lose. We get ahead of ourselves by putting too much emphasis on the outcome. Comments like these are heard during tournaments and show how different players feel pressure from a variety of sources: "What will such and such say?" "My ranking will not improve if I lose this match." "I am letting my team down if I lose." Or "my dad/mom will be really upset if I don't win this one." Comments from parents and coaches are also sources of pressure. Such as: "We have never lost to such and such player" and the list goes on!

Another very common situation happens when a player has a look at his or her draw for a tournament and makes inappropriate predictions about outcomes. Such as "First round should be no problem, second round, I beat him two years ago, third round I get a seeded player; we'll see." Another player may look at the draw, and tell some of his or her friends how they should be able to get to the semis pretty easily. And win his/her first three matches without too much difficulty, and so on and so forth.

Are we getting the picture? This player is getting ahead of his/her time and others' time, and placing needless pressure upon himself or herself as well as others. This player is obviously overconfident and will very likely lose earlier than he or she is anticipating!

Let's start by stating that all pressure in a Tennis court is self-imposed. Tennis is still a game, not a life and death situation. To my knowledge, nobody has got killed yet because they lost a Tennis match. So, how do we deal with all this pressure? Is the fear of losing as bad as the fear of death? I guess it should not be, but in some instances it almost is. All serious Tennis players need to learn how to cope with pressure and how to minimize, eliminate, or use it to their advantage. It is a hard thing to do because of the pressure of expectations.

WHAT TENNIS PROS DON'T TEACH (WTPDT)

Focusing on performance and not the outcome will help a player dissipate pressure. In fact, failure to do so inhibits performance, and a player will not be able to have the results he or she wants. Why? Because he or she is thinking about the outcome and the player's concentration is on the result of the match, so how can one perform? Focus on things directly under our control, the outcome of a match is not. Let me say it again; concentrate on doing the right things all the time. Detaching ourselves from the potential result of the match is of utmost importance, to being able to perform well under pressure. Allowing our game to surface naturally and beautifully and to playing free, happy, hopefully allowing ourselves getting in the zone. Understand the zone as an ideal state of mind/body working in perfect harmony.

So, what is the right thing to do? Let's make a list, placing all our efforts on things directly under our control:

a) Managing the in between point time (reaction, relaxation/recovery/breathing control, concentration, rituals, visualization)
b) Sticking to our strategy and playing within our boundaries
c) Drinking water on changeovers
d) Sitting down on changeovers staying within our tempo or pace
e) Going for the right aggressive shots when in good position and having an open court
f) Playing defensive when the opponent is attacking
g) Give credit to our opponent when he/she hit a great shot. Remember we do this for our opponent as much as we do it for ourselves in order to stay positive.
h) Always project confidence
i) Control negative emotions and concentrate on the next point
j) Off the court stuff like making sure we sleep enough, eat right, do our fitness training as prescribed by our coaches, hit the warm-up courts with sufficient time, and do our daily stretches

There are other things under our direct control not mentioned here, but this illustrates the point well enough. A player has to have fun all the time, he or she needs to be enjoying the whole process. In fact, if a player does not love every step of the way, he or she will eventually quit Tennis. Why would anyone want to do something they don't love to do? That is a tough question to pose at this point, but in reality it speaks volumes of what humans are made of. Think of it this way; we only do things we don't love doing because of others' needs or others' demands! And if we do something we don't enjoy doing it's because of our own demands, and we are in reality on death row!

Failure to follow these instructions will result in lots of frustrations, lost matches, and possibly quitting the game. Tennis should be fun. Loving every minute of it needs to be in place before anything worthy of mention is accomplished. So, go wander what ingredients are needed to make it a love affair, a lifetime commitment, something a Tennis player can count on looking forward to every day no matter what!

Pressure can be destructive, but no matter what we do as players we are going to feel it. One thing is for sure, whether on the Tennis court or at work or with family or just friendships, we will feel this pressures coming from all sources.

However, pressure can also be viewed as a good thing, without it, we cannot evolve or learn. As humans we need this pressure to grow; we need pressure to develop in all endeavors. From the moment we are born; we are subjected to pressure. Pressure to be born! The thing that is hard to figure out is how much pressure to apply before breaking something or for that matter someone! When subjected to more pressure than capable of handling, stuff breaks. Cars, for instance, need an oil change every so often, children need breaks, and professionals need to take vacations. These maintenance pit stops; vacations and breaks have to be administered smartly. Too many breaks and vacations lead to weakening. Think of it as a muscle we are trying to make stronger. We subject it to weight resistance over and over. At some point we need to rest it, or we'll injure it, and then if we don't work it enough it will not stay strong, it will go weak again! Such is the mind as well, just like a muscle. That is part of the reason sports science has come up with so many complicated techniques, theories, and systems to apply to athletic performance.

Emotional and physical stress needs to be administered increasingly, building it up a little at the time to the point where we finally get to our desired goal. To sustain that goal, we still need to continue to apply pressure. As an athlete, a father or mother or as a child developing, learn to know when it is time for a break. Pushing the right amount a little at the time until we become so strong mentally, physically and spiritually we can deal with just about anything that is thrown at us.

Playing poorly and having a bad day will happen in Tennis as in any other sports. Having bad days is part of everyday life. All players have bad days, and all players have great days! Even the best of the best can have several bad or off days during a season; where it is very difficult for them to win. How we deal with these bad days is what marks the difference between greatness and just average. Good players will figure out ways to win matches on days when they are not hitting the ball at their best, or moving their best, or even thinking clearly or at their best. We need to be mentally prepared to have a bad day every time we get on the court! By being prepared mentally and physically for poor performances, we are not being negative; we are just realistic! At this point, a John McEnroe quote comes to mind that went something like this as some media person asked him "Why are you always so negative?" McEnroe said, "I am not being negative, I am just realistic." Bad days can result from bad timing, poor footwork on days when a player cannot get his/her energy flowing or is too nervous to let it surface, or negative thinking. Pressure will aggravate all these.

A true competitor will dig deep under these circumstances to get out of trouble and figure out ways to move forward. Far too many times, have I heard students and players from all different levels say, that their goals for such and such matches or tournaments is to play well and to win. These players are just imposing tremendous added pressure upon themselves. We have to understand that playing good and winning comes from above, and it is something not under our direct control and we need to tackle this situation with what tools we have at hand. These tools are everything we know how to do on a Tennis court; our number one tool here is our brain, so we have to use it as much as we can. Apply all our knowledge, all technical, tactical and spiritual tools when on bad days. And yes, we need to believe firmly and have faith that we can do it even if things are not going the way we want them! When having a rough time out there dig, dig and dig! Utilizing everything we have learned we may find the key to the puzzle. Again quoting John McEnroe's famous line: "There is always a way to win." Or the hammered old saying "When the going gets tough, the tough get going." Some of this stuff may sound repetitious to the reader but believe me, we need to sit down and really think about it a lot, in order to fully comprehend it.

Making mistakes, and losing is part of the learning process. It is okay to lose matches, to make mistakes, to go down sometimes. As long as we can get back up and go at it again and again, striving for a slightly higher goal each and every time!

HOW MUCH IS TOO MUCH?

This is a difficult question to answer because every player is different. It is true that if we play a lot of tournaments, we get match-tough and perform better at them. At the same time, we need to be careful of burnout. Watch for signs of burnout all the time as explained earlier in this book. We need to be at the maximum matchplay allowed by a player without crossing this invisible barrier; we just have to go with our gut instinct on where this barrier is. For a 12-year-old it may be about 10 evenly spaced tournaments in a year, some can handle a lot more. Maybe a 15-year-old can play in 17 tournaments in one year. More is definitely not necessarily better. We need to find the right balance for the player, and this is usually pretty obvious. If a player is not fully excited about a tournament or seems tired, we better watch it. Observe the player in practice; is he giving it 100% emotionally, physically and spiritually? Or is he/she coasting? As coaches and parents, it is very important to look for all these signs very closely. Refer to the subsection on Burnout.

There are different ways to go at it; we may get started with some casual point play with a kid; this helps them understand shot selection and strategy. Play lots of friendly tiebreakers, or just play a bunch of points where we serve a ball and play the point out. Don't keep track of the score, when keeping track of the score everything changes and some children cannot handle it. Let them serve the ball to us and play the point paying attention to shot selection and basic tactical stuff such as positioning. Again, as soon as we start keeping track of the score if they are not winning with some consistency, they start getting upset and lose motivation by getting all frustrated. Do this non-scoring point play practice a lot, until they get better, and then, little by little, play some short games or sets. Again, play lots of 7 and 10-point tie breakers rather than full sets and matches. As kids get ready and understand better how to play points, we can start signing them up for some lower level tournaments and start playing full sets and matches for practice in a gradual manner! Every kid is different, so the right balance for each and every player needs to be met by the coach or the player himself. For the most part, parents may need to talk to the coaches in order to figure out whether a child is ready for tournament play or not.

DOUBLES! WHAT COULD BE MORE FUN IN TENNIS?

Doubles in Tennis is the fun part. Not to say that singles isn't fun, but in doubles there is a lot less pressure, and Tennis becomes a team sport.

In doubles, players communicate and share the whole Tennis experience with a partner. For the most part, they almost always get to choose their partners. The social aspect of doubles makes it very attractive to children, as well as adult players. Doubles partners can even wear matching uniforms.

23) These are JK and Anasazi going for a high five. These two girls were 10 years old when this picture was taken and have played in tournaments for a few years now. They just love it and seem to have so much fun together on the court. They fill with anticipation when they know they have been signed up for a doubles tournament. They practice together and have developed a friendship through Tennis that will last a lifetime.

WHAT TENNIS PROS DON'T TEACH (WTPDT)

There are several lessons to be learned from doubles that are harder or impossible to learn in singles. And there are several reasons for having juniors and any aspiring players practice a lot of doubles as a way to develop their game.

In doubles, players are exposed to net and transitional point play a lot more. For doubles players, it is mandatory to communicate with one another for strategy and encouragement.

The recommendation is to learn to serve and volley for more effective doubles at least for all the boys and for girls in the 14s division and up. A good spin serve, is conducive to good serving and volleying since the ball is in the air longer, allowing the serving player to reach the net in time to catch the ball out of the air, as he or she moves in towards it.

In doubles, a higher percentage of first serves is necessary. Players have to add more spin to the ball to reach this goal; 70% to 80% first serves is a desirable statistic in doubles play.

Accuracy is important when returning serve because less of the court is available due to the player at the net. In reality, players have more court because of the doubles alleys, but tactically it is less court since there are now two players on the court guarding it across the net. Returning serve in doubles has to be cross court the great majority of the time. If a player returns down the line, he or she needs to be accurate in that the ball has to be low, and fairly fast up the alley, when the opponent at the net is poaching a lot. Another interesting thing, about returning in doubles that makes sense, is to hit a lob off the return. Lobbing returns of serve hardly ever applies to singles. In fact, doubles will involve a lot more net play, and therefore lobs are important as part of a strategy.

Effective doubles play requires returning low. What is known as *chip and charging* is nothing other than slicing a return and rushing to the net behind it. It is a great strategy if the player has what it takes to execute it. Players need to be fairly proficient at slicing the ball for this strategy to be effective. If the opponent is serving and volleying, a player concentrates on chip-and-charging low, and if the server is staying back, then the returning player may need to chip and charge low, but also with some depth, or maybe wide to try to open the court, as he or she comes in for the volley.

If unsure about shot selection, hitting low down the middle is always a good idea regardless of the circumstances or situation.

Positioning in doubles gets confusing. The server gets to set himself out wider from the center mark as needed for the regular or traditional doubles formation. Positioning along the baseline should vary depending on how the returning player is dealing with the serve. The traditional formation is midway between the center mark and the doubles line for serving in doubles. But this should vary depending on strategy. I personally like to serve out wide near the doubles line since this gives me more court to shoot into. By doing this, I get to aim over a lower part of the net, and really opens up the court if I am able to get the ball pretty wide. Also, when serving from this position, it takes some adjusting from my opponents since for the most part everyone is used to dealing with servers taking positioning from inside the singles line somewhere. When serving in the traditional way, the net player should stand centered in the service box, not near the alley. The partner of the returning player should be one or two steps inside the service box and mid-way between the center service and singles line. Sometimes a player is recommended to be closer to the center to pressure the server and cover some more of the court in case the opposing net player poached and went down the middle.

All types of variations do happen from what is being explained above. When dealing with aggressive players with solid serves and volleys, a doubles team may have to play it more defensively when returning the first serve or even both serves by having both players stand back. Or maybe have the net player start at the net only if the server missed the first serve.

There are also variations in the traditional serving formation in doubles. The best-known formations are Australian formation and the military formation, also called the I formation. For the most part, these formations are used to neutralize the returning players' crosscourt returns. By utilizing these formations, players are virtually putting pressure on the opponents to go down the line with the returns. Generally, a player who is great at returning serve crosscourt will probably not be as good hitting down the line.

When serving in the Australian formation the server will position himself near the center mark, and his or her partner will be hunched down near the center service line on the same side as the server. For the military or I formation, the net player stands on top of the center service line. In both cases, the net player needs to be located about midway between service line and net.

One of the great things about these doubles formations is that players are forced to communicate and think through tactical stuff at the start of every point. The server needs to know in advance where his or her partner will be moving to at the net as soon as the serve is hit; this keeps the opposing team guessing where and how to return! Also, when serving, a player wants his/her partner at the net to know in advance what type of serve he or she will be going for. A lot of good doubles teams use hand signals. I personally don't care for them because I prefer just to talk and communicate verbally with my partner between every single point.

Remember, strategy is about neutralizing the opponent's strengths and maximizing our own!

See images below of different court formations and positioning options in doubles:

Fig. 24) Traditional doubles positioning when serving and returning players. Bottom of picture is the serving side.

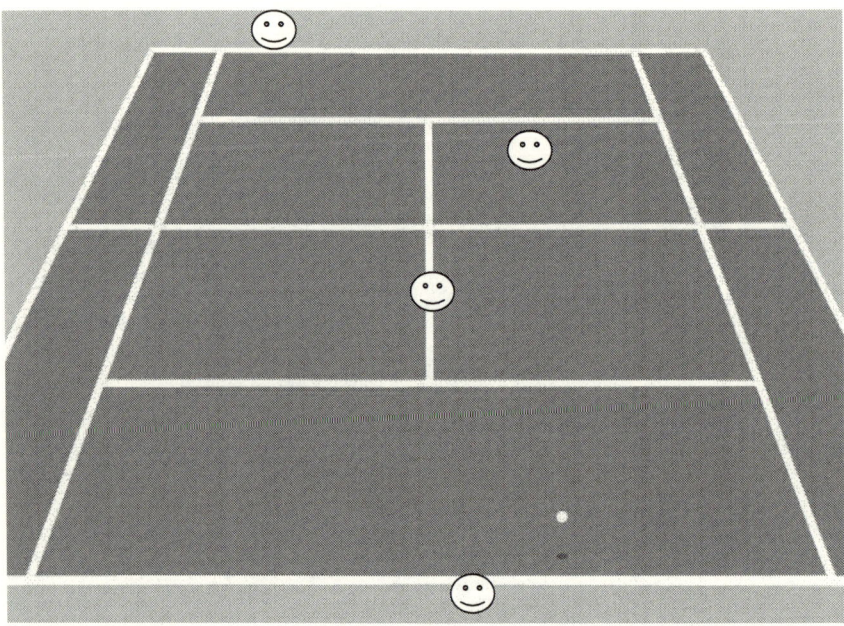

Fig. 25)Military or I formation. Here the serving team is virtually aligned one behind one another and the net player has to squat down really low to avoid getting hit by his serving partner.

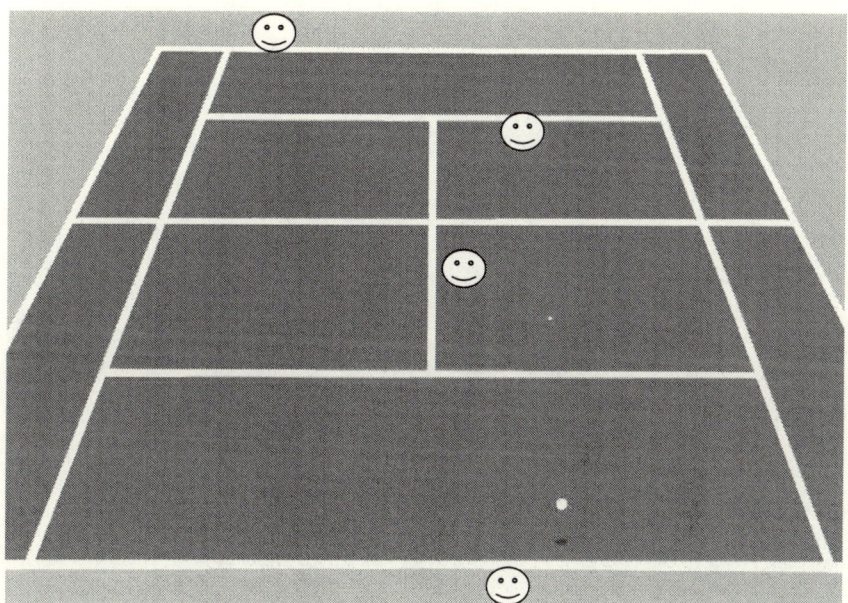

Fig. 26)Traditional Australian formation. Bottom of picture is the serving side. The Australian and Military formations force you to think and communicate with your partner before the start of every point; this can be achieved via hand signals or verbally; I personally recommend verbal communication.

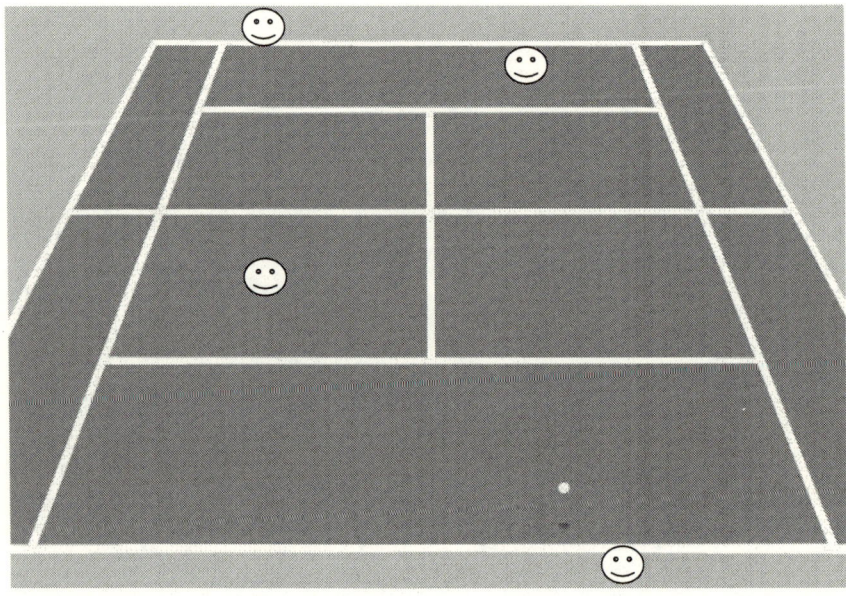
Fig. 27)Defensive returning formation. Player on bottom of picture is the server. Returning team is on top of picture

WHY NOT DOUBLES INSTEAD OF SINGLES? ARE WE MISSING THE BOAT?

Doubles in Tennis has been suffering a continuing decline in junior, college and professional Tennis over the last 20 years or so. It is a sad and bad thing for the sport at all levels. Tennis organizations around the World have gone from full matches back in the 70s and 80s to the well-known format of the 8 game pro set. This whole idea, of doing away with doubles a little at the time, is disappointing; especially when it comes to junior Tennis.

Several reasons for giving doubles the deserved importance come to mind. I often ask myself why Tennis organizations and federations have neglected these ideas. Here are a few:

1- If we put some thought into it; we come to the conclusion that about 95% of all the juniors today will be playing doubles in their 30s, 40s, 50s and beyond.
2- Doubles will develop a kid's game as a whole. Juniors will better understand transitional Tennis and especially the net game. Chances are; we would see a resurgence of the serve and volley game. An American Tradition and the emblem of almost all the great American players of the past; this trend has been lost in time and space. Part of the reason this style of play is out the window, has to be due, in part or as a whole, to the lack of intense doubles practice and competition in the early stages of players' development.
3- Understand and learn the importance of serving percentages, and the value of precision and accuracy over power in Tennis; finesse comes naturally in doubles, not so much in singles.
4- Burn out rate would be reduced. We need to emphasize doubles as being a lot more important than singles because in reality it truly is at the grassroots levels. A small example of this, was my daughter when she was beginning to play in a few tournaments, at

age 7, telling me she only wanted to play doubles because she made friends that way and got help from her partner!
5- When we see kids playing doubles they seem to be having a good time, we usually see them smiling, doing high fives, and loving it. We hardly ever see smiles in singles, and instead we see tears, temper tantrums and frustration, especially in the lower divisions.
6- Doubles will make our singles players better and develop more exciting Tennis for everyone to enjoy. Doubles yields better, more creative singles players and a potential resurrection of the all but lost serve and volley style that was so exciting and beautiful to watch and play.
7- Effective promotion would yield more doubles involvement. Simply said, if more importance is placed on doubles, more kids and parents would support this development. As a Tennis Professional, I've witnessed too much burnout throughout my years coaching Tennis. And if I could have told those kids only to play doubles with full support from parents, friends and Tennis organizations, these kids would still be playing today and eventually might have put more effort into singles.
8- More efficient utilization would come from time and space. Four players on one court playing a doubles match count twice as much as four players playing singles on two courts. Not only that; but singles matches tend to be longer than doubles matches.

Some alternatives to the problem of too much emphasis on singles play could be:

- Have 2 out of 3 set matches doubles tournaments in the 10s, 12s, and 14s, and reduce the singles to the 8 game pro sets. Or just add or substitute some of the traditional tournaments for doubles only tournaments. From the developmental point of view, this makes all the sense in the World. Players fully develop their game and have fun; everyone comes out on the winning end.
- There should be only one individual ranking; as many individual points should be granted to doubles players per round as would be granted to the singles players. This means; players that do well in doubles will have similar rankings as the kids that do well in singles. This will give equal opportunity to kids that are not ready

- for individual competition, and love the team spirit. And at the same time, there will be room to accommodate the kids that like singles and being out there on their own.
- In my own personal opinion, these rules need to be applied to the 10s, 12s, and 14s divisions only. Once players turn 15 years old, they, for the most part, will be ready for singles, mentally and socially. Once playing in the 16s, have separate tournaments and dates for singles and doubles. This way we continue to emphasize doubles, but we add weight to singles events. Maybe then, rankings could be separate again.
- Doubles draws and tournaments should also have a consolation bracket whether full feed in or the first round loss type.
- Doubles play needs to be sold at all levels. We need to educate parents, coaches and Tennis organizations of the criticality of resurrecting doubles and placing it back at the top of the hill for what it means to Tennis as a whole.
- Tennis will eventually die, and it will be a thing of the past that will only be found in the history books. With more emphasis on doubles, the life of this wonderful sport will stretch into the next millennium!

The popularity of Tennis won't be saved by singles, in my view. Singles is a little egotistical, and singles takes a lot of space and time, and it is too individualistic; for as much as I love it for what it is, "one warrior against the World!" But humans are fundamentally social creatures, and we function better and are more effective working in groups.

In hope that nobody gets the wrong message, I personally believe we need more and better singles players. And my belief is that within a few years, we will have more effective and entertaining singles players, because of these changes and new rules. Players would soon develop better techniques and strategies as well as more solutions to solving problems against tough opponents.

Ever since John McEnroe was competing professionally, we really have not had many great players who played doubles and singles in recent history with few exceptions like Stefan Edberg and Patrick Rafter. Doubles play will improve singles games. But it has also been a way for many players to express themselves professionally and improve at many levels. Take, for instance, the Bryan brothers: They are not only well known for their doubles prowess but have become the most successful doubles team in the history of Tennis. Without doubles, many players like them would not have a way of making it. It is also true at the college level in that we have some doubles specialists who are intelligently used by coaches to form their doubles squads. Doubles today is still very much a part of Tennis and plays a very critical part of the game at all levels and ages.

If we were able to place more emphasis back on doubles, it is not difficult to visualize a pseudo-resurrection of Tennis, by generating new and different players, who are not just great from the baseline, but also rush the net and play a super athletic style.

We should really think seriously about this!

PRESSURE AND BURNOUT IN JUNIOR TENNIS

Pressure and burnout in Tennis come from very different sources: Self-inflicted, parents, coaches, and friends. It is not hard to identify a junior player suffering these two diseases. For the most part, one leads to the other. Consistent pressure leads to burnout and eventual quitting. Sometimes too much pressure leads to injury! A player under too much pressure will usually show anger, frustration, and low energy or fatigue on court during practices and tournaments. Once a player is in the burnout state, he or she will start tanking matches as a way out, and to save what little self-esteem might be left in him or her.

Most of the time, excess pressure will come from parents. Parents and coaches need to be on the look out for the symptoms. As soon as burnout signs appear, a meeting with parents and coaches is necessary to identify, exactly, what the problem is and figure out ways to solve it. Especially for juniors under 12 years old, since at that age it is not rare to see them suddenly quit or lose interest. Burnout will usually show its ugly face in advance of a junior quitting or losing motivation, and we as coaches and parents need to be on the lookout for these signs all the time.

Excessive pressure can also lead to injury. It leads to faulty technique, low-intensity conditioning, and poor practices, creating the potential for rolled ankles, Tennis elbow, hard falls, as well as other horrors.

Burnout is 100% preventable. Parents and coaches need to remember, that when a junior player signs up for Tennis and experiences good results, Tennis should never become so important that it steals a kid's childhood. Unless he or she is not bothered by this loss. Learning Tennis for a junior player should definitely not be a race to see who gets there first. It is more about enjoying the process every step of the way. Tennis is a great character building tool if administered correctly in children. But if there is excessive emphasis on winning it can make family relations horrible and destructive. If administered wrong, Tennis can instill the wrong values, instead of developing the autonomy, resiliency, and independent thinking. The kid can become totally reliant on others to get everything done; especially when parents and coaches are overprotective of the players.

Good coaches take the time to analyze each and every player's needs and only help them get to solutions of problems to the point they can figure it on their own. Great coaches teach foresight and anticipation of problems and how to start solving them before they become a serious threat.

In an attempt to be even more empathetic, let me say again: Tennis should be a blast every step of the way. It should promote the building of character, friendships, the learning of resiliency, discipline, autonomy, emotional control, how to deal with pressure, as well as teamwork skills. This is why intervening in burnout is so important.

Burnout in any field can be defined as too much of something, whatever it is, and Tennis is no different. We have to look for these signs and solve the situation early before it hits us.

Sure signs of burnout and too much pressure include but are not limited to:

- Too much time spent on the practice court.
- Not enough time on the practice court, leading to boredom.
- Too many tournaments (too much challenge).
- Not enough tournaments (lack of challenge).
- Playing the wrong competition (such as going for too tough a division, or too easy a division).
- Excessive fitness training.
- Inappropriate fitness training. A player may be working hard at the gym or track, but the results are not getting better. Possibly the training regimen could just be fatiguing or stiffening him/her, hampering performances. As a result, the player is feeling the pressure of ever increasing fitness loads.
- Too much babying of the players by coaches, parents or both. It is pretty common to see overprotective parents limiting mental toughness or fitness development. Causing players to have a lower pressure threshold. As a result, these players break up more easily and start showing signs of burnout for insignificant causes.
- Not enough communication from players, coaches or parents or all; something may be going on at home or school, and the player or parents are not communicating with the coach. Or something is

happening on the court or traveling tournaments and the coaches or players are not communicating with dad or mom. This situation will cause limited performance due to issues that could be easily resolved with better communication. A simple example of this would be a player needing more time at home to study for his tests or to make up his/her grades. But the parents, coaches or players are not talking about it, this issue keeps the player worried, reducing his or her performance on the court. When the report card or test results come home, the parents finally realize the need to make some adjustments to training loads and priorities.

- Practicing the wrong things or at a low-intensity level; spending endless time practicing the wrong things not really impacting the player's ability to improve; this makes players grow stale and bored. A player with solid groundstrokes needs to hit more volleys, and fewer groundstrokes or a player with an awesome serve may need to work more on his or her return of serve, etc... Also, when the level of intensity is too low, the player may feel that he or she is putting in the time and not improving. Sooner or later this player starts losing confidence and motivation; matches that he or she should be winning and letting things go downhill. Remember that what we do on the practice court will reflect itself during tournament matches. Low-intensity practices lead to mediocre results that are unsatisfactory and lead to pressure and burnout.
- Practicing with the wrong coaches or practice partners; this means a player may not be getting challenged enough with who he/she is hitting or practicing with. Players in this situation may get bored and lose motivation pretty quickly and need to be listened and paid attention to, in order to make the right adjustments to their training routines. Also, the opposite could be true if the player is getting challenged too much. He or she may be feeling pressure from coaches and practice partners. This player may not belong in the training group he or she is in and may have to be moved to a lower intensity level group.
- Placing too much emphasis on winning; players may be getting unintended messages from different sources about the importance of winning matches and may be feeling the pressure; while coaches are unaware of this situation. This also serves as a good example of the importance of everyday communication of players with coaches.

- In some instances burnout and lack of motivation will also derive from coaches and parents not showing any genuine interest in the player's Tennis; however, this may be preferable to too much interest in some cases. Parents, coaches and players have to figure out the right balance.
- Stuff going on outside Tennis could be causing added pressure and lack of motivation or concentration in players. Human relations and friendships are of extreme importance to players of all levels and ages. If things are not going well with friends or family; it is difficult for a player to stay focused or motivated for any length of time.

WHAT IS MENTAL TOUGHNESS?

Here we are talking about emotional, physical, mental and even spiritual control when under pressure. Without this control, players can be easy prey to their opponents. When we speak of spiritual, we are referring to the player's inner and firm belief that he/she has what it takes to win a match or get out of a tough situation.

Players need to suppress negative thoughts and emotions. Mental Toughness is being able of turning around after losing a tough point, do a quick analysis of the situation and move on without mental disturbance. It's about being fiercely cool, using all our mental, physical and spiritual energy and available time to proceed through points one at the time intelligently until the match expires. Mental toughness means to be able to manage our time on the court, sticking to the business at hand regardless of the score, who we are playing against, or other distractions.

Confidence and faith in one's ability are everything on a Tennis court. Players have to believe they can win successive points in order to win a match. So acting confident even if we are not feeling confident will eventually make us start feeling confident. Having sufficient mental and emotional control to be able to do this are key to competitive Tennis. The quality of a player's Tennis on any given day depends upon his/her frame of mind.

Recall my section on watching television. Here's another reason related to mental toughness. Watch the great players and observe everything they do on the court. Watch their expressions, how they walk in between points, and how they vent frustration. Pay attention to what they do before the start of every point. We will detect their mental toughness in all of these activities.

Having a routine for in between point time is key to mental toughness. What we do and think a few seconds before the start of every point, is going to impact directly what ends up happening during the actual point, these routines are of extreme importance. According to Dr. James Loehr, founder of the Human Performance Institute in Orlando, Florida, players need to develop a set of routines that helps them focus on the task at hand. Instead of getting carried away by crazy uncontrollable emotions. He called it THE 16 SIXTEEN SECOND CURE, and it goes something like this:

Stage 1) Positive Physical Response: this is the reaction that happens immediately after a point finishes. We need a two to three second positive reaction after a point is either won or lost. Players need to be trained to have a positive reaction to both circumstances. A positive physical reaction can be a fist pump. If the player lost a point or missed a shot, then it can be the physical rehearsal of the stroke with the corrective technique and visualization of the ball going to the spot intended. If a verbal, or physical reaction is preferred, then the player needs to say something positive whether or not he or she won the point. Such expressions as "come on," "move your feet", "see the ball", "play more aggressive", "just think", "hit the ball", etc... Please remember that when executing a physical response we need to be respectful of our opponents and the spectators. The *in your face* attitude is wrong and should be discouraged. The fist pump or verbal response needs to be directed away from all public and opponents. In some instances, a physical response may not be necessary. I have worked with a few players that preferred to just turn around, regardless of what may have happened on the court, and go to the next point. I worked with this awesome Asian girl that was such a player. When I started working with her, I tried to get her to get more fired up by having a physical response. As we started training for this, I noticed how hard and unnatural it was for her to do a fist pump or even a low verbal positive remark. So I decided to desist from this and let her just be herself. She won a lot of matches and at one point in the 14s she was ranked No. 1 in the USTA Southern Section and top 30 in the nation with only like 7 or 8 tournaments played! She was truly awesome! Her name was Tiffany Tang.

28) Physical response: The fist toward the side fence, plus a positive verbal remark are good physical response routines during tough matchplay situations.

Stage 2) Relaxation/Recovery Response: as soon as the player is finished with the reaction stage, he/she enters the relaxation/recovery stage. He or she should pass the racquet to the non-dominant hand, and carry it in a relaxed, horizontal position. Walk with an upright, confident posture that looks strong. The eyes should be focused on nearby balls to be picked up, or on the ground 7-10 feet in front of the player. Moreover, players are trained to breathe deeply in a controlled and trained manner into the next point or changeover. These strategies provide a player's mind and body a little mental timeout by concentrating on deliberate walking and breathing. By deep breathing, a player lowers his/her heart rate and is able to bounce back to 100% physically and mentally, ready for the next point. This stage should last from 5 to 12 seconds as needed.

29) Relaxation/Recovery Response: Strong, deliberate but relaxed walking, followed by some toweling off while deep controlled breathing is the way to recover and relax to get ready for the next point.

Stage 3) Preparation Response (concentration stage): this stage starts as soon as a player is done with the relaxation/recovery stage. The player picks up the balls, then comes to a position near where he/she needs to be for the start of the next point, but not facing straight to the net or the opponent yet. The racquet comes up, and the right (or dominant) hand goes to the strings of the racquet. A player can straighten his/her strings or rest the hand there; his/her eyes need to be on the string bed for eye control. While in this position, the player should think about strategy and tactics and concentrate on the next point; this stage should last 4 to 6 seconds.

30) Concentration response: During this stage, it's a good idea to fix our hands and eyes on the strings of the racquet, while we plot out our tactics for the next point.

Stage 4) Ritual Response: This is nothing other than the physical and mental execution of a series of habits before a point begins. A player may jump up and own a little, tug or fix his clothing, hair or bounce the ball, etc. At this stage, it is a good idea to have a verbal expression such as "I can do this" or "Intense footwork." Players are executing a series of individualistic and unique routines. Most bounce the ball; some bounce it differently, or a lot more than others; or they might tug with their shirt or shorts. A lot of them get rocking the racquet side to side in the serving or returning positions, players may spin the racquet in their hands as they get ready to return (Watch Roger Federer). Watch the pros and analyze each individual's prep habits. A cool habit is the player looking down at the strings as he or she plays with them crouching down to return serve. A few skip on toes side to side or up and down, or just flexing their knees up a little and so on and so forth. All these rituals deepen concentration and get the player in point play mode. This stage lasts 4 to 7 seconds as needed. It is recognized that the most ritualistic players have better concentration and are mentally tougher! Who has not seen Rafael Nadal and his array of rituals to serve and return? It is hard to think of anyone mentally tougher than him!

31) Ritual Response: In this stage, the player will execute his/her rituals right before the start of the point. Bouncing the ball before serving, or fixing the strings before returning are typical rituals as observed in mentally tough players.

Stage 5) Visualization Response (This stage I added out of my own observations and is not part of the original work of Dr. Jim Loehr's *16 second cure*). In this "response," the player simply looks at his target whether serving or returning and visualizes his or her first shot. This stage should last one or two seconds max. Also, different players do the visualization immediately after the preparation or concentration response and right before they go into their rituals.

32)Visualization response: In this stage, the player will typically see or imagine what his first and even second shot will look like.

See the What Tennis Pros Don't Teach video of the in between point time five stages mentioned above on www.youtube.com at https://youtu.be/ylzLGTHq5FY

For more detailed information on *The 16 Second Cure*, look for Dr. Jim Loehr's material. I feel this is probably the best work and research that has been done on the subject of mental toughness, and it is a good start point for all players to get stronger in the upstairs department.

DIG, DIG, DIG!

In Tennis, as competitors, we can always find ways to do more when we are out there in the heat of the battle. Even if we feel like we are giving it a 100% effort, there is more we can get out of ourselves. Someone might say "How is that possible if we are at 100% already?" But are we? We may be exhausted physically while our opponent may be playing great as we are running out of options and time. Can we go up a notch or maybe even two? In Tennis, as in no other sport, absolute silence and stillness is mandatory from all audiences; because, of course, a state of very deep concentration is needed to perform at the top of our ability. This is where the dig deep philosophy comes into play. How deeply can a player concentrate? We sometimes see players in like a sort of trance or self-hypnosis state during matches. Yes, the zone! How did they do that? Through deep concentration, we can see it in their eyes as they get ready to return or serve. Trying hard to concentrate, calm ourselves and focus on the task at hand at the start of every point is paramount to achieving this state of mind. We can always dig deeper... I mean concentrate deeper! Are we getting the picture?

Also, during changeovers, as players sit down on their bench, they have to question themselves how badly they want to win? That is another way of digging. How deeply are we yearning for winning? We hear that during sports events all the time. Okay, said in other words, we can always get more out of our brains and our hearts! We can always give the extra by digging deeper within us!

As my then ten-year-old daughter Anasazi walked off the court after playing a practice match one day, I gave her a big smiling hug because she was working hard out there. However, she still lost the match 8/2 to one of her practice peers. A few minutes later, we had the chance to talk a little about the match. I tried to explain this digging deep philosophy to her. It was hard for her to understand it to say the least. She got irritated fast saying that she had worked hard the entire match, which may seem true. One has to be careful in explaining things to children. As coaches and dads, we have to be sensitive to their feelings. A more detailed explanation was necessary for her to get it. After a little while, she grasped the concept. Even though, an athlete may be giving it everything physically, there is always room for more mentally and emotionally! The dig deep philosophy stems from the fact that our brains and our hearts know no limits!

PLAYING A CHEATER AND HIS/HER PARENTS

Nobody likes to play a cheater; it is not a question of whether we have to deal with one or not but of when. There are lots of them in Tennis at all levels. Let me start by saying that during my career playing a cheater always made me want to beat him that much more. If I got a couple bad calls, I would get so much more focused and committed to the match. Let me also say that as Tennis players, we have to learn to deal with cheaters and figure out ways to win matches against them with or without them cheating or n spite of their cheating.

In junior Tennis, it is not that uncommon to find situations where a kid is playing, and he/she may be making bad calls, while his/her dad or mom may be going, "good call", just as they made a terrible call at a crucial moment in the match. And then after the match they act like nothing happened, and that it is a normal thing to win matches this way. It is also sad to see dad or mom trying to coach the player. Instead of helping, they distract and fray the nerves, making it impossible for either one of the two players on the court to have a fair match.

Of course, the right way to deal with these situations is to call an official. Officials are available for the most part in all sanctioned junior events. The problem is, they usually come for a few minutes, may ask the players to make fair calls, watch two games and leave. At this point, a cheater will go right back to cheating, and the player needing the help may not be willing to call for another official. In close matches, officials need to stay on the court because a couple of bad calls can be the defining factor that will determine who wins this match. A player needs to ask the official to stay for the whole match, and the official has the obligation to do so.

It is important to question bad calls from cheaters. How we question these calls has everything to do with whether we get them to arrest or at least slow down the cheating. The familiar "Are you sure?" way of questioning adopted by most juniors does not cut it. How about, "Hey, the ball on the line is good", or "The ball did not even bounce on the line, it was inside it, how can you say that was out?", Or even, "Come on, that was way in... Is this how it is going to be?"

Ultimately the better player will win in most situations. As mentioned above, if the match is really close, cheating needs to be stopped because it can and will be the determining factor in who walks out the victor. Two or even three bad calls will not change the outcome of a match if one of the two players is clearly better than the other and will win no matter how much the other one cheats.

We cannot let cheaters get into our heads. We need to keep them in perspective and focus on the task at hand. A player needs to deal with them as best as he/she can. But if we let them get into our heads, we are going to play more nervous or more hot-headed. A cheater can make us play bad if we allow it. That compounded with the cheating, may make enough of a difference that we end up losing the match. We need to let chatters know that we are well aware that they are cheating and breaking the rules. Also, there are many different ways to cheat in Tennis. Bad calls, scoring disputes, coaching, unneeded bathroom breaks, obnoxiousness on court, creating distractions deliberately, and all sorts of gamesmanship situations to try to gain an unfair advantage or distract the opponents. If someone is making bad calls, deliberately hit the ball further inside the lines of the court to keep them from being tempted to call shots out. Beat cheaters, in spite of their cheating!

VISUALIZATION AND IMAGERY

Visualization is nothing other than getting into a deep state of relaxation and concentration (sort of like self-hypnosis). Followed by seeing oneself doing what we want to be doing, will be doing or should be doing. In a very detailed, descriptive, enjoyable, focused, controlled, fully engaged, fully submerged, fully intense, but relaxed, energetic and fun way! It's like watching a movie of ourselves doing or saying things.

Imagery is similar to visualization, but instead of seeing ourselves as outside observers, we view ourselves from the inside. In other words, we are feeling, seeing, and doing in our mind everything mentioned above. In other words, we are actually doing what we want to do. We are feeling it, and seeing it. To illustrate this technique, consider this example: "I can imagine myself in the serving position. I am about to hit a second serve to the add side of the court, I am seeing my opponent (Victor Smith, who is a good player and I have never beaten him) standing on the opposite side of the net ready to return. It is match point! I go for a high kicker to his backhand, and he lays a short return with a little topspin. I move in and hit a clean winner crosscourt as he anticipates to his left covering the down the line shot instead... Yay! I did it!" Does that work? I am not even doing this for real, but I can feel the adrenaline and excitement in my body as I write it. It is the next best thing to the real deal! Try it!

Visualization is a neglected technique, but it plays an important role in sports performances. 100% of all Tennis players do some sort of visualization, sometimes voluntary, and most other times involuntary. A very small percentage of them utilize visualization in a methodical way or as a training tool. At the professional level, many players are using some imagery or visualization routine on a weekly basis. We don't have to attend a yoga class or go to a sports psychology guru to get started on this.

There are several good books on the subject. One of the-all time best books in Tennis that goes into detail with this is "The Inner Game of Tennis" by Timothy Galloway. Another one that I found was very good, and a bestseller was "Creative Visualization" by Shakti Gawain. A simple 5 to 15-minute routine a couple times a week will add confidence, purpose, motivation and inspiration to a player's training menu. It takes no physical effort and is highly recommendable at all ages and levels. Another way to apply imagery or visualization can be on the court right before we serve or return. On changeovers, during the 90 second break, a player can take a full 20 seconds or so to do some deep visualization with his/her eyes closed. I remember the great Arthur Ashe with his towel over his head sitting down on changeovers... mmmhh! Wonder what he was doing? Meditating? Visualization?

Give it a shot, do some research, watch some of the great ones out there and notice their routines. We can tell they are visualizing at the start of every point... All those rituals, ball bouncing (Djokovic), rocking the body (Del Potro), spinning the racquet (Federer), tugging the shirt (Roddick), rubbing the Tennis balls on your shirt or shorts (The great player from Mexico in the 70s Raul Ramirez), pacing back and forth or swinging her racquet in the air (Maria Sharapova). Rituals deepen concentration; they are a method of visualization. Just before that brilliant ace serve, Federer was probably visualizing that exact outcome!

DO RULES MATTER? HOW WELL SHOULD I KNOW THE RULEBOOK?

Rules do matter a ton. To not know the rules and most of its hidden cases and situations is the equivalent to having a weakness on stroking technique! Players who know the rules in detail have a definite advantage over players who don't.

A lot of the rules are learned through experience in tournaments. Once a player achieves higher levels of competition, such as at the State, Sectional or National levels he or she better be paying attention to rules and maybe even studying them.

In a close match situation, the kind of match we really would like to win, a bad decision on a rule against us could be the determining factor for losing the match.

One good way to learn the rules is through watching Pro Tennis on TV and paying attention to not only the Tennis itself but to what is going on with the chair umpire, line judges, etc... A simple local competitive Tennis match will start educating us. The best way is through playing tournaments and learning the hard way. Hopefully, players will be knowledgeable enough by the time they start playing at the national or international levels.

Get a current rulebook and keep it in your Tennis bag and have it always there for reference. Also, all rules are in PDF format on the Internet. Just in case a clarification is needed to be researched, and no one has a Rulebook. Also, Look for the 101 section of this book and the subsection on *101 Rules that matter; Special cases on rules*. This sub-section will give us a really good start in being more knowledgeable on rules that can and will make a difference when competing.

SECTION IV

MATTER OVER MIND

FITNESS AND CONDITIONING

By no means do we mean that the physical or fitness demands are more important than the mental or the emotional ones. But without the fitness component, players cannot compete at a high level; it could be said that the mental and the physical components complement or enrich one another.

Fitness and conditioning are serious subjects in Tennis. Training for Tennis needs to be specific, and, as in many other disciplines, players need to go from the general to the specific. They do have to include basic hand-eye coordination, flexibility, mobility, etc... as well as a good cardiovascular base. Players can improve these qualities with specific training routines or exercises. Conditioning refers to the attainment of the right level of fitness to be able to compete at a high level whatever the player's age. It is all relative. What does an 11 and under player have to do to compete at his/her level? Or what conditioning and fitness levels are required for college players to be effective and able to maximize what they are demanded by opponents our own game on a Tennis court?

Tennis players need to be able to play matches that will last for up to 3 hours in the heat and sometimes with a minimum of breaks in between points, games or sets. They have to be able to react quickly to very fast moving balls. They sprint and stop, or slow down before taking a hard or a soft swing at a ball that may be moving fast or maybe it is just driven softly over the net. Tennis players have to be able to get back to a smart position on the court and immediately react to the next shot. After a 20 second break, they must repeat this effort all over again. Long points may last up to 20 shots or more. For some of these shots, the player may have to sprint, stop, hit, and explosively recover. The heart rate goes way up during a long point. And then, these players need to have the capacity to let it settle back to an almost normal rate before the start of the next point within the little 20 second break allowed between points.

In Tennis, players need to jump high and hard upwards, backwards, to the side and forward. In other words, players need to be able to jump suddenly, high and hard in any direction! Tennis players need to have unequaled balance and power on the move. Great intensity and speed combined are required continuously, in almost every point. At the same, time a player has to be relaxed enough to think with clarity and execute a solid hit on a fast approaching ball. Tennis players need to have superb capacity for physical, mental and emotional intensity simultaneously. On top of all of that, they need to be able to think clearly and act with absolute control, relaxation, and accuracy under extreme conditions such as heat, cold, wind, sun, as well as pressure from opponents, parents, coaches, the public as well as self-inflicted.

Obviously all these things are not easily attainable, and they require years of hard and disciplined work to achieve.

So here lies the great difficulty of our sport in that it is not just about learning how to strike the ball with the right form and technique. A developing player will also have to be able to hit consistently and with the proper shot selection repeatedly during the course of a match while he or she is moving all over the Tennis court.

In the following subsections, we will find detailed information on the different disciplines regarding fitness and training. We will start by providing parameters from which we can extrapolate and get a feel for where a player is at in his or her training.

TENNIS TRAINING TESTING

Some Tennis organizations around the World have devised different Tennis training protocols. The USTA, the ITF, and others have an effective set of measurements and tests to determine where the player is at in his or her quest for development towards being fit to compete.

Here are some of the most relevant fitness tests. Some of these are my own and others come from different sources of information:

Spider Test: Place 5 balls at the following intersections: 2 balls at the baseline and singles lines, 2 balls at service line and singles lines and one ball at service line and center service line. Draw a 12 inch by 18 inch box directly behind the center mark off the baseline just outside the court. The player starts with one foot on the center mark, and at a signal, he/she has to get the balls from each location, into the small box behind the baseline, and go back and get the next ball. Balls have to be picked up in a clockwise fashion and one at the time (also test with counter clockwise pick up). When placing balls in the box, they have to stay in the box. Time the player from start to finish; 16 years of age and older should complete this test under 18 seconds. Allow longer for younger ages and a little faster for older kids. If the balls roll out of the box add 0.5 seconds for each ball, and if the balls are picked up in the wrong order disqualify and start over. Allow three chances and take the best score achieved.

Hexagon Test: Draw a hexagon on a court 24 inches per side. If the test is done on a hard court, children's street chalk can be used which easily comes off with a little water. On a clay court, the lines are drawn with a finger or a pencil or pen on the surface of the clay. Have the player stand inside the hexagon, he or she has to jump in and out the six sides on the hexagon while facing forward in a clockwise fashion. The player needs to continue to face forward at the person keeping time the whole time. The player has to complete three full laps (the three laps are completed when the player touches the ground inside the hexagon on the last lap). Allow three chances and score only the best time. Conduct the test jumping clockwise and counter clockwise. If players steps on a line or miss the sequence or spin around as they jump, add 0.5 seconds. Kids 16-year-old should be able to do this under 12 seconds! Extrapolate accordingly.

20 Yard dash: Time sprint from behind the baseline to the service line on opposite sides of court. Run through the outside of the court and net poles. Allow three chances. Record the best time obtained. 16-year-olds should be able to do this in less than 3 seconds.

Medicine ball chest pass: With an 8 pound medicine ball, do a chest pass from the outside of the baseline. The player cannot go over the baseline as he or she is throwing the ball, and he or she cannot take steps forward to gain momentum. He or she just stands outside the baseline, to make the throw. Measure distance as accurately as possible with measuring tape, over 16 years old should be able to throw 12 feet or longer.

Forward leap: With both feet behind the baseline, and without taking extra steps, jump into the court without stepping on the baseline. Measure the jump with measuring tape, allow three chances, record longest jump; players 16 years of age and over should do 5 feet or longer.

20 Touch Centerline to Singles line: Stand in the center of a service box facing the net, with a racquet in dominant hand, at the signal sprint touching the center service line and then the singles line. Do 20 touches of the tip of the racquet to the lines. Players cannot spin around and should be facing the net all the time without turning backwards, if a player misses the line with the tip of the racquet add 0.5 seconds, to his/her score. Allow three chances to achieve the best possible time. Let players recover between testings (up to 2 minutes). Score fastest time. Kids 16 and older should be able to do it under 19 seconds.

Vertical Jump: Next to a wall or tall post, have a player jump as high as he or she can without taking additional steps to impulse him/herself in a comfortable position. Allow three chances to obtain best possible result. With a marker or chalk draw a line at the standstill height and the peak of each jump, record only the highest jump. 16 and older should be able to jump 12 inches or higher.

Flexibility forward: Sit the player down with feet together on a flat surface. Without bending the knees, reach forward to the toes. Measure the distance to the toes or past the toes. All kids should easily be able to reach the tip of their toes with the tips of their fingers. Allow three chances. If not quite to the toes, use a negative sign (-) to score in inches, and if past the toes, use a positive sign (+).

Shoulder flexibility: Reach over the right shoulder with right hand's middle and index fingers try to reach or touch left hand's thumb behind the player's back. Measure the distance in inches such that if not touching, then use the minus (-) sign, if touching and if past the touching point use a (+) sign. Do the same with left arm over left shoulder in a reverse way and score results. Most children under 12-years-old should be able to touch fingers on both sides. It is normal that a Tennis player will display more flexibility in the right arm over than left arm over because of the naturally increased range coming from the service motion.

Leg spread flexibility: Sit the player down on the center of the baseline or service line in a way that the spinal column is directly on top of the line. With legs spread and extended apart as far as possible, hands should be off the ground. Measure the distance from the heels straight down to a line out of the sitting position, record the distance from both heels. Divide the distance from heels to the line from the spread out position and divide it by the length of the legs (distance from the line to the end of the heels with both legs together). This gives us a fraction and the smaller the fraction, the better the flexibility. Good results range from 0.4 - 0.2

Trunk twist flexibility: Sit on top of the center of the baseline or the center of the service line with legs crossed. The spinal column should be directly above the line. Reach as far as possible with the right hand around the left side of the body and draw a line on the clay or make a chalk line on the surface. The other hand should be off the ground at all times, give player three chances, he or she can swing to try to reach farther. Measure distance to the centerline from the spine on both sides of the body. Use a + sign if past the center line, and a − sign if not all the way to the center; all juniors should be able to score at about + 4 inches on both sides.

100 jump rope test: Jump rope 100 times as fast as possible. It is faster and more efficient if the player alternates feet as he or she jumps, but the feet together are okay for testing purposes, time the 100 jumps. 16 Year olds and older should have no problem doing this under 30 seconds, much faster times (like 23 seconds) are possible with better technique.

One mile run: Go to a track at the local high school or college, run 4 laps plus 9 meters (9 meters equals about 10 yards). One mile equals 1609 meters. Time the run with a stopwatch. 16-year-olds should be able to run the mile under 5 minutes. Older athletes may be able to do it under 5 minutes. Only a handful of about 5 or 6 high school age kids has ever made the one mile run under 4 minutes. My best personal time as a teenager was 4:21 minutes when I was 16 years old!

Push up test: Do as many pushups as possible in one minute. Pushups need to be done in such a way that the elbows bend to 90 degrees and then back to full extension of the arms. Pushups not done right or above 90 degrees should not be counted. Boys 16 years of age and older should easily be able to do over 50. Girls will be in the neighborhood of 30 or maybe more.

Sit-ups: Do as many setups as possible in one minute. The player should lay down on a flat soft surface such as a towel or carpet with his or her knees bent together to 90 degrees and both feet on the ground. With arms crossed over shoulders and elbows down, the player should rise and touch the elbows to the thighs. 16-year-olds should do 50 plus easily. Girls are better at this and sometimes do over 60 or more.

WTPDT FITNESS TRAINING PROTOCOL

Following there is a chart with all the testing mentioned above and the acceptable ranges. This chart facilitates scoring for a group of kids; it gives us a parameter for comparison, and it's easy to file for future reference.

This chart shows acceptable ranges based on results obtained from kids 10- 17-years-old. Low scores are from 10-13-year-olds; intermediate or in the middle scores are from 13-15-year-olds and high scores come from 15-18-year-olds. At the same time, flexibility ranges are based on a scale from good for the high scores, okay for the middle of the road scores, and poor for the low scores. Depending on the different flexibility tests; these tests are not so dependent on age but more so on the physical maturity, athletic development and previous training each player has had. The ranges give us a foundation from which we can extrapolate and identify where our players fit in order of establishing training targets.

In these tests, we are covering fitness in general with tests for endurance or cardiovascular testing, flexibility, power, agility, and speed.

More than compare to others, we need to evaluate every 6 months to a year and train the player to spend more time in areas that yielded low scores:

WTPDT Fitness Testing Form

Test Name:	Obtained Result:	Acceptable Range:	Comments:
Hexagon Test:		10-17 Seconds	
Spider Test:		16-23 Seconds	
20 Yard Dash:		2.5-4 Seconds	
100 Jumps:		23-34 Seconds	
20 Touches:		16-25 Seconds	
Medicine Ball Pass:		4-14 Feet	
Shoulder Flexibility:		+3 to -3 Inches	
Trunk Flexibility:		+3 to -2 Inches	
Forward Flexibility:		-3 to + 4 Inches	
One Mile Run:		4 – 8 Minutes	
Vertical Jump:		4-15 Inches	
Pushups 1 Minute:		20-70 Reps	
Situps 1 Minute:		30-70 Reps	
Leg Spread Flex:		5-13 Inches	
Forward Leap:		3-7 Feet	

Fig. 33)WTPDT Fitness Testing Protocol Form. These exercises were designed with the idea of testing and having a comparison or parameter chart, but they can definitely be used for regular weekly training. They are good because the player is always trying to beat his or her previous scores thus getting the feeling of achievement and improvement.

See www.youtube.com video of What Tennis Pros Don't Teach Fitness Testing at https://youtu.be/cH4LAdo2se8

By no means should we consider the previous list of test exercises exhaustive. More information can be found on the Internet and in fitness literature, look for publications by Jack Groppel, Pat Etcheberry, Todd Ellenbecker. Other sources of information are the ITF's and the USTA's websites.

SPORTS SCIENCE, WHAT IS IT? HOW DO WE APPLY IT?

The idea of sports science has been around for a long time. It is nothing other than science-based principles applied to sports. In this case Tennis. The areas covered by sports science are nutrition, fitness training, biomechanics or technique, and mental toughness training. The amount of available information on sports science can be overwhelming if one gets really looking for it.

If interested in tackling some of this information, a coach or player needs to start by doing some research on the Internet about subjects, books, and publications. The ITF, USTA, and other Tennis associations and federations around the World have many publications and periodicals specific to Tennis. Some authors I personally recommend are Jim Loehr, Tim Galloway, Brad Gilbert, Jack Groppel, Pat Etcheberry, Paul Roetert, Todd Ellenbecker and Carol Dweck among others.

The thing to do is to look for practical advice on the different fields; stuff that is easy to understand and can be applied on a day to day basis.

Note: Look for the 101 practical sports science based tips for Tennis players in the 101s section near the end of this book.

PERIODIZATION

Periodization is a term used by World class athletes and coaches in all disciplines. It is scheduled or programmed training for high-performance competition. This principle came from the training of Olympic track athletes, and it has now been applied to nearly all the different disciplines such as soccer, football, Tennis, etc... The principle of periodization aims at having an athlete reach his or her peak during the most important competition periods during a predetermined cycle. This cycle can be 3 months, 6 months, a year, etc... The length of it depends on the discipline and the timing of the competition periods where we want the athlete to perform at his/her best.

A sample of an appropriate periodization schedule for a competitive junior Tennis player who is starting serious fitness training is presented here.

Let's assume this player is 15-years-old and plays four major events throughout the year, and we want him/her to peak for those four events marked with asterisks. The higher number of asterisks the more important the tournament. The starting dates for the tournaments are indicated with the asterisk tournament level. Notice the number of tournaments is a total of 19 events. This is a reasonable number of events for 13-18-year-old juniors and a pretty well thought out schedule. Consider the level of the different tournaments as well; as coaches we want this junior playing a lot of matches. We should schedule in such a way so as to not have to travel too far for all the level * tournaments. We may have to travel a lot more for the level *** tournaments.

Another consideration of great importance about doing a schedule such as this is that the family can budget their expenses based on this schedule. Once we have this document, we pretty much know exactly how many lessons, drills, trips, even the number of stringing jobs players will require week-to-week and month to month. Most parents go at it randomly. Before they know it, they're broke and must cut a tournament out of the schedule.

Periodization, therefore, is good for planning purposes as much as training purposes.

Below I am presenting definitions with explanations of all the different activities players need to be doing during their periodization cycle. These definitions are numbered for reference in our periodization schedule. Different percentages of each activity are prescribed. An athlete and his/her family can easily follow a guideline like this for the day-to-day training and scheduling.

1) Drilling: Stroke production (repetition), technical work. This type of training may be done anytime during the season, but it should really taper down as we approach top competition; at this point, all the drilling turns to hitting, point play and match-play. As we approach competition, the player no longer has time to be messing with technical stuff. Fed balls or dead ball drilling is not specific to real Tennis training, but it helps to isolate a stroke and make technical corrections.

2) Point play: Tiebreakers, lots of serve and return followed by playing out the point, without keeping track of the score. Play lots of random points, let the players mess with different strategies and try out new things. Make lots of tactical and shot selections observations. Players want to engage in this type of training most of the year. This type of training is a lot more necessary as players approach top competition and an absolute necessity for the developing junior.

3) Matchplay: Have players play as many full sets, full matches, and lots of regular and match tiebreakers as time allows. This type of training should get started as much as three weeks prior to tough competition. Different players require different amounts of match play to get match tough. Players may want to do match play two days in a row followed by a transition day and then match play two or even three days in a row to simulate tournament play. The closer we get to top competition, the more full matches the player needs to be exposed to. It is a good idea to consider smaller tournaments for training purposes and provide more realistic matches as we get closer to top competition. It is a great idea to throw into the equation lots of doubles matches intermixed with singles.

4) Cardiovascular training: Cardio training refers to activities such as long distance running, swimming, biking, or even rowing helps

with endurance. Cross-training in sports like soccer or mountain biking is a good idea that keeps the training fresh and athletes motivated (be cautioned of not getting injured doing contact sports as training tools). This kind of training should be done in the low season when the player is involved in lower level competition and tapered down as training gets more geared towards top competition where speed and explosiveness training is necessary. Long distance training should also be done on alternate days. Long distance running or cardio training on consecutive days is also conducive to injury. Every other day up to three times per week is a good recommendation. Keep in mind the importance of calisthenics and stretching.

5) Endurance weight training: This type of training is used for building a strength base. This means doing high repetitions and low weights. This kind of training should be consistent throughout training periods except when the player is about to enter a cycle of explosive training two to three weeks before tough competition.

6) Explosive weight training: This type of weight training is aimed at adding some mass and power. Gradually add weight and reduce repetitions in weight training routines. Players can start this type of training as much as a month in advance building up to top competition, done every other day two to three times per week. Make sure to do calisthenics and stretching before getting started to prevent injury.

7) Maximum power weight training: This training is aimed at developing maximum power and explosiveness. Very few reps with pretty high loads are needed. Please be extra careful to avoid injury. If possible, always have juniors training under professional supervision! Powerlifting should only be done prior to tough competition no more than two weeks beforehand and should be done two or three times a week on alternate days.

8) Plyometric training: Good for explosiveness, power, and speed on the Tennis court. When doing this kind of training, junior players should also be extremely cautious to avoid injuries. This type of training requires some hard impact on the ground that puts pressure on the player's joints. Be extra careful making sure to warm up well and stretch before and after training. Plyometrics should be done a week to two weeks before big competition and

should be supervised by a professional. Make sure the athlete does calisthenics and stretching before starting. Plyometrics should be done on alternate days, two or three times per week.

9) Resistance and overload training: This type of training requires an overload. Sprinting uphill or on a horizontal surface with someone holding the athlete back like a horse on a chariot or doing push ups with a 20 pound disc on the player's back. Most of this type of training should be done a week to two weeks prior to top competition on alternate days maybe two or even three times in one week. It is the kind of exercise that builds explosiveness and thus it also has the potential to cause injuries. Better if supervised by a professional.

10) Interval training: This is where a circuit is set up for the athlete to do different activities in a sequence. For instance jogging 50 meters, then 15 push-ups, plus 10 lunges, sprint 30 meters, do 15 jumping jacks, shuffle 20 yards, hit 15 balls down the line from the baseline going side to side, sprint 20 yards, hit 10 serves with a weighted racquet, start over with jogging the 50 meters. This is a simple example of how to interval train for Tennis. Does it sound familiar? Is this similar to cardio Tennis? It's an awesome way to train! Come up with the right interval training circuit for the specific player or group of players, based on the cycle in the periodization schedule. This type of training can be done any time of the year depending on where the athlete is on the schedule. It is a very flexible way to train, and it is fun and easy to set up. Be creative!

11) Cross-training: This is a great way to get the fitness training out of the way in a fun and entertaining manner, using other sports to address certain areas of players Tennis training needs. For instance, if a player needs better cardiovascular resistance, get him or her into a soccer league for a few weeks. Or if we want our player to develop better balance and body control, get him or her into gymnastics, Yoga, Taekwondo, Ballet or other similar sports or disciplines. Also, if we want resistance training, get him or her into wrestling or Judo. Again a word of caution is necessary to be very careful to avoid injury. Another good example is baseball, where pitching and throwing can improve the service motion. I have yet to come across a student whose serve did not benefit from baseball. Cross-training is fun and makes it easier for juniors to deal with the

physical demands Tennis imposes on them. This type of training can be done anytime during the year. Cross-training can be designed for any season so be creative and come up with the right balance in accordance with the needs of the player.

12) Time off the Tennis court: This is done when a player has had too much Tennis and needs a break. Another obvious time to get off the court is after an injury or to prevent an impending injury. The length of time off the court can go from three to five days to as much as two weeks. If no injury, it is recommendable to do some cross training during this time to maintain the fitness levels or address fitness needs. If there is an injury or impending injury, some fitness or cross training can be done that does not involve the injury area.

13) Calisthenics: This refers to getting warmed up before stretching and training on and off the court, involving exercises like push-ups, lunges, and jumping jacks. Always do a little stretching or dynamic stretching after the calisthenics. Begin slowly and allow the joints and musculoskeletal system to maintain and even increase the range of motion by stretching. Calisthenics should be done every day, year-round.

14) Stretching or flexibility training: Very important after calisthenics and should always be incorporated into the training routine on and off the court. Even more important is to work on flexibility after gym sessions. Weight training, overload training, power lifting and Plyometric training are all conducive to decreased flexibility. A session of deep stretching, up to 20 minutes or more is recommended following all these types of training, avoiding losing range of motion, and maintaining or increasing flexibility. Stretching is especially important after tough tournament matches. Dynamic stretching should be part of the regular stretching routines. For example, in dynamic stretching, a player may swing a leg side to side in increasing ranges to warm-up and increase range of motion. This exercise should be done after some calisthenics and be administered gradually in order to avoid injury.

15) Maintenance training for top competition: A player who has to play two or up to three tournaments in a row has to design a training routine for maintaining top performance. This training blended in with the tournament matches. It should include several of the training definitions described above; namely, 16, 14, 13, 11, 10,

9, 8, 7, 6 and to a lesser extent 1 as well. This is where it all should come together. A coach needs to be careful to come up with the appropriate combinations of everything. Surely, time is of the essence, so a miniature version of the regular training routines is applied as needed. For instance, if a player is not moving great, a few sprints and Plyometrics are in order. Or if a player is not hitting with enough juice, a little power lifting or Plyometrics may be applied. If a player is getting too tired on long matches, they should run some long distance. It is hard to find the right balance for this type of training, but it can be done on days where easy or no matches are played and applied at the discretion of the coach or player.
16) Sleep and rest: Obviously, we need to monitor amounts of sleep, and it can and should be considered part of the training routine of any athlete. Without adequate sleep, high-performance athletes cannot yield as expected and good results will not be possible.

Note: If doing Overload, Plyometric or Explosive training on the same days, make sure not to overstress athletes with too much. Again, be extremely careful in preventing injuries.

For more detailed and customized periodization schedules see a fitness training professional. For a fitness coach to come up with the right periodization schedule for a High-Performance Tennis player, he or she needs to understand the physical demands of the individual, and know his/her tournament schedule, in order to be able to program the different cycles.

MOCK PERIODIZATION SCHEDULE

Jan14	Feb12	Mar15	Apr13	May5	Jun7	Jul22	Aug27	Sep15	Oct2	No26	Dec3
*	*	**	*	***	*	*	*	**	**	*	*
	Feb19	Mar30	Apr20		Jun21	Jul29		Sep30			Dec10
	*	***	**		***	*		***			*
16	16	16	16	16	16	16	16	16	16	16	16
	15		15		15						15
14	14	14	14	14	14	14	14	14	14	14	14
13	13	13	13	13	13	13	13	13	13	13	13
12			12		12		12			12	
11	11		11		11		11	11	11	11	
10			10	10			10		10	10	
	9		9		9					9	
	8		8		8					8	
	7		7		7					7	
6	6				6			6	6	6	
5	5		5		5		5		5	5	
4			4		4		4		4		
	3	3					3	3			
2	2	2	2	2	2	2	2	2	2	2	2
1	1						1		1	1	

Fig. 34) Schedule for fitness and Tournament Calendar combined for a competitive 15 year old High Performance Junior Tennis Player. Tournament competition denoted by the stars (*); One * lower level or caliber tournament, two stars ** medium caliber, and three stars *** high caliber event. Below the date and stars the numbers refer to the different activities the player needs to have programmed during the given cycle. As can be seen it is getting more and more complicated as the level of play gets higher. In order to come up with the right schedule, we need to take a dive into all this stuff. A deep understanding of the player in question, the game of Tennis, tournament structure, physical demands, mental demands, tactical and strategy demands, nutrition, etc… is necessary here.

WEIGHT TRAINING

Tennis players have been known to do training in the gym. However, this should only comprise about 20%-30% of all the training of a competitive or high-performance Tennis Player. Most players and athletes should be cautious about weight training and get professional help if in doubt about how to proceed. Weightlifting has the potential to ruin players' ability to play at their normal Tennis level for a while or, worse yet cause an injury.

Tennis Players don't need big muscles. Tennis players need strong but resilient, flexible, and powerful muscles. There is an important difference. As players grow a muscle, say a bicep, the muscle gets stronger and bigger. However, as the muscle grows larger, its range of motion gets smaller, and this is a terrible consequence in Tennis. In Tennis, players need their range of motion and flexibility at fullest potential. Without sacrificing these two qualities, we want to get these muscles as strong and powerful as possible. Notice I added the word powerful: power as in explosive strength!

One of the risks of losing range of motion and flexibility is injury. Getting hurt is possible since we will be straining some of our ligaments, joints, and muscles to create the needed racquet acceleration in certain shots or movements.

So there arises the question: How do we achieve power and strength without losing range of motion and flexibility? Athletes have to train in a very deliberate and specific way and at the same time apply the principles of periodization.

We are not going into detail as to how Tennis players need to train in a gym, but I will provide some general guidelines. For more detail information, it is better to go to a professional fitness training specialist or do some research.

A Tennis player will benefit from fitness training in a gym maybe two and no more than three times per week for about 45 minutes to 1.5 hour workouts. At first he or she may start going for 45 minutes and then increase the time gradually to the 1.5 hour as he/she gets stronger and adds to the prescribed routines.

For the first three to four weeks, Tennis players should do high reps and low weight. They want to have a routine that encompasses the whole body. The deltoids or shoulders, abdominal muscles, and quadriceps are of particular importance to Tennis players. I would focus more on these areas than anything else without disregarding the rest of the musculoskeletal system. Joints are very important, and we need to make them stronger by impacting all the muscles leading to the joint in question. So if we want to prevent Tennis elbow, we want a gradual strengthening of the forearm and bicep muscles. For rotator cuff injury prevention, strengthen the shoulders by doing all the different exercises to increase strength and flexibility in that area, or if wanting to protect the ankles, then reinforce the calves and so on.

As athletes get stronger, they can add weight gradually, and decrease reps by a small percentages. Say for forward leg curls, go from 30 reps at 90 pounds to 25 reps at 100 pounds; do this for two weeks and then go to a maximum weight of 120 pounds with 20 reps. As athletes get about one week to ten days away from important competition, we may add even more weight and lessen the reps to about 12 to 15 per set. After the competition is done, go back to higher reps and less weight.

The key to avoiding injury is to avoid lifting absolute maximum weights. We want to be able to do at least a good 12 reps of whatever exercise (this holds for High-Performance Tennis Players only). When an athlete gets too close to max weight, he or she is entering more into the area of body building, and this is not good or necessary for Tennis.

Periodization is all about timing our training on and off court. Tennis players want to peak a couple of days before important tournaments and can keep the peak going for up to three weeks in a row, and sometimes even longer. Sustaining peak training longer than this is dangerous in that we start pushing the athlete's body, and again risking injury.

There is plenty of literature on periodization training and weightlifting. In reality, this subject applies more to High-Performance junior players, college players and professional players. If a player is headed this way, he/she might as well develop knowledge in this field.

Last but not least, let's talk some more about stretching. Obviously, the more players weight train in the gym, the more a conscientious stretching routine becomes necessary. Stretch before training on and off the court. But make it a serious point to stretch for 10 to 20 minutes after weight training.

Serious Tennis players need to stretch as part of their training routine as much as they would do it as part of their cool down routines after time spent on the Tennis court hitting balls. After training in the gym, players need to get serious about stretching. Instead of stretching lightly for 5 minutes, they need to really get into it and do it for 10 to 20 minutes as part of the training regimen. Again, talking about periodization, more stretching is required as players approach peak training seasons and for as long as they sustain these peaks.

The subject of stretching should not be taken lightly. It is important that we understand this. Stretching will help us sustain and increase range of motion and flexibility. Stretching will help prevent injuries big time. Stretching is of extreme importance before, during and after practice, tournament matches and training of any sort. Stretching is very relaxing, and it can be considered almost a way to get down earth mentally. Take advantage of the time devoted to stretching to meditate and think about all we do and how it all comes together. Stretching should be an awesome part of our training that is enjoyable and feels good. We can socialize or have a nice conversation while stretching. We can even use stretching time to pray!

STRETCHING FOR TENNIS

Some of the really good players and juniors that I have known throughout my career paid very little attention to stretching. Even at the professional level, we don't see players devote enough time to stretching. Stretching is neglected by a lot of athletes bringing terrible consequences in the form of injuries and bad results.

Players need to warm up lightly every day and put their body through a light stretch that should last about 7-8 minutes before hitting any Tennis balls. After training or matches, a full 12-30 minute routine should be mandatory for all competitive players regardless of age.

Static stretching has been proven to reduce power output in some studies. Dynamic stretching is preferable for warm-up purposes. Static stretching is still very helpful in increasing range of motion and flexibility and should be included in the everyday training routine of an athlete.

We should hold stretches for a minimum of 20-30 seconds each if stretching for cool-down and about 12-15 seconds for warm-up. If we are doing stretching not just for warm-up and cool-down purposes, but for training. Because we need to increase ranges of motion or just as rehab for some injury, we should stretch for a full 30-90 seconds for each stretch. The way to maximize results is to stretch one way, and then go the opposite way. For example, after a lower back stretch, done by folding the upper body forward, and touching our feet with the hands while knees are bent slightly, we should do the antagonistic or opposite stretch, by putting our hands on the hips, and leaning as far back as possible, without getting hurt, slightly bending the knees, and holding for an equal amount of time. If we have the time to do this two or three times per stretch, we will notice the results in a very short period of time, resulting in increased flexibility and range of motion, as well as reduced soreness from a tough workout, or a long Tennis match.

Players who are stiff and prone to injuries should do stretching as part of their training, not just as cool-down and warm-up routines. This will prevent injury and result in much better mobility and reach as well as more power on some of the longer swing shots such as the serve, overhead, and some groundstrokes. Increased rotational capacity will impact an increased angular velocity and power on just about all shots in Tennis, including volleys.

So what are we waiting for? Go stretch for a while. If our coach is not providing stretching routines, we need to find help if we don't know how to go about it.

INJURIES

All players suffer injuries sooner or later during their careers. It is a lot more common to see juniors with injuries once they hit their teen years as they suddenly find themselves hitting the ball harder. However, these juniors don't have the muscle mass yet to prevent the pulls, strains or tears that come with this increase in intensity. Once players get into their teen years, they start growing rapidly, and also getting stronger causing them to be borderline all the time while they train or compete.

When a player suffers an injury, it is important to pay attention and listen; neglecting pain can result in chronic re-injury.

Only the player knows how bad it is. The question to ask the injured player is whether or not he or she thinks the injury is getting worse if continuing to play or train. If the answer is yes, then the player should stop immediately.

If someone gets injured, and he or she stops before the injury worsens, the injury should usually go away within a few days. In this situation, ice and some over the counter anti-inflammatory like Advil or Ibuprofen is recommended in adequate amounts for a good three days at least. If these instructions are followed, players should be injury free in a week and ready to go at it again. However, to be stubborn about it, trying to play through the injury, can result in much more serious problems. An athlete will most likely end up at a doctor's office having to stop training for a much longer period of time, and even contemplating the possibility of surgery.

When applying ice, we want to do it in a plastic bag for a good 30 minutes without removing the ice from the injured area. The first few minutes really hurt, but once the area goes numb, an athlete cannot feel anything and will be fine. Ice a good two times a day for the duration of the injury. Most people use ice incorrectly, applying it and removing it when it starts to hurt not really allowing the cold to reach deep into the injury and reducing inflammation. Don't worry; the player will not get frostbite!

For ankle sprains, it is a good idea to submerge the whole foot in a bucket of ice water above the injury area. Such a routine can be pretty painful, but the swelling will subside quickly and allow the player to recover much faster. Remember 30 minutes!

My friend Carlos Palafox (cousin of the famous Davis Cup player Tony Palafox) sprained an ankle pretty bad during a tournament match against me. The format was round-robin. He really wanted to finish his matches because, at the time, he was an up and coming player. He went ahead and did the icing of his foot as prescribed above up to five times per day for two days! The huge inflammation went away very fast, and two days later he was playing again with a light brace on his foot! Icing works!

Rather than talking about injuries, since we have all sorts of them in Tennis, let's talk about preventing them.

As Tennis players, we want to be able to hit the ball harder, move faster, be more flexible and more explosive in all our movements. We want to have quicker reactions and reflexes. At this point, anyone would think I am now talking about fitness. Fitness and injuries are closely related to one another. A high-performance player who neglects fitness training or observes the wrong training will get injured sooner or later. While players who train well will also sustain injury, they will recover much more quickly and stay healthy for greater periods of time. A player who adheres to his/her fitness routines will have a much better chance of a quicker recovery from just about any injury as compared others who do not do any fitness training. Fit athletes will recover quicker, due to the fact that, the injured area does not have to go through as long an adaptation period as the one suffering injury who is not fit. Tennis is not a contact sport, true? However, let me ask then: is it not? Tennis comes with its own form of contact. As Tennis players, we are in contact with the ball and the ground. A high percentage of movements of the body and the racquet are explosive, and we make these explosive movements repeatedly. This is a formula for disaster unless players are fit and smart in preventing injuries.

Preventing and recovery should include adequate warm-up routines, strengthening, recovery through weight training, technical corrections on different strokes and lots of stretching.

When getting on the court, a player needs ease into the warm-up a little at the time. It is recommendable to do a little jogging, shuffling, and running to get our body temperature up, and our muscles loosened, some dynamic stretching is in place followed by some static stretching. Warm up and preparation for a match or practice session does not need to take more than 12-18 minutes. Players should start by hitting the ball softly, moving slowly to approaching balls. A good way to warm up is to hit short from a couple feet behind the service line down the middle, keeping the ball inside the service box. Follow this by some up close volleys down the middle, focusing on ball control and footwork. Once players have done this for another 5 minutes, back up to mid-court, and continue to bang balls more or less down the middle of the court keeping the feet moving without hitting the ball too hard. After another 3 minutes, go back to the baseline to continue rallying, and after a couple other minutes, players can start hitting harder.

This gradual warm up is crucial if players don't want to get injured right off the bat. Let me add that in my experience, a fairly high percentage of all injuries occurred during the first few minutes hitting balls!

Once players are done with groundstrokes, they should go back to the net, hit a few more volleys one up one back and add some overheads. Increase power and speed gradually a little at a time.

A very sensitive area is the deltoid muscle of the shoulder or rotator cuff while serving. When warming up serves, I see juniors smashing at the ball right off the bat. This is incorrect since Tennis players should start off hitting the serve softly, at about half their regular speed and effort, gradually increasing power.

It has been found that the areas most prone to injuries are the rotator cuff, elbow, knees, ankles, lower back, and hips. Maybe in that order; I see ligaments, tendons, muscles and joints getting injured quite often. As we get older, we will obviously get injured more or be more prone to injuries; therefore, we should double our warm-up and stretching routines.

It has been my own personal experience that any area that is hurting or prone to injury can be helped in the gym through high repetition low weight training. Just to give a couple examples. For a chronic lower back pain, we want to do three or four different types of sit-ups, two to three times per week: Normal crunches, leg lifts, and leg extensions, for instance. Do four sets of each with 25 to 40 reps each! Yes, that is a lot of reps. Believe me; this routine will fix lower back problems. The whole routine takes about 15-20 minutes if we go at it hard. For rotator cuff pain, we need three different types of exercise with light weights; military press, arm lifts forward, and arm lifts laterally. The amount of weight should be low enough so the athlete can do four sets of at least 20 reps each.

This type of recovery will only work when the injured area does not require surgery. If an injury keeps getting worse, seek a specialist since most likely a different path to recovery will have to be followed.

    Solid technique is the foundation of a healthy athlete. If a stroke looks or feels strange, typically injury is impending. Technique has to be smooth and solid to avoid injuries. Fixing technical issues is often the easiest way to deal with and recover from an injury. Moreover, improving technique will impact a player's results and his/her time on court will be more enjoyable, pain-free, and will result in better winning percentages. Injury-free players can spend more time on the practice court and devote their full concentration and efforts to improving their games and tournament matches.

CRAMPS

Cramps are very common in Tennis. For the longest time, if a player cramped during a match, he was just given time to recover, or he or she would just retire on his or her own. There are rules now, and these rules have been changed over the years.

Cramps, are really not injuries but in the majority of cases the result of lack of hydration and poor eating habits. Cramps can also be attributed to lack of fitness or just plain fatigue. Cramps happen when a muscle or group of muscles are pushed beyond certain limits. They are common in players who don't hydrate properly. Drinking sufficient water and electrolyte-rich drinks, as well as proper nutrition, will prevent them. Cramps are a lot more prone to happen in hot and humid environments when dehydration is more of a possibility.

A lot has been said about preventing cramps. From experience, I just tell players that they have to drink enough liquids before their matches to the point they urinate almost totally clear, and then keep drinking lots during their matches. Players may have to take some bathroom brakes on changeovers, but that is preferable to cramping.

Electrolyte drinks are good but not in excess, since they can cause stomach discomfort. It is a good idea to dilute them with water to about 50%. Also, immediately after finishing a tough match, drink a lot of water and electrolytes, eat some easy to digest carbohydrates, so the body can start recovering, gradually getting back to 100% for the next round.

In the event of cramping, it is difficult to stop them from continuing to come at us. We want take some anti-inflammatory pills like Advil immediately in order to help relax the muscles, applying ice to them in order to keep the cramping at bay. Ice will stop them almost instantly. Obviously, we want to stretch the muscle in question to take out the cramp. Some muscles are difficult to stretch, especially if a player is already cramping! Examples of muscles that can be tricky to stretch are the inner and outer thighs, groin muscles, and certain parts of the abdominal muscles. Ice will do the trick. Put on an ice bag and apply it liberally to the cramping area. As temperature drops, the cramp will dissipate. My wife knows the drill well. Because, for the longest time, on days when I abused my body by playing too much Tennis or teaching too many good players, where I had to hit a lot of balls back to them for hours on end, dehydration was almost inevitable. So at nights at home at the dinner table, or during the middle of the night I might start screaming with pain because I was cramping. The first few times this happened she thought I was having a heart attack or something of the sort. But now, she knows to run to the freezer, get some ice in a bag and apply it to the area cramping to make it go away... ugh!

Only the player can tell if he or she can continue to play through a cramp. If the player in question is able to continue to move enough on the court to return balls, and is able to keep the cramps more or less under control with ice and stretching, then, he/she should consider finishing the match, if it looks like he or she still has a chance to win. Now and then, the cramps may go away allowing the player to finish his/her match without further trouble. Remember Michael Chang at Roland Garros versus Ivan Lendl serving underhand? Winning? Beating Stefan Edberg in the semis and Boris Becker in the final to win his only Grand Slam title? If he had retired, no Grand Slams for him... Can you imagine? Sometimes we just have to continue to play and believe that we can win.

For now the rules allow treatment to a player for cramping in one occasion. For all subsequent cramps after that first treatment, whether it is the same muscles cramping or not, the player will have to deal with them on his/her own. For more detail on rules and medical timeouts, look at the 101s section of this book in "101 Rules that matter."

Cramps are pretty much a part of competitive Tennis. We should carry a couple of plastic bags in our racquet bag, in case we end up cramping and need to ice the affected area. However, let me say it again, the best way to deal with cramps is to prevent them!

NUTRITION, HYDRATION, AND SLEEP

PROPER EATING

Whatever it is we do with our dietary habits is a personal choice; whatever these habits are they better be helping us perform at the peak of our ability physically, mentally and emotionally. If this is not the case, then we need to be monitoring what we swallow. Here are some reasons we should watch what we eat; lack of concentration, lack of mobility, lack of stamina, lack of resistance, lack of energy, lack of power, and lack of mental toughness. Also, excessive weight, or not enough weight, as well as, hyper or hypo activity during matches or practices, etc... If there are signs of any of these conditions, consider how they might be related to diet. Some of these situations may have to be referred to a professional dietitian or doctor.

The diet of a high-performance junior player needs to be: 60-80% carbohydrates, 20-30% protein, and 10-20% fats. This is obviously an oversimplification. But it is a nice starting point. Lots of carbohydrates are needed such as cereals, grains, salads, fruit, juices, pastas, and breads. Not so much should be taken in as protein, red meat, fish, and milk. And very little fat, fried stuff, greasy meals like pizza and very cheesy meals are not good for an athlete. Different age kids have unique nutritional needs. If a kid is ready for gym work, then they maybe should increase the intake of protein-rich meals. If more detailed information is needed, see a dietitian or a professional in the field.

The ranges mentioned above are pretty wide because no two athletes require the same nutrition. A competitive Tennis player needs discipline in his or her eating habits and needs to pinpoint what works best under different circumstances. One major point is to understand our body's digestion. Eat properly and in the right amounts and timing before matches and practices. It is not uncommon to see a player throw up on the court after a few games during a match, because he or she ate too much or interrupted his/her digestion with all the movement of intense Tennis.

HYDRATION, DRINKING, AND ELECTROLYTES

If Tennis players are hydrated properly, everything works better, their muscles will be more responsive, they feel more energetic, and they think and concentrate better. There is scientific proof of this. We have to drink lots of water before, during and after matches; especially when it is hot and humid out there. How much is enough? Remember that by the time we are actually thirsty, it is already too late, so drink plenty on changeovers. Don't allow thirst to set in. Players of different ages and sizes have different needs. But a general rule of thumb, is to drink three to five full gulps of water on every changeover, six to eight in extreme conditions (1 gulp more or less = ½ ounce, 1 paper cup = more or less one gulp, 3 cubic centimeters = more or less 1 ounce). Cold water is better in warm conditions since it helps our system to cool down.

Energy and electrolyte drinks are fine to a point. A player may start drinking electrolyte and energy drinks towards the end of the first set, or at the beginning of the second set if the match is close and if conditions are tough. It all depends on different factors. Players are probably asking themselves the following questions: If these energy and electrolyte drinks are so good, why don't we drink just that and forget all about straight water? The answer to that is simple. Water requires very little effort from our system to be absorbed. Electrolyte and energy drinks may take a lot more effort from the stomach to digest and actually lead to stomach cramps, nausea, vomiting and more dehydration. Instead of helping, they become a problem. These are symptoms of hypernatremia and hypercalcemia, caused by the excessive consumption of minerals in drinks, such as calcium, sodium and potassium. We see too many kids out there drinking nothing but energy or power drinks, and all they are doing half the time is actually keeping their bodies and minds from performing at their best. Also, remember that a lot of these sports drinks have a lot of sugar, and if we are trying to monitor or control weight, by drinking sugary drinks, we will actually be putting on weight, if we are not burning it on the court. A good rule of thumb, here again, is to drink the power, and the electrolyte drinks diluted 50% with just cool water.

One drink that I have found useful in hot, humid conditions during tough summers is just plain bubbly mineral water. It seems to have the necessary amounts of minerals in it without the added sugars of sports drinks. Give it a try; it may just be the ticket to prevent dehydration and cramping.

SLEEP

Sleeping is fundamental for top performance. Kids under the age of 15 need at least 9 hours of complete sleep to fully recover and to be 100% for their matches or workouts the next day. After that, 7 to 8 hours should be sufficient for most, although some kids who are still growing may need more; it all depends on the individual. Less than 7 is just plain unsatisfactory.

Tennis players do have to get up early to start getting ready for their matches. According to studies, it takes up to six hours to be fully awake after a full night's sleep. Of course, this is an extreme. We need to get up as early as common sense dictates. Getting up an hour before a big match is a mistake, in such situations it is better to just get up earlier, and deal with the lack of sleep in other ways.

Avoid going to sleep with a full stomach. Players forced to a late dinner due to late matches, are better off eating lightly, so digestion is not an obstacle to sound sleep, and they feel rested the next day.

When possible, try to get used to siestas (midday or afternoon rests or naps) during the day. These are of great value to help the athlete get a little extra sleep, especially when not enough was had the previous nights. Don't go for siestas before matches, this can backfire if not enough time is allowed for the player to be fully awake and energized to go at it by the time he or she gets on the court.

A WORD ON COFFEE

Coffee can be misunderstood in Tennis. Coffee, if not in excess, can make the difference between winning and losing. I don't disagree with some players who drink one or maybe two cups of coffee before some matches. Coffee can boost metabolism; that means having the needed energy available so we can perform at the peak of our ability in early-morning matches. Coffee can help players wake up and be more near 100% physically and mentally by the time they step on the court. We have to figure out a way to be full of energy and as wide awake as possible by the time we get on the court. What if we play a match at 8 am? This is actually the norm for most tournaments. We probably need to be up by 6 am, take a shower, have a light breakfast with some coffee and get on a court hitting balls a full hour before our match. And oftentimes, right after warm up, we should maybe take in some more coffee as we get ready to go check in at the tournament desk.

As a former professional player, let me say that we used to follow a routine similar to this. We even drank some coffee for midday or late afternoon matches sometimes, depending on how we were feeling. Of course, coffee has its downside. Coffee can get a player jittery, hyper, and causes some dehydration because it is a natural diuretic. So we need to know ourselves to make sure we drink the right amounts. The dehydration part can be countered by drinking two full cups of water for every one of coffee. Sandwiching the coffee with one full cup of water before and after the coffee is a good idea.

Read about all the coffee drinking benefits in the 101 scientific based tips section of this book.

SECTION V

GEAR AND EQUIPMENT

RACQUETS FOR CHILDREN

Here in the US and the rest of the World it is common to use smaller racquets for children. They come in as small as 21 inches and can be found all the way up to 27 inches.

Kids starting Tennis at ages 3-5 should go with a 21 inch, 5-7 go for 23 inches, 7-9 a 25 inch racket is more or less normal. For ages 9-12, racquets in the 26-27 inch range are recommended. At age 9 a lot of kids are big and strong enough for a 27 inch racquet. At this age, they can maneuver and swing a 27 inch frame with good accuracy and consistency as long as the racquet is light. It all depends on where kids are with their development physiologically as well as their Tennis skills. Juniors that have been playing for a couple of years are usually more capable of dealing with a heavier racquet since their arms and shoulders are already stronger, and more conditioned for the use of a racquet. Also, we need to take into consideration where the child stands developmentally. Some kids who are developing in competitive Tennis will probably be able to handle a regular size racquet at 9 years of age. Manufacturers make full-size racquets in very light weights for this purpose. Very light 27 inch racquets range between 8 and 10 ounces. Seek advice on this from coaches and dealerships.

In the US, it is a rule for competitive juniors, to have to play with a 25 inch racquet or shorter in 10 and under sanctioned competition on 60 foot courts.

The weight and length of the racquet are important considerations in a racquet of choice for children. If a ten-year-old has been playing for a couple of years, a light regular-sized racquet should be fine. A heavier racket will minimize injury rather than amplify it. Given the right biomechanics are in place, a heavier racquet will help a child hit harder because force equals mass times acceleration, one of Newton's laws of Physics!

Go for the headlight frames and stay away from the head-heavy racquets that distort the natural swing and are more conducive to causing injuries in young players.

RACQUETS... THE TRUTH!

Tennis racquets come in all sizes, shapes and colors. What we go for is very much a personal choice. All manufacturers make quality rackets. And all of them have top of the line models. Also, all of them make at least one model a specific player should be able to adapt to. But it is also true that all manufacturers make lots of worthless junk. In fact, most racquets on the market are of very low quality.

Opposed to popular belief, it is not hard to pick the appropriate racquet, but it does require a little knowledge. All a player has to do, is match his/her sex, build, and playing style to that of the touring pros, good club pros, or quality players in the area. And "voila"! Play with what they play with. Obviously, asking the local Tennis-pro should be the way to go. But, unfortunately, a lot of club pros go for the easy, fast, and most convenient sale.

Another point of interest is the problem with extremely powerful, head- heavy and unforgiving frames. These are to blame for Tennis elbow problems, as well as wrist and shoulder injuries. So the recommendation is to stay away from very stiff head-heavy racquets, for the most part.

Graphite or carbon is the way to go as far as materials are concerned. Stay away from entry level metal racquets. Post the wood era and for a while, metal was considered the best material available for racquets; aluminum, titanium and steel were in high production in the 70s and 80s. Tennis players should play with as flexible a frame as possible without hurting their game too much. More flexible frames have less power but are more forgiving on arms and joints. Also, consider the head size and length of the racquet. Oversize frames are better for volleys, returns, blocking the ball back, and finesse shots. Oversize may be better for serving, too. I would also say that at the recreational level, oversize is better for doubles than singles. Midsize and midplus racquets will usually enhance your groundstrokes. They have better control off the ground and yes usually less power.

WHAT TENNIS PROS DON'T TEACH (WTPDT)

The standard length of a Tennis racquet is 27 inches; that is a good length for maneuverability and feels good on the hand. However, there are some manufacturers that offer 27.20, 27.25, 27.5 and even 28 inch lengths. These frames have advantages and disadvantages. Groundstrokes will suffer from a longer frame. But these longer racquets are good for volleys and serves, for slicing and dicing, for finesse shots. And if this is a big part of someone's game, then he or she may definitely want to consider them.

Keep in mind that a racquet is only as good as its stringing job. Make sure to read the section on stringing. A sports car with pickup truck tires will probably feel more like a pickup truck than a sports car. Think about it, Tennis players want a quality string job that fits the racquet and enhances their game.

Nowadays there are some extremely light racquets out on the market. My feeling about them is that they are ineffective. Racquets weighing 10 ounces or less in weight should really be considered only for children or some senior players. Lighter racquets are a lot more prone to cause injuries; due to the fact that most of the impact of the ball on the racquet, will vibrate up the player's arms joints (wrist, elbow, shoulder). A heavier racquet will absorb a lot more of this shock! Also a moderately heavier racquet, will deliver more power to the ball than a light one. Tennis players should go for the heaviest racquet they can handle with a good degree of comfort without sacrificing ability level.

Another thing to stay away from is the extremely stiff racquet. First of all, these super stiff racquets don't feel good at impact, and they too are to blame for a lot of arm joint injuries. Much if not all the shock goes to the arm at impact due to the great stiffness! So stay away from them. Very stiff racquets feel like bone cracks, and they are not pleasurable to hit Tennis balls with.

Here is an interesting piece of statistical information: 100% of all touring professionals weight and balance their racquets with lead tape! Adding weight to a frame, in order to achieve certain qualities in the racquet, is called racquet customization. And it is nothing more than messing with the racquet's weight and balance to fit or enhance a player's taste and game. Some players add as much as two ounces of lead tape on the head, handle and the throat of the racquet! What is the Moral? Add some lead tape (weight) to our racquets! Get someone who knows what he/she is doing to help us with this project!

TENNIS BALLS

There are all kinds of Tennis balls. Wilson, Dunlop, Penn, Slazenger, Babolat, Gamma, Tretorn, Spalding, etc... They all have to conform to the ranges stated in the rules of Tennis. The size, the weight, the bounce, and the composition! For all of these variables, the rulebook will allow a range for each one of the different categories. Because of these ranges, different Tennis balls from different manufacturers or specifications may feel very different to a player. Some of them feel great, a lot of them not so good, and the majority of them just feel average on the strings as we impact the ball. Some balls last longer than others. Some keep a robust bounce better. To a certain degree, durability and playability, depend on who is hitting the balls, and on what surface the balls are being played on. Players who hit hard and with a lot of spin, will wear them out a lot quicker than someone that hits flat or softer.

Extra duty felt balls are designed for hard court surfaces. They typically have more, or tighter felt in order to survive the more erosive nature of hard courts. Hard courts are coated with a silicon sand rich plastic paint that eats up the felt on the balls. Some of them have a lot of it to slow down the bounce of the ball in order to make them play slower to allow longer or more pleasurable play. Extra duty felt balls may be a little heavier and at the top limit for the maximum weight specification as per the rulebook. Regular duty felt balls are made with a little less felt and are designed to play better on soft surfaces like clay or grass, or maybe synthetic grass or artificial clay. For the money we pay, we need to use Extra Duty Felt since typically they will last longer under most circumstances. Personally I like a heavier ball; it gives me a more wholesome feel on hard hits. It also doesn't travel as fast as a regular duty felt and makes for better play where it is harder to finish the point.

For the most part, Tennis balls come in a pressurized can; this is necessary to make the balls bounce according to specifications. There are also pressureless balls. Pressureless balls are sold in little cardboard boxes.

Pressureless balls are usually preferred for playing at locations where the altitude is higher than 3000 feet above sea level. Pressureless balls will typically last longer than pressurized balls but will feel very different, being stiffer and woodier as we hit them. Pressureless balls are considered High Altitude regulation balls. They are extensively used in areas that are mountainous and where it is very difficult to play with regular balls. In fact in several places where Tennis is played at high altitude, a regular ball will not meet bounce and weight specifications due to the balls lighter weight, thinner air, and lesser gravitational pull. It is very difficult to play Tennis with regular balls in a high altitude area. Our shots will fly all over the place, kind of like birds let out of a cage, and it is very hard to keep the ball on the court if we hit hard at all. Enormous amounts of spin are required and having to hit a lot lower over the net.

Tennis balls must conform to certain criteria for size, weight, deformation, and bounce to be approved for regulation play. The International Tennis Federation defines the official diameter as 65.41-68.58 mm (2.575-2.700 inches). Balls must weigh between 56.0 g and 59.4 g (1.975-2.095 ounces). Yellow and white are the only colors approved by the USTA and ITF, and most balls produced are fluorescent yellow (known as "optic yellow"). The color first introduced in 1972 following research demonstrating they were more visible on television. Tennis balls are filled with air and are covered by a uniform felt-covered rubber compound, although some manufacturers have produced balls filled with small polystyrene spheres inside them.

Tennis balls begin to lose their liveliness as soon as the can is opened up, and the balls are exposed to the regular atmospheric conditions. A ball is tested for bounce by dropping it from a height of 254 cm (100 inches) onto concrete. A bounce between 135 and 147 cm (53-58 inches) is acceptable (if taking place at sea-level and 20°C / 68°F with relative humidity of 60%; high-altitude balls have different characteristics when tested at sea-level). Modern regulation Tennis balls are kept under pressure (approximately two atmospheres) until initially used.

CLOTHING FOR TENNIS

On court clothing and fashion have changed a lot. We have gone from all white, cotton clothing to all kinds of colorful synthetic materials.

Designs have gone from kind of tight and short for men, all the way too baggy and very loose, and now the tighter fashions are returning again. For girls, it seems to be moving from tight, small fitting Tennis clothing to even tighter and smaller. In women's clothing, we see even more of a tendency to lean towards synthetic fabrics and less and less cotton and natural materials.

This book is definitely not the place for telling players or anyone how to dress on a Tennis court. But I would certainly like to mention a couple of things in suggesting what is considered classy, and also, what is smart to wear.

For men, the classic colors are white, navy, and black. Nowadays we see a lot of green, optic/neon colors, brown and tan. They all look okay. It is hard to beat all white if we really want to stand out and look impressive on court. T-shirts are less classic looking than collared Polo and Lacoste style, but it may be more comfortable. The obvious downside to the all-white look is cleanliness and the challenge to keep it looking good throughout the day. I don't know how many times my mom and now my wife had a perfect, spotless white outfit ready for me to wear the next day! I love it! However, as soon as I have it on, I stained it with coffee, ink, salsa or whatever else; it never fails!

As far as materials are concerned, the new synthetics are acceptable; however, they tend to be sticky in hot, humid weather, and very cold in cool weather.

It is hard to beat a good quality all cotton shirt, t-shirt or even shorts, and warm-up jackets and pants. Cotton absorbs sweat well in humid or hot weather. If a shirt gets too wet, we can always change into another one. In cold weather, cotton keeps us at a comfortable temperature. The other thing about good quality cotton is that it is durable. Unfortunately, most cotton garments sold these days are poorly made, stiff or rough, and the designs are unimaginative. The drawback here is that good cotton Tennis clothing will be pretty expensive and very hard to come by. Good cotton material or fabric is usually thin and very flexible and comfortable, thus not inhibiting performance on the court, adapting to the contours and movement of the person wearing it.

Wearing a hat or visor in Tennis is a must today; especially in some southern and southwest states. A good quality cap, visor or Australian style hat are great to have on a bright sunny day. Nothing stops UV rays better than a good hat. It makes for more comfortable play, keeps our hair under control, and for the most part it looks good.

When playing in cold weather, layering is important. A cotton t-shirt as a bottom layer, followed by Tennis shirt or another t-shirt, maybe even a long sleeve t-shirt. As an outwear layer, go for a sweatshirt and maybe even a jacket or hoodie may be necessary. We may remove layers as needed during the day or as we get warmed-up practicing or playing a match. We want all materials to be flexible and fitting just right, and that garments don't inhibit us from moving as needed to execute our shots and run around the court!

TENNIS SHOES

Tennis shoes are probably one of the most important pieces of equipment. Tennis shoes are definitely more important than clothing. The bottom line is, that if our feet are not comfortable, our shoes are not the appropriate ones for the surface or our foot type. If the fit of our shoes is not right for Tennis, we will probably not move very well, or be very comfortable that day on the court.

    Let me start by saying that the right fit for Tennis on shoes is not the same that we would have for say running or other sports. For Tennis players need a snug to slightly tight fit. Our shoelaces have to be uniformly tightened and laced-up. Our foot should not be sliding inside the shoe back and forth or side to side as we move on the court. Not only will we not be able to move well, but we are a lot more prone to injury if we don't have the right shoe/fit combination. Obviously the most common injury is the ankle sprain. But Achilles tendon/heel injuries are just as common as other plantar injuries on the ball of the foot, arch, as well as toes. Blisters are injuries due to wrong shoe/fit combination as well and should be prevented at all costs since it is next to impossible to move well on the court with blistered feet.

    Shoes should provide solid support all around the foot; especially at the ball of the foot area and the forward edges of the shoe. A good cushioning sole, especially towards the back of the shoe is an absolute must. And if we play on different surfaces, we need to have hardcourt shoes, clay court shoes, and even grass court shoes, if we can afford the luxury of playing on grass courts. Hardcourt shoes tend to have a larger size grid. They are usually a little heavier since they have to withstand more wear. Clay court shoes are better identified for having the grill style grid on the soles for better grab on the clay surfaces without harming it. For grass, we need something similar to clay. It will be slippery for the most part, but that is the nature of playing Tennis on grass courts. Every year at Wimbledon, we see professionals falling and slipping on the grass all the time, this happens a lot more during the first week of the tournament since the grass is newer, therefore, a lot more slippery.

A good solution to preventing ankle injuries is to wear mid top Tennis Shoes. For a while, they were very popular. Players with weak ankles or ankle injuries can still find some of these in a couple of the different brands. Basketball shoes are okay for Tennis, and they do make a whole lot of different styles in mid top models; the sole is usually okay for clay or hardcourts, and they last reasonably well. For the longest time, I wore only basketball shoes for Tennis with good results. A lot of professionals wear ankle braces full time during matches to prevent injuries. However, these ankle support braces may indeed prevent injury, but they may also weaken areas of the foot and legs prone to injury. One downside to ankle braces is that, for the most part, they do look weird and bulky. If a player is wearing any type of support for preventative measure, it is recommended that he or she does not wear it all the time on the Tennis court. Maybe only during tournament competition or days of intense practice and match play sessions. Taping up the ankle or foot is a good proposition if the player knows what he or she is doing or knows someone who does. At most sanctioned tournaments, we can find trainers who are experts in doing this sort of stuff. If a player is having issues with foot or ankle injuries, I highly recommend that he/she talks to them before getting on court and they will advise on whether to tape the foot or not.

For added support, it is a great idea to wear gel heel inserts under the shoe insoles. This practice dramatically reduces the impact to the ankle/knee/hips/lower-back junctures as we run around and lunge for balls on the Tennis court. I have been doing this for years now with great results! In fact, I wear double gel heels on both feet all the time.

A couple seasons back, I purchased a pair of running/gym shoes. They were super light and very comfortable. They felt like gloves on my foot. Also, they did not look like your typical running shoe with the big spikes or stalls and super tall and wide on the hill. They actually looked a little like a regular Tennis shoe, so I decided to try them for Tennis. Oh! Could I move on these shoes! They were awesome and light and extremely comfortable. I kept on using them for about two weeks. And then, they started to virtually disintegrate before my eyes. The bottoms came unglued, the light side support peeled off, and in two weeks they looked like they were six months old already. I took them back to the store, and they replaced them with a new pair; this happened like 3 or 4 times. I finally decided that it was not the ethical thing to do. These shoes had not been designed for Tennis, but for moving, walking and running straight forward, not the side to side, in an explosive way, on rough surfaces required for hard Tennis.

It really is too bad that manufacturers have not figured out a way to make a Tennis shoe that is super comfortable, durable, light, and that looks good. Tennis shoes are always going to have to be pretty heavy compared to Running shoes or gym shoes. They need all kinds of support and reinforcements all around in order to protect our feet from injury, provide good footing and last a reasonable time for the player using them. Some very intense and active players can wear out one pair of shoes in one week! I have done this on a few occasions. A funny such anecdote happened to me at a pro tournament in Veracruz, Mexico, when I had to finish a qualifying match by applying racquet head tape to my shoes since the sole had completely worn all the way through, in the middle of the first set. I would put the tape on the shoe on all changeovers; the good thing was, I never run out of tape, but was close! Unlike other sports, Tennis is played on all kinds of surfaces. In the US, Tennis is played on hard courts that completely eat up Tennis shoes the great majority of times. The rigors of Tennis are indeed tremendous. That is why it is so important that we find the right Tennis shoes in order to not only avoid injury but to be able to play our best Tennis.

SOCKS FOR TENNIS

It does not matter whether or not we purchase the proper shoes if we are going to end up with the wrong socks. Socks are simpler in that the right fit is easier to obtain. Remember, Tennis players need to have a snug to tight a fit for their shoes. The way to custom fit our shoes is to get the right sock(s) combination to go with them. Socks made out of cotton are great, and they are the best at absorbing sweat, but we may have to change pairs in long matches. Whether cotton or synthetic materials are preferred, we do need good cushioning in the heel and the toe areas. Since the different shoe manufacturers size their shoes differently, we will need to have in our Tennis sock drawer at home different kinds of socks all the time. Meaning some may have to be thicker than others or wider than others in order to get the right fit for our Tennis shoes. I prefer crew height socks for clay since this keeps the clay from getting in my shoe and directly in contact with the skin of my foot. The crew look is not popular with women, and they deal with this issue differently by changing socks a lot more often than men do. Women prefer the short or tin look which is just barely over the edge of the shoe itself.

All manufacturers make socks specifically for Tennis. They make them in different degrees of thickness and utilize cotton as well as synthetic fabrics. Also, consider basketball socks for Tennis. They are popular for Tennis and are of good quality.

Finally, let me say that personally it is hard to beat the double sock combination for Tennis. Wearing double socks allows what no single pair of socks can achieve. A player can wear a synthetic and a cotton combination to find the perfect fit, as well as good breathability. I have done this my entire life, and I know this is definitely the way to go. A lot of people think a two-sock combination is too hot, but this is not accurate. Two layers of fabric in between the player's skin and the actual inner surface of the Tennis shoe makes for a bigger gap of air circulating inside the shoe, thus a cooler and more comfortable shoe. In cold weather, the two layers will keep our feet warmer. As we tighten the shoelaces, we actually put pressure on the two pairs of socks and not directly on our feet, allowing better blood circulation and a better more comfortable fit. Double socks also permit a perfect fit by combining just the right sock thickness necessary to have our shoes fit just right. It is a good idea to make sure to wear two socks when trying on new shoes at the store to get the right sizing. If buying shoes online, we need to go for brands that we are familiar with and models that we have worn before to avoid having to send the pair back because they were too tight or too big.

STRINGS, STRINGING MACHINES AND RACQUET STRINGING

It seems that nowadays racquet performance is all about the different strings on the market. Tension is not given enough consideration. The new polyester strings are in vogue these days. Gut is definitely taking a back seat to this all new, revolutionary string material. The truth is that Polyester (which has been around for over 20 years) strings last a lot longer than all the synthetic and natural gut strings of the past. Polyester plays very differently in that it is less resilient than its counterparts. Poly strings are great for topspin, or just spin, in general. String manufacturers are capable of producing a geometrical cross-section in the shape of a square, a star, a triangle, a hexagon and so on and so forth, in very thin gauges with good durability. The thin gauges and geometry of the cross-section creates unequaled grab/bite on the ball's surface. Poly strings in 18 and 19 gauge are not uncommon nowadays. Whereas with the multifilament and synthetic guts of the past, this gage was like money down the drain since they would break in less than 30 minutes of hard hitting. I remember the first time I tried a 17 gauge synthetic gut. I started hitting and loving the feel, but in about 20 minutes I busted the strings. Synthetic gut, nylon strings, natural guts, and multifilament strings are just too soft, and not as smooth on the surface, therefore denting or notching a lot quicker than the smoother surfaced, and much harder materials of the polyester strings.

What a lot of touring pros are doing nowadays is known as hybrid stringing. Let me say that hybrid stringing is not a new idea either; it was very popular in the 80s and 90s also. Hybrid stringing is nothing other than the combination of two different strings. Main or vertical strings are the load carrying strings, and the ones that, for the most part, will dictate what feel, control, and power we will get. The main strings are the ones that usually break as they get worn out by frictioning themselves with the crosses. The crosses or horizontal strings don't receive much wear and fill in the gaps, per say, to complete the string job on a racquet. In a hybrid string job, we will have one type of string on the mains and another one on the crosses. A string with decent durability and fairly nice feel, should be used on the main strings, and one of good feel, and, for the most part, much thinner (17, 18 or even 19 gauge) will be desirable for the crosses. But today, a lot of the good players are going for poly on the mains and synthetic gut, multifilament or even natural gut on the crosses. Some use the opposite combination. So if the main strings are going to determine what kind of feel a player gets. Using the synthetic gut or multifilament on the mains, and poly on the crosses, then we will basically get the feel of the synthetic gut or multifilament as we hit the ball, but the durability will not be as good. By doing this, we will get the added advantage of the indenture of the poly on the ball for added spin. A few years ago, I got lucky and was able to buy a Wilson Pro Staff 2009 US Open autographed Roger Federer racket at a silent auction for charity. It is strung kind of loose, at like 51 pounds or so. It has Natural Gut on the mains in 17 gauge, and Luxilon Polyester on the crosses, probably in 18 gauge. This combination probably gives Fed the best of both worlds, in that it will have great feel from the 17 gage natural gut, nice spin control with the aid of the Luxilon poly, and okay durability, since durability is based on the main strings and not so much the crosses. Although I wouldn't think, Fed is worried about durability! Since he probably has 6 or 7 racquets in his racquet bag and can get them strung whenever and as many times as he wants to!

On the subject of durability, further explanation is needed. The reason poly strings last so long is that the polyester surface is so smooth and hard. This diminishes to a great extent the friction between mains and crosses, extending the life of the string as much as triple and quadruple comparing to traditional nylon, synthetic gut, and natural gut strings. My favorite combination is a star cross section string in 17 Gauge in the mains and a smooth cross section in 19 gauge on the crosses. This gives me great feel, due to the super thin gage and very good spin control because of the star cross section and ball biting qualities of polyester. For durability purposes, go for poly string on the mains and the thinner gauge poly, synthetic, or multifilament on the crosses.

There are different degrees of poly string quality. Prices range widely. Some of the most expensive are over $20 per set. The less expensive polyesters come in 660 feet reels with 21 sets per reel at $40 per reel. Doing the math--we can see how buying string by the reel is a lot cheaper! Generally, low-quality poly, will last longer but will not have the feel or consistency. Another disadvantage of the treated top dollar polyesters is that they tend to lack springiness or forgiveness and end up feeling a little too much like a synthetic gut or multifilament. The one thing I love about polyester is its springiness.

One of the big drawbacks to all poly strings is the tension retention qualities of the material. It does not hold nearly as well as a fine multifilament. A lot of the top quality polyester strings are heat treated and alloyed in order to help them sustain tension; however, this usually makes them softer, and they don't last as long. In my mind and like in many other things in life; the best of both worlds lies somewhere in the middle. My own personal recommendation for now is the Pro Supex Blue Gear Platinum 17 gage in the mains hybridized with Pro Supex Micro 19 gage on the crosses. Not super expensive, but nice.

Talking about polyester strings, let me also add that once we have gotten used to them, it will be very hard to go back to the traditional strings. Players will get used to that extra spin and springiness and will immediately miss it if trying to get back to what they used in the past.

Going a little into detail on synthetic gut, multifilament, Kevlar and natural gut strings:

First of all, let me say, that anything written now may be obsolete tomorrow. Technology, innovation, and new string materials are hitting the Tennis industry all the time, and ten years from now, none of this stuff may be applicable anymore.

Synthetic Gut strings have been around for a long time. Basically, these strings are made out of nylon material. There are all kinds of different grades, and they come in all colors and gauges from 15L to 19 gauges (the higher the number in gauge the smaller the diameter of the string) for Tennis. Generally, these strings are pretty forgiving with good feel but not great durability. Just to give a comparison, a string job of a modern poly string will last up to five times longer than its counterpart in nylon if restrung at the same tension and on the same racquet. However, a lot of players still use nylon synthetic guts because it is forgiving on the joints and has a good feel. An advantage of these strings is that they are relatively inexpensive in comparison to top dollar poly or multifilament strings.

The best synthetic gut on the market is heat treated and also hybridized with either gut or multifilament. For a good while, Kevlar strings were very popular, and they always came hybrid with some sort of synthetic gut for the cross strings. Kevlar lasts well and plays fairly nice. I played some with it in the late 90s and had a good time with it. Kevlar is relatively expensive but worth its price. Just for testing I recently restrung one of my racquets with a Kevlar/Synthetic hybrid combination, and was pleasantly surprised at how nice it played. Kevlar tends to be stiffer and cups the ball less with less of a trampoline effect. In other words, Kevlar has a kind of dead feeling to it, but it still performs beautifully (meaning the strings don't deform very much upon impact of the ball since it is so stiff). However, when Kevlar strings were put on the market, the idea was to offer a string that lasted a long time, and I can confidently say that Kevlar; will not last as long as some polyester strings, under the *all other things being equal principle*.

Multifilament is one of the best values we can get for our money as far as playability, forgiveness and feel. Compared to real natural gut, it is relatively inexpensive, and it plays a lot like it. It usually comes in natural color; although I have seen Babolat and Technifibre come up with colors as well. It can be found in all the different gauges, and it plays well, except that it is not as durable as Polyesters or even some synthetic guts. For feel and great stability as well as affordability, tension retention, multifilament is probably still king of the hill. Natural gut, generally, plays better, but it is so much more expensive and not too many players can afford it.

Natural gut lost a lot of its popularity over the last 30 years or so because it is so expensive, and because it is more difficult to string. One set alone of quality natural gut is going to cost up to $45 USD and more. Stringers or Tennis Shops just about everywhere, will come up with a markup (stringing labor of natural gut, will cost as much as twice the regular string job of other strings) for stringing it, because of added difficulty when stringing since it is so delicate. A string job with natural gut will run $60-$80 or more at the local Tennis shop. My feeling on this is that manufacturers and stringers everywhere would have to drop their prices in order to make it a competitive alternative. Nowadays less than 1% of Tennis players everywhere use natural gut; I would know this since only one out of every 400-700 hundred string jobs done will be a natural gut requests. At our Tennis shop in NW Arkansas, we string up to 100 racquets a month and in 8 years at this facility we have done less than 20 natural gut string jobs. Another thing that needs to be mentioned here is that natural gut requires protection from humidity and dampness. Water or excess humidity on the balls will ruin it. A player using it has to protect the string in a sealed plastic bag once strung to keep the strings from absorbing humidity. Also, it is a good idea to get some beeswax and apply it as a sealant after playing. I remember my uncle, Manuel Guerra, who introduced me to Tennis when I was 8 years old doing this very thing.

He used natural gut, and I remember him applying the wax to his Wilson Jack Kramer racquets before storing them in his locker at the Guadalajara Club in Mexico.

Natural gut offers by far the greatest feel and stability on the string bed. Unequaled control and good tension retention come along with it. Durability is not bad if regularly waxed. Definitely worth it if a player can afford it. Natural gut can be a good option for players that don't break the string often since they don't have to worry about paying for string jobs all the time.

A lot of the top touring professionals go for hybrid string jobs with natural gut on the crosses and some high-quality polyester on the mains. This combination offers, as mentioned above, the best of both worlds. And when I say top professionals I mean exactly that; some of them use this combination as part of their sponsorship package. Very few if any of the players ranked lower than top 100 in the World get natural gut as part of a sponsorship, so they opt out of it for some of the other strings.

BREAKING STRINGS

It is an exciting thing to see a child break strings for the first time. My daughter broke hers when she was just barely 8-years-old. Her racket was strung with some 17 gauge synthetic gut. However, an up and comer junior player, hitting his/her early teen years will become a string breaking machine. When I was like 14 years old, I started breaking strings like a maniac. My Dad did not understand, and for a while my stringer would just put a patching job, but 3 or 4 days later I was back for another patch. My wooden racquets had all kinds of knots in them and different types and colors of strings; I wish I had some pictures to show. But I learned my lesson soon, so I got myself a little table-top stringing machine and started doing my own.

My recommendation is that if a player only has one racquet, he/she has it inspected by a knowledgeable player before tournaments and have it restrung if need be one or two days before the event. If two racquets, then use only one until the strings break, so the player will always have a freshly new string job on the 2nd racquet in the bag. Here is a personal anecdote from my junior years. Playing a doubles match in a national tournament in the 16s in the Club España in Mexico City, I had broken strings on one of my two racquets during my singles match earlier that day. We lost the first set like 6/4 and then I broke the strings off my second racquet, one of our opponents said he could let me borrow one of his which was a very nice gesture. As we got into the second set, we started winning pretty handily, and at that point, the guy that had let me borrow his racquet went, "I think I need my racquet back now, this one is not feeling good anymore". So I had to give it back and played with someone else's that was way different, and I could not hit a ball in the court to save my life. We ended up losing the match, of course. If I'd had one fresh string job in my bag, that would not have happened to me! If a player has the luxury of 3 or more racquets, then he/she can use them randomly keeping an eye on the different string jobs before tournaments.

WHAT TENNIS PROS DON'T TEACH (WTPDT)

Another important recommendation for player with 3 or more racquets is to have one strung at a slightly looser tension. It comes in handy when hitting into the wind, or for the days we just cannot hit the ball with any pace, and need a little extra help from the looser strings in trampolining the ball a little further, harder, or deeper.

STRINGING MACHINES

There are several types of stringing machines. Prices oscillate from $100 to $7000 US Dollars and more. Size and shape vary just as much. However, a good stringer will get the job done regardless of the stringing machine. One of those state of the art electronic machines that costs a small fortune, will do about the same job, as a $200 Drop Weight Table-Top model, provided the stringer is fairly experienced, and knows what he or she is doing.

So, if someone is thinking about buying a machine for family or personal use, he or she does not need to go invest a lot of money on this. Target the mid-range tabletop models that are easy to store, and can actually be thrown in the trunk of a vehicle, to take to tournaments. If a player would rather not mess with learning how to do string, and want to get his/her racquets done at some Tennis-Shop, create a relationship with a trusted pro-shop. Talk to the person getting the stringing done, and find out a little about his/her experience stringing racquets. It would be fair to say that almost anyone who has been stringing racquets for over three years or has strung at least 100 or 130 rackets should be knowledgeable enough to deliver consistent and reliable results.

Also, when getting racquets strung by someone other than the usual Tennis Shop, study the stringing jobs of the local professional for tension, uniformity, etc... Look at the knots and ask them what the tension is on the different racquets inspected and see if they seem to be the right tightness. By moving the bottom strings near the throat with the index and the thumb fingers and by hitting the string bed with the base of the hand, anyone can get pretty good at estimating tension.

Players with a lot of power and spin will break strings all the time, and it would be a good lifetime investment to buy a stringing machine. However, if a player does not have the time or does not want to do his/her own stringing. Stringing racquets takes time, devotion for the skill and patience, then he/she needs to make sure to at least buy his/her own strings. This way he/she can control this variable, always getting his/her racquets done with the string of choice. Also, the stringer will only charge for labor. Labor can vary from $6 to $30 in the US. In some Latin American Countries, it goes for as little as $3 per job. On the other hand, when the string is not provided by the player, the stringer or the Tennis-Shop, where the stringing is getting done, will most likely double or triple the price of the string itself, on top of the labor cost. This is why, in the US, stringing can get so expensive. The average string job being between $30 and $40 USD (unless we provide our own) it is easy to see how it can get very expensive fast; if dealing with one of those juniors who breaks strings daily, or at least two or three times per week.

Stringing machines can be divided into two major groups: power-operated and mechanically operated. Under the power-operated machines, we have Electrical, Digital (nothing other than electronic or computerized), and Pneumatic. And under mechanical operated we have the crank system (probably the most common type), hand drop weight and pedal drop weight.

Within these two groups it is important to mentioning that all crank systems stop applying tension as soon as the crank clicks or locks; this happens as soon as the desired tension is reached. After the crank clicks then the person stringing puts the clamps on the string to hold the tension, but no more tension is being applied to the string. This is seen as a weakness in these machines since they are not what are known as continuous tension machines, meaning they no longer are pulling but just holding the tension. But in my mind, that is a bunch of bologna, since the same exact thing happens as soon as we clamp the string on all other kinds of machines. All strings will stretch a little as they are being pulled. The theory goes, that if the string is not done stretching when the crank clips, then we lose tension due to its continued stretching. With continuous tension stringing machines, this stretching continues until the string is clamped, rendering, in theory, a better more accurate tension level on the racquet. The solution is simple, double crank or slowly crank or add one or two extra pounds of tension to the racquet being strung. The time the stringer takes to clamp the string will indeed allow a little more stretch; we are talking two or maybe three seconds longer.

An experienced stringer knows that if a newcomer wants a string job, he/she needs to make sure to know what this newcomer is looking for. If he or she usually gets his or her racquet strung with a continuous tension machine, and we as the stringers use a crank system, we are going to either crank slowly, double crank or add one or two pounds to compensate for the stretch of the string. As a stringer of many years, I can say with confidence that a client will always rather have his/her racquet a little tight opposed to looser than what he or she is used to! With some strings, especially natural gut, it is recommended to pre-stretch the string. This process involves fixing the string to the machine, stepping away, and stretching the string for about a minute by hand. It's like making pasta; we got to follow a precise routine to come up with the right consistency; this makes for a more accurate string job. It is a terrible thing for the stringer to have a player come back disappointed about a string job because it was not tight enough, and now the racquet has to be restrung again.

Over the years, we have had many experienced players return their racquets because the tension was too low. In all those occasions, the frames had to be restrung again, sometimes even two more times. As stringers and Tennis players, we owe it to our clientele to deliver precisely what they want, no excuses here! So here comes Jackie's mom, Jackie is a hard hitting and serious player, she needs her racquets done at 67#, fairly tight for today's standards. We get the job done, and when Jackie gets her racquets back and tries them, she complains about the tension being low, and does not come back because she went to the competition that has a continuous tension, cutting edge, state of the art machine. So we lost a valuable client, someone who breaks a lot of racquets every week. Why? Some Q and A from the stringer was in place when they brought the racquets in. What kind of player is Jackie? Does she hit hard? Does she use a lot of topspin? How often does she break strings? Where does she usually get her racquets done? Do we know what kind of machines they have there? If we don't know, we need to find out... and so on! This way, we make sure to deliver exactly what Jackie wants every time! There are some demanding customers who require perfection, and perfection must be delivered in the quality of the string job, color of string, as well as playing characteristics. When anyone is looking for fairly high tensions, it is always a good idea to clean up the supporting system in the machine. Use a clean cloth and alcohol to make sure we don't lose tension from slippage of the string in the clamp or bars as we release it from the pulling mechanism in the machine. All this stuff is pretty technical and for more information the reader will have to do some research. One excellent source of information is the USRSA (United States Racquet Stringers Association) and other racquet stringers associations in the World in Europe and Asia.

The support system in a stringing machine is what keeps the racquet frame from deforming on the machine as it is subjected to pressure and tension from the machine and the string. We want at least a four-point support system. Some old models come with only a two post support system; this is fine granted the posts are sturdy, and the stringer does a good job attaching the racquet to the stringing machine.

There are two types of clamps for holding the string tension: floating and stationary clamps. Floating clamps are like pliers that are independent of the machine. They clamp onto two strings at a time to be functional. These clamps are very common on drop weight machines and are supplemental equipment on all other types. The beauty of the floating clamps is that we can use them regardless of the machine. So it is a good idea to have them on hand just in case the fixed clamps fail. Floating clamps are relatively inexpensive and easy to find. Stationary or fixed clamps are actually attached to the machine. On most machines, these are easy to use and reliable, but some can be awkward to use requiring stringers to tighten them twice for each string pulled, rendering them slow and inconvenient. Most stand alone (stationary) machines use fixed clamps. Unfortunately, clamping is not standardized, and each machine brand has its own set of fixed clamping system, and, for the most part, it does not fit machines of other brands.

Digital (Electronic) machines are obviously the most state of the art and have the latest technology. They are accurate and fairly easy to operate. They can be table top or stationary. We will see some of these in the more sophisticated Tennis Shops. They can be incredibly pricey, some going for up to $13 000 US Dollars. I do not recommend these stringers for home use. One advantage, however, is that digital machines are continuous tension pulling the string until the string is clamped. This usually promotes a more accurate and uniform string bed on the racquet in question. The support system is solid with a 4 to 6-point support system.

Electric stringers pull the string with electric power. They are fairly easy to operate, and they also keep the string tension until clamped. These stringers are a lot less expensive, and they range from $500 to $2000 depending on how sophisticated we need it or want it. Some of these come in good table top models but still not recommended for the regular home stringer because they require electrical power. On trips, we have to find that electrical outlet to be able to string racquets. These models usually come with a 2 to 6-point support system.

Crank System stringers are the most popular type of machines. They are extremely reliable and easy to operate. One disadvantage is that they do not keep pulling the string before clamping. Once the crank clicks, they no longer pull the string but only hold it, producing a somewhat lower tension on the racquet than requested. The huge advantage they do have is their simplicity of operation and reliability. Another huge advantage is that these machines are very fast, allowing an experienced stringer to get the job done professionally in less than 15 minutes! We have strung over 20 000 racquets on our Winn Pro II Stringing Machine over a 25 year period, and it has never faltered mechanically even once! Crank System Stringers can be tabletop or stationary. Tabletop models are fairly portable and a good recommendation for home or personal stringer. They range in price from $600 to $2000 depending on manufacturers and how state of the art we want it. These stringing machines can also be found with a 2 to 6-point support system.

Drop Weight: These machines can be pretty accurate granted the person doing the stringing knows what he or she is doing. The principle is very simple: As the weight drops, the rod that suspends the weight needs to come to the horizontal position consistently. If this is not happening, the tension on the different strings is going to have a variation, rendering a non-uniform stringing job. The obvious disadvantage of these machines is that they may not be as accurate as their counterparts. The person doing the stringing has everything to do with the quality of the job here. However, there are some huge advantages these machines have over the others: reliability and simplicity are two of the main ones as well as the fact that they are continuous tension machines. They are very simple and easy to operate. Also, these machines are portable, making them a good option for do-it-yourself players. I have strung racquets with these machines on pickup tailgates, restaurant tables, bars, and even on the ground sitting down. Another good advantage is price; they range from $100 to $600. Most of them come with a two post support system but can be found with 4 and 6-point support systems at a higher price. These machines can also be very fast in the hands of an experienced stringer.

Here are a few things to consider if learning how to string:

a) Sound (pitch) testing the main strings before we get started on the crosses, is one of the best ways to know the stringing job is a solid one. Simply snap them with the fingers like a guitar player would and compare to the equivalent string off to the other side of the racquet. The sound should be equal or at least close. The 6 or 7 center strings should have a very small variation in pitch; this variation comes from the different lengths.

b) Making sure the frame is fixed or clamped properly on the machine is paramount to keeping the frame from deforming upon compression from tension on the main strings. I don't know how many times I have seen rackets with the head deformed from this situation. Inexperienced players may not notice this problem, but it will cause the racquet to play differently. Also, it greatly increases the frame's chances to breaking when in use, or during the stringing process; due to the added stress inflicted upon it by the deformation from the stringing machine. Back in the early 80s, in my first job as a Tennis-Professional in Manzanillo, Mexico, I once had an American client who brought a Prince Boron racquet for stringing. Someone who has been playing for a while will probably remember that these racquets sold for about $500 USD. I had just purchased a drop weight stringing machine to take care of the stringing demands at my little Tennis-Shop. I was probably 24 years old, fresh out of college, and when playing college Tennis I had only strung racquets with an old Serrano drop weight, the foot pedal type stringer. This machine was very robust, and the frame clamping system was solid, so we never had a problem with it.

But let's get back to my Prince Boron story. My little drop weight was anything but a sturdy machine, and it only had a two post clamping system. As I was stringing the middle main strings, I heard a crack and immediately noticed a fracture on the side of the frame at about 2 o'clock. I removed the racquet from the machine and decided not to mess with it anymore and just tell the owner what had happened. The next day, here comes this man in his 50s to pick up his racquet. I told him what happened, and he looked at me surprised. He was nice enough to not charge me for the racquet and just send it back to Prince for a replacement as a manufacturer's defect. The truth is the frame had not been clamped tight enough on the stringing machine, and that is why it broke. Prince replaced the frame without a charge. To this day, I feel a little guilty from having broken such an expensive racquet!

c) Make sure when stringing a racquet the string and pulling clamps are free of dirt, especially grease or the string will slip and lose tension as we release it to the clamp. The clamps and pulling clamp or mechanism have to be cleaned with alcohol or water often to prevent this problem. Newspaper and simple napkins make a good simple way to keep bars and clamps clean.

SURFACES FOR TENNIS

Tennis is the only sport on the planet that is officially played on several different surfaces. Hard courts, clay courts, grass courts, carpet, artificial grass courts, manure courts, cement or concrete courts and wood courts.

Not too long ago I read an account of Davis Cup matches played on manure courts of Mexico VS India in India.

I played several official matches in College on wood courts inside a gym and on concrete courts in public facilities like High Schools, etc... I must confess that I've never played on manure!

Having grown up playing in Mexico, my favorite surface is red clay. Red clay is pretty different from Har-Tru or green clay courts. Red clay is a lot more unpredictable and unstable. On red clay, one can slide a good 30% to 60% more on average. When it is dry, a red clay court is powdery, and the red dust gets everywhere: our socks, shirt, underwear and even our face. One has to love it and has to taste it... it is awesome! A red clay court is composed of crushed clay bricks; it is actual clay material. The court changes substantially in how it plays depending on humidity, temperature and surface dampness. So how the court will play on any given day is not a given. A player can step on a court and be surprised by a pretty fast surface if the humidity is low and the surface is pretty dry. Under these conditions, players will slide a lot more and have a harder time maintaining balance. It is fun, and this is where we can identify the really good clay court players from the rest of the herd. Clay court players fanatics like me love a pretty dry court, and they move well on it sliding/gliding/surfing to the ball every chance they get, with awesome balance and control. Those poor souls who don't understand clay will be scrambling/falling/stumbling, and at the same time getting pretty irritated. I remember playing a pretty tight match on court 1 in Club de la Colina in Guadalajara Mexico against a young player. The court was very dry and extremely slippery. My Tennis shoes had very little grid on them, and I had fallen about 4 or 5 times already, as we approached the end of the first set, the grounds crews kept on asking us if we wanted the court watered. But I insisted to not water it because I was having the time of my life gliding and surfing on it, and also because my opponent had fallen twice as much as I had! I ended up winning the match with a few minor scratches as I walked off the court, but my opponent had more scratches and was limping! As per the rules back then, both players had to be in agreement for watering the court!

Har-Tru courts are considered clay courts. But in reality it is not clay. Har-Tru is crushed stone; HAR-TRU is made from billion-year-old Pre-Cambrian metabasalt found in the Blue Ridge Mountains of Virginia. This material is also found around the South and the East in the US. Therefore, there are lots of green clay or Har-Tru courts in those regions. Green clay also follows similar patterns as the red clay but to a lesser extent. Green clay is probably more predictable, but it too will play faster and allow the player to slide if the surface is not watered and dry conditions prevail. Green clay courts will probably be more stable and a lot easier to maintain than red clay courts. This surface is also known as fast dry because when it rains or if it is watered, it will quickly suck up the water on the surface and can be used in a very short period of time.

Red clay courts can also be made into fast dry surfaces. The way to do this is to lay a bed of full clay bricks under the smaller crushed pieces and then finally laying a film of about 1/8-1/4 inch of powder clay on top. This type of surface will also be playable fairly fast after a downpour.

Most clay courts, green and red, use plastic tape as lines. But in some places on red clay they will use white concrete lines. This makes for pretty unpredictable bounces. The advantage of this is that one does not ever worry about the lines. If a shallow area develops, all that has to be done is to fill it to the height of the lines and the court will be okay. Powder chalk is still used here and there as lines material on clay, kind of like a baseball field. They dissolve it in water and paint the lines of the courts every day! Such were the courts of my youth!

Obviously, clay courts need to be rolled almost every day. They need lots of water and care. They are living surfaces, and if we want to have a decent court to play Tennis on, grounds personnel have to pay attention to it and be on the lookout for developing imperfections. As players, we can request a watering or brushing before we get started on a tournament match. It usually should be no problem to please an eager Tennis player. Ground crews usually are proud of their courts and want to provide a nice surface for all players and matches. They love to hear compliments about how smooth and good their Tennis courts are! So, say to them something like, "Hey, thanks for the awesome courts, they play very uniform and are beautiful, it's an honor to be able to play on such good courts." Chances are, next time we are about to play on these courts, they will be even better. A bad court can get in our heads as Tennis players. The bad bounces usually favor the weaker of players, and it can get pretty frustrating.

In my mind, nothing beats a nice red clay court's beauty. In some private homes, country clubs or Tennis clubs around the World, red clay courts are considered decorative. There is a lot of material and literature on clay court maintenance and clay court construction, so we will not go into detail here. Suffice to say that if we want to play Tennis on the most ancient and awesome surface there is, go for red clay courts!

Grass Tennis courts are also extremely beautiful and decorative. The maintenance on them is crazy in how much detail, work and money they require. A grass court is like a green on a golf course but without the undulations and slopes. It takes the right weather to have good grass courts; they require a lot of compacting and rolling. They also need adequate amounts of water and yes, the grass must be mowed every two or three days to keep a consistent surface. Although I never did play at Wimbledon, I have had my experiences on grass. I can tell the reader that the bounce, for the most part, is extremely low and rather unpredictable. That is why a grass court is said to be the fastest of the many surfaces because the ball virtually does not bounce very much at all. If we were expecting an approaching ball to bounce three feet, it will only bounce two feet or less, subtracting from the time we have to hit a return. Grass courts definitely favor players who hit low slice shots and flatter balls. Netplay and volleys will be more effective on grass since our opponent has so little time to make the hit or passing shot. For the most part, he or she always has to hit the ball from below waist level. And there is a decisive advantage for the player at the net since he or she is not letting the ball bounce, meaning he/she will not have to deal with the super low and fast bounce.

Grass court tournaments can be found in almost all divisions. But to get ready for one of these, players will probably have a pretty hard time finding a court nearby because grass courts are rare. I remember running sprints and doing agility drills and exercises as well as hitting Tennis balls on a Golf green in Club Campestre Juarez in Northern Mexico back in the mid-80s. If I had been caught by the maintenance crew, I am pretty sure they would have beaten me up and sent me to jail. But I was friends with the Tennis Pros, and we would go there at times when there was no golf activity; to play Tennis on a green that was sort of flat, in order to get used to the bounce and the footing as we were getting ready for a national grass courts tournament in Santa Barbara California. This green was out of sight from the Golf Shop and the homes surrounding it!

Let me just say that grass courts are beautiful, difficult to play on, very rare, especially good ones, and very difficult to maintain.

Hard courts are also a full load as far as finding quality facilities. Although a lot more common, I have yet to see a perfect court. Most will develop cracks that are repaired year to year or every two or three years. We can expect to find decent hard courts more consistently than clay or grass. It is very annoying though to find in the same tournament and many times within the same Tennis facility hard courts with inconsistent playing characteristics. Some of them are newer or have been resurfaced more recently and usually play slower. Others play a lot faster while some have horrible cracks. A few hardcourts will even have difficult to see uneven spots that make the ball either kick to the side or bounce higher than normal or skid low unexpectedly.

And as mentioned elsewhere in this book, the only sure thing about hard courts is that they will have cracks, have had cracks, or are about to develop cracks.

Hard courts do promote more solid footing, but the harder surface means more impact to our joints and body, in general.

Some manufacturers are offering hard courts with some cushioning. I was pleasantly surprised to find them fun and pleasurable to play on. They do take some getting used to. The ball seems to bounce a little less but still kicks high enough. As the ball bounces on the cushioned surface, it will bounce a small percentage less than normal, and a lot of times the bounce of the ball sounds hollow. These cushioned surfaces do take some of the impact and beating off the players' joints.

Hardcourt manufacturers have different kinds of finishings; some surfaces are kind of rubbery; others are just normal paint. Others are acrylic, which makes them a little more resistant to wear but are a little slippery. Most manufacturers will put a finish on the court to the specifications of facilities or private court owners; they can make courts play slow, medium or fast. Most hard courts are pretty slow to medium in terms of speeds. By this I am referring as to how much grab or bite the surface will have on the ball as it bounces; this is determined by the finishing material being used.

As courts get worn and old, they tend to get faster since a little of the grainy silicon topping is rubbed off every time someone plays on it. If we want our courts to remain fairly consistent throughout their life, go for a fairly fast finish. This way we will minimize the amount of silicon or sand added to the paint and a lot less will be removed from the running, bouncing or just normal wear of the surface.

Hard courts are the most common surface in the World due to their simplicity and ease to build and maintain. I personally would not recommend them for private courts; however, I do see a lot of hard courts in private subdivisions that look pretty good and add the possibility of Tennis to the community. Hard courts are an attractant to kids on wheels using scooters, roller skates, and skateboards. These ruin the surface and should be prohibited.

Personally I don't find hard courts very attractive or decorative. I think they fulfill a necessity and functionality. I do appreciate their practicality and the fact that the maintenance required to keep them in playing condition is minimal.

Synthetic grass is nothing but a rug with a grass-like surface filled with sand to about half the length of the grass sprouts. The more sand we add to it the slower it will play, and the more it will resemble clay in playing characteristics. If we add less sand, the court will play a little more like real grass. These courts can be played on even when pretty hard rain is coming down given players don't mind getting a little wet and playing with wet heavier balls, remembering to caution those with natural gut strings. Synthetic grass courts require very little maintenance. We do have to brush them with a heavy brush to get rid of the deep divots. Occasionally we may need to add more sand in certain areas where sand has been pushed off the main playing areas of the court. Synthetic grass courts are pretty expensive to build, and have lost appeal due to their high initial price range. These courts are a lot more popular in Australia and other countries than in the US and other North American countries.

Manure courts, concrete, carpet, wood; these surfaces are rare, but they are out there. Different types of carpet courts are used extensively during the indoor season at professional tournaments around the World. The average player rarely has access to these courts. Concrete is what we will find in a lot of high schools, college campuses or public facilities. Wood courts can be found in gyms. The surface is usually shared by other disciplines such as basketball, volleyball, and gymnastics. Manure courts are something I have only read about. Apparently they are common in India and maybe other Asian countries. I would assume this surface will play like clay with a very consistent bounce due to the fine powdery characteristics of the pulverized manure.

Here and there we can even find dirt courts. Made of just about whatever soil material is around the area, the surface is flattened; some lines are taped or drawn with chalk, and *voila!* We now have a Tennis court! The net can be made from just about any cloth or netting material. Some nets I have played on in my youth were made of chain link fencing; others were made of cloth sacs attached or sewed together. The back fencing was made of chicken fencing. Several courts I have played on had no back fencing and, yes, I did spend a lot of time fetching Tennis balls! As a kid 4 to 10 years old, I used to spend the entire summers at my grandparent's huge ranch in northern Jalisco State in Mexico. I spent my days fishing, hunting, and exploring on horseback or burro back for that matter. I have some very fond memories from back in those days. However, when I started getting into Tennis at age 8, I grew reluctant to spend my whole summer at the ranch because there were no Tennis courts anywhere for me to practice on. My grandma Laura missed my absence so much she went ahead and built a Tennis court outside the main hacienda house. I wish I had some pictures of it; it was a perfectly hand flattened surface with some chicken fencing all around it. The net poles were thick mesquite tree branches, the lines drawn with chalk powder, and the net sewed from ixtle sacks. It was super cool, and I did spend some time playing on this court. However, I still had the dilemma of not having anyone there with whom to practice on a regular basis, so I would spend a lot of time in one of the huge back rooms; banging Tennis balls on one of the walls. Some of these hacienda rooms were huge by today's standards, something like 40x20 feet, so this made for lots of space to move around and practice all my strokes!

All Tennis courts should be a flat surface. Outdoor courts need to have a slope side to side for the entire surface in order for them to drain properly when it rains, or when watered, in the case of clay or grass. The ITF recommendation is a ratio of 1:120 for most surfaces including hard courts and artificial clay or grass. In the case of grass or clay courts, the recommendation is 1:200. Indoor courts do not need a slope and should be a perfectly flat and leveled surface.

Orientation of Tennis courts should generally be North and South as per ITF recommendations. However, depending on latitude, the time of the year the court will see most usage, as well as other structures around the court that can cast shadows on the surface during peak play hours, other orientations should be considered. A court near the equator, for instance, is recommended to have a 15-25 degree Northwest to Southeast orientation, in order to avoid having the Sun on the server's eyes earlier and later during the day.

SECTION VI
CONTROVERSIAL STUFF

DAVIS CUP, FEDERATION CUP, OLYMPICS, GRAND SLAM AND JUNIOR TENNIS

Grand Slam and Davis Cup are the events that get all the fluids going in Tennis around the World. These are the real deal for Professional Tennis and easily the best possible Tennis we can watch. While it is great physically attend an event like a Grand Slam, Tennis is much better watched on TV than at the actual stadium. Unless we can afford the $500 plus US Dollars of the front row in the Stadium, preferably next to the chair umpire. The same is not the case for Davis Cup. Davis Cup is usually played in much smaller stadiums and tickets are readily available and a lot less expensive. In some ways, Davis Cup competition has lost some of its luster partly because prize money is a lot less than in the Grand Slams. Also, because it's hard to get good sponsorships for it, so the promotion, marketability, and overall attractiveness is not there. My feeling about it is that the ATP along with the ITF should embrace it and add some serious ranking points to all players participating in it. Make it into a two-week event instead of a year around one where all the participating teams meet (Soccer World Cup Style) for some awesome Tennis and an electric atmosphere. There is so much involvement and commitment from players, coaches, National Tennis Associations and Federations during Davis Cup; to me it is an attractive and worthy event that has not been maximized. As a kid, one of the things that kept me going was the dream that one day I would be able to play Davis Cup for Mexico. However, I never did make it, though I battled for a spot for a few years. The AMTP (Asociación Mexicana de Tenistas Profesionales) in conjunction with the Mexican Tennis Federation, organizes a professional national tournament, guaranteeing a spot in the Davis Cup squad every year, for the next Davis Cup season, to the winner of the singles event. So the tournament is played towards the end of the season in November, and players go for it since it usually has good prize money and, of course, the possibility of a spot in the Davis Cup squad. I played in this tournament during my 20s and early 30s and would advance a couple of rounds but eventually I would get knocked out. It is a fantastic event, and one that I really miss playing in. Several times I had to play in the qualifying rounds having to win two or three matches in order to make it to the main draw of the event.

One of the main reasons Grand Slam Tennis is so awesome is because the top 20 players in the World will for sure go all out on these events, especially the top 4 or 5. Unfortunately at a lot of the smaller events, for a lot of these top athletes, playing all the tournaments is just business. By that I mean they sign up for it because of guaranteed money, prize money, and practice. Yes, that's right, practice! But if a player is already peaking, playing well and wants just to chill for a few days before the bigger grand slam event starts. He or she may just tank on the first or second round, in order to save or sustain his or her peak for the following week! So don't be fooled to see No. 1 or 2 in the World lose in the first or second round of a smaller tournament, when we are one, or maybe even two weeks before the start of a Grand Slam event!

Another point of great controversy right now in the US is in junior development. A few years ago, the USTA came up with a mandate forcing sanctioned events in 8s, 10s and 12s to use the ROGY system. ROGY as in Red, Orange, Green and Yellow Tennis balls for children. Red for 8 and under, Orange for 10 and under (38 foot courts are needed for the Red balls, and 60 foot courts for the Orange balls), Green for 10 and 12 and under (it changes from state to state), and finally the regular Yellow balls once a kid has mastered all the other colors.

It's a little crazy because ROGY complicates things exponentially for coaches, parents and Tennis facilities. For coaches, it means a lot more equipment is needed because of different carts of teaching balls and the smaller nets and courts. For the players and parents, the rules are somewhat different, and for Tennis facilities, this means they now have to construct these smaller courts or paint or draw the lines for them on top of existing courts. This makes a regular hardcourt look like the gym at a high school; where multiple lines are drawn on the wooden floor for basketball, volleyball, badminton, and Tennis.

A few years ago, at Burns Park, a twenty-something court facility, in Little Rock, Arkansas, they made courts 1, 2, and 3, into small little courts for QuickStart Tennis. Those three courts used to see a lot of use before for warm-up, lessons, and drills. But ever since they built those little courts, every time I go there, and I have been there several times over the years, those courts are empty! That's right, not a soul using them. During tournaments now, players have to struggle to find practice courts off-site, because, all the other courts are being used for the huge tournaments that are run out of that facility.

Some coaches and Tennis professionals are opposed to the change based on the premise that a mandate is never a good thing or that it was not negotiated or researched enough. Apparently there is no scientific data or grounds that indicate it will be better for American Tennis or junior development for that matter. Some well-known coaches are fighting it from different angles. I have read blogs on the Internet where multiple coaches from all over the World put in their two cents worth, with very interesting opinions and comments. One big argument is the *mandate* issue, in that nobody likes to have a mandate to have to do something a certain way. Another one speaks of the philosophy and belief that easier should not and is not necessarily better, in the long run. Yet another one relates to children having to relearn a whole new array of skills all over again for each transition. Advocates are saying that the ROGY system is easier, more fun as well as more inclusive in that it will bring in more juniors to Tennis and will help in keeping them in Tennis.

Several things remain to be said and done. A full conclusion of the results coming out of this mandate will not be known for a few more years. In the meantime, the controversy will continue. I must say that I am not a big advocate of the ROGY system. My personal feeling and experience on it is that it slows down development rather than accelerates it. (Look at the Subsection on Quckstart for more details on the ROGY system)

THE CODE
(changing the culture of our team)

If we want or *need* to change the culture of our team (players, coaches, parents, and all involved in a Tennis Academy or junior program for that matter) develop a code. I've tried the rules approach (as in a rulebook describing rules to team members for all the do's and don'ts, or Totem and Taboo) and had little luck with it; then I thought of the code as implied in the rules of Tennis. This is the part of the rulebook where officials; players, and parents place the most emphasis, and it is the most respected part of the rulebook. So, I developed one that I simply called The Code. I found that it really turned attitudes around! All I had to say to someone is, "Are you following The Code?" That, believe it or not, pretty much worked. Of course, I leaned my head a little to the side, looked down, and lowered my voice a little to not sound too aggressive. I make it semi-formal by giving them a copy of The Code and then have them sign an official looking document that they swore to The Code for the length of our working relationship. Everyone really loves little ceremonial and secret team things like this. Trust me. It really drives the message home.

My Tennis Tips are a standard part of my e-mails; these tips are not always Tennis related. They are brief little reminders and practical lessons. However, sometimes they are not put into practice by the members of my team.

Some of these Tennis tips tell players, parents and all involved what to do under different circumstances during practice, travel tournaments, or just around the Tennis facility. Based on some of these principles we also have a code of conduct. The Code will guide us and will provide a basis for all actions in and out of the Tennis courts. We will see a dramatic shift in the culture of parents, players, assistant coaches, and other team members.

The CODE:

- Respect is our core value. Respect for the team, for coaches, players, and parents, for equipment, and for others, also respect for officials and most importantly, respect for ourselves.
- As coaches we create lifelong friendships and working relationships for our players and their parents; this is a big responsibility. Parents become our friends and supporters as well.
- Pursue excellence every day, all day. We can always get better.
- *Never* compromise on quality or the standards no matter what we are doing in relation to our team and our Tennis as well as everyone else's Tennis.
- Aim high, think big and do whatever it takes to exceed others expectations and our own… The whole team, coaches, players, and parents should become raving fans and supporters!
- As coaches, special requests for players and parents are never a problem; if we can, we will! Find more ways to say "yes we can." And as players and parents, too, they are willing to come through with helping other members of the team in anything they need or want, be it a coach or another player.
- Good enough is never acceptable. There is no room for mediocrity.
- Every Tennis related activity (lessons, drills, tournaments, trips, camps, junior socials, etc…) is a "live show", so we must put on our best performance every time, remembering we only get one shot to make a first impression.
- Ensure that our students, players, and parents are the happiest right before they leave; rather than when they just arrived at the courts or to a tournament.
- *Talk daily* about what we do right and what we didn't.
- Remember that every task, every job is of equal importance. From explaining a technique or strategy, or helping parents understand what/where his or her child is in her/his development, or writing a report or evaluation, or answering the phone or an e-mail, or programming the year, or setting a personalized developmental plan for a junior player, or running a clinic or drill, or just having a casual conversation with a student on the way to the courts, or promoting our program all the time, or helping a junior re-grip his or her racquet, stringing a racquet, or traveling to a tournament,

- etc… etc… Every little detail contributes to a magical experience and a magical program that produces results.
- Very special people have come together to develop a very special Tennis Program. We will continue to surround ourselves with exceptional people. We all need to be exceptional in order to fit the equation for this team's success; are we always exceptional?
- Learning is our strength. We will ALWAYS be learning! And always be looking for new things to add to our understanding of Tennis and the art of teaching it and learning it.
- *We are a TEAM.* First, last and always! Being part of a World class team means watching the back of our teammates and never putting personal agendas before the welfare of the team's interest. But at the same time be on the lookout for someone stranded or in need of individualized help!
- Do we want better results? We need to ask ourselves better quality questions. Refocus our mind to what can "I" do to make improvements or how can I take "personal responsibility." Questions that start with "Why", "When", "You" or "They" take our personal power away. Always be ready to serve and help others achieve their goals in order for them to help us achieve ours!
- Never give up in the light of competition. Strive to run down every ball, and try to win every point. Strive to take full control of all things directly under our control. Be accountable for all our acts on and off the court and apply the principles of sportsmanship on and off the court as a player, as a coach, or as a parent.
- When possible, if a teammate is playing a match, stop and cheer a little. Doing this really helps the battling player feel the support of his/her team.
- When competing against another member of the team, show even more respect and make it a win/win situation. Let the best one for that day win the match, shake hands and congratulate each other on a good friendly but yet competitive match.
- As parents, stay out of the way of juniors competing. Let them act on their own and follow the natural process of learning through making mistakes. Don't worry, others have survived and became successful men and women.

- Never engage in an activity or conversation criticizing a team member; be it a player, a parent or a coach. This means to not be critical of other team member's failures or achievements in a negative way. Avoid doing something to hinder anybody's progress or development, or the team's progress or development.
- Remember that a lot of the pressure is induced by teammates and the team itself. We have to figure out ways to minimize pressure coming from us for all our teammates.

Create a code for a team operation and tell me about the results. I challenge everyone to try this philosophy out. Remember that the definition of insanity is doing the same thing over and over expecting different results. My belief is that to reach a higher level of success we need to do things a little different than the majority. Try it; The Code is an awesome force.

DEVELOPING OUR PHILOSOPHY

Let me talk about a few things regarding Tennis philosophy. Why do we play Tennis? (See the 101 reasons we play Tennis section) But wait, that is not good enough. What is the main reason to Play? It really has to do with who we are and what we are trying to become; our deepest self, our soul, our transcendental other. There has got to be a link to our inner self or entity through Tennis. Really good players will tell us: "We will get to know ourselves on a Tennis court" and "we will really get to know others on a Tennis court." Tennis needs to be special in our life and pretty high on our list of priorities. Maybe the hierarchy of things that matter in our lives needs to go something like this: God, Family, Tennis, and so on...

    As a kid on any days off from school or any other responsibilities, I'd just head to the Tennis courts and played matches all day! It was by far my favorite thing to do. Most Tennis players I know put Tennis way low on the list. I will never forget a kid (former student) who once said to me that he was not coming to Tennis because it was his day off. What the hell does that mean? His day off from what? Tennis is not important or dear; Tennis is a damn obligation to this poor kid! Things do not work out this way; that kind of philosophy towards Tennis is wrong! I am sorry if I am insulting anyone out there, but playing Tennis as a mandate from parents, coaches as an obligation is wrong! Please, don't play Tennis or expect kids to play Tennis or win matches if Tennis is last in the hierarchy of things in life. Tennis needs to be a priority in order for it to accept us and for us to fully understand it, and so we, maybe... just maybe! Might become a great player one day! And then again, only If the Tennis Gods want us to! Yes, I am treating Tennis as a live entity, as someone I know who is special to me, a really good friend whom I trust! Let me also add, players, junior or adult, parents especially, don't expect to win or expect kids to win if the commitment, love and proper priority for Tennis is not front and center. I hear a lot of comments like this: "Well, David has not yet won a match in a tournament." This is a kid that has been playing in tournaments for three years! But if we look at the commitment level... there is the answer! David arrives late to practice every day to

skip the warm-up and fitness routines. On the court, his energy level is always low. He never, never goes the extra mile by staying longer, after regular junior drills, to hit some serves, play a set, do some extra fitness. He uses serving practice to socialize and in the process distracts everyone else. Why does he lose? Go figure!

In order to overemphasize the idea a little more, I guess we could almost say: "Tennis should be a sacred way of life." The lifestyle that springs from Tennis has certainly forged my life, my family's life, and yes, I make a living at it. How can it not be important to me? And how can I not absolutely love Tennis and feel so indebted to it?

Make Tennis a high priority! We have to get on the court thinking this may be our last chance to strike a Tennis Ball. Go all out every time, be it a tournament match or not, go hit Tennis balls as much and as often as time and health permits. Every time I get on the court and hit Tennis balls for me, outside of a lesson or tournament, just for pure pleasure or exercise or both, I know that I will get something in return, more health, a better mindset for the rest of my day, and so many other tangible and intangible benefits. So playing for fun just for oneself is an awesome power and opportunity to grasp some momentum in life. I do this often, and everyone should do the same thing. I see John McEnroe with his senior tour, he is having so much fun, he has made Tennis the center of his life, and look at the guy, he looks really good, at his age. In some ways, he is a great role model and a great promoter of Tennis and all it can and should be.

Exercising our values and ethics while on the court is important so we can reinforce them. Tennis players have to let the World know who they are and what sportsmanship means to them. Learn from every experience, from every ball hit. And from every shot, savor the glory of success, and when defeated, always be thirsty for more. Fix it, fix it, and fix it again! Be it a stroke or the head or the fitness or whatever it is, fix it! Problem-solving and digging deep is learned when we are losing on the Tennis court.

Tennis is larger and bigger than any player alive or who has played in the past, bigger than the Grand Slams and Davis Cup. These events represent and form part of what Tennis ultimately is, and what it represents, a celebration of majestic proportions. Grand Slam and Davis Cup, test the best protagonists at their skill, balance, and strength; a balance that can only be achieved with enormous sacrifice and an uncompromised work ethic.

There are millions of Tennis players across the Globe of all ages, races, and levels. We all have a lot in common. Ever wondered why Tennis became so popular? Why it continues to be so unique?

We cannot fail Tennis… We have to grasp it for what it really is. We cannot disappoint Tennis. We have to embrace it as part of who we are, make it dear to us as we would our home, our family, our land or our whole self, material and spiritual.

Tennis will always find a way to get back to players what they put into it. Sooner or later it will pay back. I'd bet my life on it!

SPORTS THAT ROBBED FROM TENNIS AND COMPETE WITH TENNIS

Tennis has existed for over 200 years. The game of Tennis as we know it today came from Jeu de Paume (The palme game) this is a ball-and-court game that originated in France between the 14th and 16th centuries. A sort of ball was hit with the hand; then paddle racquets were used first, followed by the introduction of strung racquets later in that century. All racquet sports come from Tennis. Racquetball, squash, badminton, even ping pong. These sports have taken away from Tennis in different degrees. Some of these sports have been around longer than others, but Tennis is the oldest easily, the toughest to learn, and most popular. None of these other sports compare to Tennis in magnitude as a way to one's forge life. Let's all continue to promote Tennis, and remember the place that Tennis holds as the Hulk of Racquet Sports! If someone was having a hard time learning Tennis, don't just go to squash or racquetball; stick to Tennis. The rewards in Tennis will always be bigger, guaranteed. As a simple example of that, let me ask, how many other racquet sports win scholarships in prestigious colleges and universities around the World? With the opportunity to travel and play in far away Tennis courts and places? Tennis will take longer to master, but it has so much more to offer to its advocates than the alternatives. Tennis is a very international sport through which players can open doors, do business and make friends. Through Tennis, we can expand our horizons way more than we could with any of the other racquet sports! Push and promote Tennis. Engage and commit to a lifetime of Tennis; Tennis will always pay back what effort, time and resources are put into it!

    There are many other none-racquet individual sports that compete with Tennis. A lot of these sports have sprung up over the last 20 years or so. Skateboarding, mountain biking, spinning, and Pilates. Some of these sports or disciplines may complement Tennis. Pilates offers cardio, whereas Tennis has difficulty providing this benefit in a natural or automatic way. Tennis will not and does not look to compete with them. In reality, some of these cardio or fitness sports are not sports at all but disciplines. So, for anyone advocating any of these or other similar individual sports, I don't want to say "give it up," but I do want to say, experience Tennis, or if already involved in it, keep at it. Don't substitute for one of these lesser sports. None of them will be as beneficial, satisfying or as spread worldwide as Tennis is. Also, for anyone who has never tried Tennis, please give it a shot. Tennis is for those willing to put in a little time and effort. Tennis will reward its followers big time, Tennis will add dimension and health to one's life like very few other endeavors we may undertake, and again, Tennis will pay us back what we put into it ten fold!

POLITICS AND DRAMA, THE DARK SIDE OF TENNIS

Tennis as a sport and a medium for self-growth is limitless. However, there is one side of it that will sometimes make people look elsewhere for entertainment, fitness and discipline. What I want to talk about is obviously politics and drama in Tennis.

Politics and drama in reality should not have anything to do with Tennis. But since Tennis has grown so much, and there is so much money involved, time and effort invested in it everywhere; there are lots of interests that arise from the organized form of the sport. Big, medium, and small tournaments, Tennis associations, federations, and organizations, Tennis committees, and groups of players, enthusiasts, and aficionados everywhere. Sometimes make a big deal out of some of the rules, regulations, and other outside influences of the game, to the point that we end up with some drama and a bunch of unhappy players!

Adverse politics and drama take place the moment a group of people or individuals throw their personal interests into the equation. These interests are not always for the betterment of the sport but for fulfilling their own ego, promoting individual players in an event, or for financial pursuits. Anywhere money is involved there is also power, and those two combined create envy and jealousy, corrupting the sport and its culture, making things ugly sometimes to the point of being unacceptable.

My point here is this, If someone belongs to a Tennis organization, a Tennis committee or any group involved in Tennis, or if he or she is thinking about joining one. Let this person go in with one and only one thing in mind: anything done or said needs to be for the betterment of the sport, leaving behind any hidden agendas. Whoever he or she may be, needs to be 100% sure of this. If this person is not, then he or she should not get involved. It will be better for the Tennis organizations or events and the overall Tennis culture. I don't know how many times I have seen situations where personal interests were the main motivator for someone putting major time and money into Tennis events or Tennis associations or federations. Corrupting a Tennis event with the sole purpose of controlling it or to satisfy personal agendas is wrong. There are also those getting into Tennis organizations to gain a business advantage or build a business platform from the already existing structure of a Tennis association or committee. This is also the wrong motivation, and this person should be rejected. Anyone looking to make money out of Tennis needs a job in Tennis related businesses or offices, not in a Tennis committee.

If we are joining a junior Tennis committee at a club or association, it would be wrong to do it because we have kids who play competitive Tennis, and we are looking to gain favor or their promotion. This is very common, and it is a perfect example of how people inject personal interests into their involvement. In most cases, this will cause problems for the committee. It will keep it from performing its duty or tasks in an unbiased, efficient and effective way. Another common example of this occurs when the head of a business or corporation sponsors an event with big money. But he or she has hidden agendas other than the promotion gained from the advertisement for his/her business or corporation. These agendas can be of various natures; personal business, favor players, or simply to show off or impress the Tennis community. These motivators are wrong, and Tennis would be better off without such sponsors. Going to a public facility and finding benches, gazebos, or other furniture with the names of the individuals who donated money for them, stamped or placked on this furniture, ticks me off!

Some of the drama happens at the club level, namely league or club Tennis. Enmity between two players or families may cause one to exclude the other from a tournament or promote denigration or gossip. Stuff of this sort should be avoided. Stay out of it as much as possible. As ethical Tennis players, we need to lead by example on and off the court. Don't criticize others. Be a role model for adults and kids. Regardless of the level of play, we can help things get better, keep things the same, or make things worse; our actions on and off the court will determine that. Be honest on court… play fair and straight; always walking off the court, or out of the Tennis facility with full satisfaction, and with the willingness and urge of coming back. Who needs to suffer favoritism or ill-treatment in situations such as league play? Chances are, a player suffering rejection or experiencing drama or adverse politics at a Tennis facility or event, will be looking for an alternative place to play. A lot of times, this might be the one thing that just pushes him or her out of the game. My wife Carmen reached a nice level as a player at one point, but after a couple of seasons in league Tennis, she decided to quit competitive Tennis, after experiencing some unpleasant situations dealing with favoritisms and drama. One awful example of drama comes into play when juniors from different families develop rivalries and end up playing very tough matches, and there is animosity over calls, scoring or even racial implications. Here are two such anecdotes of such unfortunate incidents (the names have been changed for privacy purposes):

Marcela a Latino girl and Michelle, an Anglo girl, are playing a singles match at a local 12s sanctioned event for the nth time. They both have beat one another in close matches, and they both are students of mine. This time, it is no different in that they again are playing a very close match. Michelle calls an official because she feels that Marcela has given her some bad calls. The official comes into the court and overrules two of Michelle's calls and none of Marcela's. Marcela ends up winning this one, but during the match both families present were heavily involved with a little more than just pretty intense cheering. An hour later, an open posting from one of Michelle's older sisters appears on one of the big social media websites, telling about how her little sister got cheated out of a match in a Tennis tournament by this player who, according to her, always cheats in her matches, but no specific names were mentioned. Now I would know who makes bad calls or who does not out of my own students, and I know Marcela plays pretty straight and makes good calls. If in doubt, Marcela will always grant the benefit of the doubt to her opponent. Of course, Marcela and her family soon learned about the posting on the Internet, and they are devastated because they know they are talking about the match that was just played. A once friendly relationship amongst families disintegrated, and two girls that practiced together and were once friends, never talked to one another again, and one of them eventually quit my junior program! How is that for drama and bad politics?

Another such example occurred following a similar path in a boy's junior event at the local level. Ernesto and Connor are playing a closely disputed match in the finals of a 14s event. Connor has already questioned several of Ernesto's calls. Both families are present, and there is a lot of tension in the air. As in the previous story, these two players have met numerous times with divided results. After an official came on court, Connor ended up winning the match, but it was ugly because of the *in your face* attitude of both players. Ernesto had just joined my program, and they were working together almost every day. Making things work out for me was challenging since these two kids just don't get along well, and I have to watch them every second of every practice. I have spoken to both families in an effort to make them understand how they need to get along in order to take advantage of the opportunity to have two of the best juniors in the State practicing together. Neither kid will have any of it as they continue to have fist pumping attitudes against one another every day. After a couple months of this, Connor's Dad and Mom have me over at their house for a meeting. They just wanted to let me know that Connor was dropping out of my program and joining a newly started Tennis academy nearby. Things were just not fun anymore, and Connor wanted to be anywhere but on the same court where Ernesto was. A year later, Connor, a great competitor, and an excellent athlete drops out of Tennis! What exactly pushed him out of this awesome sport? It is hard to quantify the answer, but one thing is for sure, drama had something to do with it, drama, drama, drama... ugh!

One extreme example of how politics can adversely affect Tennis happened in my youth when Mexico advanced to the Semifinals of the Davis Cup versus South Africa in the 70s a couple of times. Because of South Africa's then Apartheid regime, Mexico withdrew from the semifinal. Both times it was Mexico who needed to travel to South Africa to play the Davis Cup match, and both times South Africa got a bye in the semis to the finals! This left a very bitter taste in me as a child and made me think a lot about how lucky we were without wars and segregation as seen in many other places and times in the World's history. Raul Ramirez was the lead player for Mexico back in those years. Just imagine his frustration, sadness and how upset he was as a person and player. This was his opportunity to help his country and his people, but he was denied this opportunity because of Apartheid!

In Mexico as in many other undeveloped Latin-American countries it is extremely hard to generate players at the professional level. Some argue that the lack of money is the issue, but I wonder if this is true. Mexico, Central and South-American countries have had, continue to have and will always have incredibly talented and unbelievably skilled junior players. If we were to take any top three juniors from Mexico, and make them face any other top three juniors from any other country, especially those who consistently produce top players, I guarantee we would be in for a real battle! I have seen this happen first hand on a few unique occasions! The problem arises when they have to make the transition to professionals. In developed countries, their respective Tennis associations and federations will come up with all kinds of grants, scholarships and coaching to aid players in financial need.

In Mexico, as in many other underdeveloped countries, unfortunately, what little money the Mexican Tennis Federation is able to muster goes down the drain to tournaments and sponsorships that hardly ever produce anything.

Big money is spent running some pretty big events where Mexican players, especially top juniors are not even protagonists. At least some of this sponsorship should go to junior development. It would not be difficult for FMT (Mexican Tennis Federation) to come up with a rule where, any sanctioned tournament organized, and all sponsorships, should grant a small percentage, in the order of maybe 3%-10% of all entries and sponsorship money, to a Junior Development Fund. This fund could be utilized exclusively to hire the right coaching, and grant the financial aid necessary for some of the top and most promising juniors in the country (14-18-year-olds) with financial difficulty, to help them take off into the professional arena. This money could be used to travel with a group of four to eight juniors worldwide to the different tournaments and competitions with a coach, and hopefully even a trainer, for maybe a couple of years, or until they had success, and could continue on their own. Of course, there would have to be a strict code of conduct, ethics and rules for the players, as well as the coaches! Instead, the money typically ends up in the pockets of all the wrong people. All these Latin-American countries continue to be in a trench from which there is no way out and generations upon generations of unbelievably talented, hard working junior players continue to be produced and wasted. As mentioned elsewhere in this book, junior players find that dead end when they finish their junior career. They go to either work or college and quit Tennis altogether. At best, they end up playing college Tennis for four more years then quit in frustration, for not having had the opportunity to take their game to the next level! To me, this is the worst way in which politics or personal agendas affect Tennis negatively around the World!

SECTION VII

WHO WE ARE

TENNIS PRO'S IMAGE: WHO ARE WE? WHAT DO TENNIS PROS DO?

As if the Tennis Pro's image was not degraded enough already, nowadays we allow just about anyone to label themselves with the title: Tennis Pro. What does that mean? Why Tennis pros are sometimes labeled as womanizers, opportunists, adventurous, and dishonest? These good traits can be found in just about any other profession or occupation; including priesthood. A few famous former Tennis pros have received more attention than they should have, forging an image for this profession we don't deserve. Oh… and don't let me forget to mention that opposed to popular belief, we don't make crazy money either!

Many Tennis Pros are honest, hard working; family oriented, well-meaning individuals. In Tennis as in any other professions, there are good, okay and bad Tennis pros or coaches. A player looking for Tennis lessons will usually get what he/she is paying for, but not always. It is important to do the research on potential coaches. Don't go for the sweet talker. Or the super nice guy, either. Parents or players have to find a coach who will tell them the honest truth about their kids or their own game. It is important to have good channels of communication, and there should be good chemistry in a coach-player relationship for it to work out well.

Some Tennis professional organizations have worked very hard to try to change this twisted image that has developed in regard to Tennis Pros. These organizations have been somewhat successful. However, as long as we continue to allow just about anyone that knows how to hit a Tennis ball in a half-assed way to teach Tennis, we will not see a full turn around in this regard.

The very nature of Tennis as a sport and as a game lends itself to having created this image. We play Tennis at a Tennis Club, Country Club, or Tennis facility. It is done for the most part outdoors, and it is supposed to be great fun and good exercise. When enthusiasts arrive on the Tennis court, they are usually smiling, looking forward to a good time. The Tennis Pro, who has already spent five or six hours outside under the elements, smiles enthusiastically as Tennis players trickle in and out of the Tennis courts. This Tennis Pro will probably not be as clean and tidy as he was early in the morning. Also, consider Tennis parties. Everyone meets at the Tennis facility for a get together. For all but the Tennis Pro, this is a time to socialize and have a good time. The Tennis Pro has to be fully engaged in doing and saying the right thing while everyone else is probably drinking and having a good time. Sometimes it happens that some of these Tennis aficionados start flirting with the pros and things get out of control (especially if the Pro starts drinking too). Next thing we know someone's dating one of the Pros or people begin acting funny around the Tennis facility, and the rest is history.

This story repeats itself often. Tennis pros are sometimes victimized due to the nature of their job and stigmatized as a result of this. Tennis Pros are not bandits, reckless, or dishonest; Tennis Pros are just human beings! Normally we will interact with them in a way that makes them look casual about what they do. The game of Tennis is their business and their profession. And everything that happens around Tennis is not essential to life... right? Wrong! What Tennis players do and how they do it on a day to day basis has direct life implications and consequences! This is why Tennis as a sport and discipline has grown to be so huge around all corners of the World for individuals from all walks of life. The uneducated, not versed in this philosophy, those not treating Tennis as a sport, a passion, and a true discipline, but just as a simple game, done for entertainment reasons, are those that cause trouble, and got us into this negative image situation.

Tennis Professionals are not lazy, either. Tennis Pros just want to be respected, recognized and understood. It seems to me that in Tennis if we don't win a Grand Slam tournament or coach someone who did, we are nobody, and no one will pay any attention to us or what we have to say; or for that matter even acknowledge us. For Tennis Pros, Tennis is a way of life; Tennis as a profession is a lifestyle, and as Tennis pros we don't usually live lavishly or wealthily. For us, Tennis was, at one point, pure love and joy, and for a lot of us it still is, but it is also work... Tennis as a profession is taxing physically, mentally, emotionally and spiritually. The moment money is thrown into the equation, Tennis loses its purity and gets corrupted. Some people tell me how lucky I am to make a living of Tennis. I do agree with this, but make no mistake about it: being a Tennis Professional is no easy job and definitely not for the weak, both from a mental and physical standpoint. In my lifetime, I have seen many potentially good Tennis pros come and go, a lot of them did not have what it took to make it, and walked away to other professions!

Sometimes I see a Tennis court as a jail! Four fences too high to escalate and a life sentence attached to it. Other times a Tennis court (especially a red clay court) is such a beautiful thing. A Tennis court can be a mystical place, like a temple of knowledge, where one goes for learning, for mentoring, for cleansing, for suffering, for praying and sacrificing. But one also goes there for joy, for fun, for understanding or self-healing, and for pure love!

WHY I STARTED PLAYING TENNIS AND HOW?

Some of the stories presented here should hopefully serve as inspiration to some children and readers. As a child coming from a very large family, my Mom and Dad were way to busy for much individual time with us. Each one of us had to figure our way out in life, and mine was Tennis.

As a kid, I was very active in different sports, I guess not too different from what a lot of kids are doing today. I played a lot of soccer, loved to hunt with my dad and by myself, sometimes with homemade bows and arrows and sometimes with a slingshot or BB gun. I also played some basketball and baseball.

One day, my cousins and older brother got mad at me for some reason I cannot remember but we had a bad fight. We were at the Guadalajara Club in Mexico. It was a kids' paradise covering all the sports including 13 red clay Tennis courts, an Olympic size pool with ten, five and three-meter trampolines. My uncle, Manuel Guerra was an avid Tennis player of many years. So I decided to blow off my cousins and brother and watch my uncle play for a little while. When I got there, he handed me one of his wooden Jack Kramer racquets with catgut strings, a couple of white wool balls, and walked me to a concrete wall down by courts 5 and 6. The surface on the wall was also red clay, with lines and just like one of the regular courts. He briefly showed me how to hold the racquet, and how to practice on that wall. I was there for over an hour messing with it. I guess I must have had a pretty good time. I started coming back to that wall two or three times a week. Anytime I had a chance I would go and hit some balls. It's funny because now that I think about it, my brother, cousins, and virtually our entire families also started playing Tennis after that incident. My uncle gave us a key to his locker, so we could use his racquets since we did not have any of our own.

Tennis grew fast in me. Tennis was very unique and especial, so different from all the other sports that I had tried so far. The Tennis Pro, Rubén Nápoles, all dressed in white with his long Tennis trousers, V collared sweater and collared Lacoste style shirt was an impressive figure around the facility. He had beautiful and powerful strokes. I learned quickly from watching him hit or play. The white clothing, the wooden racquets, the orange dirt clay courts, the deaf wooly sound of the ball when hit, the smell and dampness of the whole place inspired and called me. It was all so beautiful, so powerful. On top of all that Tennis was an individual sport. I did not have to get along with teammates or anything like that. It was just me and whatever effort I put in; that was what I got out. All these things combined appealed to me very strongly.

That was 1967. A lot of things have changed since then. Shorts soon came into vogue and became the norm since in sports greater athleticism always leads to innovation. A few years later, color clothing was allowed by the ITF and subsequently by the different Tennis Associations and Tennis Federations around the World. I remember Arthur Ash with his fat striped-collar shirts and Rod Laver with his yellow shorts and shirt. At first I did not think anything of it, but deep inside, it made me sad. We had lost one of the most distinguishing characteristics of this marvelous sport. Not much later the optic yellow balls arrived and along with tighter clothing came the new faces of Bjorn Borg, Vitas Gerulaitis, Guillermo Vilas or Manuel Orantes after the hoard of great Australians. They were awesome for the sport. Some of them had great sportsmanship and unbelievable games and strokes for their time; others had fiery personalities but were incredibly interesting to watch, like Ilie Nastase or Jimmy Connors. Although this is not a history book, all this stuff is part of what makes Tennis today. It is worthy to note how each and every one of these players added their individual contributions to the game.

Nowadays, of course, you have Rafael Nadal, whom Tennis has benefited from so much. And who will ever forget Roger Federer. Pete Sampras is, of course, worthy of mention here since he did so much so quietly. Even though Federer has broken his record, I don't see him pull the great serving and exciting net play that Sampras brought to the game.

Tennis is interesting because it is always evolving. Compare strokes from today to what they looked like 20, 30 or even as recently as 10 years ago; more power, better or more refined techniques, and fitness is what we see. Rules change, fashion changes, equipment changes, even the court has changed officially worldwide for the younger ones. The surfaces change and new ones are added every so often. Tournaments and Tennis events all around the World change. Innovations in Tennis can be a pretty fast ride. It is hard to keep up with these changes being made to the sport. It is kind of like computers and electronics. We buy an electronic gizmo for $300, and the next thing we know a few months later is that it is obsolete already. The newer, faster, and better one will cost $230. Honestly, manufacturers have us by the throat. When they come up with a new racquet model, they sell a zillion of them. A year later, they come up with an "improved version" of the same racquet. A lot of times, it is just a different paint job, but here we go again, another zillion sold.

A lot of respect goes to guys like Courier, Sampras, Federer, Edberg and many others who have played, and some of them continue to do so with the very same racquet for many years! This shows us how little the racquet really does for us on a Tennis court. It is the player... yes, whoever is hitting the balls will be the only one that can do it correctly and manipulate that racquet to his or her advantage. There is only so much the racquet itself can do for us! I was kind of surprised when some time ago, I had one of my wooden collector's racquets with me. It was an original Donnay Bjorn Borg, with the super long leather grip, strung with gut strings; as I was getting ready to give a lesson to my daughter Anasazi, who was only 9 years old at the time, "I want to hit with that racquet Dad" she said, "why not, go for it," I replied. As I started feeding balls to her, she started nailing the ball dead center, and as she got warmed-up she was hitting the ball solid, with great topspin without too much of an issue at all! The grip on this racquet is a 4-5/8s, and it is at least 13 ounces in weight! After a little while, she missed the crisp feel of her Babolat and she traded. This little example goes to show how unimportant the racquet and the equipment itself really are. I am pretty sure that Roger Federer could beat almost anyone in the World with just about any racquet that was handed to him.

Personally and because I am sentimental traditionalist, I don't care too much for all the changes that have taken place over the last 45 plus years since I started playing Tennis. However, I recognize that without all this stuff, Tennis would be dead today. Yes, Tennis would have vanished a long time ago. Instead, Tennis is alive and strong because of change. And yes, its essence remains. Tennis for what it truly is; continues to be an awesome sport that will grow in our hearts and teach us a way of life.

When I see a child coming to the Tennis courts for the first time, I think of my uncle, Manuel and how he made that very first experience a good one on those red clay courts, and that concrete wall in Mexico. I always want to make sure that this child starts a lifelong relationship with Tennis like I did, and maybe, 45 years later, he or she will be writing about it like I am doing now.

HANGING WITH THE RIGHT CROWD

Let me start by saying that in my lifetime, most people I have met, I met through Tennis. Some of my best life-friends and mentors, are or were Tennis players. Some of the most important people that I have respected or admired, and that I have had the privilege to meet, happened around Tennis courts or Tennis events. The best and most fun times of my life have come through Tennis. Some great relationships, as well as good business, and all kinds of connections were possible for me because of Tennis. Finally, my deepest emotions, satisfactions, and feelings have come through playing Tennis and around Tennis circles.

What more do we want? Tennis has forged my life in so many ways... One cannot go wrong looking into Tennis to solve any problem in life. I guess this whole concept of using Tennis as the foundation to make any decision in life is not that easy to grasp. Even for Tennis players themselves, but believe me, it's hard to go wrong doing that because Tennis offers so many hidden benefits that come with it! "What? Don't buy it?" Just get in the Wisdom 101 section of this book and read down reasons we play Tennis. Or why are there millions of people of all ages playing Tennis worldwide? And why is Tennis the most internationalized sport in the World? Not the most populous, but most internationalized for sure, because Tennis is awesome!

So, sign up for lessons for the whole family, or just go to the Tennis courts and start hitting balls. Sign up for Tennis tournaments and spend the day doing that. Make a vacation trip out of it, invite some friends, and Tennis will reinforce the friendship and the bonds, and everyone will be better off for it. Good times, better health, better friends, etc... If I need to meet someone, invite them for some Tennis, and talk to them on the Tennis court. My daughter Anasazi wants her birthday party to be a surprise Junior Night Out Tennis party at the Tennis facility for the 3rd year in a row. Tennis parties are great fun; everyone is in a good mood, usually pretty good eating and a nice atmosphere.

WHAT TENNIS PROS DON'T TEACH (WTPDT)

Tennis has been my niche in life for a very long time. Tennis will continue to be a special, kind of sacred place for my loved ones and me for as long as I am alive. As a family, we will continue to make friends and expand our World because of Tennis.

So, who will we be hanging out with? Tennis friends? Work friends? School friends? Family and relatives? Loved ones and close ones to our hearts? The answer will obviously be our loved ones and close ones. But I suggest the majority of the rest of the time; we go to our Tennis friends. Of course, we will hang out a little with all the rest. But our Tennis friends will be the ones we will be having the most fun with, and the ones we will be able to trust the most on our day to day lives.

REMEMBRANCES IN TENNIS AND STORIES FROM THE PROS

As I completed my four years of college Tennis, I decided that I wanted to give the pros a try. In fact, I had decided that I wanted to do this when I was still a high school kid. I had no idea whatsoever what I would be getting into because it was all me, and I had no coach, money or mentor. I was a little overconfident to say the least back then.

After my college graduation in 1982, all I had to show for the last four years of my life was an undergraduate diploma in Physics and some stories to tell about collegiate Tennis in the US. I needed to enter the real World and after a tough experience working at a foundry operation in Mexico I went to work as a Teaching Pro at a resort in Mexico. All along I continued to hit Tennis balls in a random way not really knowing what to do next. So I started traveling some, playing for prize money or pro tournaments. One thing I knew is that my chances were slim of making it in the pros, but I went at it with an open mind. I figured that at worst I would get some experience and would be able to use that to my benefit regardless of what I ended up doing in the future. Like 99% of all 22 or 23-year-olds, I had no idea then of what I wanted to do with my life, so I figured, I had time, so why not try to enter the larger stage of professional Tennis. I had played junior and college Tennis semi-successfully, and I say semi, because I won a lot more than I lost, but I never really felt I was getting that much better through the level of training, coaching and competition I was exposing myself to. I never really had a coach, so I was it. To clarify, I was my own coach/manager, and I was doing things as best as I knew how to; based on what knowledge of the sport I had back then. As I got out of college I had lost a little of the fire and motivation for the game, and attempting to play Tennis professionally rekindled that diminished fire.

As a junior, I participated in several professional events. When I was 16 through 18, I played regional pro tournaments sanctioned by the FMT (Mexican Tennis Federation). I won a few matches here and there but was also destroyed a few times. I had some pretty respectable results in doubles, and I felt I was beginning to get some recognition and a name for myself nationally. I hate to say this, but my father, whom I loved to death, never really believed in what I was doing. We were a huge family with four brothers and four sisters, I was third from top to bottom, so the financial support was definitely not going to come. I had to teach some lessons (if we can call them lessons because I didn't know what I was doing) to my admiring friends and some kids younger than me to make money for traveling. Some of these kids thought I was the real deal because I was the State and Sectional No. 1 player in the 16s and 18s, but I knew I was no Tennis teacher, that's for sure. My Mother, bless her heart, which worked part time her entire life, sometimes handed me some money under the table; she wanted to help me have this opportunity, never expecting anything in return.

I played in San Luís Potosi, Aguascalientes, México City, Acapulco, Manzanillo, Colima, Monterrey, Ciudad Juarez as well as Guadalajara, of course since this was my hometown. All in all, I probably played in 25 to 30 tournaments for prize money. I knew I should not take money because I had the aspiration of playing college Tennis in the US, and as per NCAA rules, I had to maintain an amateur status. Regardless of the little money I made, as it turned out, I did play college Tennis. The NCAA never found out I had collected some cash from different tournaments in Mexico. NCAA rules regarding amateur status were a lot stiffer regarding prize money back then than they are nowadays this happened between 1975 and 1978. But being in Mexico and not highly visible, since I did not win all that much, I was not scrutinized in any way or form. Now with the Internet and all the ways we have of communicating, if someone takes prize money from a Pro event, it is easy to trace it down.

In 1976, an exhibition round robin competition was organized with the best four juniors in the Western Section of Mexico's FMT (Mexican Tennis Federation), to earn a spot to participate in a huge pro event, as a motivational invitation to the best junior in the area. I was in the zone when I beat Joel Nápoles, Esteban Rocha, and Victor Esparza (the other top juniors in the section) in matches that went to three sets, and I walked off the winner on all three occasions. I was only 16 years old then, and the Jalisco Tennis Association had organized a promotional tournament with the sponsoring of Marlboro Cigarettes. The four players to face each other in an exhibition quadrangular tournament were Bjorn Borg, Guillermo Vilas, Rod Laver, and Ilie Nastase. What a combination this was, this event changed my perspective on Tennis forever. Those guys played each other two out of three set matches, a couple of doubles matches as well. I don't remember who the man behind this was. I believe it was Fernando Palafox (cousin of the great Mexican Davis Cup player and John McEnroe's coach, Tony Palafox) and others, but never since that occasion, has anything even remotely close to that event happened again. As it turned out, they did not allow me to play with those guys. I was deeply disappointed. The organizers said they had miscalculated the schedule, and there would be no time to include me in the program. However, I earned the spot, and nobody can take the memory away from me. Incidentally, Fernando Palafox was the first serious Tennis player who took an interest in me as a junior when I was maybe 11 or 12 years of age. He once sponsored me with some money out of his own pocket to help me go to a national tournament in Mexico City. And later, had some former Davis Cup players from Mexico, practice with me on different occasions when they were in town. He was quite influential and always willing to promote Tennis and help many up and coming juniors.

So I attended college in the United States and played intercollegiate Tennis for 4 years on 100% scholarships. However, I didn't improve partly because the coaching was ineffective. I lost some motivation because I was so disappointed that the coaching level was nowhere near what was needed for me to continue to develop my game to its potential. But when I got out of college, as mentioned earlier, I got thinking about it again. Getting out of college in 1982 was tough; I wanted to try to play pro-Tennis, but I also wanted to go to graduate school but did not have the financial means. My Tennis game deteriorated for a short while. Since my grades were good but not good enough to apply for some sort of an academic scholarship, hence I had to go to work. Welcome to real life! I was at that crossroads, that dead end that so many young players hit sooner or later in their Tennis careers; it's a tough and lonely place to be at! It's kind of like standing in the middle of a huge desert without a compass or help from anyone!

Instead of grad school, this is when I ended up working at my Dad's foundry as mentioned above in Guadalajara, Mexico. It was a fun job with lots of challenges. My dad put me and my Physics degree on the production line, and then in maintenance. I was there for two years. The pay was awful. I could not even afford to buy an old car or go out with my girlfriend. After a year, with the help of my mom, I did end up buying an ancient VW bug that was like 20 years old and pretty beat up. But it got me around, and I was excited! I remember driving it for the first time sitting on a milk crate since it did not have seats when I first got it! But I was smiling, no doubt! Later of course I got some seats from an old wrecker's car yard for it.

While at the foundry before I got my VW bug, I would walk or ride my bicycle to work, it was about two and a half miles each way, up and down a mountain. The readers must think by now I was crazy, and now that I find myself writing about this, I think yes, I must have been. Yes, I was living with my parents. We lived on a forested mountain south of the huge city about 10 miles out in the suburbs. One of the neighbors had a Tennis court in his backyard. A concrete wall served the court as backstop and practice backboard. Once or twice a week I would go there to bang balls on this wall. Part of me missed the Tennis courts, the clay courts, the exhilarating smells of Tennis.

Since I was back in my original hometown, little by little, I started reconnecting with some of my old Tennis friends from the high school years. Within 6 months of having been back I was hitting Tennis balls more regularly and playing matches on weekends. My sister Alma, who had been a top junior in Mexico, was now playing college Tennis in Mexico. But it was nothing like the NCAA. In Mexico, College Tennis is only a shade of what it is in the US. Her coach invited me to their practices. So whenever work allowed it, I would participate. Suddenly Tennis was becoming fun again.

The coach was Suresh Bangara. He played Davis Cup for India. He was a medical student at the Universidad Autonoma de Guadalajara. Suresh was a solid player in his early 30s. He provided pretty good practices and some good advice. And now that I think about it, I can see that I did not make the best of the opportunity of finally having access to some real coaching. It deeply upsets me to write about this since I can now see with clarity that this could have been the opportunity I had waited for so long passing before my very eyes going unnoticed by me! It makes me terribly sad! How can it be possible that at this stage of my career and my life, I finally realize that I did not have the vision and wisdom to have taken advantage of it? A lot of times, opportunity goes by unnoticed. Tennis players, especially juniors, need always to have their eyes open, being on the lookout for chances to make another stride and be thoughtful of daily events or individuals or players they might meet.

The Jalisco Tennis Association and the Guadalajara Racquet Club organized an intercity pro league, the tournament's name was The Jet Set, and I had been recruited for a team that I ended up captaining. Don't ask me how we did it, but we ended up winning the whole thing. I played some doubles and mixed doubles mostly, and a little singles. I was hooked again. Since I was the captain, I got to keep the huge silver team trophy, which I still have to this day.

One day, my brother in law, Miguel Azanza, visited at the foundry for some business. He was an automotive mechanic. Casually, he said: "Manuel, I don't know what you are doing in this place; you should go become a Tennis Pro." He went on: "My friend Jaime Del Toro called me today saying they needed a Tennis Professional at Club Maeva in Manzanillo, Colima." Manzanillo is 200 miles southwest of Guadalajara. It is a resort area on the beaches of Jalisco, Mexico. Two weeks later I was on a bus on my way for an interview.

To make a long story short, all went well, all they needed was someone to oversee the Tennis facility, a very small Tennis Shop as well as teach some lessons and clinics. The salary and benefits were okay, and they gave me a super nice villa inside the resort complex with all meals and expenses paid for. Tennis rewarding me again for all the time spent on the court banging balls!

At Maeva, I started hitting balls every day for fun and practice with Mario Correa, who was a pro at Club Santiago. He had been a junior rival of mine. Maeva had 12 hard courts. Club Santiago had 6. Before we knew it, we were traveling to tournaments together. We even organized some good prize money tournaments ourselves, sanctioned by FMT.

Another good thing at Maeva was that I was able to save almost all the money I made. I ended up with nearly $20,000 in cash. I kept my money in US Dollars inside the air conditioning unit, in the ceiling of my room. The Mexican Peso was not stable, and I needed to keep the money in US dollars to make sure it did not suddenly devaluate. Back in those days it was not possible to keep or open a bank account in US Dollars, so I had to keep the cash with me at all times. While working at Maeva, my appetite for Pro Tennis returned.

With my savings, I ended up enrolling in the engineering school at the University of Texas, El Paso. I knew my money was not going to last me very long, so I got a job at the El Paso Tennis Club teaching juniors.

I soon made connections with some of the best players and pros in the El Paso area, like Sal Castillo, and, later, Ross Walker. I was back to my teenager routine, except that I had to work to support myself now going to school in the mornings, working, and traveling to tournaments in the US and Mexico. I would work hard for a month, save some money, go play a tournament in Chihuahua or Tucson, come back home and do it all over again always traveling to different places. Sometimes I would travel for two and up to three tournaments in a row with permission from my professors at UTEP and of course work.

I also played in every open or prize money tournament in El Paso area. UTEP teachers and my boss were flexible and encouraging. Sometimes I would be gone for weeks at the time. It was awesome. In 1987, I finished the year ranked 12th in Mexico's pro circuit.

Even though I was a little old to be pursuing Pro Tennis, I went for it because part of me subconsciously knew I was investing in my future. Through 1984-1987, I probably played in over 20 tournaments per year!

As much as I have always loved singles, my results in doubles were better. I won a few doubles events in Chihuahua, Durango, Torreon, Guadalajara, and Aguascalientes, but I also experienced some very close singles matches against top players in Mexico.

Playing doubles kept me in the tournaments longer; rankings were different for doubles and singles, so unfortunately doubles results did not impact my singles ranking. Typically I could win one or maybe two matches in singles and three or more in doubles.

In singles, I could play pretty close against some of the best players. But I just could not break through and beat them with any consistency. Now and then I could get a good win, but that was it. For the most part, if I had to play against a top seed I was going to be out of the tournament.

Now that I think about it, it makes me wonder how close I really was to breaking through. If only I would have had someone to give me more hope and kept me motivated to continue practicing and staying in this chase. But I had no coach. My practices were self-designed. Basically, I was my own coach.

As a group of players and friends, we traveled as a team. Sometimes there were four of us, but most of the time it was just two of us. Very rarely was I by myself. Traveling with partners lowered costs, and it was easier to set up practices and warm-ups. As players and friends, we coached one another all the time, and we would also advise each other on strategy to deal with other players. I guess we were a real team. If we had to play against one another, it was always a friendly but very competitive match.

I have no regrets about spending all that money and so much time on the road. Those years and experiences are an integral part of what I am today and who I am as a Tennis coach and person. I did make a few bucks.

In Aguascalientes, I was handed $2,500 USD after reaching the quarterfinals in singles and semis in doubles. In Guadalajara, I made $2,000 in doubles. In Torreon, it was maybe $1,500, and I pocketed some more money in other tournaments in Cancun, Mérida, Veracruz, Toluca, Zacatecas, Acapulco and Cabo San Lucas. But I knew I had to go back and teach some more if I wanted to continue. The prize money was nice, but never enough to survive on.

In 1987, I made it to The Masters for the Mexico pro circuit to be held in Leon Guanajuato. Only the top 16 for the year were invited. I went to Manzanillo with my friend Mario Correa for training for a week before the tourney. Believe it or not, I injured my left leg pretty bad water skiing. So I limped into The Masters with a big bandage around my torn left quad muscle. I played and lost handily but collected a good $3,000 check. Someone might say this was a little unethical, but believe me I needed the cash!

I never did make it into the bigger tournaments. I played in qualifier events for bigger tourneys several times but could not make it passed the first or second rounds. One time I advanced to the last round of the qualifying tournament in a huge Challenger San Luis Potosi event. I had already won three rounds to reach this final stage and faced Jose Lopez, a top 5 player in the nation. I went on court thinking I had a chance but knowing I was in for a real fight. I had a good strategy; Lopez was a solid baseliner, and I was an all-court player. San Luis is at least 5000 feet above sea level, and the clay courts felt pretty fast. I could serve and volley and mix it up some. I felt I should be able to hold serve pretty consistently. Lopez had a weak serve, especially his 2nd delivery and a sort of iffy forehand. Part of my strategy was to rush the net obviously; off the return of serve some of the time and force him to go for it. I was known for being very fit, and pretty fast and athletic around the court; my serve was definitely the foundation of my game. As it turned out, something got in my head in the middle of the first set and lost complete confidence in my serve. I ended up double faulting like 15 times; I was still able to get a few games, my score was something like 6/3 and 6/1, but that was it, I was out! Again!

A few times, having advanced to the last round of the qualifying tourney, I lost and entertained the possibility of a lucky loser. A lucky loser is someone who advanced to the last round of the qualifying event but lost that last match. This player gets first bids for entering the main draw event as an alternate if someone withdraws or does not show in the first round of the main draw. I was never handed a lucky loser pass into the main draw of any tournaments. I typically always made the main draw by effort, except for the one time I was handed a wildcard at tournament in Aguascalientes. I was making a comeback for the nth time, and I had some relatives and supporters there that could pull some strings for me.

The tournaments in Aguascalientes were special to me. I played several times at the Club Campestre de Aguascalientes. I was 15 years of age when I first played there. I reached the finals of what was then called the semi-pro division and collected $900 USD. I came back to Aguascalientes on and off at least ten times. They always had their pro tourney over Easter week. My Mom was originally from that area, and I could count on having housing and meals taken care of as well as a great cheering squad from all my cousins, uncles, and other relatives. Every year was a special and memorable experience!

It was in Aguascalientes that, after three qualifier rounds, I faced José Cortez, back then a top player in Mexico. I won the first set 6/4; he won the second set 6/4, and we went to a tiebreaker in the Third Set. He got up on me 6-3 in the breaker, and I came back to win 8-6 after some fearless serve and volleying and chip and charging. I do not remember ever being nervous and did not realize how close I was to losing this match until I had actually won it. On match point, I just served a high kicker to his forehand, and he swung as hard as he could and the ball went three feet out. I saw the ball sail by my right side two feet high over the net, but the ball had very little; to no topspin and I knew it was going well out. There were at least 150 people watching. Some of them were sitting on a concrete bleacher. Others were seated on folding steel chairs. Others were just standing or sitting on the ground. It was magic! Talk about being in the zone!

I was also in the zone in Abilene, Texas. My freshman year in college, after the short fall season, we traveled to a prize money open tournament in this West Central Texas town. We knew we could not accept money if we won. First round, I played a top Texas junior and killed him 6/1 and 6/1. It felt good; yes, the zone again. In the second round, I was zoning in yet again, and easy win. In the third round, top college player Jeff Williams from Central Texas College was my opponent, and the zone stood on my shoulder. I won the first set 6/4, lost the second set 6/4 and won the third something like 6/3. Williams went ballistic during the whole match. I just kept playing great but was never aware of it. Nothing could disturb me I had no problems, no pressures other than learning English and making my grades. Hitting Tennis balls was fun, and competing was frosting on the cake. I loved being on the Tennis court. At this point, the fire; still burning strong, and I, still dreaming of playing Davis Cup one day. My teammates, who had been out of the tournament long before me, were all following me match to match cheering and supporting. It was like my private support team that week; they would lay down on the ground behind the court and watch under the windscreens with their head supported by their hands having fun and socializing in the process.

Another match that I cannot forget happened when playing doubles in my junior year at Truman University in Kirksville, Missouri. It was a home match. We were playing some school from Chicago. I had already won my singles match at No. 2 in straight sets, something like 6/3 and 6/1. I was playing in the zone that day. Jeff Hammerschmidt our No. 3 player and I were in deep trouble in doubles. We were getting killed. Things were not happening for us. The score got to where we were down 0/6, 0/5 and 0-40 in game 6. At Love-40, I was playing the add side, and Jeff the deuce, we were receiving serve. When the serve came, I just ripped a winner return crosscourt. Then we won the next point, then he next, then the next and the next. It was 1/5 now, and to make a long story short, we ended up winning this match 7/5 and 6/1 in the third. I don't know how we did it. We were playing in the zone, and all I can remember is Jeff tossing his Prince Woody racquet 20 feet in the air as he run toward me, and we hugged. That was a once-in-a-lifetime comeback. I am pretty sure those guys we beat that day still remember the match also. Later on, trying to figure out how we did it, Jeff and I never knew what we did differently. It was all automatic pilot, and that is all I can recall!

And don't let me forget some of my matches against Ross Walker. Ross was Director of Tennis at El Paso Tennis Club back in the mid-80s. He is English by birth and was part of the English Davis Cup squad at some point in his career. I ended up working for him as a Staff Professional for four years. To players like Ross or myself, there is not such a thing as a practice match. We played all out regardless. Until I met Ross, I always thought I was a decent player. Ross, however, was a fantastic player. Back in those years, Ross was serious about getting himself ready to play USTA national tournaments in the 35s and 40s. I was just excited to have the opportunity to play with him. We would play for hours on end. We would play sets or full matches. He beat me pretty bad most of the time. He was solid all around.

Ross had absolutely no weakness in his game. He was fit, smart and disciplined, very serious about his training routines. I have to confess I never did beat him, and the closest I ever came was on the red clay, probably his worst surface and my own best one. This happened on the Campestre Juárez Tennis courts across the border from El Paso as he was getting ready to play clay court nationals. That year Ross had already won hard courts and indoor nationals I think it was 1986. That day, as we were driving across the border, he said to me: "Manuel, I think you have an inflated opinion of my game. I feel we should play a lot closer." Anyway, to make a long story short, that day I probably played some of the best Tennis of my life. I guess what he said to me, really got in my head and gave me confidence, but something happened to me that day that I could do no wrong. I won the first set 6/3. He won the second 6/4. In the third, we played neck and neck all the way to the point he was serving at 4-5, and the score was 15-30. I had been hurting him with my chip and charging strategy off his second serve. He was having a hell of a hard time passing me at the net.

He missed the first serve. I prepared for another chip and charge kill. I was winning the great majority of points on Ross's second serve. So he served to my forehand; I chipped it down the line. It looked good. As I moved forward, suddenly, he appeared like a phantom at the net and volleyed my chip down the line for a clean winner! I was completely thrown off mentally. He had not done this the whole match, and to come up with this move at such a crucial time was just beyond me. If I had won that point, I would have had two match points! As it turned out, he ended up holding serve and breaking my serve beating me again 7/5 in that third set.

Ross Walker was awesome; in my mind he could have been a top professional player but was plagued by injury early in his career and could not play consistently. Ross was and still is a great coach. He really helped my game and forged part of my coaching style and philosophy. I consider him a true friend and a mentor. Back then, I would just sit down on the side of his court and watch and listen to him teach our top juniors for hours on end every week.

Let me add a small anecdote about a match versus the great Sal Castillo from El Paso, Texas. Sal was also my friend and we practiced together on and off. Sal was also a very good player although somewhat younger. In a small prize money tourney in Carlsbad, New Mexico we met in the finals. Sal was a smooth mover, extremely talented with great serve and volley skills; plus lots of spin on his groundstrokes and serve. Ross and Sal knew each other well because they had played a few times in the past; a day or two before heading to Carlsbad, Ross gave me some insight into his matches versus Sal. He told me that one of my key tactical things was going to be the lob, since

Sal really crowded the net. Man was he right, over and over I hit lobs over Sal's head when he came into the net and closed for the volley kill shot!

Again, a similar scenario; Sal serving at 4-5 in the third set, 15-30 the game score. Sal served and volleyed, I played a low backhand slice crosscourt return. He hit a weak backhand volley. The ball sat in the middle of the service box for me to put away with a forehand passing shot. As I prepped for the shot, a mosquito or some sort of bug decided to land in my eye! Swinging hard, I hit the ball with the frame, and Sal put it away. I lost the match 7/5 in the third set.

I could play them close but could never quite break through and beat some of these really good players. I had similar matches against former Davis Cup players from Mexico like Jorge Lozano, Ives Lemaitre, Hector Ortiz, and others...

In my late teens and in the juniors as well as in my early twenties, I was less aware of my surroundings and less aware as a Tennis player. My theory is that this triggered playing in the zone for me more often. There are numerous occasions I played in the zone, but it was not something I knew how to reproduce at will. In several matches, I could enter the zone but could not sustain that condition.

In doubles, at Truman, Tim Shnicklauss and I went 19 and 0 for our 1981-1982 season before we tanked against some school in St. Louis because of some irritating acting by our coach. What coach had said or done, I cannot even remember now... it was obviously not a big deal, and tanking the match was obviously the wrong thing to do about it. Maturity and wisdom, what awesome things to have! Unfortunately, the only way to gain them sometimes is through aging!

I am proud to say that I won more matches than I lost, but there are a few loses that I will never forget. One such occasion happened during my sophomore year in college playing in a little tournament in the spring of 1979 in Navarro, Texas. I was playing this kid from India. He was very smooth and unbelievably quick. It was windy, so conditions did not lend themselves to good Tennis. We went to a tiebreaker in the third set. Back in those years the tiebreakers were played first to five with a sudden death point at four all. I got up to 4-0 in the breaker, and ended up losing 5-4. Don't ask me why this happened. All I can remember is playing all those match points tentatively, and when I lost, I boomeranged my racket under the net from baseline to baseline along the ground all the way to the opposite fence. My coach Bob

Chaloupecky kicked my rear pretty hard; not for losing the match, but for throwing my racket... of course!

Another painful loss in the juniors that I will never forget happened when playing Jorge Lozano. He was probably 14, and I like 16 or so. I won the first set 6/1 and was leading 3/0 in the second when it got too dark to complete our match, and there were no lights on court 6 in the Guadalajara Club. The next day I was a bundle of nerves and could not hit a ball in the court to save my life. He ended up winning that second set and the match. For some reason, this match still weighs heavy on my mind! It happened over 40 years ago! Tennis... mmh!

To finish on a good note, let me tell about my match versus Mexico's Davis Cup player Octavio Martinez. This match happened way back like in 1974. We were playing in a pro event in Club Santiago, Manzanillo, Mexico. The match was played on centre court. At that point, I was a promising 15-year-old junior. Octavio was fresh out of college and playing a lot of tournaments. We were neck to neck the entire match. Of course, I was feeling no pressure at all. We went to a third set, and he ended up winning 7/5. It was a late afternoon match, and there were a lot of spectators around the court. As I was getting off the court, everyone wanted to talk to me, telling me how great a match that had been and how well I had played. They just kept going on and on about how I had a really good chance of making it into professional Tennis. Octavio himself congratulated me and talked to me about college Tennis in the US. He had played for Lamar University and said he could help me make some connections to some schools that would be very interested in recruiting me for their team. I was excited and motivated.

In that same tournament, I also played in the semi-pro division. I played solid, winning the tournament in the third set against junior rival Victor Esparza in a tough three set match. Victor was in full control of the match at 6/2 and 5/2. For a short guy, Victor had a really good kick serve, and I could not break him to save my life. At 5/2, it occurred to me that I should try to return his serve from 4 feet further back. Suddenly, I was able to see the ball a little better and started making better returns. I broke his serve and ended up coming back to win 7/5. In the third, set I still had the momentum and won 6/2. A little adjustment in tactics was all that was needed to change everything in that match. I was happy!

SECTION VIII

WISDOM TENNIS 101

101 TENNIS TIPS WITHOUT DIAGRAMS... MY WISDOM TENNIS CONNECTION

These tips were created with the idea to instill something in a player's mind in a simple and understandable way that can make a difference on a Tennis court. This know-how material can save us when in trouble fighting to figure out ways to come back in a match or to counter problems. Some of these tips did not come from this author; they came to be on their own, and could be credited to Tennis itself as a living entity.

1- High Tension on the strings of the racquet provides more control on hard shots but less touch and feel on finesse shots. Low tension gets us more power on hard shots and more feel on finesse and touch shots!

2- In doubles, we should not only try to go to the weaker player as much as we can, but hammer the weaknesses of the weaker player as much as we can!

3- Anything that happens on a Tennis court, we either made it happen, or we let it happen!

4- In a close match situation, the player who wants to win the most usually ends up winning the match! So, are we hungry?

5- A generally good idea when losing is to do to our opponent(s) whatever he/she/they is/are doing to us. This usually works!

6- The only way to play our best Tennis is draw from a sense of joy, fun, and enthusiasm! Our best Tennis will never surface out from feelings of confrontation, frustration or condemnation!

7- As in the laws of physics, there are also laws of Tennis. How we practice, we will play! Want it or not. If we practice in anger, we will play matches frustrated and angry. If we practice without focused concentration, our mind will be fragmented in matches. If we have no intensity in practice, don't expect to be dynamic and alert in matches. Matchplay will always be a reflection of practice!

8- The simplest way to improve our mental toughness is to shut our mouth! The only time we open it is to say something positive such as "Come on," "Let's go," "Make the shot," "Concentrate," "Run down the ball," "Hit the ball", etc... And, of course, to call out the score!

9- When dealing with a tough opponent, avoid his or her strengths and concentrate on their weaknesses! Playing too much into our opponent's strengths will make them more confident and tougher to deal with!

10- On retaliation calls, I am by no means suggesting a player to resort to this measure when someone is making bad line calls. However, if we are getting hooked badly and there are no officials on hand to help with some line calling; a retaliation call may not be that bad an idea. It will help make our opponent stay honest and think about it before he/she makes the next bad call. So we are not retaliating to cheat per se, but trying to keep the opponent honest!

11- Any movement of our body that is not contributing to making a stroke better, is probably contributing to making it worse; therefore it should be eliminated!

12- Anything that is not a strength in a Tennis Player is probably a weakness! And anything that can be a strength in Tennis can also be a weakness!

13- Each point played in a match is bound to repeat itself. Having said that, if our opponent is serving wide, in order to open the court on the deuce side, and winning the point consistently, figure out a way to prevent that. Likewise, if we hurt our opponent by running around our backhand when returning on the add side, then we have to make damn sure we repeat this as often as possible; looking for variations during points, to make this strategy even more effective!

14- A thinking player needs to be sensitive to small changes in strategy. Failing to do this usually means losing matches he/she could otherwise win!

15- Take care of the ball first... Then worry about the opponent(s)! We get distracted by what our opponents are doing or about to do. Focus on the coming ball only and go with whatever comes to mind first!

16- We have to let our instinct be our guide! It is the only way to go. Taking our eye off the ball when it is in the air is a capital sin in

Tennis, and it will not be pardoned! We will pay for it by losing the point most of the time. We should be able to keep track of our opponents positioning on court through peripheral vision!

17- Always change a losing game. Never change a winning game. This tip is obviously not mine, but it could be anyone's, it is as timeless as life itself!

18- Wear two pairs of socks. We want our tennis shoes to fit a little bitty tight, and we want some space between our skin and the wall of the Tennis shoe. Wearing two pairs of socks increases that gap and allows for a little more air circulation inside the shoe; two pairs of socks increases the cushioning and fills the gaps where the shoe may not fit perfectly!

19- Anytime we have lost three games in a row we most likely need to modify our strategy. If the games were close, a small modification might be necessary. But if we've only won three or four points in three games, then a radical change in strategy may be necessary!

20- How old are my strings? It is pretty easy to figure out when our strings are about to break. Near, or right on the sweet spot of the string bed, move down two or three of the cross strings, sight down one of the cross strings, and see how deep the notches are on the main strings. When the strings are worn or notched about one-third or more of the string's diameter, that is a good indicator they are about to break. Also by sliding the cross strings down back in place if a clear snap is heard as the cross strings fall back into position that is another good sign that the strings are pretty worn out. If about to play in a tournament, it is probably a good idea to get our racquet restrung. Hard hitters who use a lot of spin and break lots of strings, have to have at least 3 fresh strung racquets in their bag all the time!

21- Smart tournament players should be aware of when they are about to break strings and switch racquets during matches before they actually do break. Breaking strings will most likely cost us the point. Some players break strings every day, some twice a day! I work with a 19-year-old that hits a very heavy ball that breaks polyester strings in 16 gauge once or twice a day! He is a nightmare to keep up with… for our stringers!

22- In a close match, one point can and will make the difference; a Tennis player cannot afford to lose a single point out of lack of awareness and sloppiness!
23- The type of string and string tension needs to match a player's style. Hard baseline hitters usually require more tension, finesse players like it low, and all else fall somewhere in the middle. If a player likes spin, it is hard to beat the new polyesters with thinner gages and geometrical cross section!
24- To slide on clay courts, players need to lean back or put their weight on the back foot, in order to allow the front foot to skid/surf/glide/slide on the surface!
25- To stop when sliding on clay, a player has to lean forward and transfer his/her weight to the front foot, keeping a low center of gravity by getting down close to the ground, for maintaining good dynamic balance!
26- Sliding on clay is an art. Most players get used to sliding on clay with the same foot (right foot for right handed players and left foot for lefties) to move in all directions. The more gifted or hard working players are capable of sliding with both feet. We should be able to slide open stance or closed stand as needed! (see sliding on the clay techniques video at https://youtu.be/hCyMUh4QFR8)
27- A player's choice of racquet should match his/her game or playing style. The best way to figure out what racquet to go with is to find an advanced or professional player that can be modeled. This player should be of similar physique and playing style, the racquet he or she uses will probably be a good fit!
28- In a less than a perfect World, spins are a necessary aspect of Tennis. The reason we use spins so much in Tennis, is because we cannot always hit the ball perfectly, and we need spin to compensate for our inadequacies as humans and as players!
29- More spin will give us more control but less linear speed and depth. Too much spin can be counterproductive and can lead to a ball that is moving too slowly through the length of the court or fall short!
30- Resolving one problem only exposes the next immediate one, there is no end to this, even for great players. If we are able to make our backhand better, then we may have to work on our forehand or serve or whatever that next weakest link is!

31- On fast surfaces, don't hit behind the opponent, just go to the open court when punishing the ball; the fast court will work in our favor!
32- If we are playing against a slow player, don't try to hit behind him/her too often, because most likely, they will still be on the same side of the court by the time we hit the ball back to them, so, just go for the open court instead!
33- We will only be as good as the best competition we can find! This tip is obviously as timeless as the game of Tennis itself. But it is obvious and easy to understand and apply!
34- Less than 10% of juniors who are extremely successful in the 10s, 12s, and 14s make it to the pros! This is a published statistic from a few years ago, so go wonder what our junior players need to be doing!
35- It's almost as if we'd rather not have our kids do well in the early stages of their development. The reason for this, obviously, is that at those early stages, kids don't play Tennis the way they will be playing when they are older, and there is a really good chance that if they played the way they did or continued to play the way they did when they were little, they would lose a lot of matches!
36- In Tennis as in life, it's all about enjoying every step of the way... It's not the destination, but all that will lead us to it, that we need to focus on!
37- Each and every ball a player hits on a Tennis court has the potential of either making him/her better, keep him/her the same or make his/her game worse! It's like a giant staircase where each ball we hit with full concentration gets us up one step, keeps us the same or makes us go down one step. At the top is excellence, and very few ever make it all the way up. Every ball should be hit with a purpose!
38- No lead is enough in Tennis! Don't be too complacent with a lead. Doing so is wrong and conducive to allowing opponents the opportunity to come back. In Tennis, unlike other sports, each game is like a whole new mini match, and each set, is a fresh start. This is so because of the weird scoring system in Tennis!
39- Tennis is a battle of two players' minds, as much as it is a battle of strokes and physiques. Those who are capable of imposing their terms on others, physically, mentally, emotionally and spiritually are those who will win most matches and tournaments!

40- Develop an instinct for the location of our opponent(s). We should instinctively know where they are when the ball is in the air. Concentrate on our own positioning and the ball moving in the air!

41- Players who make it to the top in Tennis and other sports learn something completely new in three months, and they can also change a technique radically in the same amount of time! For all others, normal human beings, it will take us longer, and in most cases too long!

42- If we want to have fun and play our best Tennis every now and then, we just have to play our normal game... But if we want to win more matches, we need to think outside the box, and sometimes win playing someone else's game!

43- There are no rights or wrongs on a Tennis court! What works for one player may not work for someone else, and what works for all or most, may not work for another player... Each and every player is an individual!

44- We have to figure out ways to make our opponent play into our strengths! A simple example is what John Newcombe used to do when returning serve. On big points, he would stand way to his left behind the doubles alley in order to force his opponent to serve to his huge forehand!

45- All other things being equal, if we want to hit forehands, we need to hit to our opponent's forehand. Or if we want to hit backhands, then we need to hit to our opponent's backhand. If our opponent wants to break from this pattern, he or she has to go down the line, which is lower percentage! Voila!

46- If we want to hit crosscourt shots... then we need to start crosscourt rallies first. If we want to hit down the line; then start down the line exchanges. If our opponent wants to break away from this, he or she has to redirect the ball, and that is lower percentage! Voila!

47- Tennis players need to establish their own pace during matches. If losing, we need to try to veer away from our opponent's pace. Is he rushing us? Or is he making us wait? We can call it rhythm, pace, or tempo on court. How fast does a player play? We have seen this before. Lendl could play very slow, and the tougher the match, the slower things got. He drove many players crazy. Agassi played super fast, and he seemed to be rushing things all the time!

WHAT TENNIS PROS DON'T TEACH (WTPDT)

48- Anticipation is the only way to cover the court. After a player hits the ball, he needs to get his/her behind moving towards the largest opening on his/her side of the court!

49- A Tennis player has to treat each and every ball as if it was the last ball he or she would ever hit... Play every point on a Tennis court as if it was the last point he/she will ever play... Play every game, set and match as if it was the last one he/she will ever play... Live every second of our life as if it was the last second we will live!

50- Hard hitters who are a big string breakers, wanting to save money on stringing need to buy their own string and only pay for labor at the local Tennis shop!

51- Players needing to make some extra money need to string their own racquets and their friends' racquets too. Buy a portable stringing machine and learn how to do it. With a little practice, it should not take longer than 20 minutes to string a racquet from beginning to end. The machine will pay for itself pretty fast!

52- If we want a free Tennis lesson? All we have to do is take a close, comfortable seat near the court where a good Tennis coach is working with a player with a similar problem as ours. Listen, learn... and take some notes. We can even film! With permission, of course!

53- Another way to get free lessons is by watching TV. The amount of information on the screen is overwhelming. Watch the player, not the ball. Follow the footwork patterns. Understand court position and strike zones. Write down some notes!

54- Not always go for what the commentaries on TV are saying. Be a little skeptical here because sometimes they are full of bologna. Really good commentators are few and far between. Some of the best are Cahill, Gilbert, John McEnroe, Courier, Fernandez, Navratilova, and Stolle. Arias used to be good, but he was a little tough and rough to listen because he could be a little too direct and critical of some players, but very interesting nevertheless!

55- Tennis players need to make their decision on positioning as soon as they hit the ball. Sometimes as they are hitting the ball they already know where they need to go as the ball is traveling away from them!

56- In Tennis the exception confirms the rule. Sometimes positioning will be determined by our opponent and the circumstances and not by us!

57- A Tennis player makes his/her decision on shot selection as the ball is approaching. Stick to what comes to mind first. Deviating from this simple rule will cost the player the point!

58- If dealing with hardcourt resurfacing and new hard courts, don't bend over backwards trying to prevent cracks or get rid of them. The only solution to cracks on hard courts is to accept them. And the only truth about cracks is that they will appear sooner or later. And if we have them fixed, it will not be a matter of if, but a matter of when they will reappear!

59- Be prepared mentally to deal with some bad bounces when playing on natural surfaces like clay or grass. Clay (or dirt) was the original surface when Tennis was invented. The first Tennis courts were rather crude in nature and construction. Some of today's clay courts are awesome in comparison!

60- The reason we do Australian formation in doubles is to neutralize the crosscourt return of serve. Same goes with the so called the Military or the I-Formation. Both formations are very similar!

61- During a baseline crosscourt rally playing singles, breaking away from it switching to down the line, sometimes is a sign of breaking down mentally and technically! Unless a player gets a weak shot that he/she can really punish or put away. We have to sustain that crosscourt rally and let our opponent make the switch to down the line; he will be the one taking the extra chance of a lower percentage shot!

62- Junior Development is not a race! Working with juniors takes time, and everyone should work at his or her own pace. It is not about who gets there first, but about who actually makes it to the end line in the developmental process!

63- Hitting a Tennis ball should feel good! If it does not, then something is wrong! Hitting a Tennis ball should be pretty effortless, if it is not, then something is wrong! Hitting Tennis balls and playing Tennis should be fun and enjoyable as well as a learning experience. If it is not, then something is wrong!

64- Volleys and the net game are not about power but finesse in Tennis. Volleys are about redirecting the ball into the opening on the other side of the net. Volleys are about keeping the ball low and a lot of times just short. Volleys are all about agility and quick reactions and pure athleticism and beauty!

65- Power in Tennis belongs to the server and the aggressive baseliner. Groundstrokes can be hit very hard and deep. Some hard groundstrokes can have formidable power and require lots of force!

66- Besides neutralizing tough crosscourt returns in doubles, the Australian formation really enhances communication between partners. This is absolutely necessary for success in doubles. Both partners must know and agree on serving patterns, also the net player should let his or her partner know in advance which way he or she is going to move!

67- Start a private Tennis Journal. Write thoughts and ideas, about other players' strengths and weaknesses, about different Tennis courts played on, records for stringing and equipment in general, and use as reference. Always have it in the Tennis bag. A small hardcover journal with a thick rubber band around it will stand up to hard use!

68- String dampeners don't really help reduce arm injuries. All they do is silence/dampen the vibration and sound from the strings. This vibration is not what causes injuries in Tennis. The kind of shock produced by the impact of the ball on the strings goes to the frame and passes to our arm's joints, and that is what causes the injuries. In my mind, dampeners take away feel from the player. We can feel the vibration of the strings and listen to them as we stroke the ball, and this information helps develop better understanding of what kind of shot we are hitting or need to be hitting. Dampeners do change the feel and the sound of impact. Once players are used to them, it is hard to break away from them. A dampener is just one more gadget. The thing of it is, if a player is able to get used to hitting without one, then he/she will not want to go back to them, because the feel of the hit without one is actually more fulfilling!

69- Be cautious not to hammer too much on our opponents' weaknesses because we may strengthen them!

70- When the ball is in the air, we should be running, really moving with the ball in flight. But for most solid groundstrokes, it is better to hit the ball with both feet down on the ground!

71- Avoid doing fitness training before match play or practice. It is better to hit balls first and then head for the gym or the track!
72- Singles play is a lonesome affair, doubles is a social encounter! As Tennis players, we can have either or both to enrich our lives!
73- It is one thing to know how to hit a ball, quite another knowing where to aim it. Knowing how to hit the ball correctly is only part of the equation. Matchplay is essential to the development of players!
74- Tennis players or athletes for that matter have to consider sleep and rest part of their training. During tournament competition, sleep and rest become even more important. Allowing our body to heal and our system to recover is a big part of being successful on the Tennis court!
75- In junior development, we need to ask our kids the right questions after each match, lesson, and drill: Who are they becoming because of Tennis? Did they have a good time? What did they learn today? Don't ask: What was their score? Who won? Who did they play against?
76- Our emotions and what flashes through our mind 3 to 5 seconds before the start of every point is most likely what is going to transpire when the ball goes into play. We need to be relaxed but intense, and we need to concentrate, ritualize and visualize in those 3 to 5 seconds. This needs to be a very deeply embedded routine that happens automatically before the start of every point!
77- If we are playing a pretty close match; chances are we probably have the right strategy. If we lost the first set 6/3 or 6/4, we could win this match if we make subtle changes in strategy and believe we can do it. Radical changes in strategy should only be done when we are pretty much getting blown off of the court. If we lose 3 or 4 games in a row, we probably need a more radical change!
78- Tennis can be anything and everything we want it to be. Tennis has that flexibility to accommodate, and it should be okay. Tennis will tolerate us even if nobody else does!
79- Sports science has much to offer the developing and the serious player. Study some nutrition, fitness training, and mental toughness training; there is lots of material out there!
80- As coaches we sometimes lose students to other programs or coaches; this should not be the end of the World. 90% of the

time, it will be the wrong move. But do let a student go to another academy or program when his or her time comes!

81- In Tennis, as in anything else in this life, there is no substitute for hard work. Sometimes, we fool ourselves thinking we put in two hours on the court, when the whole time we were not really at 100% intensity mentally, physically, and emotionally; that would account for only about 30% of the two hours… about 40 minutes worth!

82- Junior players ages 13 and older should be doing their fitness training on their own. As coaches, we can design a program for them, but they have to pursue it on their own. As Tennis coaches, we don't have time to do everything. When the player is on the court he/she needs to be concentrating on Tennis!

83- Familiarity brings confidence. Tennis players have to get familiar with what they are not good at in Tennis. Net play is a good example. Players need to spend a good portion of their practices at the net hitting volleys and learning to be comfortable with this skill and little by little they will get much better at it!

84- The overhead is a very psychological shot; in that a player should be able to put it away most of the time. Missing a few, however, can breed tentativeness. If we hit a successful overhead, we get more confident, and our opponent now is more reluctant to give us lobs. This forces him/her to go for tougher and lower percentage shots such as passing shots when we are at the net! So we have to practice overheads a lot especially if we are net players or all court players!

85- Learn to volley with one grip only. The best grip for this is the continental grip. If we have a two-handed backhand volley, we can probably get away with an eastern forehand grip for all forehand and backhand volleys. But if we have a two hander… it would probably be worth our time to learn a one handed backhand volley; this will for sure increase our skill at the net!

86- Consistent tossing is one of the main ingredients of great serving. Without consistency, players will never develop a good serve. The key to developing a solid toss and serve is not swinging at bad tosses. As we toss the ball, identify if the toss is good before swinging. If not good, just stop the ball and try again!

87- Tennis is life and life is Tennis… We have to build our life around Tennis and not our Tennis around life! Is life like Tennis?

88- If a player is winning; he may step up the tempo a little bit! If he/she is losing, slow down the tempo a little! But stay within the boundaries of ethics and rules!

89- Playing with sunglasses on a court full of dappling shadows is not a good idea. Chances are we will be having a harder time tracking down the ball, and it probably is harder to track it down if less light is allowed in our eyes!

90- If we are winning don't argue about scores, line calls, rules. Let our opponent have his way... but keeping up our momentum. Momentum in Tennis is very fickle... It shifts all the time at the slightest provocation. Momentum is kind of like the wind!

91- When losing... players have to identify two or maybe three causes for getting beat during a Tennis match. Thus, we can probably counter if we have the tools. These tools may be mental ones much of the time!

92- Always sit down during a changeover, even if we are not tired; this is a good habit and solid routine. Go figure why the pros always sit down. Nobody knows best!

93- Matches we will always remember are the ones where we came back from being way down or down one or more match points! But also the matches where our opponent came back after being way down or down one or several match points!

94- When at the net or approaching the net, follow the ball's path as it moves away from us after we hit it; this applies to doubles and singles equally. The ball wants to come back to its original impact point, and by following it as we hit it, we have a much greater chance to intercept it as it comes back over the net!

95- If we want our opponents to hit lobs; then hit lobs at them. If we want our opponents to hit hard, then hit hard at them. If we want them to hit slice, then give them some slice shots... This tactic is a good rule of thumb. It does not apply to all players, but it sure is a good one to know for tactical purposes when we face troublesome opponents! Do to them what we want them to do to us... in other words, make them play our game!

96- Although not always the most effective thing to do, Tennis is more satisfying when hitting the ball hard. We need to hit the ball as hard as we can hit it with some sort of consistency!

97- No shot in Tennis pays higher dividends than the serve, this means we need to spend more time practicing serves and less time on stuff that pays fewer dividends; like rallying down the middle of the court for hours!
98- Backboards, hitting on rebound nets, and other training and teaching aids are great ways to improve and polish our game... Make some or all of these tools available!
99- The "I have nothing to lose" kind of mentality is wrong... We hear that line in sports all the time. Coaches and players who use it are way off the mark. If we have nothing to lose, we have basically already lost! Mentally that is... To see someone overcome that as the match goes on is very rare... I would say that 99% of the time when a player says something like this before a match, he or she or they will lose that match! There is always something to lose!
100- Staying close in the score to our opponent during a match is a good idea... Let him feel comfortable. Just stay close! As each set nears its end... Take it up a notch or two and steal the set! It works!
101- Hitting on a wall is probably the least appreciated form of practice, the least expensive, and oftentimes, even at the highest levels, one of the most effective ways to sharpen our game, polish our strokes, and learn new ones!

Here are a few extra tips:

102- The bottom line is that Tennis players should hit the ball with the smallest swing possible that will achieve the purpose! Be it a regular groundstroke, a kill shot putaway on midcourt, or a volley as we close the net. I think this summarizes the idea pretty well! Stay compact and economize all movement of the racquet and body!
103- Players initial position--be it the ready position when returning, or the initial serving position or the ready position at the net--has everything to do with how well we will execute the next stroke! The player needs to be in a very relaxed position, arms down with either forehand or backhand grip for returns or continental for serving or volleys. Arms should be relaxed and pretty much just hanging down from shoulders, gripping the racquet loosely, trunk leaning slightly forward and heels off the ground. The ready

position with the arms straight out and up at eye level for net play is wrong; the serving position with the racquet pointed too far way away from the service box is off the mark. It's also a no-no having the arms too high above waist level as you set up for serving. The hands should be pretty close together and relaxed, hanging down, the non-dominant hand cradling the ball properly in the crevices of the first joints of the index, middle and ring fingers along with the thumb. For the ready position at the net, arms relaxed down, and racquet head up is best, crouched down, off our heels and really ready and engaged!

See www.youtube.com video demonstration of the ready position for net play and returning at https://youtu.be/4ijQnTa I80A, as well as the serving position at https://youtu.be/N_Fk QCV2wqc, and proper ball hold or cradle for tossing at https://youtu.be/RFI4WnKDKtw

Fig. 35)Baseline return of serve ready position. Note upright stance. For groundstrokes this initial position is more appropriate for return of serve and baseline play since most hits will occur at about hip to shoulder level.

WHAT TENNIS PROS DON'T TEACH (WTPDT)

Fig. 36)Ready position when at net needs to be squat down a lot more. Player looks a lot more like a goal keeper in soccer where a penalty shot is about to be kicked at him. This position allows you to jump or lounge very fast. The lower ready position more readily allows the player to handle all kinds of volleys with more ease. This position reminds me of a tiger ready to strike its next meal!

104- On the subject of racquet weight, all other things being equal, heavier frames are better than lighter. Heavier frames are more conducive to solid hitting and better technique! Head heavy racquets are not great for instilling proper technique either. Also, be aware that light racquets and head heavy racquets are conducive to injury!

105- The more I lose, the closer I get to winning! And the sweeter it will taste when I finally do win! As hard working Tennis players, we need to realize this statistical fact and not lose heart because of lost matches. If we are persistent and consistent, we will learn and eventually start adding up the wins. We learn by making mistakes. So go on, make lots of mistakes; this is how children learn. The hard way... Is there any other way?

106- Every time a player touches the ball he/she has the potential of finishing the point; it is up to this player to have the right selection!

107- A dead ball that we can stick in the middle V of our racquet is a great way to add some weight to the racquet for warming up. It even provides a good way for a junior to learn correct swinging paths (overload training). Swing it over and over... After a while remove the dead ball; start hitting, and the swing and the hitting feels so light and easy!

108- As tournament players, we don't have to check in at the desk 30 minutes or 15 minutes before the assigned time; this is okay to do and a courtesy to the tournament organizers. As long as we do check in a couple of minutes before the assigned time we should be okay. If we want to check in but we are not ready to get on the court and play, we can do so but make sure to mention that to the tournament desk personnel. It is better for them to know that a player is already present and that he or she will let them know when ready to start. The officials or people running the tournament desk cannot force players to start before the assigned time unless they agree to it!

109- For higher percentage Tennis hit the ball back to where it came from. Players making too many errors should try this for a few games until they get the confidence to go for more. This tactic is generally a good strategy, and a foundation to build a game plan or a winning strategy!

110- In order to play the point, we have to play the ball first. Focus on the ball and hit it; then worry about the point!

111- In order to understand better the proper forehand grip, it is a good idea to put the index finger through the V in the racquet and grip it, this makes it possible to see the right angle of the racquet face and shaft in relation to our arm and hand. Hit a few balls like that, get a feel for it!

112- To better understand the path the racquet face follows in a topspin forehand, try a few swings with the hand extended out. Starting from hip level and as we finish the swing, point the thumb to the top of the opposite shoulder!

113- All points in Tennis count the same, but not all points in Tennis weight the same! 15/30 or 30/15 are important points, especially in no add scoring situations. Anytime the score is such that the next point won or lost will generate a game point in favor or against is an important point. Also, the first point of each and every game allows a player to grasp a little momentum to hopefully close out the game without too much difficulty if serving, and maybe break serve when returning!

114- Considering the weight, the different games carry during a set in a match, getting to that No. 5 is huge. If the score is 4 all or we are up at 4-3 or 3-4, winning the next game will put us within striking distance of the set. Getting to No. 5 is magic; once accomplished, we should know and believe we can win the match. Another important game during a match is the first game of the second and third sets, and to a lesser extent the second and third games!

115- As coaches if one of our students/players is threatening to leave us; set them free to go, if they come back they were ours, if they don't, they never were! From the well known Richard Bach poem!

116- Get in shape to play Tennis... Don't play Tennis to get in shape!

117- In doubles, the single most important thing we can do to be successful is to make our partner feel comfortable playing with us... If he or she is doing the same thing, momentum and rhythm will work in our favor. This is especially important in doubles teams where one player is stronger than the other. Stronger players need to have his or her partner feel comfortable helping him focus on boundaries, strengths, and solid tactics!

118- In Tennis technique, all shots could be said to be a two stage process: wind-up and unleash, or back swing and forward swing, or load and unload!

119- A Tennis player ought to try to MASTER all skills. It is a never ending battle; even the best of the very best have new stuff that they can add or learn for their games!

120- In doubles strategy and positioning, anytime my partner moves, I also move. I have to move along with him/her side to side or back or forth. Or if I make a move, he/she has to move with me. We call this the rubber band theory... Also, as soon as the ball is in the air moving, we also have to move with it!

121- The dig deep philosophy stems from the fact that we can always concentrate deeper or have a deeper yearning for winning a match... Remember that the heart and the brain know no limits!

122- In Tennis we need to move in relation to where the ball is. If the ball moves, we move... Also, in doubles, we move in relation to the ball, but also to what my partner is up to. If he/she moves, I have to move, and if the ball moves, we need to move as a team. If my parner is moving and I am standing still, I am getting in trouble already and will probably lose the point!

101 SPORTS SCIENCE AND SPORTS MEDICINE BASED PRACTICAL TIPS

This book is not a medical journal, of course, but there is some smart wisdom in the following tips. These tips came from studying, and research, and are applicable in a practical way to most high-performance athletes.

1- Get some carbohydrates into a player's body 30 to 45 minutes after workouts or matches. Not doing so, will create a deficit in recovery, and he or she will not be at 100% for the next match or the next day!

2- Hydrate enough to where a player urinates clear yellow or totally clear before getting on the court for tough matches in the heat and with high humidity indexes!

3- For High-Performance Tennis athletes, the percentage of body fat should be a little higher than for most other sports since Tennis matches are so long, and often players have to go at it back to back. Boys 12-20% and girls 15-25% is pretty acceptable. These percentages, for the most part, would not apply to a bodybuilder, a sprinter, a marathon runner or a football player!

4- To learn a new technique or to make a technical change in stroking technique, players need to make about 150 reps of the same technique daily for three to six months. The length of time varies with individuals. The best players in the World those who reach their potential at an earlier age are usually the ones who learn the fastest!

5- Only 10% of all extremely successful juniors in the 10, 12 and 14 and under ages ever make it to the top of their ability; this information is based on statistical research!

6- Apply all kinds of learning approaches; vision, hearing, and touch or contact to illustrate a technique. Almost everyone learns through visualization, but there are some who have to listen to a detailed explanation for them to decipher how to execute a technique. Others may have to be moved along the different motions where they are feeling the movement guided by a coach or instructor. Try to figure out what works best for each individual. Do some testing with these three ways of learning and figure out the most effective learning tool!

7- Understand and apply the periodization principle. Periodization is a great tool to get the right loads of work on and off the court and the right nutrition for different ages!

8- It's a good idea to train players to win streaks of three points in a row. Statistics show that the player who wins the most bundles of three will win the match. Also, statistics show that the player who ultimately wins more points (not games) will win the match! This illustrates how all points in a match are of equal importance to the final outcome!

9- Pressure and nervousness make us blink our eyes a lot more. As a result, we don't see the ball as well, and we end up framing and mistiming more shots than normal!

10- When stretching for training, not just for warm up and cool down, it is a good idea to stretch the joints, ligaments and muscles in sets of two: Stretch down and then up. In other words, make the reverse stretch immediately after the first. For instance, lean down to the toes and then lean backwards, or twist your trunk one way, and then the other way; this allows increased range of motion and improved flexibility!

11- Black and dark colors in the summer make sense if we can handle the heat because black and darker colors block more UV rays than light and white colors. Darker colors have a lot more SPF than white and light colors. Darker colors also make for more efficient workouts by making us hotter and burn more calories from the extra heat than lighter-colored outerwear!

12- It is not productive to subject prepubescent kids to rigorous fitness programs; this only makes them tired and oftentimes encourages burnout or injury. Instead, it is better to get them involved in cross-training activities like soccer, gymnastics, etc… to develop them further as athletes!

13- Organic food is no different from non-organic in that it has the same nutrients and is absorbed by our body, in the same way.

There is no evidence that organic is better, cleaner or purer than the alternatives. So far, there is only one substantial difference; the price is higher!

14- Eggs are good for us on a regular basis. We can have one or two eggs, two or three times per week. Eggs are very nutritious and contain lots of goodies that our body needs. The cholesterol content is rather small, and they contain no trans-fats which are the culprit for high cholesterol, clogged arteries, and heart disease. One large egg contains 2 grams of saturated fat, about 10% of daily value. For most of us, eating eggs, there should be no problem because our body will simply make less cholesterol!

15- Too much sugar is bad for us. I guess this is obvious, and everyone knows it! Too much sugar puts us and our children at risk for Type 2 diabetes. For Men, 9 teaspoons is a daily max and for women, 6 teaspoons. Nice and simple!

16- To control our weight we need to eat a low-fat diet, not a low carbohydrate diet. For Tennis players, we need to ingest lots of carbohydrates for energy availability. We do have to keep track of carbohydrates, though; Eating carbohydrates is good for us… eating too many carbohydrates maybe not so good!

17- It is true that cooking vegetables above 118 degrees F will deactivate plant enzymes. But these enzymes are not beneficial for humans. Plant enzymes are needed by plants themselves. Therefore eating raw vegetables is not necessarily better for nutritional purposes than cooking or steaming them. The enzymes in plants are for the most part eliminated during the digestion process. It is also a myth that enzymes are limited and that we only have so many available in our lifetime; the enzymes are produced by our body as needed!

18- It's not true that we have to combine two sources of protein foods in the same meal in order to get the full benefit of the protein itself in these meals. We can have the two sources of proteins in different meals and still get the full benefit of all the proteins in both meals!

19- It is not true that calories eaten at night are more fattening than calories eaten during the day. Calories are calories are calories, and it is the total number of calories that exceeds the amount needed by our body that makes us fat. One thing is true: if we have a calorie loaded meal right before we go to sleep, we may not sleep very well that night!

20- Microwave cooking is no different from regular cooking in that all it does is to apply heat to the foods we eat. It poses no danger of exposed radiation. Foods cooked in microwaves sometimes taste different because the heat is applied from the inside of the food as opposed to from the outside like on a source of fire. Personally, I don't care for microwave cooking because it makes food taste and feel different in my mouth. There is a danger if cooking in a plastic container or bag in the microwave in that these plastics may release some unwanted chemicals into the meal and enter the body. Make sure to use microwave safe containers when cooking in microwaves!

21- It is the amount of time we cook our food that makes it lose some of the nutrients, not the speed of the cooking. Microwave cooking can actually lead to keeping nutrients in food better because it is so much faster than traditional cooking. When foods are cooked for extended periods of time they tend to lose some vitamins and thiamin (a form of vitamin B)!

22- We don't crave for foods that have the nutrients our body needs. We crave based on emotional state and routine diets. If we are bored with what we eat every day, we may crave something completely different from what we are used to. One thing humans crave for is iron, but instead of craving iron-rich foods, people crave for stuff like ice cubes, clay or even cement. This weird phenomenon, according to some scientists, is a malfunction of our appetite mechanism, that has not been explained or understood yet!

23- Eating small meals throughout the day do not control weight. It does accelerate our metabolism a little but not to the extent that it makes us burn calories that much faster. On the other hand, eating two or three meals a day only in the traditional style sometimes makes a person so hungry that they end up eating way too much, thus losing control and putting on weight. We have to watch how much we eat period!

24- Tennis does not burn much fat because it is basically an anaerobic sport. We may lose some weight if we play back to back matches day in and day out; this is because we just cannot eat enough to supplement. The energy we utilize for Tennis comes primarily from our muscle system that stores this energy for immediate utilization. Unless we hit the aerobic plateau, fat, as energy, is not accessed by our body. When we hit Tennis balls without breaks, like we would on a wall, with a ball machine, or by hitting with someone with great consistency, we can get to our aerobic threshold, and start getting our energy from our fat reserves. That is why it is recommended to do aerobic work for at least 20 minutes to make sure to sustain this fat burn for long enough to make a difference. Energy in Tennis comes from glycogen stored in our muscle system for the most part and not from fat reserves. When playing a match, we are taking 15 to 30 second breaks every point, and 90 second breaks during changeovers. During these little breaks, we are allowing our system to replenish this glycogen into our muscles, not accessing fat energy!

25- Fasting does not help us eliminate toxins as commonly believed. The only thing we have that does that is our liver and kidney systems. Instead, try to eat foods low in toxin levels!

26- A gluten free diet does not necessarily mean better nutrition or digestion. This type of diet is only necessary for people with Celiac Disease (damage to the small intestine)!

27- Concentrated juices are not so great for us since they usually have more sugar than real juice!

28- Frozen foods contain a lot more fat than regular foods, and, for the most part, should be avoided. Nothing beats eating fresh stuff out of the field!

29- Wholewheat bread slows down our metabolism because it is harder to digest, and that will make us gain weight. Thus, we should not eat too much of it. However whole-wheat easily beats eating white refined bread for nutritional purposes!

30- Our brain regulates performance and balance as well as all psychological systems. Fatigue (or slowing down) is the result of this regulation which happens before any total or complete physiological failure occurs!

31- Physiological failure or fatigue is the result of lactate accumulation and an oxygen deficiency in the blood and the body. Breathing in a controlled way and pacing ourselves around the court are extremely important from beginning to end in a Tennis match!

32- Athletic performance is regulated; not determined by physiology. All psychological implications need to be taken into account as well!

33- Reaction time and peripheral vision training will increase sports performance!
34- No one knows (sports science does not have the answer) how an athlete kicks into a second and even into a third wind during a long performance. A runner sprints fastest the last 400 meters of a 10K run or a Tennis player suddenly goes into turbo in the last 20 minutes of a 4.5 hour match!
35- Fat loss due to wearing heavy clothing or a wetsuit is a fallacy. What we do know is that this practice does cause dehydration!
36- Regular exercise and the right diet help reduce cholesterol levels dramatically!
37- It is true that red wine and dark grape juice help reduce the bad cholesterol levels by aiding its transformation into good cholesterol. Red wine needs to be the type that is more acid like Cabernet or Shiraz, and the grape juice has come from dark grapes. Scientists don't know for sure what it is that makes this happen yet we know it does happen. The alcohol content in these red wines is not in any way responsible for the lower bad cholesterol levels!
38- Body size and muscle strength are definitely determining factors in hitting the ball harder. However, it has been proved that technique and biomechanics are the main factors in generating racquet head speed. Bigger muscles have the tendency to reduce range of motion and also get injured more easily since they are not as flexible!
39- In professional Tennis there are considerably more injuries on clay and grass surfaces than on hard courts (clay and grass are soft surfaces) due to the unpredictability of the footing and bounce of the ball!
40- In our body, we have 206 bones and 600 muscles plus a heart that circulates blood 1,000 times per day. Athletes better pay attention if they want optimal performance!
41- Exercising two or three times per week for 30 minutes or more in a sport like Tennis reduces your chances of death by all causes by as much as 50%, all ages included!
42- For mature women or young girls (although this holds true for men too), drinking a lot of coffee regularly, has been proved to promote the formation of cellulite due to the accumulation of toxins, coming from the caffeine, on the outer layers of the skin!

43- Sports science relies on high tech instruments to defray (analyze and help us understand) player's moves or athletes moves; some of these instruments are high-speed video, internal movement sensors, and computer analysis. Some of these tools are available for free in the Internet. One such free tool is High-Speed Video!
44- Eye control and knowing what to look for and when to look makes the difference between amateur and professional Tennis players! Professionals know their opponents' positioning on the court through peripheral vision but also track down and see the ball better at impact!
45- Kinesiology tape (KT Tape) does work and what it does is to help in stabilizing muscle groups and helps relieve pain!
46- Our body can store one-half a day's worth of glycogen. If we consume more glucose than we can use as an immediate energy source, this turns into fat!
47- Sodium is part of what sweat is formed with, and it is what makes it salty. That is why sports drinks all contain sodium! But don't be fooled. Our body needs natural water first and foremost!
48- Aerobic exercise is nothing but continued non-stop activity for extended periods of time of at least 15 minutes. Anaerobic is described as strenuous start and stop exercise every few seconds or minutes. Our body and brain need both for excellent health. A Tennis player may hit 7 or 8 shots during a point, for a couple of these, he/she may have had to sprint to get to the ball and exert maximum racquet acceleration while hitting, and at the end of the point, he/she walks around the court getting ready for the next point. Tennis can be very anaerobic!
49- Common sports injuries are cramps, pulls (Tennis calf), back strains, shin splints, tendonitis (Tennis elbow), plantar fasciitis, etc... All can be prevented with the right regimen of fitness training and good stroking technique!
50- Altitude training does not work! Physical deconditioning can occur and sometimes takes months to take effect. It is better, and it would make more sense to live at altitude, and train at sea level for top athletic performance!
51- Static stretching has been proved to reduce power output in some studies. Dynamic stretching is preferable for warm-up purposes. Static stretching is still very helpful in increasing range of motion

and flexibility and should be included in the everyday training routine of an athlete!

52- Hot showers are bad for our skin. The outermost layer of our skin called the stratum corneum is composed of naturally produced oils that protect our inner skin layers from excessive dryness and cracking. Long hot showers will effectively remove this layer of oil and expose our skin. Granted this is not all bad. The same oils that provide moisture to our skin are also the ones that trap dirt and odor which are removed as we shower every day. We just don't want our showers to be so long and hot!

53- Use ice to treat cramps; ice allows the muscle to relax by reducing inflammation and ease pain fast!

54- Stretching a muscle that is suffering a cramp will eliminate it most of the time. We need to stretch the muscle in a way that it counters the direction of the cramp. In other words forces extension of the cramped up fibers!

55- Another good solution to muscle cramps is the application of an analgesic balm. There is only a little scientific evidence that it actually helps; some examples are Tiger Balm, IcyHot, BioFreeze, and Iodex from India!

56- It is also a good idea to take in some over the counter anti-inflammatory like Advil or Ibuprofen to relax and prevent the cramps from coming back!

57- Sports science applications uses scientific assessments. Results can be used to compare to elite athletes in the same discipline, evaluate athletes strengths and weaknesses, assess the effectiveness of a training program, provide short term goals, enable athlete to perform more consistently, assist athletes in identifying the best techniques for enhancing sports performance, evaluate an athlete's health status, identify an athlete's readiness to resume training and competition. Sports science involves applying science and its principles to sports and helps athletes improve their sports performance in a variety of ways: physiologically, psychologically and biomechanically!

58- Performance analysis cannot be 100% accurate; there are too many intangibles in sports that science cannot take into account because they are not measurable. Making a prediction will usually have a margin of error of less than 10% if taking into account all measurable predictors. Some intangibles are individual. Others are things like illegal substance intake or stuff as simple as an injury or a bad day where the athlete is not at his best. These predictions can be said to be based on pseudoscience and allows us a degree of acceptable uncertainty in sports. Performance analysis is never exact!

59- Statistically, taller is not always better in Tennis. On a day to day basis and depending on what our opponent does, taller can be an advantage or a disadvantage. Defining tall as 6'3" for men and 6'1" for women or taller, we will find that many players exceeding this height have not dominated Tennis. There have been plenty of former No. 1s shorter than 6'3": Laver, Borg, McEnroe, Hewitt, Agassi, Connors, Nadal, and Federer. At the same time, there are several players taller than 6'3" who have won grand slam championships. The obvious advantage is in the power generated serving as well as other strokes due to the longer kinetic chain, as well as their wingspan. However, there are strong disadvantages. Taking into account the size of the Tennis court and the nature of the sport, tall players tend to have a hard time with mobility, dealing with low and short bouncing balls. A higher center of gravity severely hinders directional changes, on top of the fact that a lot of these players are more prone to injuries in the lower back, knees, and hip areas. In women's Tennis, the lack of super tall women who dominate the game seems more pronounced with Billie Jean King at 5'5", Chris Evert at 5'6", Martina Navratilova at 5'8", Martina Hingis at 5'7", Steffi Graf at 5'9", Arantxa Sanchez 5'6.5", Justin Henin 5'6" and more. Nowadays we have Serena Williams at 5'9" and Maria Sharapova at 6'1", taller on the average but definitely not super tall; Lindsay Davenport at 6'2" and Venus Williams at 6' 1" could be said to be the exceptions rather than the rule!

60- It is not possible to formulate the perfect training program for individuals because there are too many variables caused by personal and situational differences. However, it is possible to optimize the effects of training by considering the scientific evidence related to the specific physiological demands of Tennis!

61- Science versus tradition: In sports it is not always clear cut what training methods are most effective. A coach or player may be biased by what traditionally has worked for him or her in the past and base training on these ideas. This helps the athlete/coach relationship stay happy and confident. It is probably better to have a happy athlete before competition, than a super trained one that is upset or embittered. Because he or she was imposed a training routine based on scientific methods and information rather than what has been known to work in the past. Each player and coach is different, and we have to find what works for each individual!

62- Open versus closed kinetic chain training for rehabilitation refers to training a joint, muscle or group of muscles. In closed kinetic chain training, we rehab an injury without moving it, by just supporting or laying either the foot or the hand on a surface at the appropriate angle, and make the muscles flex, and the ligaments move without bending the main joints, be it the knee, the hip, the shoulder, or the elbow. In open kinetic chain training, we bend the joint to achieve the desired results!

63- If an athlete engages in a weight losing diet, coaches need to be careful about how to go about it. If he/she goes into anaerobic training, enough glycogen should be stored in the muscle system. If this is not happening, the athlete will be burning protein from muscle tissue, and a lot of times the weight loss will be from muscle loss and not fat!

64- We cannot lose fat weight without losing some muscle weight; this is how our body and metabolism works. Engaging in a weight losing regime, needs to be closely monitored by professionals in young athletes. Eating protein rich snacks minimizes this process and a Tennis player engaged in heavy training should always have some of these in his or her racquet bag!

65- Weight loss can only be achieved by creating a caloric deficit on our daily routines. We either eat less calories or burn more than we ingest or a combination of both!

66- If an athlete is achieving weight loss, but maintaining endurance and appropriate levels of strength, he or she is doing a good job at ingesting enough protein rich foods. For high-performance athletes, we need double the RDA (recommended daily allowance) of protein 0.8 gr/kg/bw/d (grams per kilogram of body weight per day)

67- Sitting is the new smoking! Every hour sitting watching TV cuts up to 22 minutes of our life span! Smokers shorten their lives

by 11 minutes per cigarette. (Oct 2012 British Journal of Sports Medicine scientific study)
68- Going Paleo or barefoot training: According to some scientific studies running barefoot or shoeless has been shown to minimize structural impact, it is more economical and efficient physiologically and financially!
69- Flavanol rich chocolate and cocoa products may have a small but significant effect on lowering blood pressure levels by 2-3 mm Hg in the short term. It is the 70% cocoa rich chocolate or dark chocolate that has this benefit!
70- Fluoride in drinking water can significantly reduce IQ development in children. Neurotoxicity due to fluoride in H2O has been found in scientific studies conducted recently!
71- Drinking coffee on a daily basis in moderate amounts (two to three cups per day) is really good because it boosts metabolism and gets us going!
72- Caffeine is the number one used stimulant in the World. It effectively blocks an inhibitory neurotransmitter in the brain leading to a net stimulant effect. Caffeine makes for improved mood, reaction time, memory, vigilance, and general cognitive function!
73- Coffee can help us burn fat and improve physical performance. Caffeine increases metabolism and increases the oxidation of fatty acids. Caffeine was found to increase athletic performance by as much as 12% on the average!
74- Coffee may drastically reduce your risk of type II diabetes. Type II diabetes has increased ten-fold in a few decades. The reduction risk varies on different individuals from 23% to 67%. The more coffee an individual drank, the less the chances of contracting the disease according to studies conducted on over 500,000 individuals!
75- Multiple studies have shown that coffee can reduce our chance of having cirrhosis by as much as 80%!
76- Other studies on coffee have also shown that liver health has been directly linked to coffee drinkers, and liver cancer can be prevented as much as 40% by drinking coffee every day!
77- Coffee consumption has been associated with a reduction of chance of death by all causes by as much as 30%; Scientific studies

conducted over a 20 year period with a large number of individuals confirm this information!

78- From a nutritional standpoint, coffee has a large amount of natural antioxidants as well as several vitamins and minerals in it. Coffee is the biggest source of antioxidants in the modern World. Two or three cups per day are recommended, and the benefits add up and are good on a day to day basis. A cup of coffee contains 6% of the RDA for Pantothenic acid (vitamin B5), 11% of the RDA of Riboflavin (vitamin B2), 2% of the RDA of Niacin (vitamin B3 and Thiamine B1) and 3% of the RDA for Potassium and Manganese. It may not seem like much, but if we drink several cups of coffee per day, this quickly adds up!

79- There are minor health issues in association with coffee, jitteriness, anxiety, heartburn, insomnia, loss of calcium in urine and dehydration. All of these are far outweighed by the benefits that come from coffee drinking. Doctors and health professionals are more concerned with all the stuff we add to coffee, especially sugar, syrup, cream, and all kinds of sweeteners that make it into a calorie bomb instead of just a simple and delicious drink!

80- Coffee ground made into a paste is a treatment for cellulite as it is applied topically to the areas of the skin affected by this ailment!

81- Tennis players run the risk of skin cancer due to overexposure to damaging UV rays from the sun. Avoid sunburn by using a quality sunscreen cream regularly, meaning at least every two hours of sun exposure!

82- When playing Tennis wear dark colors that don't allow as much light through them to keep UV rays from filtering in. Typical white cotton t-shirts offer SPF about 2-7, depending on the thickness and of how tightly woven the fabric is. The darker the colors we wear on the court, the more UV ray protection we will have!

83- A wide brimmed hat will cover our face, ears and neck up to 200% more than a visor or baseball cap. Also, utilize quality UV protection rated sunglasses!

84- Another way to battle skin aging is to have a skin healthy diet: fruit, vegetables, nuts, and fish should make our menu three to four times per week!

85- One of the main ways to combat skin aging is to make sure to stay hydrated all day, especially when exposed to the sun for extended periods of time!

86- When wearing a traditional Tennis visor, while it may be more comfortable, don't forget that our scalp will be exposed to UV rays. It is better to wear a baseball cap or brimmed Australian outback style hat that will cover the top of your head as well. Hair alone will allow a lot of UV rays into our scalp producing sunburn and potential skin cancer!

87- Iodine in the air is beneficial to our health. It is a lot more common in areas near the ocean because that's where most iodine originates. Problems with the thyroid gland may emerge from an iodine deficiency. If we live in areas that are pretty far away from the ocean, we may experience some iodine deficiency. About 400,000 tons of iodine escapes from the oceans every year; some of it will enter our lungs as we inhale air, and a lot of it will deposit itself onto the surface of the earth, entering a bio-cycle, ending up on our plate!

88- Tap water can be just as good for us as bottled water in terms of Calcium and Magnesium content depending on where we live. The drawbacks to bottled water are obvious: expense and pollution!

89- It takes 3,000-5,000 reps to learn a motor skill, but 8,000-10,000 to master it! In Tennis, this should be no secret. It takes tons of repetition training on court to get any degree of mastery at it. How many per day? It will be anywhere between 50 and 150 reps per day or per training session. The big gap is due to the different capacities different athletes have to concentrate on only one thing at a time for that period. The learning curve definitely flattens out as we start going over 150 reps in most individuals!

90- Chess makes us smarter... It has been proven by scientific studies that Chess is closely associated with higher IQs, by increasing brain power, arithmetical skills, verbal skills, critical thinking, emotional intelligence, psychosocial skills, and preserving mental acuity in the elderly. Some of the great minds of humanity have been chess players! The introduction of Chess to children as early as 6 and 7-year-old and to 2nd and 3rd graders is highly recommended!

91- Plyometrics are exercises designed around having muscles exert maximum force in as short a time as possible with the goal of increasing speed and power. Plyometrics are very effective to increase power in a very specific way, meaning Plyometric exercises can be designed specifically for different sports and disciplines. The drawback of Plyometrics is that it can also lead to serious injuries if the athlete is not conditioned, warmed-up, and he or she does not understand the different exercises well. At least for a while, an athlete starting Plyometric training for the first time needs to tackle it under the supervision of a professional trainer or coach! For instance, a 17-year-old junior Tennis player getting ready for a big tourney, may do some plyometrics given the fact that he or she has been following a firm fitness regimen leading up to it. Before starting the plyometric training; a nice warm-up and stretch has to be done. The plyometric workout proceeds in a gradual fashion starting with light plyometrics followed by harder ones!

92- The principle of overload in athletic training refers to engaging in physical conditioning routines under harder conditions and/or loads than the athlete would encounter under normal competitive circumstances. Our bodies can and will adapt to progressive loads of work thus becoming more resilient, strong and better fit for tough competition! This type of training too can lead to injuries if not done well and merits the supervision of a professional trainer or coach!

93- The principle of specificity in training refers to training our body, muscles, or groups of muscles in a way that they directly mimic the way these muscles will be working when utilized in the different disciplines. This means, specificity training in Tennis for speed, would have to be done in a way such that the moving or speed training, is practiced in an area about the size of a Tennis court, with sprints and bouts of about the same length, direction, and duration as they occur during intense Tennis play. Simply running for distance such as running in a 10 Kilometer race is not specific to Tennis. Short sprints with recovery times of about 15 seconds in between is a lot more Tennis specific. And so on with all other methods of training. Specificity training needs to be monitored and dosed by a professional trainer or coach!

94- Adaptation refers to our body learning how to cope with new loads in training activity in a progressive way! It takes 4 to 6 weeks for our body to adapt to the new levels of stress applied to the different muscles. Therefore, it is a good idea to increase the loads or change the activity or training routine every six weeks or so to avoid stagnating at a plateau we already have under control!

95- Progressive training is a modified method of periodization training referring to gradually augmenting loads leading up to the competitive periods or events! It is a solid way to tackle fitness excellence but should be treated with the utmost caution in youth athletes since it can lead to injuries. Professional training and supervision are mandatory!

96- Interval training has been around for a long time. It deals with training stations or modifying the load or intensity of training every few seconds or minutes. A simple example of Interval training for Tennis, could be something as simple as running a 10 yard sprint, doing 10 push ups, and then going to five jumping jacks, followed by 7 lunges forward. After that, we take a 10 second break and do it all over again until we have completed 17 rounds or so! It is super effective and has yielded great results to high-performance athletes for decades!

97- Yoga as a means of increased athletic performance has been around for a long time, also. A well-balanced yoga training regimen, can lead to increased capacity to reduce injuries, faster recovery after tough competition, or exposure to physical strain, reduced aches and pains in the body overall, improved breathing control, and technique, improved flexibility, greater strength, higher capacity for relaxation, etc…

98- Cross training refers to utilizing different disciplines or training in other sports to further enhance our fitness level, avoid boredom of routine training, prevent injury from overuse by doing the same exact exercises over and over, etc… We want to engage in cross training keeping in mind the principle of specificity. Good examples of cross training for Tennis would be track and field for cardio resistance or power, basketball for hand-eye coordination and footwork. Soccer is great for increasing cardio capacity and improves footwork. Baseball, is a good way to learn the throwing motion, which fully transfers to the service and overhead motions in Tennis, which are so important, etc…

99- Transfer in sports training refers to training in other activities than Tennis that would help the athlete's performance on the court.

WHAT TENNIS PROS DON'T TEACH (WTPDT)

There are sports and other disciplines that do not transfer to Tennis. For instance: Table Tennis does not transfer to Tennis because we use our arm and wrist a lot more than in Tennis. In Tennis, we need to use our whole body to generate enough power to hit the ball with authority. Playing a lot of Ping-pong can be detrimental to Tennis players! Another good example of bad transfer training would be distance running. While some distance running is good, and a necessary part of fitness training for Tennis, too much of it, will make the player slower on court, and can also inhibit recovery after strenuous point play since Tennis is more anaerobic!

100- It seems that at least once a month we hear breakthrough information on eggs in the news and whether they are good for us or not. Endless scientific studies seem to indicate that eating eggs two or three times per week is extremely good for us! By now, we all know that eggs contain cholesterol and are high in fat content. However, these factors have the tendency to be more of a risk factor for those with an existing condition of diabetes or heart disease. If we are healthy already, go ahead and eat some eggs. They are really good, with an endless list of vitamins, minerals, protein and carbohydrates!

101- Egg shells are a great source of calcium and other minerals. They can be eaten by pulverizing in a good blender and thrown in as part of a protein shake! No scientific evidence has been found that the sharp edges of eggshells are dangerous! Eggshells have been an inexpensive source of calcium for cattle for years! Of maybe even of more importance is the consumption of eggshell membrane. Eggshell membrane has been found to be a great source of the necessary nutrients to keep healthy joints. Studies seem to indicate that it far outperforms Glucosamine and Chondroitin, with measurable results in as little as a few weeks!

More Tips:

102- Stop eating while you're still hungry... Our brain takes a full 20 minutes to let us know our stomach is full. Instead of continuing to eat, drink some good water. Give it a few minutes and hunger will go away. This is a good way to keep our weight at bay!

103- Skin cancer is by far the most common type of cancer. The areas of the skin of most incidences are the neck, head, ears, calves and arms. Use a sunscreen daily, and frequently reapply it if we are exposed to the sun a lot.
104- Smiling has been proven to help us perform anything and everything we do better. We can make more money if we smile while doing business. If we smile before the start of a point in Tennis, we will likely hit better and harder or more accurately since smiling makes us relax. Smiling makes us a better person automatically because it helps others trust and accept us. Smiling will improve our health and help us live longer since it helps dissipate stress in our lives. Smiling makes us look more confident, and it actually makes us feel more in control of different situations. When in doubt about anything, smile... and a light may just start shining!
105- It has recently been found through scientific research that as we add fat to your body composition we reduce the size of our brain! Okay now... is this a good reason to stay fit and slim or what?
106- It is not true that lettuce or salads have no nutritional value. Due to its extremely low-calorie content and high water volume, romaine lettuce—while often overlooked in the nutrition World—is actually a very nutritious food. Based on its nutrient richness, our food ranking system qualified it as an excellent source of vitamin A (notably through its concentration of the pro-vitamin A carotenoid, beta-carotene), vitamin K, folate, and molybdenum. Romaine lettuce also emerged from our ranking system as a very good source of dietary fiber, four minerals (manganese, potassium, copper, and iron), and three vitamins (biotin, vitamin B1, and vitamin C). Various scientific studies have shown lettuce to be a preventative of different types of cancer!
107- Grunting makes your opponent slower and less accurate. Some scientific studies results are unequivocal, showing that extraneous sound interfered with the participants' performance, making their responses less accurate and slower!

101 RULES THAT MATTER... SPECIAL CASES

Of course, all rules matter, but here is a list of rules that make a difference if a player knows them. Players that don't have a deep knowledge or understanding of the rules will be at a distinct disadvantage on the Tennis court under the heat of competition. This list was prepared including the rules in Tennis that are not so obvious or clear. A simple read before tournaments makes sense to refresh our memories. Carrying a copy of this list in our Tennis bag is probably a good idea.

1- A player who breaks a string or racquet may continue to play with the racquet unless prohibited by a tournament rule or may ask someone to retrieve a replacement. A player who leaves the court is subject to code violations for delay under the point penalty system.
2- In some events or divisions coaching is permitted during authorized periods. Before the start of a match tiebreak (3 minute break, on court) or a third set (10 minute break, coaching can be off court). Coaching is not permitted during bathroom breaks, equipment adjustment breaks, court repair or adjustment of the net breaks, slight rain timeouts, bleeding or medical timeouts, 2 minute set breaks, etc... (These coaching rules do not apply everywhere or in all divisions. We may need to check with an official or referee to make sure we are not getting our players in trouble).
3- A player may bring written notes to the court and read them during breaks. A player is not allowed to use any type of electronic devices such as a cell phone, radio, mp3 player, or any device capable of receiving information. A player can use hearing aids, watches and any electronic device not capable of receiving information.
4- The name or the logo of a sanctioning body can be placed on the lower part of the net so long as it does not interfere with the vision of the players or the playing conditions.

5- If a singles stick falls during play the point stops immediately and is replayed. Singles sticks are used for singles play only and they are placed three feet out from the singles lines to emulate the net pole's distance and height as is set up for doubles play.

6- A broken ball and/or a soft/dead Tennis ball or dead ball, not within regulation, should be removed from the court for official play. If a ball breaks or goes soft during the point, play should be stopped, and the point replayed. If a ball breaks during the act of hitting, the player is entitled to a let or replay, even if he or she missed the shot. But if a ball goes soft and the point is played out, the point stands. Only if the point is stopped as the player(s) found out the ball was soft, but before the point was over, will the point be replayed.

7- Vibration dampeners can only be placed outside the pattern of the cross strings of the racquet. That is below the first bottom string or above the first top string.

8- Batteries of any sort may not be placed on the racquet. The so-called smart racket is not within regulation. Okay for training purposes, although.

9- A server may be required by an official to call the score before the start of every game and every point. If an official is asking a player to do this and the player does not do it then, the server will be subject to code violations for unsportsmanlike conduct.

10- If the server states that the score is 40-15, but the receiver says it is 30-30. The players agree on who won every point except the second point. In this case they should replay the second point from the add side of the court, and if the server wins the point, then the score is 40-15, and if the receiver wins it, then the score will be 30-30. The next point will be served from the deuce side of the court.

11- If during the warm-up it rains or play is delayed for whatever reason, and the players leave the court, the toss stands but the choices the players made can be changed. The toss or coin flip should be made before the warm-up starts.

12- An out-call, can be made after the player making the call has already hit the ball, as long as the ball he or she hit is still in the air, and has not bounced or has not been hit by the opponent.

13- If a ball in play touches a permanent fixture after hitting in the correct court the player that hit the ball wins the point. If a ball touches a permanent fixture before it hits in the correct court the player hitting the ball loses the point.

14- If a ball hits the net outside of the singles sticks, and then falls inside the correct court, the player hitting that ball loses the point because the net outside the singles sticks is considered a permanent fixture.

15- If a singles match is being played on a court without singles sticks, and a ball hits the net pole and falls in the right court, and the opponent failed to return it, then the player that hit the ball wins the point since the entire net and poles are part of the court when no singles sticks are available.

16- Serving order or choice of receiving side can be altered at the beginning of a match tiebreaker but not at the start of a regular seven-point tiebreaker.

17- In a doubles match, unless it is clear that more than one racquet touched the ball, it is legal to clash racquets when making contact with the ball; in an attempt by both players to return it to the other side of the court.

18- A receiver may call a foot fault; if he or she has tried to get an official on court and failed, and has warned the opponent about his or her foot fault, and the foot faulting is so flagrant as to be clearly perceptible from the receiver's side.

19- The server cannot deliver the serve until the receiver is ready, and they have made eye contact for about two seconds. If the receiver is not in the ready position, the receiver can just call "not ready" and force the server to serve again. At the same time, ethics and sportsmanship, as well as rules call for the receiver to play to the server's pace within reason. A receiver that is not ready repeatedly and is delaying play deliberately is subject to a time warning and point penalties if the behavior persists.

20- The 20 second rule for time between points does not apply in the case the server missed the 1st serve and before the second serve. In this case, the server should serve the second serve immediately within reason for normal rituals and concentration.

21- When the server is interrupted during the delivery of the second serve; he or she should be entitled to 1st and 2nd serves again.

22- When there is a delay caused by the receiver between 1st and 2nd serves, such as a broken string, the server should be granted a 1st

serve again. But if the delay is caused by the server himself, due to broken strings or any other reason, then the server should proceed to serve the 2nd serve. If the interference is caused by an external source such as a spectator's cell phone or adjacent grunt from another player the player should not be granted another 1st serve. When a ball from an adjacent match rolls in the court between 1st and 2nd serves, the receiver can grant a 1st serve, based on the time it took to clear the ball out of the court. If too prolonged a 1st serve should be granted.

23- Only an official or a player can call a let. And the player can only call a let on his entire court; this means a player can call let based on something happening on either side of the net. The exception happens when a player is causing an interruption of play such as dropping a ball or his or her hat or a ball from his/her pocket. In this instance, the player cannot be the one calling the let.

24- A player does not lose the point if he or she crosses the imaginary extension of the net before hitting the ball into the other player's side, as long as he or she does not touch the other player's court or the net.

25- If a player hits the ball with any part of his or her body, clothing or shoes and gets it back on the other side, this player loses the point.

26- If a player succeeds in tossing the racket in the air at the ball to try to get it back, he automatically loses the point. The player has to be touching the racket when the ball makes contact with the racquet. Hitting the ball back on the other side of the court with anything other than the racquet, is not allowed by the rules. The ball cannot be hit with any body parts, clothing or gear other than the racquet.

Here is a little story: Back in the 80s Peruvian Davis Cup player Pablo Arraya played a match in a small pro tournament versus the American youth and prodigy Jimmy Arias. During a much-disputed point, Pablo lost his racket when at the net, as he made the shot over into the other court, Jimmy hits it back, but Pablo was able to get one of his Tennis shoes off, and hit the ball back over the net with it for a winner. Who won the point? Anyone who knew these two players can only imagine the argument that followed; both were very competitive and would strongly defend their point. Under rule 26, it would be Arias's point. But under rule 27, it would be a let if Arias or an official called a let as soon as Arraya dropped the racquet!

WHAT TENNIS PROS DON'T TEACH (WTPDT)

27- If a player drops his hat or any of his or her gear on the court while the ball is in play, the opponent can ask for a let the first time it happens, and gets the point for any subsequent similar happenings. The player dropping the hat cannot call a let himself.
28- If a vibration dampener comes off the strings of the racquet while the ball is still in play and hits the net or the opponent's court the player that lost the dampener loses the point.
29- If a player drops his or her racquet immediately after or as he or she is hitting the ball for a clean winner, this player wins the point.
30- If a ball is laying on the court, and the ball in play strikes it, the point goes on and the player dealing with ball on his or her court can try to hit back either of the two balls in motion within one bounce. The player that left the ball on the court on his side loses the point if he fails to return either one of the balls over to the other side.
31- A shot cannot pass between the net and the net pole, this is considered a through and the player hitting this shot loses the point.
32- If a ball hits a bird that is flying across the court; the point should be replayed since this is considered a hindrance.
33- If a player's cell phone rings while a point is being played, this player loses the point. If the cell phone rang in between points, then the player will be subjected to a time violation warning, and he should turn off his or her phone.
34- If a match tiebreak was to be played in lieu of a third set, and the players only played a seven-point tiebreaker, but shook hands in acknowledgment of the end of the match, the score stands and the match stands as played. By shaking hands, the player that lost is accepting in good faith that he/she lost the match.
35- If playing two out of three full sets, and the players go for a match tiebreak instead of a full third set as they split sets, and they have started the second point of the tiebreaker, they should finish the tiebreaker and the winner wins the match.
36- If two players have started playing the 2nd point of the 5th game of a third set they should finish the set if they were playing a full 3rd set instead of a match tiebreak mandated by the tournament rules.
37- Bathroom breaks should only be taken during set breaks. Only under true emergency circumstances should these breaks be allowed any other time. Bathroom breaks can be taken at any time

during game changeovers as long as they are taken within the 90 seconds allowed by the rules.

38- If a player reaches over the net to try to hit the ball after the ball has bounced on his or her side of the court, and if he or she makes the shot, the ball continues to be in play as long as the player reaching over does not touch the net or the opponent's court. This only happens as a result of heavy spins or wind making the ball bounce back over the net immediately after bouncing on the right side of the court; it is a pretty common occurrence.

39- A player can reach over the net after he or she has hit the ball on his side of the court as a result of a follow through. If he touches the net or the opponent's court, he loses the point.

40- Ball mark inspections can only be made on clay courts. If a player touches or erases the mark, he or she concedes the point.

41- A player may not cross the net to the other side to check a mark or for any other reason during a game. Doing this is subject to a code violation for unsportsmanlike conduct.

42- In doubles, players should not talk when the ball is moving towards the opponent's court. It is okay to talk as the ball is coming towards them or as they are hitting the ball on their side of the court. Singles players should not talk when the ball is in play.

43- A player may move once the ball is tossed in the air. Any exaggerated and not normal movement prior to that with the intention of distracting or breaking the concentration of the opponent is against the rules.

44- Extreme grunting or loud noises are considered hindrances of play and should be controlled by an official. If a grunting player is to be penalized, he should be given a warning ahead of time before penalization. If an official deems that an opponent lost a point as a result of loud grunting, the official can order a replay of the point. An official cannot order a point to be replayed if the grunting or yelling on a court affected the outcome of a point on an adjacent court.

45- Stalling is subject to penalties under the point penalty system. Examples of stalling can be bouncing the ball too many times before serving, taking longer than allowed to towel off in between points or on changeovers, walking really slowly to serve or receive before the start of points, taking time to talk to spectators or partners before the start of a point or a game, taking time to stretch out once the match has started, etc...

46- When new balls are specified for a third set in a tournament; new balls shall be used unless all players agree otherwise.

47- Clothing or towels are not permitted to be placed at or on the net. Towels can be placed at the bottom of the fence in the periphery of the court at ground level.

48- A referee should make a reasonable effort to give comparable rest periods to winners of matches who will play each other in the next round.

49- A junior player should be given a minimum of 12 hours from the end of a match one day and the start time of a match the next day.

50- In the 10s, 12s, and 14s divisions no match should start or if suspended be re-initiated past 8 pm. And in the 16s and 18s divisions matches cannot start or be re-initiated after 10 pm.

51- If regular scoring and full two out of three set matches are being used in a tournament; the maximum number of matches allowed per day in junior Tennis is three. More matches per day are allowed anytime shorter formats are utilized, such as when playing a match tiebreak in lieu of a third set, or no add scoring, or short sets, etc... (Check rulebook for more details on number of matches allowed for shorter format tournaments)

52- Parents or coaches can retire a player from a match or tournament as a disciplinary maneuver. When this happens during a match, it is considered a default if the match had started already, or as a retirement if the match has not started yet.

53- Withdrawals from tournaments for reasons besides injury, illness, or personal circumstances or emergency have consequences and can be penalized by the governing body of the tournament. Also withdraws from one tournament because a player was entered in two simultaneous, or overlapping events can definitely have consequences and penalties apply as per the rules and the governing bodies of the tournaments involved.

54- Rest periods between full best of three tiebreak sets should be one hour. Less when a shorter format is being played. Equal or equivalent rest periods should be given to two players meeting the following round. More rest may be permitted if, playing conditions such as extreme heat or very high humidity indexes or length of matches dictates players need more time.

55- A player who needs a toilet break or attire change before a match tiebreak can do so after the 3-minute break. If a player wants to take the toilet or attire break during the 3-minute break he can do so, but he forfeits on-court coaching. No coaching can be done outside the court during the toilet break. If the toilet break is taken after the 3-minute break, the other player should remain on court and no more coaching should be permitted since the coaching is limited to 3 minutes only.

56- Maximum time a player is granted for a medical timeout is 15 minutes. The evaluation and treatment should not exceed this time limit. If two different conditions exist, then the player should request the timeout for the two simultaneously, and the timeout would still be 15 minutes. In the case of bleeding on court, the timeout should not exceed 15 minutes. The only time resumption of play may take longer happens when the court is dirty, and it takes longer than that to clean it up. The standard MTO should be 2 minutes for evaluation and up to 3 minutes for treatment.

57- The ITF rules of Tennis no longer distinguish between injuries and natural loss of physical condition. This means that cramps are now treatable. Although only one timeout will be granted for all cramping and heat-related conditions, even if the cramping occurs in different muscles and parts of the body.

58- The only exception to the above rule, occurs when one timeout is taken during warm-up. In this case, another timeout for cramping or heat related conditions may be granted during the regular development of the match.

59- If a player already had code violations, a point penalty, a game penalty, and starts cramping after having already run out of cramping timeouts, and this is happening during a changeover, if the player fails to resume play within the changeover break, the player should be defaulted.

60- A player who leaves the court to get a replacement or borrowed racquet because his strings broke or for any other reason is subject to code violations under the point penalty system.

61- During an authorized intermission in all divisions other than juniors, the referee may permit practice on the match court. In junior divisions, no player may practice on any court during an authorized intermission. Practice with the match balls should never be permitted. During a rain delay, players in all divisions may practice on any courts during the delay and before matches are resumed.

62- The size permitted for a manufacturer's logo or any other logo on Tennis attire is 2 square inches per garment. The ATP allows logos up to 6 square inches on either or both sleeves and up to 4 square inches on front or back of shirts, shorts or skirts. To avoid confusion and problems check tournament regulations for different Tennis organization or events before play.

63- An abusive spectator or person associated with a tournament player may be asked to leave the playing area or Tennis facility. Failure to follow instruction to leave by an official will subject the player to a code violation and the point penalty system.

64- A player shall not enter two tournaments at the same time. When entries close, a player shall not be entered in two or more sanctioned tournaments if any part of the tournaments overlap unless each Tournament Committee involved understands the situation and concurs in writing. After a player has been eliminated from a tournament whose schedule of play partially overlaps with that of a second tournament the player may enter the second tournament. Any player breaking this rule is subject to suspension points under the rules of Tennis.

65- Unsportsmanlike conduct includes but is not limited to the following:

    a) Verbal abuse
    b) Visible or audible obscenity or profanity
    c) Racquet abuse. Throw or break a racquet in anger or frustration during the normal course of a match
    d) Ball abuse. Hitting or kicking the ball out of the court in frustration or anger, especially if the ball hits an opponent or a spectator, or comes close to doing so
    e) Physical abuse. Threatening or actually hitting or holding anybody be it another player or a spectator
    f) Unauthorized coaching during a match
    g) Failure to follow instructions from an official

66- When both players or doubles teams are equally responsible for delay of play in a match; any penalty will be imposed upon the server.
67- A player making a retaliation call (this is an obvious bad call as retaliation for a perceived bad call from the opponent) is subject to a code violation for unsportsmanlike conduct and the point penalty system.
68- Time violations should be applied in the following order: First offense is a warning, and each subsequent offense will be one-point penalty.
69- An official may immediately default a player for a single flagrant unsportsmanlike act. Examples that justify immediate suspension or disqualification are, physical attacks, injury to an official, player or spectator through an act of racquet or ball abuse. Also, spitting on a person; and racial, religious, or sexual orientation slurs.
70- Even if courts are not available, players not checked in at the tournament desk on time will be subject to the penalties for lateness once the official has called the matches.
71- Consecutive time violations could and will be treated as code violations, and will be subject to the penalization of a point, a game and the match, if the circumstances warrant that the offending player is utilizing this time violations in an unsportsmanlike way to disrupt momentum and the natural flow of a match.
72- If a player is overruled on some line calls by an official more than once, any subsequent overrules may be treated as unsportsmanlike conduct and be subject to the point penalty system.
73- If a player has loud outbursts in a language that the official does not understand, the official can warn the player to either speak in a language he or she can understand or to stop the talk. If the player fails to do this, he or she will be subjected to the point penalty system. At the same time, all cheering should be done in a language that officials can understand. Otherwise, the player in connection with the people cheering, will be subjected to unsportsmanlike conduct and the point penalty system.
74- Cheering and clapping in good faith are acceptable during an official match. But cheering in a foreign language that the official does not understand can be treated or considered as coaching, putting the

player in question at risk of the point penalty system. The official should warn the person cheering that this is against the rules.

75- A player who has been defaulted for misconduct during a singles match in a tournament will also be withdrawn from the doubles event or any other events that the player may be signed up for in the same tournament.

76- A ball hit around the net pole, clearly below the height of the net of a singles or doubles match, that lands inside the playing area is good.

77- When a code violation occurs during a doubles match; suspension points are applied only to the doubles player who committed the violations.

78- A player who signs up and plays in a tournament during a suspension will be subjected to ranking suspension points under the rules of Tennis.

79- A player who does not give his or her best effort to win a match will be subjected to ranking suspension points under the rules of Tennis and code violations. The point penalty system also applies.

80- In junior Tennis doubles tournaments, 15% of the ranking points earned in doubles count towards the singles ranking as well. This may be different from organization to organization.

81- A player loses his amateur status if he or she accepts prize money based on the round he or she advanced in a specific tournament.

82- A player may receive a scholarship for a Tennis camp as a prize earned at a specific tournament.

83- A full-time student of high school or college grade may get hired as an assistant Tennis instructor as a salaried employee, not an hourly per lesson basis without affecting his amateur status.

84- Only reasonable expenses may be reimbursed in connection with the participation in a specific tournament.

85- Documentation of all expenses incurred in connection to tournament participation will have to be made available to the tournament organization for proper reimbursement and as proof of expenses.

86- Tournament expenses reimbursement may not be paid by someone else (for example a sponsor) unless the amateur actually returns the payment in due time to the sponsor.

87- Value of prizes for amateurs may not exceed $250 USD per event. If a player is participating in singles and doubles, he may receive $250 for each event entered. These prizes cannot be given to the player in the form of cash.
88- If a thunderstorm is approaching, apply the 30-30 rule, which states that if less than 30 seconds elapsed from flash to bang, the storm is too close, and cessation of all matches and warm-up should be immediate. Resumption of play should occur 30 minutes after the passing of a storm.
89- Points played in good faith stand. This means that if it is discovered that the net was 4 inches low after having played several points, the points played stand. Likewise, if the wrong order of serving or receiving in a doubles match is discovered after a few points were played, these points stand as played, and the right order of serving and receiving should be reinitiated immediately.
90- A player may decline his or her right to warm up. If he or she does this, the opponent may get anybody to conduct his or her warm up on the designated match court.
91- In doubles, partners may warm-up with one another if they please to do so. This means that their opponents can do the same thing as well.
92- A player can only make calls on his or her side of the net. In doubles either player can make the call of out, even if the ball was not coming toward him or the ball is away from him when the ball landed on his side of the court. This situation applies with the exception of the first serve; meaning a server may call his 1st serve out himself if the ball was clearly out and not called by opponent. The other exception that applies to this is in the case a shot hit by a player is clearly out, then the player hitting this shot may call it out as well.
93- Any shot that cannot be called out immediately is automatically good. Any time a player is in doubt of a call the player loses his or her right to call that ball and the ball is deemed good.
94- A player may request the help of the opponent in making a call, if, for some reason, the player was not able to see where the ball landed. Spectators are not allowed to make calls for the players, or interfere in any way in making calls in or out under any circumstances.

95- A shot that neither of the players saw with clarity, and they are not sure, is automatically called good.
96- Deliberate double hits are not allowed; this happens when a player obviously is hitting the ball twice in an attempt to get it back to the other side. If a player hits a ball, and it seems as if the player framed the ball, and then the strings, and then the other side of the frame, but did it all unwittingly and in a single motion, this is allowed, and if the ball lands in the correct court, it is considered a good shot. Unintentional double hits are within the rules.
97- Any player in a singles or doubles match may call a let serve. If the serve is an ace, the call shall be made promptly in order to avoid confusion. Let serves are played as good under NCAA's rules in Division I Tennis.
98- In Tennis there is no rule prohibiting alcoholic beverages or smoking on court during tournaments. However, most Tennis clubs, public courts, and Country Clubs don't allow smoking or drinking on court!
99- An official or tournament committee can suspend play during a tournament for extreme heat, humidity, wind or cold temperatures as well as rain and other climatic conditions.
100- A player who uses a Tennis ball to absorb perspiration, or as a towel to dry or wipe sweat from his or her forehead or body, should be warned and be subjected to a code violation and the point penalty system, if the behavior persists.
101- A player may not receive an injection of any type for recovery or treatment purposes with the exception of an insulin injection in the case of diabetes.

More rules that matter:

102- If both players are out on a 10-minute break between the second and third set, and one of the players is more than 5 minutes late he shall be defaulted. If less than 5 minutes late, then he or she gets penalized one game only. Similar rulings apply to both players being late for the start of a match.
103- If a player yells, "come on", or anything else, as he or she hits a great shot, thinking he or she already won the point, but suddenly the opponent is able to hit the ball back in the court, the player

yelling automatically loses the point because of hindrance. This situation happened at the 2015 Australian open women's' final between Maria Sharapova versus Serena Williams, deep into the 2nd set tiebreaker; as Serena hit a huge wide serve on the add side, but Maria returned it somehow. The chair umpire correctly granted the point to Maria calling it a hindrance by Serena. There was no argument about it at all.

104- The code in the Tennis rulebook is nothing other than a list of rules to go by in unofficiated matches. Most matches in Tennis are unofficiated. The exceptions are obviously in professional Tennis, Division I college Tennis, and some national and international junior and senior competitions and tournaments.

105- In some tournaments where a roving umpire or official is overwhelmed with too many courts and matches to cover by himself/herself, the official can and will deputize an spectator or volunteer to help in calling the lines in a match, or help with supervision of all the courts.

106- A parent, coach, or player exploding in rage at the tournament desk, can be asked to leave the premises immediately. If he/she is a player, he/she will be defaulted if he is playing a match at the moment of the assault. If he/she is not playing at the moment, then he/she will be withdrawn from the tournament. If he/she is the parent or coach of a player, his/her player could be defaulted or withdrawn if he/she fails to abide by the official's or tournament personel's instructions.

107- Cell phones do not need to be turned off on vibrate mode during an official tournament match. But if a player answers a call or looks at his/her cell phone during the match, he or she will be subjected to a code violation.

108- During a tiebreaker, if a player mistakenly served in the wrong order, meaning he/she served when it was not his/her turn, the order of serving is kept the same on even points, and changed on odd points. Any points played in good faith, will stand as played.

101 QUOTES PLUS MORE FROM THE PROFESSIONALS

Who doesn't like quotes? I personally love them, and I think most hardcore Tennis players do too; especially some really good ones that have been around for decades. There are all kinds of quotes in Tennis books and the Internet. Here is a list I gathered of some of my most revered ones. A great amount of wisdom comes from these quotes. As we read them; it is a good idea to take them in slowly, and think about them a little, in order to appreciate them to their fullest in their content, force, and flavor! Quotes in Tennis should be treated like a good Shiraz or Cabernet wine!

1- Writing free verse is like playing Tennis with the net down… Robert Frost
2- Tennis is just a game. Family is forever… Serena Williams
3- When you do something best in life, you don't really want to give that up, and for me it's Tennis… Roger Federer
4- Played Tennis for years, but you can't improve at Tennis beyond 50. You get to be in your 40s, and suddenly you're a doubles player… Jack Nicholson
5- You always want to win; that is why you play Tennis because you love the sport, and you want to be the best you can at it… Roger Federer
6- I don't want to be remembered for my Tennis accomplishments… Arthur Ashe
7- Later I discovered there was a lot of work to being a good Tennis player… Arthur Ashe
8- I want my Tennis to speak for everything… Maria Sharapova
9- I know my serve stinks, but I was a pretty good Tennis player… George H. W. Bush
10- 'Oh and 'Oh is a Tennis term… It's a nice way of saying you took your opponent to pieces… Venus Williams

11- I've been playing against older and stronger competition my whole life. It has made me a better Tennis player and capable of playing this level despite their strength and experience... Maria Sharapova
12- The depressing thing about Tennis is that no matter how good I get, I will never be as good as a wall... Mitch Hedberg
13- I enjoyed the position I was in as a Tennis player. I was to blame when I lost, and I was to blame when I won. And I really like that because I played soccer a lot too, and I could not stand it when I had to blame it on the goalkeeper... Roger Federer
14- A great Tennis career is something that normally a 15-year-old does not have. I hope my example helps other teens believe they can accomplish things they never thought possible... Maria Sharapova
15- Tennis is a perfect combination of violent action taking place in an atmosphere of total tranquility... Billy Jean King
16- I was just another long-haired teenage with visions of grandeur, summoning a Tennis racquet or a broom in front of his bedroom mirror... Jon Bon Jovi
17- If I did not play Tennis I don't know where I would be... Venus Williams
18- Tennis has given me this wonderful life, and I am very grateful for it... Maria Sharapova
19- Tennis is mostly mental. Of course, you must have a lot of physical skill, but you can't play Tennis well and not be a good thinker. You win or lose the match before you even go out there... Venus Williams
20- To stay interested in Tennis I have to mix it up with other things... Venus Williams
21- It was simple reality... most competitive Tennis players in my day were privileged, spoiled, entitled and white. Also, many of them were beautiful, fit, tan and of good stock... Great big hair and white teeth and long legs... Then there was the rest of us... Anne Lamott
22- In Hollywood people lie to each other and cheat each other and then they go and play Tennis... But I don't want to be a Tennis player... David Geffen
23- I spent a whole year when I was injured and just trying to get my arm back to the point where I could hit a Tennis ball for more than

30 minutes a day. I'd hit for 15 minutes, and it would feel as if my arm was going to fall off... Maria Sharapova

24- I'd like to imagine that in order to beat me, a person would have to play almost perfect Tennis... Venus Williams

25- I guess Tennis is my main art, but fashion is definitely very close... Venus Williams

26- If you can react the same way to winning and losing that's a big accomplishment... That quality is important because it stays with you the rest of your life, and there is going to be a life after Tennis that's a lot longer than your Tennis life... Chris Evert

27- Tennis is a mental game. Everyone is fit, and everyone hits great forehands and backhands... Novak Djokovic

28- The poet Melvin B. Tolson once said" A civilization is judged only in its decline." That made sense to me, would imagine the same is true for poets and Tennis players... Nikki Giovanni

29- I am here to play women's Tennis. I'm a lady. Predominantly, most of the time I always like to play ladies... Serena Williams

30- Team sports aren't my thing. I find it easier to pick something up if I can do it at my own speed. And you don't need a partner to go running; you don't need a particular place, like Tennis, just a pair or Trainers... Haruki Murakami

31- It was very unusual for a boy to play Tennis in my country... Novak Djokovic

32- My father had never watched Tennis, never liked Tennis too much. He said, 'Ok, we buy a racket, we watch together, 'because we didn't know anything. It was a process of learning together that made it more interesting... Novak Djokovic

33- I definitely want to get out of Tennis and try something completely different... Marat Safin

34- Ever since that day when I was 11 years old, and I wasn't allowed in a photo because I wasn't wearing a Tennis skirt, I knew that I wanted to change the sport... Billie Jean King

35- It's only a Tennis match. In the end, that's life. There are much more important things... Rafael Nadal

36- Tennis is my life; I need to focus and win, but it is not the only thing, I am not going to play Tennis forever... Novak Djokovic

37- Tennis is best of three sets, so even if I lose the first set, I still have a chance... Li Na

38- My mother said I would have more chances to become a Tennis player than a football player... Marat Safin
39- As Tennis players we're always playing in center courts that feel like arenas. And when we get on the court and the crowd cheers your name and salutes you... it's like you're a gladiator in the arena... And everyone is cheering – and you're an animal, fighting for your life... Novak Djokovic
40- There is no life for girls in team sports past little league. I got into Tennis when I realized this, and because I thought golf would be too slow for me, and I was too scared to swim... Billie Jean King
41- Golfers are forever working on mechanics. My Tennis swing hasn't changed in 10 years... Pete Sampras
42- There is a fear of emotion in Tennis... Andy Murray
43- Tennis is an individual sport, and I am quite a self-conscious person... Andy Murray
44- Tennis is a psychological sport. You have to keep a clear head; that is why I stopped playing... Boris Becker
45- You know my dad pushed me to believe that I was going to be the best, I just never thought of life without Tennis, even looking forward... Andre Agassi
46- I always had a powerful serve. It's one of the best in women's Tennis. It's very good to have a weapon like that... Li Na
47- Teach a child to play solitaire, and she will be able to entertain herself when there is no one around. Teach her Tennis, and when she is on a Tennis court she will know what to do. But raise her to feel comfortable in nature, and the whole planet is her home... Joyce Maynard
48- What is the single most important quality in a Tennis Champion? I would have to say desire, staying in there and winning matches when you are not playing that well... John McEnroe
49- It's a pity that Tennis is going down the drain. Every year it's getting worse and worse. There has to be a radical change, and I hope it will be really soon... Marat Safin
50- Tennis has given me soul... Martina Navratilova
51- I grew up a little girl in the Soviet Union playing at a small sports club... Tennis gave me my life... Anna Kournikova

52- To be a Tennis champion, you have to be inflexible, you have to be stubborn, you have to be arrogant and you have to be selfish and self-absorbed... Kind of tunnel vision almost... Chris Evert

53- Tennis was never work for me; Tennis was fun. And the tougher the battle and the longer the match, the more fun I had... Jimmy Connors

54- Tennis is not like other sports where the coach is hired by an independent entity, and that makes a huge difference in the dynamic... Ivan Lendl

55- I let my racquet do the talking. That's what I am all about, really. I just go out and win Tennis matches... Pete Sampras

56- As soon as I step on the Tennis court I just try to play Tennis and don't find excuses. You know, I just lost because I lost, not because my arm was sore... Goran Ivanisevic

57- Tennis has had a very positive impact on my life... Gabriela Sabatini

58- I have this terrible dark side to my personality, which playing Tennis keeps at bay... Monica Seles

59- I had a great Tennis career. I have no regrets. But to find peace with yourself and to finally be with your family - I'm probably the happiest guy in the World... Bjorn Borg

60- When I was 40, my doctor advised that a man in his 40s should not play Tennis. I heeded his advice carefully and could hardly wait until I turned 50 to start again... Hugo Black

61- Many Tennis coaches are enablers. They need the job more than the player needs the coach. And if the coach needs the job more than the player needs the coach, he can't effect change... Ivan Lendl

62- People know me. I am not going to produce any cartwheels out there. I am not going to belong on Comedy Central. I'll always be a Tennis player, not a celebrity... Pete Sampras

63- When you are very little Tennis should be fun, it should be a game... Guy Forget

64- What I want out of Tennis is not necessarily just winning... Jennifer Capriati

65- I'm not saying I'm something special. I might play a little better Tennis than other people, but it is because I was given the chance, and not many people have this chance... Martina Hingis

66- Tennis is pretty unforgiving if you are carrying weight. You are expected to wear short skirts, and you are compared to all these 16 and 17-year-olds... Monica Seles
67- I would like to see it go back to the wood racquets, to see the touch put back in Tennis... Jana Novotna
68- I did a really good job of sticking to the Tennis courts... Brad Gilbert
69- I chose to stay with Tennis, and they did not understand that at school... John Newcombe
70- Playing on grass can sometimes be a bit of a lottery... Rafael Nadal
71- I love the feeling of hitting the ball hard... and the pleasure of a rally. It is these things that make Tennis the delightful game that it is... Helen Wills Moody
72- There is a lot of ingredients go into being a good Tennis player... Rod Laver
73- Women's Tennis is two sets of rubbish that lasts only half an hour... Pat Cash
74- These girls play Tennis first and foremost; the fact that many of them are very glamorous is a major bonus for any promoter... John Lindsey
75- Whoever has played Tennis knows the court is pretty big, and you always have space to put the ball in... Thomas Berdych
76- I'm just glad Open Tennis is here. It's great for the game. That's more important... Pancho Gonzalez
77- I call Tennis the McDonald's of sports... You go in, they make a quick buck out of you, and you're out... Pat Cash
78- In these days of modern Tennis, a player is as strong as his weakest stroke... Bill Tilden
79- One important key to success is self-confidence. An important key to self-confidence is preparation... Arthur Ashe
80- There is a syndrome in sports called paralysis by analysis... The ideal attitude is to be physically loose and mentally tight... Arthur Ashe
81- The next point, that's all you must think about... Rod Laver
82- The mark of great sportsmen is not how good they are at their best, but how good they are their worst... Martina Navratilova
83- I play each point like my life depends on it... Martina Navratilova
84- Being number two sucks... Andre Agassi

WHAT TENNIS PROS DON'T TEACH (WTPDT)

85- You cannot be serious... John McEnroe
86- Experience is a great advantage. The problem is that when you get the experience, you are too damned old to do anything about it... Jimmy Connors
87- I hate to lose more than I love to win... Jimmy Connors
88- Success is a journey, not a destination. The doing is often more important than the outcome... Arthur Ashe
89- We get criticized for showing no personality; then we get penalized when we do... Lindsey Davenport
90- This taught me a lesson... But I don't know what it is... John McEnroe
91- I'm not a creature of the night mate... Patrick Rafter
92- If I can't play for big money, I play for a little money, and if I can't play for a little money, I stay in bed that day... Bobby Riggs
93- Tennis is more than just a sport; it's an art, like a ballet... Bill Tilden
94- The fifth set is not about Tennis... It's about nerves... Boris Becker
95- My game is a lot about footwork... if I move well, I play well... Roger Federer
96- If you can play Tennis while someone is shooting a gun down the street, that's concentration... I didn't grow up playing at the country club... Serena Williams
97- Life is like a game of Tennis; the player that serves well seldom loses... Unknown
98- Life shrinks or expands in proportion to one's courage... Anaís Nin
99- If you think you're wrong, you're probably right... Unknown
100- There is always a way to win... John McEnroe
101- Anything that happens on a Tennis court, you either made it happen or you let it happen... Manuel S. Cervantes

More Quotes:

102- Good Tennis players miss little, and when they do miss, they miss by a little... Manuel S. Cervantes
103- People don't seem to understand that it's a damn war out there... Jimmy Connors

104- I try to say good shot to my opponent anytime he hits a good point finishing shot... I do it for him as much as I do it for myself... I do this in order to keep myself in a positive frame of mind... Manuel S. Cervantes

105- I didn't aspire to be a good sport; champion was good enough for me... Fred Perry

106- I am the best Tennis player who cannot play Tennis... Ion Tiriac

107- Losing is not my enemy... Fear of losing is my enemy... Rafael Nadal

108- You have to find it... No one else can find it for you... Bjorn Borg

109- A smile is a curve that can straighten out a lot of problems... Ana Ivanovic

110- Winning for your country gives you a high that lasts two or three days... You can't go to Kmart and pick that up... Jim Courier

111- The great thing about Tennis is that you can't run out the clock... As long as we were still playing I had a chance... Andre Agassi

112- The roughest thing I ever said to an umpire was: 'Are you sure?' Rod Laver

113- When intensely working on a Tennis court, it is hard to hit the ball soft... Tim Mayotte

114- I have always considered Tennis a combat in an arena between two gladiators who have their racquets and their courage as their weapons... Yannick Noah

115- To err is human, to put the blame on someone else, is doubles... Unknown

116- Love means nothing to a Tennis player... Unknown

117- From what we get, we can make a living... What we give, however, makes a life... Arthur Ashe

118- Never let success get to your head... Never let failure get to your heart... Unknown

119- There is plenty of room at the top... It's the bottom that's crowded... Jim Rohn

120- There is a reason Tennis starts with Love... Unknown

121- Don't be afraid to give up the good for the great... Serena Williams

122- If you want something you have never had... You have to do something you have never done... Unknown

123- Determination is the difference between what you want and what you want most... Unknown

124- Winners are not people who never fail... But people who never quit... Unknown
125- You miss 100% of the shots you never try... Wayne Gretzky
126- Sports do not build character... They reveal it... John Wooden
127- Motivation will almost always beat mere talent... Norman R. Augutine
128- It's nice to be important... But it's more important to be nice... Roger Federer
129- Its great... Everybody rates my good strokes as outstanding... And my poorer strokes as almost outstanding... Roger Federer
130- Practice is so despicable that instead I play doubles... John McEnroe
131- If you are going to do business with someone, play him or her a couple Tennis matches first... You get to know the true person on the Tennis court... Unknown
132- Tennis rocks, I owe everything to Tennis... Anasazi Cervantes
133- Write something worth reading or do something worth writing... Benjamin Franklin
134- I am so darn consistent doing the wrong thing... Pat Harris
135- Only the ball... Andre Agassi
136- I am a Tennis player first, last and always... Unknown
137- Tennis is life; life is Tennis... Is life like Tennis? Anonymous
138- A Tennis player is nothing but his results... Anonymous
139- Never let anyone believe they can beat you... it is dangerous game... Anonymous
140- When Sampras is winning, he seems mindless... but when he is on the comeback he is a genius... Marat Safin
141- In Tennis, an uneasy feeling comes to you when you are holding serve only to have your opponent do the same thing a few moments later... Manuel S. Cervantes
142- Don't open your mouth before Tennis matches... Anonymous
143- Greatness is only available to those willing to go practice like hell regardless of what it's like out there... Anonymous
144- Anything you do in life that does not require full concentration and engagement is probably not worth doing at all... Manuel S. Cervantes
145- Get fit to play Tennis... Don't play Tennis to get fit... Anonymous

146- Unfortunately in Tennis circles there will always be opportunistic, intolerable, and dishonest idiots trying to play for all the wrong reasons... Manuel S. Cervantes

147- Walls will always have a philosophical and mystical essence to themselves. The Great Wall of China, The Berlin Wall, or the wall in Thus Spoke Zarathustra, and that mysterious wall or philosophical stone in 2001 Space Odyssey. So a wall for Tennis should also be a place of meditation, reflection, and self-regeneration to all Tennis players; especially juniors. Too bad nobody goes for this anymore. I for one; built my entire game on a wall... Manuel S. Cervantes

148- I will never play mixed doubles with my wife again... If I have to force myself that much to be nice, there must be something very radically wrong with my mind... Stu Todd

149- Work is work! The rest is life! Manuel S. Cervantes

150- Always continue to search for as long and as hard as permissible... Anonymous

151- All knowledge leads to self-improvement and self-understanding... Bruce Lee

152- Anything not written from the heart is probably not worth writing about... Manuel S. Cervantes

153- Life is Tennis; Tennis is Life... Build your life around Tennis, not your Tennis around life! Manuel S. Cervantes

154- No matter what accomplishments you make, somebody always helps you... Althea Gibson

155- We just need appreciate the privilege of being able to compete... and we need to learn how to lose better... John Bailey

156- Coaches are mentors... What a privilege! John Bailey

157- My best friends came to be through Tennis... John Bailey

158- Tennis will always be waiting... John Bailey

159- Mandate or no mandate, or in spite of the mandate... If not played on a 78 foot court, with yellow balls and a three foot net, it's not Tennis... They can call it anything they want, but Tennis? I think not, thank you... Manuel S. Cervantes

160- Pressure is a privilege... Billie Jean King

161- It's easier to master consistency than to create power... Martina Navratilova

162- Teenage juniors are in a constant state of natural resistance to anything Dad or Mom might advice to them... Yijian Zheng

163- I saw him player against someone that looked way better than him, but he just won the point... Augie Moissonis
164- As I said to Cooper, my 12-year-old student "Hey Coops, be cautious don't be overconfident", he replied "When have I ever been that confident?"
165- He is not that good, he just keeps it in play, but if you give him an easy one, he puts it away... Anonimous

How about these slogans?

1- The Best or Nothing... Mercedes Benz
2- Leading to the Top... Pinnacle Tennis, Manuel S. Cervantes
3- Just do it... Nike

And so on and so forth... always look for inspiration!

101 THINGS WE MAY NEED TO CARRY IN OUR TENNIS BAG

There is a reason nowadays we see the pros carry two and sometimes three bags into the court as they walk into the stadium to play a match. Serious Tennis players have to be prepared. There is a lot of little stuff we need to have all the time. Some of these modern racquet bags are huge in size and can carry a lot of gear.

Our Tennis bag should be full of stuff whether on the court for practice, just for fun or for tournaments. Pick and choose the must have, and the should have. Obviously we cannot carry everything listed below.

Here is a pretty exhaustive list:

1) At least two Tennis racquets restrung, and ready to use. If we only have two racquets, only play with one all the time, that way we are assured to have at least one fresh new string job in our bag at all times. If we have more than two, then it is recommended to try to mix them around, so we are used to all of them in case there are subtle differences in tension, weight, balance or strings. It is not a bad idea to have one or two racquets at slightly different tensions or with different strings for certain days, and even slightly different balance and weights. That is if a player can afford to have 6 racquets or more. Some of the pros must do this all the time.

2) Always have two or more overgrips constantly at hand. Tennis players need to get good at replacing them themselves. Tennis players should be able to easily replace an overgrip in less than one minute.

3) One or two sets of string; making sure it is the same we are used to, or familiar with.

4) String savers; if we like them. String savers help strings last longer; they are easy to install and not expensive. They go in the

intersection of the cross and main strings in an area inclusive of the sweet spot of the racquet.

5) Dampeners if we use them. Personally I don't recommend them since to me it seems like they take the feel away from the impact of the ball on the strings.

6) Sawdust in a small bag or container. I really like sawdust to suck away all sweat from my hand in very humid weather. We can get it at any construction site for free; just pick it up from the ground. I used to break racquets as a junior because they would slip out of my sweaty hand when serving. But then one day I saw John Newcombe playing in a tournament in my hometown using sawdust, and I was sold on it ever since. There is no better fix for sweaty hands, and it is free!

7) Street chalk: This really helps keep the racket grip smooth and dry; it also makes a dirty overgrip not look so nasty. Think of gymnasts chalking their hands for better hold on the bars! Street chalk also comes in handy to draw lines on a basketball court or the street for an improvised Tennis court! So we don't apply it to our hands, simply cover the grip of the racquet with it. This makes for a fun thing for kids to do since they can mess with different colors.

8) Tennis Journal for notes on players, observations and ideas. Write about our matches and other friends' matches, write phone numbers, addresses, notes about the courts played on or notes about the facility a tournament was held in, etc...

9) Pens, pencils and eraser for taking notes or signing forms, etc...

10) First aid kit containing the following:

11) Gauze tape,

12) Athletic tape,

13) Band-aids,

14) Regular aspirins,

15) Ibuprofen pills,

16) Advil pills,

17) Tylenol pills,

18) Motrin pills,

19) Alka-Seltzer,

20) Small flask of Pepto-Bismol,

21) Tums antacid pills,

22) Carmex lip therapy (for all kinds of things such as finger sores, infections from a scratch on court since it has disinfectant in it, blisters, etc…),
23) Ace elastic bands, KT tape or Kinesthetic Tape,
24) Regular bandage, or band-aids,
25) Moleskin to treat blisters and other skin problems,
26) Small bottle of disinfectant alcohol,
27) Warm up gel-like Bengay, Tiger Balm, or Biofreeze,
28) Hydrocortisone cream or ointment,
29) Small bottle of hydrogen peroxide,
30) Arnica ointment or cream, etc…
31) Eye drops for irritation or other eye ailments,
32) Tennis elbow straps or bands, knee straps or bands, ankle support, heel gel support extras, etc…
33) Ear plugs for taking a nap in the car or on a comfortable chair or couch, or simply to read or study on the road,
34) Racquet head tape. I personally like head tape a lot, and always have a roll in my accessories bag along with over grips and other stuff. Especially for juniors, head tape is great since it really extends the life of the frame by keeping it from scratching too badly,
35) Lead tape for Tennis racquets to keep your frames customized to your desired balance, weight, etc…
36) Lighter and matches. I don't smoke, but I find it useful to have with me all the time to start a grill or fire for a picnic after matches during a tournament weekend,
37) Small towel and if there is room, a regular thin towel,
38) Extra shirts, t-shirts,
39) Extra pairs of socks,
40) Extra underwear, we never know!
41) Extra pair of shoes if we can fit them in, this is important especially if we are wearing new ones, or playing in extreme humidity, where shoes get wet with sweat; and players need to change during or in between matches.
42) Extra ball caps, visors, Australian style hat, etc…
43) Bandanas and handkerchiefs,
44) Cell phone or smartphone. Obviously turn it off during tournament matches,

45) Battery chargers for cell phone and iPad or iPod, or any electronics needed,
46) iPad or iPod or portable computer for accessing tournament websites and updates on changes in schedule or e-mails as needed. Obviously we don't use this equipment during tournament matches.
47) Sticky notes
48) Wristbands
49) Headbands
50) Box of lemonade singles. Little envelopes of lemonade powder, these are easy to find, a great way to add vitamin C to our body, and it makes us drink more water because it is so good! Lemonade is a natural anti-inflammatory,
51) Snacks, granola bars, crackers, etc…
52) Stencil ink; especially sponsored players need to have their racquets stenciled properly at all times. Refresh stencil if it is worn off.
53) Pocket knife or Swiss pocket multi-tool,
54) Packet of Kleenex,
55) Mint box or Deltoids box, hard candy like Halls or Jolly Ranchers,
56) Personal cards with phone number, e-mail, etc…
57) UV protection cream or sunblock cream,
58) Mix bottle or squeeze bottle,
59) Can of Tennis balls or just lose Tennis balls inside bag for warm up or just practice,
60) Tennis Rulebook,
61) Copy of "What Tennis Pros Don't Teach" or other Tennis books needed, other books or magazines being read at the time are also a good idea. Sometimes we have to wait forever for our matches to go on during tournaments… Read!
62) Talc or body powder for chafing is a good fix,
63) Deodorant bar,
64) Lotion, cologne, or perfume. We don't want to smell like hell all day after or during our matches, right?
65) Dental Floss, toothbrush and toothpaste,
66) Dead balls for wall practice or for sticking in the V of the racquet for warm up swinging. Or even to play with our dog or someone else's dog at the Tennis courts,
67) Insect repellant,
68) Change and small bills,

69) Sunglasses,
70) Sunglass case,
71) Wallet, ID, driver's license, credit cards, etc...
72) Swimming suit,
73) Photo of sweetheart or family,
74) Good luck token or good luck amulet,
75) Small portable camera,
76) USB connection cable,
77) Slingshot... believe it or not; I always carry one because it is fun for breaks during practice! I have had my sling shot with me since I was a kid at all times... No concealed carry permit needed for it! I have great fun with kids, and I am always making more for my students because they think it is the coolest thing! Anything to keep them from electronics and be normal kids like we used to...
78) The right size rocks or BB pellets for the sling shot... Buckshot is the best size for weight and power; however, the right size rocks are fine too!
79) Rubber bands... rubber bands are one of the greatest of man's inventions... They are kind of like duct tape... good for everything!
80) Individual racquet bag of the same brand as our racquets. This comes in handy as an extra pocket inside your 12X racquet thermo bag. Also as little carry gadget bag if we go somewhere like a water park or theme park or just to the movies. We can fit in our wallet, sunglasses, etc... Strap it across the back, and it is safe, pretty roomy for small stuff and comfortable. Plus we are immediately identified as Tennis players!
81) Roll of Scotch tape, and small roll of duct tape,
82) CD/DVD player, DVDs or CDs, radio, etc...
83) Lightweight/portable chess set for waiting for matches,
84) Reading Glasses,
85) Copy of tournament schedule for season or year,
86) Copy or weekly schedule, drills, lessons, practice matches, gym, etc...
87) Copy of weekly fitness routine, and WTPDT Fitness Training Protocol Chart,
88) Copy of Periodization schedule for season, year, etc...
89) Soap. How many times have you gone to a public or Tennis club restroom where they had no soap?

90) Razors just in case we need to shave. This has happened to me any number of times.
91) Sunglass spray and cloth for keeping sunglasses and regular glasses respectable, as well as cell phone and electronics screens clean of dust.
92) Extra pair of contacts, I have seen too many juniors either losing a contact lens or having to replace it during matchplay,
93) Contacts container and wash,
94) Nail clippers,
95) Light rain gear,
96) Light jacket in case, it gets cold or rains,
97) Small umbrella for sun and rain,
98) Zip ties for attaching your umbrella under your chair or bench for shade on changeovers,
99) Portable scorecards, the kind that can mount on the net near the net pole or the fence near us,
100) Plastic bags in case we need to ice an injury or cramps, zip lock bags in medium size work well,
101) Checkbook along with deposit or withdrawal slips,

More stuff…

102) USTA, FMT, ITF, ATP, USPTA, ATA, Member numbers and phone numbers as well as other Tennis organizations and offices. These numbers can all be stored in you Cell's memory,
103) GPS Unit, if we don't already have it as an app on our smartphone. I can't think of how many times it has been easier to find a Tennis facility in an unfamiliar town or city with the aid of the GPS,
104) Small roll of toilet paper, it comes in handy at a lot of public facilities and just for general use,
105) Nail polish and remover or small flask of acetone. For girls the nail polish is obvious, but for all Tennis players that keep a stencil on the strings, the acetone/remover comes in very handy, to remove stains of ink around the frame, and keep our racquets looking smart,
106) Training aids such as jump rope, elastic tubing, grip strengthening device, relaxation grip ball, etc…

Note: By going on court with all this equipment, we are actually giving ourselves a better chance of winning matches, and to perform at a higher level. Because more often than not, we are coming in more prepared than our opponents. Going on court with everything we may need, and fully prepared, is one of those things that is 100% under our direct control and should not be taken lightly!

101 EXCUSES FOR LOSING IN TENNIS

The funny nature of excuses in Tennis and other sports will always exist. Most of the excuses we hear come from situations or variables we cannot control on a Tennis court. How we deal with these uncontrollable variables is what eventually makes a good Tennis player.

1- It was too hot and humid... horrible playing conditions!
2- It was very windy. I don't think I ever hit the ball dead center on the strings of my racquet.
3- My racket is not strung right. It never felt comfortable when I made impact with the ball.
4- My grip got undone and I could not fit it back or adjust it.
5- There were so many distractions, that I was never able to concentrate.
6- This is the worst I played in a long time. No doubt, I must be getting old.
7- He is not any good. I just couldn't get my serve in.
8- He is just a pusher; all he does is keeping the ball in play.
9- Man, I got a hangover because I probably had too much to drink last night.
10- I could not sleep well last night; my allergies and noise outside kept waking me up.
11- The speed of the court was too fast or too slow there never seemed to be any uniformity to the bounces.
12- The surface was bad full of divots, and I could never get into the rhythm of things.
13- The balls were horrible and dead.
14- I could not return his power serve. The rest of his game did not really hurt me.
15- Oooh, I was too sore from last night's tough match.

16- We need to play more tournaments; that's all. We were just not match tough… And they were!
17- Wow, those shadows on the court killed me. Could never quite see the ball well enough!
18- I hate the eco in indoor Tennis courts; it just isn't the same.
19- There was something wrong with my racket; it did not feel right. It could be that my frame is fatigued. I don't know; it felt as if I was playing with someone else's racquet.
20- This was the first time I played Tennis in two weeks.
21- My strings broke, and switched to my backup racket, and it just did not feel right.
22- My wife has been giving me a hard time at home lately, and I just could not concentrate.
23- I got too much going on in my head and cannot focus.
24- To me this was just another practice match; the outcome did not matter at all.
25- My contacts kept giving me problems, and I could not see the ball very well, or my glasses kept fogging up and just could not focus.
26- It was my shoes; that's why she beat me and I did not feel good traction on the court.
27- My passing shots were nil today. I missed every one of them.
28- My Tennis elbow problem really flared with these balls. I am used to playing with used balls only!
29- This guy sliced everything; that's no way to play Tennis.
30- I finally came up with a winning strategy, but I was too far down in the score and could not catch up.
31- An official came by for 5 minutes, overruled me on a call and completely made me lose my concentration. After that, anytime someone walked by the court, I could not focus anymore.
32- He has that annoying kind of game that is just hard for me to deal with.
33- I know I look better than my opponent, but I just could not keep up with all the balls coming back down the middle of the court.
34- He played great, and I played the worst. The combination of the two things made for an upset!
35- I kept hearing the grunting on the court next to me, and that completely messed me up.

36- I was late 5 minutes to the check in, started the match one break down and one game down. It really got in my head, and I could not fight back.
37- I am not at 100% yet, just got back into it after our vacation and could not play my A game.
38- I have been dealing with injury on top of injury, and I am afraid I will get injured again if I go all out for some balls.
39- My opponent had a whole cheering squad, and I had no one going for me.
40- He was getting coaching from one of his teammates; that's against the rules, and I had nobody helping me out.
41- He was so slow and deliberate in everything he did on the court. It took him forever to be ready to serve and/or setup to return serve, and I had no sense of tempo.
42- He rushed me and quick served me the whole match, I felt as if he was always waiting for me to serve or return. He never took a break on changeovers and did not let me establish my own rhythm.
43- I had the wrong strategy and was never aware of it; I did not realize it until it was too late!
44- My coach (dad, brother, friend, etc...) gave me the wrong strategy and did not know how to change it.
45- Darn, that pain in my leg (arm, back, etc...) and could not give it my 100% anymore.
46- The weather was my enemy. Mother Nature made me lose! It kept changing during the middle of the match, and I could not play well anymore.
47- My opponent just turned it on, and I stayed the same.
48- After the match was over, I finally figured out she was a lefty.
49- I cannot deal with players that spin everything like crazy.
50- He or she had too much power for me!
51- He/she cheated his/her way out of this match!
52- I did not get enough sleep last night and felt clumsy.
53- He is way younger than me. The age difference is too much. I cannot deal with those legs and that power anymore.
54- He was much more experienced than I am; he has played a lot longer than me.
55- That was the worst court I have ever played on. I could not even see the lines or get any consistency out of the bouncing of the ball.

56- The net was full of holes, and it was very distracting for me the whole match.
57- The fencing around the court was all bent at the bottom, and the balls kept going outside, and I would lose all concentration each time that happened.
58- There were balls from other courts rolling into mine the entire match. There was no fencing in between courts and the balls from the adjacent courts kept rolling over; it was so distracting and annoying.
59- There were no windscreens, and I just could not see the ball very well, my depth perception is not great, and I really need the solid background.
60- My grip came off, and nobody fixed it for me.
61- The sun kept blinding me all match long.
62- My clothing was too loose (or too tight) and did not feel comfortable at all today.
63- There were too many people watching the match, and I felt scrutinized and nervous about it.
64- My opponent's coach watched the whole match and mine was nowhere to be seen and felt at a disadvantage.
65- Too much drama going on in my life with family and friends for me to be able to do anything right.
66- We are not moving well together, and that's all I could think of all the time.
67- My girlfriend/boyfriend is threatening to break up with me, and Tennis is just not in my mind right now.
68- My children and the whole family have been sick, and we are just making it back on the Tennis courts after a long period of self-imposed quarantine.
69- Electricity went out last night at home for a few hours, and the air conditioner did not work. We were all too dehydrated for serious Tennis the next day because we had no A/C unit.
70- I wore a hole through my shoes and did not have another pair with me, and my toes started bleeding a little. I had to use racquet head tape to fix them on every change over.
71- It was intimidating playing in this awesome court in this huge tournament; I guess I am just a rookie.

WHAT TENNIS PROS DON'T TEACH (WTPDT)

72- I feel I am getting a little burned out, need a break from Tennis. My parents make me play and practice more than I really want to.
73- I felt I should have been able to win, and I cannot figure out how it was that I ended up losing this match 0-0.
74- My opponent went out of the court and got an official because he or she thought I was cheating; that really rattled me, and I could not play anymore.
75- My opponent was such a jerk; he kept imitating me at every chance he got.
76- No one gives a damn about my results; I have lost all motivation; how can anyone play Tennis successfully like this?
77- He had all the answers; I had none.
78- The quality of my Tennis was up there, but it still was not good enough.
79- We get what we pay for; cheap coaching will result in cheap results.
80- Tennis is just not for me; I am much better at golf, swimming, running, biking, etc...
81- I just don't have the head for this game, it is so difficult, and there are way too many variables that I have no control over.
82- I am not used to that brand of Tennis Balls; I always play with (Penn, Wilson, Dunlop, etc...)
83- The sad part is that I did not know how to win and/or close the match. When the match gets close, I fall apart like a harassed kitten.
84- Look, I was playing with this new racquet model, Ok?
85- I am hitting everything long: It must be all that weight lifting.
86- I have not been working out, and I was out of steam in the middle of the first set.
87- We only do this recreationally, and we really don't care if we lose or win.
88- It was too cold, and I could never quite get warmed up.
89- My clothing got all sweaty and was just dripping; I could not keep my grip. Sweat got in my eyes and just was soaking wet the whole time.
90- Well, I really didn't want to play in this tourney anyway. Please get off my back.
91- This guy got on my nerves. He/She was too quiet; he/she never said a word.

92- This guy just talked too much. During changeovers, he kept telling me stories about his pets at home. Concentration and relaxation were impossible!

93- I fell at the beginning of the 2nd set and got disoriented. I had won the first set 6/1, and then I fell hard at 2 all; after that I could not get it together anymore and lost the second set 6/2 and the third one 6/1.

94- I was winning, got a nosebleed and had to sit down for several minutes. I seem to have lost my momentum, and by the time I got back on the court, I had lost all rhythm, and confidence dwindled away pretty fast.

95- The country music they were playing at the pool made me lose. The tournament officials were ineffective in getting them to turn it off or at least lower the volume. It drove me crazy!

96- There was a weird smell in the air that just got to me. It made me feel dizzy and sick, and could not play at all.

97- The sound of passing cars and noise from the street on the other side of the wall next to my court was just too much for me, and it got on my nerves.

98- Towards the end I had this match figured out. But by the time I started coming back I was down 6/1, 5/1.

99- My game was suited perfectly for my opponent to drill me with his strengths and weapons, and I had not idea how to break away from that.

100- I feel I am the better player, but he just played the match of his life.

101- Every time I would counter one of my opponent's moves, he would come up with something else; I felt like I was playing catch-up the whole match. He is just better. We must admit, and we must give credit!

And the list goes on and on... Like forever!

101 REASONS WHY WE PLAY TENNIS

1- For the fun of it; because we can have a good time from day one. As soon as we start it already is fun, and it only gets better as we improve our game.
2- For the social interaction. Get with friends and meet new ones. We can benefit from Tennis at home through conversation. It is also a good excuse to invite Tennis friends over or visit their homes too. I hear people say something like this: "We got tired of hearing how great the sport was, and since everyone seems to be a Tennis player, we can be part of the conversation now".
3- For the competition and the challenge of it. Tennis really delivers here, especially in singles… It is one on one… Mano a mano… Man to man or woman to woman! No outsiders… It could also be woman to man or man to woman; or even man to wall or man to ball machine!
4- Because I love to serve aces, winners, and passing shots. For the awesome feeling of hitting a solid shot. We can really unleash our feelings and passion on the ball by hitting it as hard as we possibly can. The feeling is unequaled especially if the ball actually goes in!
5- We can be as aggressive as we want and show the aggressive side of our personality without hurting or offending anyone. Our playing style and personality on court will surface whether we want it or not.
6- Because I love net play. Through volleys I can show my talent and intelligence without anybody telling me what to do. I am free to do anything I want. All decisions are mine and only mine. Well executed, net play and volleys is a work of art for sure!
7- Because I love drop shots, and all finesse shots. Finesse shots feel great, because we are able to do so much with so little. We exert the minimum effort and obtain the maximum result when we hit a winner off a delicate, finesse shot.

8- For its simplicity and complexity. Because being so simple, sometimes it gets very complicated in a hurry. Tennis can be as simple or complicated as we want it to be. Tennis is hitting the ball back and forth over a net into a rectangle, but then if we start paying attention, there is so much more to it than just that.

9- If Tennis players want a respectful level, Tennis will demand so much out of them. 100% dedication physically, mentally, and spiritually. It is a lifetime commitment to perfection, self-discipline, and improvement. As a personal challenge, Tennis can be an awesome force for motivation and commitment. Tennis requires resiliency and courage!

10- Tennis is more than a lifetime sport; Tennis is a way of life. Tennis families and individuals committed to Tennis live, breath and eat Tennis every day, and their everyday lives are all based around Tennis courts.

11- Tennis is an international sport. We can always play tennis; whether it is on a business trip or just a vacation. We will find Tennis courts just about anywhere we go. It is very well organized worldwide. All Tennis players need; is their gear when on trips and one can find courts and other players with whom to play.

12- Because of the tradition of it. Tennis, as we know it today, is more than 200 years old, but its roots date back to as much as 500 years ago! Very few other sports offer this tradition and depth!

13- Because no matter how good we are, we can always get better. There is no such thing as the perfect stroke or the perfect Tennis player. There has never been a player who did not lose any matches! Winning in Tennis is based on the lessons learned when we lost!

14- We can always come up with good excuses. In doubles, we can blame the loss on our partner, the officials, and more. There are many excuses for losing or not performing at an anticipated level. The anticipated level is way off the mark many times. Just because we spend tons of time on the court practicing, there is no guarantee we will play well. That means that if I had been hitting the ball great in practice, I may still come back during tournament time and play awful. That is why we get nervous before matches; because we don't have control over how well we will play day-to-day!

15- Tennis is affordable. But at the same time, it can get very expensive. We can blow off a bucket full of money on lessons, gear, tournaments, etc... Or we can go low budget and still get a lot out of it.

16- It can be for the elite only, either socially or playing level. There are different Tennis circles, one for every social network. Players can surely find one where they fit just fine no matter who they are. One thing is for sure, the better we are, the easier it is to find people and places to play.

17- It is played with wool balls. Equipment is unique. As a kid, this is one of the things that attracted me to it. Wool balls, wooden racquets, clay and grass courts, gut strings... All natural materials; of course equipment and many other things have changed a lot, but it still holds its fascination. Other things that haunted me as a kid were the sound of the ball, the smell of the damped red clay, the white clothing, the long trousers the pros wore. Now it is different, but still haunting. There is something magical and transcendental about Tennis that is hard to explain!

18- It is the only sport played in 7 or more different surfaces. It is actually played on three natural surfaces: Clay, grass and manure. But also on concrete, carpet, synthetic grass, pavement, sand, dirt, wood, etc...

19- We can have a court in our backyard and hold our own tournaments without spending a small fortune. To play Tennis, we don't need a whole field and a small army of people to make it happen!

20- Players can customize everything to themselves; including the balls, the court, and other equipment. They have the choice; they choose the colors and materials as well!

21- It brings family and friends together because Tennis is such a family tradition. I am already the 4th generation. It is such a cool thing. It's like: "Do you speak Tennis?" Instead of English or Spanish, etc...

22- Even Dogs like Tennis. They love to chase and chew on Tennis balls. I had a huge Labrador named Indio who jumped over the net like a competition horse over and over chasing Tennis balls! I even wrote a book about him!

23- We can always bring our rackets with us on any trip. Tennis gear doesn't take up half the trunk space like golf clubs do. It is so practical; Tennis is 100% portable. We can take it with us anywhere we travel, for work or vacation, we can always find Tennis courts.

24- The handshake, the values, and ethics, the respect for the competition. Pros hug after matches besides the traditional handshake, and girls kiss and smile! Well, not all of them!
25- The stencil on the strings can be anything we want. Our racket is a private billboard. The racquet is a way for anyone to express something. Unlike Tattoos, we can express thoughts and ideas through stenciling on our strings, and we can always get new plain strings later without stencils.
26- We can play for money, lunch, a drink and/or gamble or for whatever we want. It is fun to place some bets even if we are not the ones playing.
27- It is always changing, or we can make our own rules if playing for fun or practice. At the same time, rules do change, and if we are into competitive Tennis, we need to keep up.
28- Tournaments happen everywhere. If we feel like playing a tournament, all we do is log on the Internet, and there are virtually thousands to choose from Worldwide.
29- We don't necessarily have to play in tournaments or compete to be part of Tennis. Social Tennis is just fine. The great majority of Tennis players around the world play socially just for fun, recreation or exercise, although most diehards are tournament players.
30- Tennis coverage is unbelievable today. We get to enjoy it 24/7 even at home when on TV, Internet, Radio, Facebook, Twitter, YouTube, smartphone, etc...
31- We can have a personal coach at whatever level we play, and guess what? It is actually affordable! We can even be our own coach if we wish. We customize our workouts to our needs, money and time availability.
32- Tennis players can drink and play and not get a citation or ticket or go to jail. Although there may be other lesser or maybe less desirable consequences!
33- Because of the fashion of it. We see all kinds of trends in Tennis. In a lot of places, it is okay to play Tennis topless. In some places, players can wear anything they want. Shoes and attire don't matter at a lot of Tennis facilities. But on the reverse side, there are some very exclusive racquet clubs that maintain the strictest attire rules. Some Tennis facilities and racquet clubs around the World still have the all white clothing rule and no t-shirts rule in place.

34- There are Tennis courts available 24/7, so we can play whenever we want. There will always be someone willing to play with us.
35- We can practice on our own on a wall or ball machine, or even by self-feeding (hand dropping balls). I do that every now and then, and I feel this really helps my footwork and strokes.
36- It does not take that long, 45 minutes of intense hitting, or playing Tennis is plenty. We can be totally exhausted if we really work hard. The great Jimmy Connors was known to limit his practices to 45 minutes of super intense hitting and point play!
37- Tennis is a great excuse to travel out of town, as a coach or with family or just to play a tournament.
38- Take full advantage of club facility. A lot of country clubs have Tennis courts, but most members don't use them.
39- Tennis provides an excuse to buy new Tennis attire, balls, shoes, etc... It is always a good excuse to spend money. And it should be okay with a spouse, for the most part because Tennis is good for us. It is not like we are wasting money on drugs, cigarettes, or alcohol.
40- Everyone is always in a good mood, almost always! Being a game and sport, when players get to Tennis courts, they usually are excited and happy.
41- Tennis educates us, forces us to develop emotional control, teaches us discipline, and determination; Tennis forges a strong and confident personality.
42- Tennis keeps us healthy physically and mentally. Tennis fights old age. Tennis keeps us younger, because of the physical, emotional and spiritual exercise. Tennis develops strong physiques for kids growing up. Helps us drop our weight and prevents diseases from attacking our body.
43- It's addicting, better than drugs and not illegal.
44- Develops rivalries. In Tennis, whether we play socially or competitively, we are bound to develop some rivalries with other players of our caliber. It is fun, and it forces us to get the best out of each other.
45- I love to take lessons from professionals, at affordable prices; however, this can be misleading because, at some facilities, Tennis lessons are way overpriced.
46- I can get a tan and be active at the same time instead of going into one of those tanning capsules that resemble coffins!

47- Tennis players serve as role models for kids, and family; since I play Tennis, everyone else starts playing too. Whether I am a social, competitive or professional player, by becoming an active and dedicated Tennis player, I become a good role model.
48- Tennis makes for a great weekend. Very few things we do in life compete with the satisfaction and benefit of a hard weekend of lots and lots of Tennis; especially if we done with family and friends. Everywhere, people pay large sums of money just to have a taste of these ingredients.
49- As a kid, Tennis got me away from drugs and off the streets.
50- In Tennis one truly learns what it takes to win, and we can do it all on our own. Therefore, we can get 100% of the credit of our results; even though these results may not always be that desirable.
51- We learn to lose and deal with it. As predominantly an individual sport, Tennis teaches us how to deal with losing. We may, for a while, make a complete fool out of ourselves until we learn to cope with defeat a little better.
52- Tennis helps us to get to know others. On a Tennis court, we get to know others better; especially if we are playing in a tournament or for money. In Tennis, we get to know players for who they really are. Don't be surprised to find out that the nice guy we met at a restaurant is in reality the biggest cheater or the worst and most disrespectful sport. I would go as far as to say that if we want to do business with someone, get them on a Tennis court a few times first and then decide if we still want to do business. Don't believe the "Tennis transforms me, or Tennis reveals my other personality." It's more like "Tennis exposes my real self."
53- As Tennis players we have to figure out ways to adapt to different playing conditions and styles, this develops toughness, mentally and physically.
54- Learn to use body and mind together successfully. We can find a balance and then apply these skills in the real World.
55- To make a living as a Tennis Professional or become a pro and make money through Tennis. It is awesome to finally; sit down and watch our students compete, and our job now becomes that of an observer. We learn Tennis and later teach it to contribute in some one's life positively; to impact them physically and mentally.

These are great rewards; better than money... but we still make a living from doing it!

56- It is s a simple and down to earth sport. What could be simpler than Tennis? Hit a ball back and forth over the net into a rectangle?

57- Because there are not as many injuries since it is not a contact sport. After playing a lifetime, we are actually still okay and not handicapped because of it like in other sports!

58- Tennis is a very well-rounded sport. Through playing Tennis, we get a healthy body and mind, increased flexibility, strength, etc...

59- Tennis gets us away from anxiety, stress, and everyday problems. It is relaxing; it distracts us in a positive way and is available whenever we need it.

60- Makes us think a whole lot. We love to have to figure out how to win and get out of serious trouble through changing strategy. Tennis teaches us to critical thinking and ways to solve problems.

61- We can switch gears and go into Turbo as needed. Or we can slow things down as needed too. We can establish our own tempo.

62- Gives me something to shoot for in life. As a teenager, go for college Tennis and get an education on a scholarship; anyone with a little discipline can do it.

63- It was a great way to pay my way through college. It helps me set goals in life; earn a scholarship to play Tennis in the US.

64- Tennis helps with maturity. I learned to deal with all kinds of difficulties on and off the court. This situation presents itself at all levels of development and tournament play.

65- Develops hand-eye coordination, like very few other sports. The whole body/mind combination has to be in perfect synchronized mode to hit solid and smart shots.

66- Looks cool to get clay all over my body and clothing. This is true when playing on red clay (the surface of my youth). I loved it, and still do. My mom as a kid did not like it so much because she was the one doing the laundry!

67- It teaches us knowledge of sports. Interest in Tennis gets us a good perspective of sports since we become part of them in our own very unique way.

68- Because we earn trophies and awards. This is not always true, but it eventually happens if we stay with it and if we are disciplined about it.

69- It provides therapy to find someone to talk to and let our thoughts out. We can be in a bad mood coming into a Tennis court. By the time we leave, we are feeling better unless we got crushed! It's a great way to vent our frustrations from a tough day at work or at home.

70- Get to play with beautiful and glamorous women or handsome and respectful gentlemen. Tennis is associated with a lot of people who like to be healthy and look good. This is not a bad place to be, no matter what walk of life we come from. A Tennis facility is probably one of the best places to find the right date regardless of our age.

71- To make business without wearing ties and suits, all formal, board rooms, meetings, etc… We can meet on a Tennis court with players to do business and to network in our area.

72- Hear all the gossip and latest news, etc… And at the same time have a workout in a good atmosphere with friends.

73- Become part of the international family of Tennis players across the World. No other sport has the reach that Tennis does as far as being so internationalized. A player will always find Tennis courts and Tennis players everywhere he or she goes, and guess what… The rules are also the same!

74- Love Tennis parties. Tennis parties have a common denominator. What gets Tennis players together is Tennis itself, and we all are happy around anything Tennis related because we love it.

75- We learn to deal with ourselves and others on neutral ground. When we face a player for the first time, with a little experience we learn to deal with his/her personality. This ability transfers into real World day to day dealings in business, social and family life. It is invaluable. It is a way to learn to cope with situations in a controlled atmosphere that gets us ready for the real World. Tennis teaches self-reliance as well as emotional and physical control like no other sport.

76- Tennis will save us, and help us continue to be alive. Tennis will set us free. Enjoy wearing shorts or skirts. Sometimes I get funny looks wearing shorts, but it is second nature to me; it feels natural to me. Tennis players don't have to shave; it is okay not to. As a Tennis Pro, I relate to how a lot of times it is actually more appropriate to not shave; it gives us that look of toughness and ruggedness. Now, though, we do have to shower, smell good and wear clean clothing!

77- It's okay to play Tennis, our significant other knows we will be more agreeable to family and friends after a good round of doubles.

78- It does not take long to get a good workout; it is practical; we can get it done in 45 minutes, not 4 hours like golf and other sports. Tennis is also more accessible than golf; it is less expensive; there are more Tennis courts than golf courses by far.

79- Teaches us to love the pain. After a good workout or match, we really feel it sometimes, but it is classified as good pain. Sore muscles and joints mean they are only getting stronger and more flexible. Because it hurts... love to work our rear off, and we actually build toward something very rewarding. Hard physical work on and off court will make us better but sometimes very sore. But this is what we have to do if we truly want to reach our potential.

80- Because it is a passion since I was a kid. No matter what, I always feel the urge to come back and hit some balls. Even nowadays 45 plus years later, I still enjoy practicing on a wall or a good hit with a partner. It is a way of life.

81- Because I love frame/string winners. This may be funny, but it happens a lot on Tennis. Of course when we frame the ball we miss more often than not, but it does happen, especially if we are one of those players that use heavy topspin.

82- We love Tennis because we can be part of a team. Team Tennis in the USA has gone to the next level, and it actually is responsible for the growth of Tennis Worldwide. We don't have to always be on our own, and it is our call. By the way, we really network through league Tennis and team Tennis.

83- This is where I met the love of my life, and therefore I am indebted to it.

84- Photography is awesome in Tennis. As an amateur photographer, I have taken Tennis pictures my entire life, and it certainly brings the two hobbies together on top of the fact that we have something to give and show to everyone.

85- The feelings and memories of a good match stay with us forever. We can even remember specific shots from many years ago. I remember several great and not so great shots and matches from

30 plus years ago, and details of just about every match I have ever played.

86- In Tennis, unlike other sports, we can come back from being way down in the score; this is because of the unique scoring system where every game starts from scratch. In other sports, say soccer, if one team is down 0-3 or 0-4, it is next to impossible to come back. All the winning team has to do is play defensive until time runs out. Or in Ping Pong whose sets are played to

87- Trying to come back when down 10-3 or something like that. Even if a player found the right strategy, chances are, he/she will not remount the score in that set. It is not uncommon in Tennis to hear of some unreal comebacks where one player was down 5-1 after having lost the first set 6-0 and come back to win the match. Back in my college Tennis days, my partner Jeff Hammerschmidt and I came back from being down 6-0, 5-0 and Love-40 to win 7-5 and 6-1. How did it happened? I have no clue; all I remember is that; after the handshake, I told Jeff, "Can you believe this? We were way down" We went on automatic pilot of course and played hypnotized. By the way, this happened in 1982! How is that for keeping Tennis memories alive?

88- We have to mix with other sports or do fitness and conditioning for our Tennis to truly reach its potential. Tennis on its own is great, but if we add sports like soccer or track as part of our training regimen, our Tennis and health really benefits.

89- Because a Tennis racket will be the key a good Tennis player will use to open innumerable doors in his/her lifetime. It has been said that a Tennis racquet is a magic wand. The better we swing that Tennis racquet, the more doors will open our way, and the more benefits will derive from it.

90- It feels good to break strings. When the strings break, there is a satisfying feel that comes from it: we worked hard and therefore wore out the strings. Of course, the downside of this is that we now have to have the racquet restrung.

91- Sometimes it feels good to break a racquet. It is a way to vent frustration. Breaking a racket is, for sure, one expensive way to ventilate temper. Breaking a racquet during a temper tantrum gets us thinking about many things and puts many other things into perspective. At the end of the day, we come to the same conclusion. Whatever made us lose our temper was probably not worth smashing a racquet in half. Breaking a racquet stays with us for a long time, and we can remember the details. I will never forget when during a doubles match a while back a bent a racquet over my left knee until it broke... Talk about pure frustration! This was a modern graphite racquet, too! Of course, I had a big bruise over my knee area the next day to remind me of my remorse for having done what I did!

92- Makes us more aware of the self and better observers. Helps us understand ourselves and others better. Tennis develops intelligence and increases our capacity to think and analyze things.

93- We can string our own racquets and actually do it for others and make some gas money. I have been stringing racquets since I was a kid; it is 2nd nature to me. I can watch TV, have a conversation, talk on the phone or listen to music while I string racquets. It is not a bad way to make some useful cash. Also, if we do our own, we save at least 50% of what we would spend if we got the local Tennis Shop to string it for us.

94- Because my personality surfaces when I am playing and don't have to pretend anymore. We can really express ourselves on a Tennis court. At the same time, we can pretend to be different from the way we really are, (this as part of our strategy), and it is okay to be like that too. Just remember that it is hard to win tough matches when we do this since to play our best Tennis all has to be balanced.

95- I can chide myself, don't need to hear it from anyone, especially when playing singles.

96- We can use our smartphone while playing Tennis; it is not against the law. Check our texts, e-mails and social media while we change over and during breaks. We will definitely not play too well using our smartphone during play, but we maybe we'll have more fun, though. However, I have seen this tried many times where the player doing it was just not concentrating at all. Remember that playing in a tournament, using a phone in any way is against the rules!

97- Tennis brings together diversity in every possible way, racial, social, political, religious, etc... This makes Tennis that much more interesting as a sport and social network.

98- We can beat players that are better than us on strategy alone and/or fitness alone. By being fit, we can beat players that are significantly better than us. Tennis brings mind and body in conjunction in an awesome way. Good thinking combined with good fitness will make an awesome Tennis player.
99- Because I love doubles, it is like a team sport, we can share it with our best friend; or who knows we might meet our best friend playing doubles.
100- Because I love singles, it is an individual sport. We are responsible for our own results. Develop our own Tennis philosophy. Develop our own playing style. We are our own team, and we can even be our own coach.
101- If we are a good Tennis player, there will always be lots of people recognizing that and inviting us not only to play, but also to lunch, or for a drink, and even on trips. Everyone wants to be associated with good Tennis players. It is such a cool feeling to have this advantage.

Here is an extra one:

102- Because it gives us access to Tennis facilities, racquet clubs, and country clubs all over the World. Some of these places are unbelievably beautiful!

Remember: Life is short... Play hard!   Anonymous

101 QUESTIONS... WHAT TENNIS PROS DON'T TEACH QUIZ

What did you learn? Here follow 101+ multiple choice and true and false quiz, plus the answers.

Instructions: Choose the best answer(s) to the questions below:

1) Mention three things we need to look for when trying to find the right Tennis coach for our children:

   a) A coach who has produced players before, a coach that takes notes in a journal, a coach that seems to be pretty fit
   b) A coach who drives a nice sports car, a coach who socializes with students during lessons and drills, a coach who does not allow kids to have fun during drills and lessons and is all instruction
   c) Someone who likes to play points with students, a pro who talks about all the things he knows regarding Tennis and junior development, a coach who brags about his students results or his results as a player
   d) None of the above

2) What is the most expensive Tennis string on the market and the one with the best feel for touch and finesse shots?

   a) Synthetic gut
   b) Finesse and touch depend more on the player, not the string
   c) Natural Gut
   d) Big Banger Luxilon Alu Power (125, 17 gauge)

e) Multifilament string in a high gauge
   f) None of the above

3) Finding the right coach would include but is not limited to the following:

   a) The Tennis pro who was a great player and is getting started coaching juniors
   b) A coach who tells us everything we want to hear and seems to be very knowledgeable
   c) A coach who seems to be out of shape, but he has been a Tennis coach for a long time
   d) A coach who has a history of developing good players

4) What could not be considered an attribute for good coaching in juniors?

   a) A coach who smokes
   b) A coach that is out of shape
   c) A coach that never hits with his or her students
   d) A coach that hardly ever watches tournament matches of his or her students
   e) All of the above

5) What is the number 1 ingredient for great junior development in Tennis?

   a) Being very athletic
   b) Starting at an early age, no later than like 6 or 7 years old
   c) Love of the game of Tennis
   d) All of the above

6) What are the most important health benefits of playing Tennis?

   a) Tennis increases flexibility
   b) Tennis increases reflexes
   c) Tennis prevents diseases and many other causes of death
   d) All of the above

WHAT TENNIS PROS DON'T TEACH (WTPDT)

7) Sportsmanship and ethics on a Tennis court teach us:

    a) That winning is worthless if the players are not ethical about the whole process
    b) That a player has to try to win matches at all costs
    c) That it is okay to bend the rules in order to win matches
    d) All of the above

8) In Tennis no teaching pro, former Tennis professional, or coach has all the answers because:

    a) Making predictions in Tennis is a dangerous game
    b) In Tennis unlike most other sports, it is sometimes very difficult to anticipate what will happen in a tournament or a match
    c) Tennis is too broad, and it is nearly impossible to have full knowledge or control of the whole spectrum of variables
    d) We hear gurus, TV commentators, and Tennis coaches being way off the mark all the time on their assessments and predictions
    e) All of the above

9) What does it mean when a Tennis professional or coach is certified by some official organization?

    a) It means we can be fully confident that the lessons provided by this coach are professional and based on true knowledge
    b) It means that we will get our money's worth in the lesson
    c) It means that a coach has experience and will most likely deliver the right instruction and assessments of the different strokes and techniques there are in Tennis
    d) None of the above

10) Basic Tennis professional certification or coach certification is equivalent to:

    a) A doctoral degree
    b) A high school diploma

c) A college undergraduate degree
d) Equivalent to 5 years of experience in the field of teaching Tennis
e) None of the above

11) How would I know if Tennis is the right sport for my children?

a) If they are independent and don't mind working on something alone
b) If they function fine in a group atmosphere
c) If they like to solve problems on their own
d) All of the above
e) None of the above

12) What are the four most important characteristics of a Tennis racquet?

a) Length, color, strings, brand
b) Grips size, stiffness level, weight, and balance
c) Material, model, string pattern, power level
d) Flexibility, width, Tension, solidness
e) All of the above
f) None of the above

13) Getting children involved in other sports besides Tennis at an early age only gets them tired and unwilling to spend enough time on a Tennis court. This only creates a competitive and technical backlog.

a) True
b) False
c) None of the above

14) What are the main two specifications to take into account when purchasing Tennis balls?

a) Brand and color
b) Altitude and surface

c) Extra duty felt and regular duty felt
d) Price and availability
e) All of the above

15) Practice hitting on a wall or with the aid of a ball machine is awesome because we can practice every single shot there is in the game of Tennis.

    a) true
    b) false

16) Involvement of the parents is crucial to junior development as long as:

    a) Dad and mom understand their and the coach's boundaries. Parents need to show emotional and financial support
    b) They get on court and pick up the balls during lessons making observations of their own at the same time
    c) Try to help by getting their kids on the courts and giving them lessons on their own
    d) All of the above

17) A junior player who is fully committed will spend most of his or her free time on the Tennis court honing his or her skills.

    a) true
    b) false

18) How long should it take to learn a stroke to a talented player who has the right motivation and passion for the game?

    a) One to five weeks
    b) One to two years
    c) Three to five weeks
    d) Three to six months

19) What is the single most important ingredient for an 8 or 9-year-old kid learning how to play Tennis?

   a) Having the right size equipment
   b) Spending several hours a week on the court hitting Tennis balls and learning technique
   c) Having the right motivation in a fun atmosphere
   d) None of the above

20) Mention three appropriate performance goals for a junior in a sanctioned tournament:

   a) Drink lots of water, take deep breaths between points, eat right during the tournament
   b) Hit consistently, serve well under pressure, win at least one match
   c) Make the opponent earn every point, be confident on the court at all times, win matches against players with lower rankings than mine
   d) None of the above
   e) All of the above

21) As far as goal setting what could be acceptable as a simple explanation of performance goals:

   a) Goals that we don't have 100% control over such as the outcome of a match or the results obtained in a certain tournament
   b) Goals that are 100% under our direct control and if we are disciplined, these goals should be reached no matter what
   c) Goals in relation to playing our best, and do our best against top opponents and in tough tournaments
   d) Goals that Parents, Players and Coaches devised together as a team for the players advancements

22) What would be a must have ingredient for the doing it on your own philosophy of learning without Coaches or outside instruction?

WHAT TENNIS PROS DON'T TEACH (WTPDT)

a) Observation ability to watch other good players on TV and Tennis courts and instilling a love of the game
b) Practicing with friends on your own on your free times at the public Tennis courts
c) Getting basic Tennis equipment, racquets, balls, and Tennis shoes
d) All of the above
e) None of the above

23) What is an easy way to get better no matter what?

a) Practicing as much as we can on our own
b) Making sure our technique is solid
c) Watching pro-Tennis on TV with a purpose three times per week
d) All of the above
e) None of the above,

24) What are three benefits of hitting Tennis balls on the wall?

a) We build our cardio, establish rhythm, really pick up footwork and instill perfect form on strokes
b) Burn lots of calories, practice without pressure, no ball pick up is necessary and we can work on anything we want
c) We can practice hard or soft hitting, quality of balls don't matter, it is okay to miss and just go on, we can take as many breaks as we need
d) All of the above
e) None of the above

25) What is the purpose of a periodization schedule?

a) To establish a well-designed routine for the players training
b) To define fitness and on court workload week to week
c) To come up with the right tournament schedule and tournament load for a Tennis player
d) To identify performance goals in the short, medium and long terms

e) All of the above
f) None of the above

26) What are some benefits of weight training for a Tennis player?

    a) To reduce the risk of injury
    b) To be able to generate more power
    c) To increase performance capacity
    d) To gain confidence through fitness
    e) All of the above
    f) None of the above

27) What can be some disadvantages of weight training?

    a) Can decrease mobility and flexibility which in turn leads to injury
    b) It tires players, and they lose the drive to spend more time on the court, makes players get hungry, and they want to eat more making them often times put on unnecessary weight
    c) Inhibits speed and agility on the court
    d) If not administered right, weight training can create technical problems
    e) It can reduce range of motion in all our extremities
    f) All of the above
    g) None of the above

28) What are some benefits of stretching?

    a) Increased flexibility on court helps us reach and get more balls back in play
    b) Prevents injuries by augmenting range of motion in muscles and ligaments
    c) Promotes players to be more relaxed on court while executing strokes
    d) All of the above

29) What are four pretty common injuries in Tennis?

WHAT TENNIS PROS DON'T TEACH (WTPDT)

   a) Thigh, bicep, chest and neck injuries
   b) Shoulder, elbow, ankle, and calf
   c) Abdomen, triceps, quadriceps and hand
   d) all of the above

30) What are two absolutely necessary elements of injury prevention?

   a) Diet and fitness
   b) Hydration and stretching
   c) Proper technique and using the right equipment
   d) Appropriate warm-up routines and calisthenics
   e) All of the above
   f) None of the above

31) Regarding cramps the one thing to do is to prevent them. As Tennis players what do we need to do to achieve this?

   a) Drink a lot of water before, during and after matches
   b) Before matches and during tournaments drink water until our urine is semi-clear yellow to totally clear in color
   c) When hot and humid or during a long match, it is a good idea to drink some electrolyte enriched energy drink
   d) Stretching before, during and after matches and practices
   e) All of the above,

32) Cramps are more likely to happen to players who did not eat properly leading up to a tournament.

   a) True
   b) False

33) Dealing with cramps includes stretching the muscle and using an ice bag to mitigate a cramp keeping it from coming back.

   a) True
   b) False

34) Having 15% to 20% body fat is unacceptable for competitive Tennis players.

   a) True
   b) False

35) For the most part, the diet of a Tennis player needs to be the following percentages:

   a) 33% fat, 33% protein, 33% carbohydrates
   b) 15% fat, 20% protein, 65% carbohydrates
   c) 5% fat, 55% protein, 40% carbohydrates
   d) 10% fat, 20% protein, 70% carbohydrates
   e) None of the above
   f) Any of the above

36) Profound and sound sleeping for 5 hours, is enough for a player to be able to perform at the top of his or her ability; granted he or she is wide awake before getting on the court for a Tennis match.

   a) True
   b) False

37) Drinking some coffee is okay for a Tennis player that has an early morning match to make sure he or she is wide awake and emotionally and physically ready for the match.

   a) True
   b) False

38) In order to get the 8 hours of sleep, it is better to let a player sleep in; until 30 minutes before his or her match, to allow further rest, than to get him or her, up two or three hours earlier, to get him or her warming-up, awake and ready for a match.

   a) True
   b) False

39) Mental toughness can be trained and should be 100% attainable under the right guidance.

   a) True
   b) False

40) Mention three elements of what makes a player mentally tough:

   a) Emotional control, eye control, tempo/pace control
   b) Rituals before play start, racquet control between points, strong image and posture between points
   c) Anger control, routine between points well established, breathing control between and during points
d Lots of smoking, drinking beer and surfing the internet
   d) All of the above
   e) None of the above

41) Mentally tough players fit which characteristic best?

   a) Not ever giving up
   b) They look like they are winning regardless of the score
   c) Are a lot more likely to come back if down in the score
   d) When playing against mentally tough players we can feel these players are not going away until the match is over!
   e) All of the above,
   f) None of the above,

42) One of the most fundamental mental toughness principles is to learn to manage in between point time.

   a) True
   b) False

43) Fitness will substantially increase confidence and mental toughness in a player.

   a) True
   b) False

44) Being well hydrated and taking care of the nutritional demands of a player in a professional and disciplined manner will increase the mental toughness component of a competitive Tennis player.

   a) True
   b) False

45) Mental toughness is not about maintaining emotional and physical control of what we do during and in between point play, but winning points and matches under adverse circumstances.

   a) True
   b) False

46) Believing and having faith that a match can be won is crucial in eventually breaking through to the next level in Tennis.

   a) True
   b) False
   c) This is not an element of mental toughness
   d) None of the above

47) Imagery and visualization can substantially help in building confidence, increasing mental toughness and the belief that a match or a point or a tournament can be won.

   a) True
   b) False
   c) Visualization is not part of mental toughness training
   d) None of the above

48) Should a competitive Tennis player study the rule book?

   a) Not necessary, that is why there are officials in sanctioned tournaments
   b) Deeper knowledge and understanding of the rules can make the difference between winning and losing in close matches
   c) It should be the coach's responsibility to instill knowledge of the necessary rules on his or her players
   d) All of the above
   e) None of the above

49) If 100% sure that we are getting some bad calls we should question the player in a more aggressive manner and in a more convincing way than to just say: "are you sure?"

   a) We just got to go with the calls, if he or she wants it that bad that they have to cheat so be it, and they can have it,
   b) It is okay to say something like: "Sorry, but the ball was on the line, or inside the line, you cannot continue to call those shots out."
   c) It is okay to let our opponent know in a respectful way that we are sure he or she is giving us bad calls
   d) Okay to give them a retaliation call to keep them from cheating any more
   e) Basically, the right thing to do is to get an official and be done with it. Refuse to continue to play if an official is not present
   f) Do get an official when the match is close. If winning handily beat the cheater and his/her cheating or in spite of his/her cheating

50) It is not necessary to carry a rule book in our bag since there are officials who have them with them, and they know all the rules and can advise.

   a) True
   b) False

51) A competitive player who does not have pretty in-depth knowledge of the rules is at a distinct disadvantage during an official match.

   a) True
   b) False

52) Cheating in Tennis is a dead end. As the caliber of play and tournaments gets higher and higher, sooner or later there will be officials who will stop unfair play and cheating will not be possible.

   a) True
   b) False
   c) Cheating players often win matches they should have lost
   d) There is no honor in winning if the player knows he/she is cheating
   e) None of the above

53) There is no value to winning in Tennis if it is done without a profound sense of sportsmanship and ethics. Children need to be reinforced in these ideas at an early age.

   a) True
   b) False

54) Parents who pretend they have not noticed their children cheating during matches are doing tremendous damage to their kids not only from the Tennis development standpoint, but the human and societal standpoints as well.

   a) True
   b) False
   c) Learning to play fair is one of Tennis's greatest lessons
   d) None of the above,

55) Tennis shoes should be fitted in a way that they are snug to tight to avoid excessive movement of the foot inside the shoe and prevent blisters, blue nails and other toe and foot injuries.

a) True
b) False

56) Wearing a combination of two socks (cotton and polyester or Dacron) usually offers the best of both Worlds as far as comfort, firmness of fit and breathability allowing more air circulation.

a) True
b) False

57) Black and dark colors are actually a wise choice for some players in the sense that it keeps a lot more UV sun rays from penetrating through the clothing material as easily as light colored or whites do.

a) True
b) False

58) Wearing black or dark colors for Tennis actually enhances our workout since these colors actually make us feel warmer or hotter making us burn more calories in hot days. In cold days if the sun is out, the reverse is also true, wear light colors to force ourselves to burn more calories because our body is working harder to stay warm. Darker colors in cold weather will help us stay warm during outdoor Tennis.

a) True
b) False

59) It is hard to beat cotton over just about anything else; as far as comfort is concerned for Tennis garments, so long as they are made of high-quality cotton, either thicker or thinner depending on the season of the year, humidity, and temperatures, as well as the players' choices.

a) True
b) False

c) Modern synthetics are better nowadays and far surpass in comfort and purpose of what cotton and natural materials are capable of doing
d) None of the above

60) Mid top Tennis shoes do not offer any extra support and are uncomfortable, heavier and awkward for Tennis.

a) True
b) False

61) All other things being equal, what is the longest lasting string material for Tennis on the market now days?

a) Synthetic gut
b) Natural gut
c) Nylon
d) Kevlar
e) Polyester
f) Hybrid
g) Multifilament

62) What advantages would a hybrid stringing job have over a normal stringing job?

a) Hybrid is longer lasting
b) Players can capture the benefits of two different strings in one string job
c) Players can combine two different colors
d) Players can secure playability plus durability in the same string job
e) None of the above
f) All of the above

63) What is the most popular string on the market today?

a) Polyester
b) Nylons

c) Natural Gut
d) Synthetic Gut
e) Multifilament strings
f) Hybrid strings
g) Guitar strings

64) Stringing at higher tensions gives us:

   a) More control on hard hit shots but less touch and finesse on soft shots
   b) More power and more control on all shots
   c) Better feel but less control on soft shots
   d) None of the above
   e) All of the above

65) The string gauge refers to what?

   a) The stiffness of the string
   b) The length of the string
   c) The color of the string
   d) The diameter of the string

66) The larger the number of the gauge of the strings the:

   a) The longer the string will last,
   b) The larger the diameter of the string,
   c) The smaller the diameter of the string
   d) Depends on the manufacturers specifications
   e) None of the above

67) Cross-section on poly string refers to:

   a) The diameter of the string
   b) The shape of the string as viewed from one end
   c) Hybrid strings of different materials
   d) The tension in the middle of the racquet
   e) None of the above

68) One easy way to save a lot of money in stringing if we don't have our own stringing machine is:

   a) Stringing ourselves at the local Tennis Shop or Tennis club
   b) Buying our own string wholesale and provide the stringer the string and the racquet for him or her to string our racquets with
   c) Buying a tabletop stringing machine model and stringing our own racquets
   d) Buying the cheapest, and longest lasting string there is on the market
   e) None of the above

69) A good stringing machine for home use would be?

   a) A tabletop model we can afford, and we can transport to tournaments
   b) Floor model that has a solid frame
   c) An electronic system stringing machine that is extremely accurate
   d) A crank system that is very simple
   e) None of the above

70) the most popular stringing machines in the World, use a:

   a) Weight system
   b) Are digital for precision
   c) Utilize the crank system or some sort of mechanical system for applying tension
   d) Are mechanical in nature but not accurate
   e) None of the above

71) A good string job will depend a lot more on:

   a) Who is stringing the racquet and not the stringing machine
   b) What kind of string we utilize
   c) How long it takes the stringer to finish the job
   d) None of the above

WHAT TENNIS PROS DON'T TEACH (WTPDT)

72) Name three basic tools besides the string machine that are an absolute must for stringing racquets?

   a) Allen wrenches, screwdrivers, scissors, crescent pliers
   b) Awl, needle pointed pliers, snip cutter pliers
   c) Hammer, Pin driver, nail clippers
   d) Tool box, extension cord, oil dispenser

73) An experienced good stringer can get a string job done to perfection without rushing in:

   a) Under 5 minutes
   b) Under 30 minutes
   c) Under 1 hour
   d) Under 15 minutes
   e) Under 20 minutes

74) What are the three most popular surfaces in Professional Tennis?

   a) Hard, clay and grass
   b) Manure, concrete, wood
   c) Carpet, synthetic grass, dirt
   d) None of the above

75) What is the cheapest surface there is for construction of a Tennis court?

   a) Concrete
   b) Clay
   c) Dirt
   d) Grass
   e) Wood
   f) Manure

76) Why is it that sometimes, top players don't do great at tournaments prior to grand slam competition?

a) They are looking to peak at the right time, and if already peaking, they don't want to burn their cartridges at smaller tournaments
b) Because they don't care to win or lose at smaller events
c) Pros only put their best effort for Davis Cup competition
d) In a lot of events, pros have a contract to participate, and if they don't need the matches to peak for upcomming grand slam, the money or the ranking, they are very likely to give less than 100% effort or performance

77) The idea of The Code, to work as a team in Tennis helps to put into perspective the personal agendas of parents, coaches, and players.

a) True
b) False

78) Why is it important to develop a philosophy in Tennis as a player, as a coach, as a parent, and as Team?

a) A philosophy helps everyone involved understand goals
b) A philosophy helps everyone understand and develop ethics and values in sports and life
c) The right philosophy teaches us respect for all involved
d) The right philosophy helps us approach competition with the right frame of mind
e) Our philosophy justifies all the time, effort and other means invested in learning a discipline
f) Philosophy gives us the necessary drive and discipline to persist
g) All of the above
h) None of the above

79) Tennis professionals, Tennis coaches, and Tennis Teachers are looking for:

a) Attention, money and fame
b) Acceptance, recognition, and respect
c) Knowledge, connections, promotions
d) None of the above

WHAT TENNIS PROS DON'T TEACH (WTPDT)

80) Name three important sources of confidence for a Tennis player:

   A) Fitness, practice, winning
   B) Equipment, strategy, experience
   C) Mental toughness, imagery, and visualization, image projection
   D) All of the above
   E) None of the above

81) A player who looks confident will eventually start feeling more confident even if he or she does not feel confident at the moment.

   A) True
   B) False

82) Hitting on the rise is very risky and should be avoided for the most part and utilized only when there is no other option.

   a) True
   b) False

83) It is very rare but not an impossible occurrence to find a great player who only had bad coaches or no coaches at all.

   a) True
   b) False

84) It is a rare but not an impossible occurrence that a great player will be fully developed under the same coach or program.

   a) True
   b) False

85) Under the right guidance, a personalized program where the player is getting coaching at one place, drilling, playing matches, and hitting at other places is not a bad idea for a lot of players. This way the player can focus 100% on his or her personal needs and not the needs of the group.

a) True
b) False

86) What is anticipation?

    A) Moving where the next shot is going before our opponent hits the ball, usually the open court
    B) Having a natural instinct for knowing where to go after we hit the ball
    C) Covering the open court
    D) Understanding the tendencies of our opponents and covering them in advance
    E) All of the above
    F) None of the above

87) The best grip in Tennis is the continental grip; it is appropriate to hit all strokes in Tennis.

    a) True
    b) False

88) What is the most popular grip for hitting groundstrokes in professional Tennis today?

    a) Continental
    b) Eastern
    c) Semi-western
    d) Australian
    e) Western
    f) Radial eastern
    g) Conservative eastern
    h) None of the above

89) The one-handed backhand has no advantages over the two-handed backhand.

    a) True
    b) False

c) The one-hander is more flexible, adaptable and offers more natural variety than the two-hander
d) The one-handed backhand fits better some players that like the all court style and the serve and volley and net rushing styles of play
e) None of the above

90) The two-handed backhand is less stable and less of a solid technique for return of serve and baseline hitting.

   a) True
   b) False

91) A competitive player does not need to work on developing at least one weapon for the purpose of winning points out right at the junior, college and professional Tennis levels.

   a) True
   b) False
   c) Weapon development is not necessary for the counter punchers at any level
   d) None of the above

92) In accordance to the principle of specificity, one could safely say that the best practice there is for Tennis is playing actual matches.

   a) True
   b) False
   c) Playing matches is not conducive to confidence building
   d) Specificity refers to the idea of practicing in a very specific way what is needed only, designed on a day to day basis
   e) None of the above
   f) All of the above

93) The games approach refers to the idea of utilizing different fun and entertaining practice games designed to develop the different skills necessary to be successful at Tennis.

a) True
b) False
c) The games approach is fun, and everybody loves it
d) The games approach, also teaches strategy and mental toughness
e) All of the above
f) None of the above

94) Developing players should devote as much as 50% of their practice time to serving.

a) True
b) False
c) Spending that much time does not allow enough time to develop the rest of the strokes
d) The serve is by far the most important stroke in Tennis, and it deserves at least that much attention
e) All of the above
f) None of the above

95) A heavy ball is one that is at the top of the range for weight allowed as per the ITF rules of Tennis.

a) True
b) False
c) A heavy ball refers to the kinetic energy the ball has in the air, combining the speed plus the spin it has, as it is hit by a player
d) A ball that when we hit it feels heavier than a normal ball
e) A ball that weighs more than a regulation ball and is not good for official play, but okay for practice

96) The right strategy should be based on strengths and weakness of both players involved.

a) True
b) False

WHAT TENNIS PROS DON'T TEACH (WTPDT)

97) A radical change in game plan or strategy is necessary if a player loses a couple of games in a row.

   a) True
   b) False
   c) If the two games the player lost were close, only a small adjustment in strategy is necessary
   d) A radical change is necessary if the player has lost two or three games in a row fairly easily and he/she only won a couple of points
   e) A change in strategy should not be adequate until the player in question has lost a set
   f) None of the above

98) Not all players need to develop defensive techniques. These are only necessary for counter punchers and all court players,

   a) True
   b) False
   c) Defense is necessary at all levels and with all styles
   d) You cannot turn defense into offense if you don't have defensive mechanisms available to begin with
   e) None of the above

99) The 4x4 rule refers to hitting into high percentage areas on the court.

   a) True
   b) False
   c) It refers to hitting the ball or aiming it 4 feet from the singles lines and baseline off groundstrokes and some volleys
   d) Tennis players need 4x4 vehicles to get around to all places to find courts where to play and practice
   e) None of the above

100) Statistics in Tennis are meaningless.

   a) True
   b) False
   c) A player can use statistics to gauge what he/she needs to be working on
   d) Players can use statistics to figure out how aggressive or conservative they need to be
   e) Statistics help players understand how effective they are with the way the play
   f) None of the above

101) "What Tennis Pros Don't Teach" is the most awesome book ever written about Tennis.

   a) True
   b) False
   c) If not the most awesome, WTPDT may well be one of the most comprehensive ones
   d) This book is just an in depth but practical analysis of Tennis as a whole

More questions for extra credit follow:

102) Tempo and establishing one's own pace on the court is not important. The only thing that matters is performance over outcome.

   a) True
   b) False
   c) Playing with a pace/tempo that is comfortable to a specific player may be the difference between winning and losing in close match situations
   d) To allow our opponents to rush us point to point makes it difficult to perform at optimal levels

103) One of the most tactical strategies in Tennis is the intelligent utilization of the drop-shot.

a) True
b) False
c) The drop shot is a desperate shot intended to finish the point earlier
d) There are two types of drop shots, tactical ones and point finishing ones
e) Drop shots are great to have, and all players should know how to hit one

104) Adopting a defensive strategy when we have a good lead in Tennis, is a good idea since by maintaining our lead, we just wait for errors from our opponent, and soon the match expires and we end up the winner.

a) True
b) False
c) Switching to a defensive strategy and playing tentatively; when we are leading is conducive to allowing our opponent to come back and bite us
d) In Tennis no lead is good enough; Tennis players need to stretch it as much as they can until they have won the last point of the match
e) None of the above

105) In Tennis, as opposed to other sports, it is very possible to come back from way behind in the score; since each new game is a fresh start, and a new set, is like the start of another match all over again.

a) True
b) False
c) Once a Tennis player is down two breaks of serve it is next to impossible to come back in Tennis
d) We hardly ever see comebacks in Tennis

106) Scouting our opponents and taking notes in our Tennis journal is a good start to having the right information and strategy once a player is on the court.

a) True
b) False
c) Scouting is a waste of time since it is more important that the player goes to rest and eat between matches
d) A Tennis journal in our bag is an awesome tool to have; it can make the difference between a win and a loss in tough matches
e) None of the above

107) What would be some must do things for players to get ready for a match

a) Go eat right after their previous match
b) Talk to their friends
c) Spend 10 minutes before check in devising a solid strategy
d) If available talk to their coach before going on
e) Hit a few warm up balls at least 30 minutes before check in time
f) Relax and rest until it is time to go on
g) Go watch their friend's matches and cheer for them
h) Hydrate until their urine is clear to light yellow
i) Eat at least two hours before their match, if possible
j) If no time to eat a full meal, eat very lightly some salad and fruit to get ready and replenished on time
k) All of the above
l) None of the above

108) Transitioning from age division to age division should be done in a very thoughtful and deliberate way.

a) True
b) False
c) Moving up a division or two to avoid pressure is wrong
d) Pressure is good for the developing player. Therefore, he or she should not move up unless he or she is fully dominating in his or her current division
e) None of the above

WHAT TENNIS PROS DON'T TEACH (WTPDT)

109) Junior Tennis, high school Tennis or college Tennis should not be a dead end. There will always be other challenges, tournaments to play, opponents to face and beat, and places to go; Tennis players can always continue to improve their game; Tennis is never a dead end!

   a) True
   b) False
   c) Some juniors feel that they have hit a dead end once they are done with junior Tennis, and they are not good enough for College Tennis or professional Tennis
   d) College Tennis is not a dead end because all players have different learning curves, and everybody reaches full Tennis maturity at different ages
   e) Players that reach full maturity under 18 years of age are one in a million
   f) All of the above
   g) None of the above

110) Developing players of all ages should include lots of doubles matches and drills since doubles teaches them how to play the game of Tennis as a whole in a less stressful environment.

   a) True
   b) False
   c) Doubles does not truly test the player
   d) Doubles does not matter anymore in Tennis
   e) Most adult Tennis players are involved in some sort of doubles leagues
   f) Some children should be signed up for two doubles divisions instead of two singles divisions in some junior tournaments that allow it
   g) None of the above

111) Anger, frustration, fatigue and lack of enthusiasm are sure signs of burnout at all levels.

   a) True
   b) False
   c) When a player is burned out, he or she may need a break or a restructuring of goals and training routines
   d) Burned out players will always quit and not come back to Tennis
   e) Burnout can be 100% preventable if detected on time
   f) None of the above

112) Sports science is one of the main differentiating factors in dictating modern fitness and biomechanical/technical development and training routines and methods as compared to the way Tennis was played in the past.

   a) True
   b) False

113) Sports science, more than the equipment (racquets, strings, etc…), is responsible for the great Tennis we enjoy today from Tennis professionals and other Tennis players of all ages.

   a) True
   b) False
   c) Racquets, strings, and equipment are more important than biomechanics in this regard
   d) Sports science is changing day-to-day, and it is hard to stay up to speed with all its innovations

114) What areas are covered by sports science?

   a) Nutrition
   b) Psychology
   c) Technique
   d) Biomechanics
   e) Fitness and conditioning

WHAT TENNIS PROS DON'T TEACH (WTPDT)

f) Sleep
g) Hydration
h) Strategy and tactics
i) Rules
j) The code
k) All of the above
l) None of the above

115) One way to unnerve our opponent is to walk on to court with no strings in our racquet and to say, "I use the frame."

a) True
b) False

QUIZ KEY

Answers:

1- a
2- c
3- d
4- e
5- c
6- c
7- a
8- e
9- d
10- b
11- a, c
12- b
13- b
14- b, c
15- a
16- a
17- a
18- d
19- c
20- a
21- b
22- a
23- c
24- d
25- e
26- e
27- d
28- d

WHAT TENNIS PROS DON'T TEACH (WTPDT)

29- b
30- e
31- e
32- a
33- a
34- b
35- b, d
36- a
37- a
38- b
39- a
40- a, b, c
41- e
42- a
43- a
44- a
45- b
46- a
47- a
48- b
49- b, c, e
50- b
51- a
52- a, d
53- a
54- a, c
55- a
56- a
57- a
58- a
59- a
60- b
61- e
62- b, d
63- a
64- a
65- d
66- c

67- b
68- b
69- a, d
70- c
71- a
72- b
73- d, e
74- a
75- c
76- a, c, d
77- a
78- g
79- b
80- d
81- a
82- b
83- a
84- a
85- a
86- e
87- h
88- c
89- b, c, d
90- b
91- b
92- a
93- a, c, d
94- a, d
95- b, c, d
96- a
97- b, c, d
98- b, c, d
99- a, c
100- b, c, d, e
101- a, c, d
102- b, c, d
103- a, d, e
104- b, c, d

WHAT TENNIS PROS DON'T TEACH (WTPDT)

105- a
106- a, d
107- a, c, d, e, f, h, i, j
108- a, c, d
109- a, c, d, f
110- a, e, f
111- a, c, e
112- a
113- a, d
114- a, b, c, d, e, f, g
115- a,b

NOTE: Max Total 174 possible right answers. The reader can grade himself/herself if interested. Divide the number of right answers by 174 and multiply by 100, and this gives us our percentage!

EPILOGUE

It is a little hard to write even more about something that I already wrote about so much. Most likely this will be my first and only book on Tennis and the reason for this is that writing about Tennis, even though it flows easily; feels a little like work. Tennis to me has been and has continued to be a passion and a way of life. Any time I hit Tennis balls for money, as in teaching Tennis; somehow a little of the fun evaporates. It's like the pureness of it evades me, and I cannot completely feel the absolute pleasure of doing it just for me, for the love of Tennis, for the passion and infatuation that I have with it. But that was not the case when I played for prize money professionally. Sometimes I love Tennis and want to hit more Tennis balls, but sometimes all I want to do is go home and enjoy some time with my family after a long day hitting balls back to junior players.

My thinking is that if I ever wrote another book on Tennis it would have to be regarding some of my own personal experiences as a player and Coach. If my Daughter Anasazi, became really serious about Tennis (she is only 9 now), I might write a book on how her interest developed, her career as a Tennis player, and about all the little experiences we went through together, to get her to realize her goals whatever these were. Part of me wants for her to know the life that I have known. Ultimately it will be 100% her decision. I can say now that I don't plan ever to retire. Instead, I'll maybe teach part time when these writers' legs and joints no longer are able to operate at the required levels. But if Anasazi decided to go all out for it, then I will never know the meaning of even part-time retirement because we have a long way to go.

Some of my friends and contributors that read WTPDT kept getting back at me saying that it sounded like someone that did not speak English as a first language wrote it. "Of course" I would say next "And that's exactly the way it should sound like, and that's the way I want it to sound". WTPDT is not a work of English literature. Some professional editors said to me that they could perfection it to make it sound clear and clean. But I opposed to that idea because they did a couple small sample edits, and they basically rewrote everything. So I said to them, "forget it, that does not even sound like I wrote it at all!"

Being a Tennis coach is a hugely satisfying job, but contrary to popular thinking, it is a tough, time-consuming, and a very mentally and physically demanding occupation; and chances are that if it is not being demanding to some coaches out there, they are probably not doing a good enough job at it.

Just like any other professional making a living, we need a clientele base. It is great when one's students are attentive and work hard; this makes for an easy lesson, and time flies by. But when the student does not really want to be there… 60 minutes on the Tennis court feels like 60 hours. Here is some advice to all parents: do us a favor, don't send children to Tennis lessons unless they are pretty fired up about it.

Tennis offers a whole universe of experiences that can easily last several lifetimes. Tennis is a whole Universe unto itself. Tennis will keep us alive and well. Go for Tennis, one cannot go wrong, fall in love with it and caress it. Tennis will pay back tenfold each and every minute spent!

So there it is, let me know if I missed anything, also about all my mistakes, I can take some critiquing; I will utilize it get better!

Contact me at: ManuelSCervantes@gmail.com

WHAT TENNIS PROS DON'T TEACH VIDEO SERIES LINKS

1- Sliding on clay: https://youtu.be/hCyMUh4QFR8
2- Self-feed cardio workout: https://youtu.be/bmFB6sqJeCU
3- Practice on the wall: https://youtu.be/r9If8bdmEKU
4- Tossing Technique: https://youtu.be/RFI4WnKDKtw
5- Footwork Techniques: https://youtu.be/9xaCNSopSXs
6- Serving Cardio Workout: https://youtu.be/4TlxkXsC1Ss
7- The Unit Turn: https://youtu.be/CRGMa0WhRcE
8- Ball Machine Cardio Workout: https://youtu.be/x3zxmfoL6Xk
9- The ready position: https://youtu.be/4ijQnTaI80A
10- Extreme shots : https://youtu.be/kxDjHFucZpE
11- Grips and grip sizing for Tennis: https://youtu.be/SCmQduNiV1c
12- The non-dominant arm: https://youtu.be/8GHJh2CluoI
13- In between point time routine: https://youtu.be/ylzLGTHq5FY
14- Volleys: https://youtu.be/YzbuiwuJUmg
15- WTPDT Fitness protocol: https://youtu.be/cH4LAdo2se8
16- Serving stance: https://youtu.be/N_FkQCV2wqc
17- StellaLuna Split Step: https://youtu.be/oMNuCzW1cbk

Made in the USA
Columbia, SC
07 June 2024